Basic Types of Pastoral Care
and Counselling

Basic Types of PASTORAL CARE & COUNSELLING

Resources for the Ministry
of Healing and Growth

HOWARD CLINEBELL

SCM PRESS LTD

334 01892 7

A revised and enlarged edition of
*Basic Types of Pastoral Counselling: New Resources
for the Troubled*
published 1966
by Abingdon Press

First published in Great Britain 1984 by
SCM Press Ltd
26–30 Tottenham Road London N1 4BZ
Second impression 1987

Typeset in the United States of America
and printed in Great Britain by
Richard Clay Ltd, Bungay, Suffolk

*To my
friends
and colleagues
in the pastoral
counseling movement*

Where there is no guidance, a people falls; but in an abundance of counselors there is safety.

(PROVERBS 11:14)

And his name will be called Wonderful Counselor.
(ISAIAH 9:6)

I came that they may have life, and have it abundantly.
(JOHN 10:10)

Be transformed by the renewal of your mind.
(ROMANS 12:2)

CONTENTS

SOME
PERSONAL
REFLECTIONS
ABOUT THIS BOOK

Let me introduce this revision by mentioning some experiences out of which the original edition of the book and later the revision grew. For over thirty-five years (which even I have trouble believing) I have been doing pastoral counseling in a variety of settings—thirteen years as a parish minister in Indiana, Illinois, and New York; two years as a minister of counseling in a downtown church in Southern California; and twenty-three years as a seminary teacher and director of a pastoral counseling and growth center. It isn't surprising that my understanding of counseling and my practice of this pastoral art have evolved through these years. My intention in these pages is to describe the concepts that now make the most sense and the practical methods that work best for me at this stage of my journey.

I can see, in retrospect, that there have been three phases in the development of my thought and practice of pastoral counseling. During the early years of my ministry, I attempted to use the Rogerian and neo-Freudian approach, which I had studied in graduate school. It gradually became clear to me that the relatively passive, long-term model of psythotherapy that I had learned was not particularly effective with many persons who came for pastoral counseling. Gradually, my conviction grew stronger—that pastoral counseling must broaden its conceptual base and revise its working model in order to flourish more fully. The efforts I made to increase my effectiveness by incorporating insights from our pastoral heritage and methods from some newer psychotherapies— e.g., TA, reality therapy, role-relationship marriage counseling—eventually produced the second phase, the revised model of pastoral counseling. This model was described in the original edition of this book, written in 1965.

In the years since then, much has happened in my life, personally and professionally. These have been years of mixed pain and joy, struggling and creativity. My own growth struggles as a client in therapy in recent years have fed the process of continuing change in my understanding and practice of counseling. This process has produced the third phase—the "growth counseling" approach, which I now recognize was present in embryonic form in the revised model. I'm pleased to have an opportunity now to update this book by incorporating the changes of the last seventeen years that seem most important—changes in my approach resulting from changes in our society, in the church, in the pastoral counseling movement, and in the flowering field of psychotherapies.

At first I planned only to update the bibliographies and remove the sexist language (of which I was unaware when I wrote the book). (I have chosen to retain some important quotations that have sexist language, written before any of us in the field were aware of this crucial language issue. As a consciousness raising device, I have inserted "sic" in the most blatant of these quotes.) However, as I began revising, I discovered that I must do much more than I had planned—I must do a *re-vision* describing the use of a new paradigm for pastoral counseling. As a result, the major changes in this edition are these: The book presents a more holistic and explicitly liberation-growth paradigm; it emphasizes pastoral care as the nurturing context of pastoral counseling; it stresses spiritual and ethical growth as central and unifying goals of all care and counseling that is truly pastoral; it highlights the particular types of caring and counseling that are normative in parish ministry and other general ministries; it seeks to show the crucial importance of the feminist perspective and of liberation theology to pastoral care and counseling today; and it incorporates methods from several newer therapies that I have found useful as a pastoral counselor, as well as in my personal growth.

This book is intended to be useful for men and women in general ministries (in congregations, chaplaincies, etc.) and for seminarians preparing to be generalists. I hope and expect that the book also will continue to be useful for training lay caring teams and will be a resource for secular counselors and therapists who are interested in the spiritual and value dimensions of their healing work.

All the case material from my counseling and growth groups used in these pages is disguised to protect the anonymity of the persons involved. The identifying data have been deleted or altered to this end.

Many people have stimulated and challenged my thinking about pastoral care and counseling. I stand in their debt! In some cases, my gratitude is acknowledged by notes or references. In other cases, the influence has been indirect, general or, I suspect, unconscious, so that specific acknowledgement is not possible. I am grateful to the many seminarians, graduate students and ministers I have taught, to my faculty colleagues, and to my friends in the American Association of Pastoral Counselors, all of whom have helped to mold my thinking and practice over these years. The responses of many pastors in training workshops to the revised model and later to the growth counseling approach have encouraged me and confronted me with the need to further strengthen these models. Another powerful influence on my thinking about counseling has been the persons with whom I have been privileged to work as counselor-therapist. Their struggles, courage, and growth, have taught me much about how growth can occur in counseling. Both the frustration of my failures and the quiet lift of those moments when counseling became an instrument of healing and growth have motivated continuing wrestling with the issues discussed in this book.

I am pleased to express special gratitude to these friends and colleagues who gave me valuable suggestions for this revision— Sue Webb Cardwell (and her students), Bill Clements, John Cobb, Gary Collins, John Griffin, Charles Kemp, Robert L. Moore, Howard Stone, Ed Wimberly, Anne Wimberly, and Peggy Way. Linda Herbert, Ray Kiser, and Christie Neuger each gave me extensive and valuable help as my graduate assistants. Christie also did the index. The faculty secretaries who did the typing—Ginny Becker, Sarah Lyon, Sue Klopfenstein—have my special thanks!

I trust that this revision communicates something of the excitement that continues to be generated in many parts of the field of pastoral care and counseling. My own energy level and enthusiasm have risen as I have moved into growth counseling and discovered how effective pastoral counseling can be when it is both explicitly wholeness centered and truly pastoral. My passionate hope, as this book is re-launched, is that it will continue to be a useful instrument in the sorely-needed, demanding, exciting, sometimes frustrating and often deeply fulfilling ministry of nurturing growth and healing in persons through each stage of their life journey! I hope that you will find in these pages some resources for your own personal healing and growth!

Shalom,
Howard Clinebell,
Claremont, California

The Present Challenge of Pastoral Care and Counseling

On a dangerous seacoast where shipwrecks often occur there was once a crude little lifesaving station. The building was just a hut, and there was only one boat, but the few devoted members kept a constant watch over the sea, and with no thought of themselves went out day and night tirelessly searching for the lost. Many lives were saved by this wonderful little station, so that it became famous. Some of those who were saved, and various others in the surrounding area, wanted to become associated with the station and give of their time and money and effort for the support of its work. New boats were bought and new crews trained. The little lifesaving station grew.

Some of the members of the lifesaving station were unhappy that the building was so crude and poorly equipped. They felt that a more comfortable place should be provided as the first refuge of those saved from the sea. So they replaced the emergency cots with beds and put better furniture in the enlarged building. Now the lifesaving station became a popular gathering place for its members, and they decorated it beautifully and furnished it exquisitely, because they used it as a sort of club. Fewer members were now interested in going to sea on lifesaving missions, so they hired lifeboat crews to do this work. The lifesaving motif still prevailed in this club's decoration, and there was a liturgical lifeboat in the room where the club initiations were held. About this time a large ship was wrecked off the coast, and the hired crews brought in boatloads of cold, wet, and half-drowned people. They were dirty and sick, and some of them had black skin and some had yellow skin. The beautiful new club was in chaos. So the property committee immediately had a shower house built outside the club where victims of shipwreck could be cleaned up before coming inside.

At the next meeting, there was a split in the club membersip. Most of the members wanted to stop the club's lifesaving activities as being unpleasant and a hindrance to the normal social life of the club. Some members insisted upon lifesaving as their primary purpose and pointed out that they were still called a lifesaving station. But they were finally voted down and told that if they wanted to save the lives of all the various kinds of people who were shipwrecked in those waters, they could begin their own lifesaving station down the coast. They did.

As the years went by, the new station experienced the same changes that had occurred in the old. It evolved into a club, and yet another lifesaving station was founded. History continued to repeat itself, and if you visit that sea coast today, you will find a number of exclusive clubs along that shore. Shipwrecks are frequent in those waters, but most of the people drown![1]

In this striking parable Theodore Wedel depicts the perennial danger confronting the church—irrelevance. The peril is especially acute in periods when the church is outwardly successful. The parable highlights the fact that the only relevance that really matters is relevance to the *deep needs of persons*—relevance to the places in their lives where they hurt and hope, curse and pray, hunger for meaning and thirst for significant relationships. Pastoral care and counseling are valuable instruments by which the church stays relevant to human need. They are ways of translating the good news into the "language of relationships," as Reuel Howe expresses it—a language which allows the minister to communicate a healing message to persons struggling in alienation and despair. Pastoral counseling is an essential means by which a church is helped to be a lifesaving station and not a club, a hospital and a garden of the spiritual life—not a museum. Counseling can help save those areas of our lives that are shipwrecked in the storms of our daily living, broken on the hidden reefs of anxiety, guilt, and lack of integrity. An effective caring and counseling program, in which both minister and trained lay persons serve as enablers of healing and growth, can transform the interpersonal climate of a congregation, making a church a place where wholeness is nurtured in persons throughout the life cycle.

Pastoral care and counseling contribute to the continuing renewal of a church's vitality by providing instruments for the renewal of persons, relationships, and groups. By reducing the crippledness of our ability to give and receive love, counseling can help us to *be* the church—the community in which God's love becomes an experienced reality in relationships. Thus, counseling is an instrument of continuing *renewal through reconciliation*, helping to heal our estrangement from ourselves and our families, from other church members, from those outside the church, and from an enlivening, growing relationship with God. It can create windows of new awareness, restoring sight to eyes previously blinded by our anxious, guilt-ridden self-concern—to the beauty, tragedy, wonder, and pain all about us. Counseling can allow us to discover fresh dimensions of our humanity. It can release our potentialities for authenticity and aliveness. It can help to release our trapped creativity—the potential creativity present in every person. By renewing us as persons, counseling helps empower us to become renewal agents in a church and in a society that desperately need renewing.

Pastoral counseling and care can be instruments of healing and growth by helping us develop what is most difficult to achieve in our period of history—depth relationships. Most of us can identify with the pain of the minister who said to his psychotherapist, "My life is characterized by a plethora of contacts and a poverty of relationships." This is the common blight that threatens the creativity of each of us in our touch-and-run culture—a culture oriented toward interpersonal superficiality. *This* is the blight that militates against the continuing rebirth of a church as a redemptive social organism, preventing it from becoming a place where persons experience transformation. This is what prevents a church from being a lifesaving station engaged in rescuing persons from our society's many forms of brokenness.

It is far from easy to relate to the depths of other persons. To do so is to come alive to their personhood—to their pain and potential, their emptiness or fullness, their unique blend of hope and despair. It is painful to relate to the depths of others because it inevitably exposes us to the dark rooms of our own inner world. Their emptiness reminds us of our own. Their anger and guilt cause ours to resonate. Yet only as we relate to others in depth can we become growth-enablers in their lives. Only those who have discovered new life in their own depths can become spiritual obstetricians, aiding the birth of new life in individuals and in the church. Pastoral care and counseling can help equip such obstetricians of the spiritual life, such enablers of the continuing rebirth that is *growth*.

When people touched Jesus' life, they experienced in him the healing power that comes from openness to oneself, others, nature, and God. They encountered a person whose life was a deep channel through which the source of all healing and growth—the loving spirit of God—flowed freely and fully.

When people touch my life or yours, what do they sense? The noisy static of our harried times, perhaps? As instruments for deepening and enlivening relationships, pastoral care and counseling can help bring continuing renewal to us as ministers and to persons in the church and in the community! Such renewal comes as a refreshing rain to a parched land.

The Contemporary Renaissance

In each period of history and every new environment, the church must find fresh ways of meeting the needs of troubled persons—new channels for its century-spanning ministry of caring, healing, and growth. Only thus can it remain relevant to the deep needs of people. The varied methods of pastoral care and counseling offer a widening channel of healing and growth in our period of church history.

One hopeful sign on the contemporary religious scene is the rising wave of activity in the field of pastoral counseling. Since World War II a surge of lively interest has been evident in the field. The ministry of counseling has been flowering with increasing vigor. Some of the signs of a remarkable vitality are: the growing availability and impact of clinical pastoral education, the strengthening of seminary education in counseling, the remarkable proliferation of church-related counseling programs, the emergence of pastoral counseling as a rigorously trained specialty within the ministry, the establishment of seminary graduate programs in pastoral psychology and counseling, the rise of the American Association of Pastoral Counselors, the burgeoning literature in the field, the commitment to restoring the spiritual and theological center of this pastoral art, denominational counseling programs, the current experimentation in the pastoral care ministry of the laity, the increasing number of women and the impact of feminist thought in the field, the growth of intercultural and global cross-fertilization in the field. It is thrilling to realize that we are in a renaissance period in the church's age-old ministry to the burdened. The challenge to each of us is to become a *participant* and *contributor*, not a mere observer, in this dynamic movement—a movement that provides fresh responses to the needs of those lying beside our modern Jericho roads, robbed of their self-esteem and beaten by the crises and tragedies of life.

If the pastoral care and counseling renaissance is to become the powerful force for growth and renewal that it can become in the eighties and nineties, certain decisive changes must occur. Pastoral counseling must find a new level of self-identity and maturity by deepening its theological roots, broadening its methodology, and discovering its unique contribution to the helping of troubled humanity, with reference to both its own heritage and the other helping disciplines. The minister as counselor needs a unique self-understanding of her or his image, role, functions, and goals. A minister's self-understanding must have a theological base derived from awareness of the grounding of what one does in the ongoing message, community, and tradition of the church. Major contributions have been made to this theological self-understanding in recent literature. The thrust of this book is toward broadening the methodology and enriching the guiding model of pastoral care and counseling.

A new chapter in the church's ministry to the heavy-laden is now possible. It can be a chapter without equal in the history of our faith. Never before have we had such rich resources as are provided by fresh developments in theology and in pastoral care, by fresh insights from the human sciences, and by innovative techniques from the psychotherapeutic disciplines. When these three streams converge in the pastoral care ministry, a broad river of healing and growth is released through a church. To cooperate with this powerful movement of the life-transforming spirit of God in our times should command our most disciplined self-invest-ment. I hope the ideas and approaches described in this book will contribute toward this objective.

The Purposes of this Book

The primary objective of this book is to help ministers (and seminary students) develop maximum skills in the basic caring and counseling methods required for an effective ministry of healing and growth. Subsumed under this generic objective are more specific purposes: (1) *It is a purpose of this book to describe a new holistic growth and liberation centered paradigm for pastoral care and liberation counseling with spiritual and ethical wholeness at its center (chapters 2, 5, & 6).* This guiding image is essentially multidimensional, focusing on the growth of whole-persons-in-their-relationships. It seeks to integrate intrapsychic and inter-personal healing and growth with constructive change in the wider structures and institutions of people's lives. This paradigm (which builds on my earlier revised model) offers a conceptual basis for integrating the other functions of ministry with pastoral care—preaching, leading worship, church management, teaching, facilitating small groups, serving the community, and working to make institutions more growth-enabling. The paradigm distin-guishes and shows the interdependence of pastoral care and pastoral counseling.

(2) *It is a purpose of this book to overview the mission, theological foundations, historical heritage, and uniqueness of pastoral care and counseling (chapter 3).*

(3) *It is a purpose of this book to review the fundamental procedures to all caring and counseling (chapter 4).* These basic procedures provide a foundation for the use of the methodologies described in subsequent chapters.

(4) *It is a purpose of this book to set forth a differential typology of pastoral care and counseling as a way* of understanding the full range of a minister's opportunities to facilitate healing and growth. Pastoral care and counseling are not one entity with one methodology. Instead they are a wide range of helping and growthing functions requiring a variety of methods. To respond to the varied needs of those who seek help, a pastor must be able to shift gears in caring and counseling—to utilize approaches appropriate to the particular resources and problems, strengths and limitations of each person. Pastors must be able to utilize different facets of their own personalities freely and flexibly. With persons floundering in catastrophic crises, for example, pastors need to use their supportive, caring "Parent" side to give such persons stability in coping with enormously stressful situations.[2] To help persons who have never achieved constructive inner values or controls to guide their lives, the minister must be a firm, accepting, but not a permissive parent figure. In contrast, counselees with rigid, punitive consciences need to experience a minister's more self-accepting, grace-full and playful side. It is not that a minister puts on a varied act in each case. To do so would destroy the interpersonal integrity that creates effective counsel-ing. Rather, the pastor employs different dimensions of his or her

multifaceted personality, responding to the varying needs of different counselees.

It should be made clear that different counseling methods often are employed at various stages of a counseling relationship, sometimes during the same session. Just as a carpenter needs a variety of tools to build a fine piece of furniture, a counselor requires a variety of methods to help persons rebuild a marriage or a destructive value structure. As experienced pastors know, the varied counseling and caring opportunities that confront them require both flexibility and ingenuity in applying everthing they know about persons and about counseling. What they have learned from their own growth struggles is often more useful than sophisticated knowledge of counseling techniques. But the more counselors know about counseling theories and methods, the better use they can make of their unique life experiences and personality resources. It is the intent of this book to encourage readers to increase their versatility and effectiveness by developing their own differential approaches to caring and counseling.

(5) *It is a further purpose of this book to highlight those types of caring and counseling that are essential and therefore normative in a persons-centered, general (nonspecialists) ministry: short-term crisis help (chapters 7 and 8); grief-related caring and counseling (chapter 9); marriage and family enrichment and counselings (chapters 10 and 11); referral counseling (chapter 12); educative and small group counseling (chapters 13 and 14); and training lay caring teams (chapter 16).* These types constitute the heart of a parish minister's caring and counseling. Most persons in general ministries do not have the time, even if they have the required training, to do long-term, reconstructive pastoral psychotherapy. This type of healing work is primarily the function of those in specialized ministries of counseling who have graduate academic and clinical education in psychotherapy in addition to seminary. The chapter on pastoral psychotherapy (chapter 15) aims at describing what persons in general ministries need to know in order to recognize those needing referrals to specialists and provide appropriate pastoral care while parishioners are ex-periencing this type of depth therapy. This chapter also points to some newer therapies that provide insights and methods useful in a generalist ministry. Ours is a period of amazing fecundity in the

field of psychotherapy. We in the church must experiment with fresh approaches as we search for resources to enhance our effectiveness in the ministry of caring and counseling.

In *Pastoral Care in Historical Perspective,* church historian William A. Clebsch and pastoral care specialist Charles R. Jaekle describe the present as a "transitional period in pastoral care." Speaking to the issue of whether it is proper for the church to draw on secular psychotherapies for its pastoral tools, they declare:

> The lesson to be learned in this connection from the history of pastoral care is simply that openness to new psychological theories and notions in fact represents and continues a powerful trend found in every epoch of pastoring. The great tradition of pastoral care stands constantly ready to receive its ideas and its vocabulary both from psychological theoreticians and from popular language about the soul. The normative feature of pastoral care in historical perspective is neither a uniquely Christian psychology nor a particular language in which human trouble must be described, but it is the constancy of the pastoral posture and of the four pastoral functions of healing, sustaining, guiding, and reconciling.[3]

In light of the pastoral care heritage, the authors recommend that in the present period of transition we remain open to the insights of various and even conflicting psychological theories. This is essential because the human capacity for trouble is intricate, complex, and inventive.[4] This heritage-informed guidance is sound. Alert openness to new understandings of personality and therapy on the part of contemporary pastoral counselors will facilitate the creative breakthroughs needed to release the potentialities of counseling as a pastoral art. Time undoubtedly will prove that some of the new methods are of limited usefulness for pastors. The road to better pastoral skill may have dead ends and detours, but the only alternative is not to travel at all! Direct encounter with the ferment of new developments in current psychotherapies can broaden the counseling horizons of ministers, deepen their general approach to pastoral care, and stimulate their interest in further reading, study, and training.[5]

(6) *A final purpose of this book is to encourage the widespread use of the reality practice or role-playing method in learning pastoral care and counseling.* Experience has proved, since the original edition of this book, that this learning method can be very useful in increasing the self-awareness and helping skills of

pastors, seminarians, and lay caring team members. It is utterly simple to use this learning-by-doing approach.

How to Derive the Maximum Benefit from This Book

Here is an approach to using this book, which will help you maximize its practical value.

Step 1: Skim the entire book. Get an overview of the various approaches.

Step 2: Go back to the beginning. Read carefully, reflecting on each chapter. Write your responses, criticisms, agreements, rebuttals, and unanswered questions in the margins. Underline key ideas. Challenge the theories and approaches. Talk back. Keep asking, "How does this apply to my caring and counseling work?" Carry on a dialogue with the ideas that hit you. If possible, discuss the major ideas and methods with another minister or theological student who is reading the book. A small group of such persons will stimulate learning through interaction.

Step 3: Find one, two, or three reality-practice partners— other ministers or theological students who are interested in experimenting with new methods designed to increase their counseling skills. Reality practice sessions with one's spouse can be a way for both partners to enhance their listening and caring skills. The reality-practice team should participate in regular (preferably weekly) sessions, using their own problems, the case material from their counseling, or the cases described at the end of the chapters on counseling methods. These practice sessions will be a kind of counseling laboratory in which seminary students can develop basic counseling skills and seasoned ministers can experiment with new methods, without the danger of mishandling vulnerable persons.

Most people feel some anxiety when they begin such role playing. The fear that they will look foolish or inept as a counselor often creates resistance to beginning this skill practice. The resistance may take the form of dismissing role playing as being "contrived" or "artificial." If learners overcome their resistance and get involved, they usually discover that their feelings and ways of relating in reality practice sessions are very real. As trust develops within the skill practice group, the fear of being vulnerable gradually diminishes and the group begins to enjoy the sessions. Significant learning of skills begins for most people within the first two sessions.

Here is the *modus operandi* of reality-practice. If only two persons are available, they alternate as pastoral counselor and parishioner. If three are involved, the role of observer-coach is added. One person begins by taking the role of a person with whom she or he has counseled or someone else whose problems that person knows well. Attempting to get within that person's internal frame of reference (Rogers) in playing that role provides valuable practice in empathetic understanding. Unlike conventional role playing, the person who is pastoral counselor plays *herself or himself* as counselor; this is why the term *reality-practice* is appropriate. After a practice session has gone on for ten to fifteen minutes, participants should stop and discuss what has happened. The parishioner begins by telling the pastor how she or he felt during the interview. The pastor then shares her or his feelings and observations. Both evaluate what has occurred, shift roles, and try another abbreviated counseling session.

An observer-coach increases the learning value of reality-practice sessions by observing things of which the active participants are unaware and giving them regular feedback. For example, one might say, "I got the feeling that you were involved in a verbal power struggle. I wonder if this was the case and, if so, why?" Or, (to the counselor), "You seemed to be attempting to solve the problem before you had really heard what the parishioner was feeling and facing." Audio or video tape recording and playback of reality-practice sessions can be very helpful. This is crucial if there is no observer-coach. Counselors who hear themselves in action are usually as astonished as persons who hear their own voice for the first time. A typical reaction is, "I had no idea I talked so much!" Since there are different learning values in each of the three reality-practice roles, it is important to rotate frequently enough to give each participant practice in all three roles during a session. If an experienced supervisor is present for a reality-practice session, it can be productive for the counselee to use his or her own real problems as the counseling case. A clinically trained pastor or pastoral counselor should be invited to meet with the reality-practice group as a consultant, as often as possible.

The value of reality-practice increases as a group gains

experience with the method. It is important that the participants become secure enough with each other to be candid in their comments. I recall one session where the parishioner said during the evaluation period: "I felt as though you were overwhelming me with words, that you weren't hearing my feelings." This was the first time that the pastor (who had done considerable counseling) had any awareness of how he was affecting his counselees. This confrontation, though painful, opened a door to self-awareness. Most participants also discover they have strengths in their personalities they fail to utilize in counseling.

Step 4: Use your new skills as counseling opportunities arise, while continuing reality-practice sessions. Current counseling situations, particularly those that are going badly, should be used as material for reality-practice.

Step 5: If you should encounter major blocks to your effectiveness, not reduced by reality-practice, by all means *obtain supervision* from a clinically trained chaplain, a minister with graduate academic and clinical training in pastoral counseling, or a competent counselor in a mental health profession. Or get some *personal psychotherapy.* Don't give up in discouragement. Growing in counseling skills and sensitivities takes time and struggle. Unless you have unusual natural aptitudes in this area, it will require disciplined practice and repeated self-encounter. As is the case with other creative skills, the way to maximum effectiveness as a counselor is straight and the gate narrow. There does not seem to be any other route to this objective. But the satisfaction of growing in the ability to be an instrument of healing and growth in the lives of burdened persons is rich indeed!

Using the Book in a Seminary

This book has been used extensively as a text in introductory courses in pastoral care and counseling. Let me share some suggestions, derived from my own experience and that of colleagues in other seminaries, regarding its use. The value of using reality-practice sessions, as described above, has been demonstrated repeatedly in seminary courses and continuing education workshops for pastors.

In my experience, students learn interpersonal skills best via a three-step process: (1) They first acquire a "cognitive map," a preliminary understanding of the theory undergirding the skill. This understanding can come from their reading, from brief didactic lectures or from both. (2) They then observe a teacher or some other more experienced person—a teacher or class member—using the skill with a reasonable degree of competence. Before asking a class to divide themselves into reality-practice teams, I usually introduce the caring skills or counseling method to be learned by demonstrating how I use it. This is done either by role playing with a student as client, or by doing a live interview in which a volunteer from the class discusses her or his actual feelings or problems. (3) Students then use the skill repeatedly in reality-practice sessions with an opportunity for evaluative feedback from peers and supervision by a person skilled in clinical teaching methods (such as those learned in CPE). The more these three ingredients can be integrated, the more functional learning occurs. One essential focus of both supervision and group reflection during skill-practice sessions should be on the psychodynamic, therapeutic, and theological concepts that illuminate and facilitate what is occurring in the role play or live interview.

The skill-practice groups, in the introductory course at our seminary, meet weekly under the supervision of an advanced student in pastoral counseling who has had one or two quarters of clinical pastoral education, several advanced theory courses in pastoral counseling, and, in most cases, personal therapy. I meet with these highly motivated supervisors each week to supervise their clinical teaching. The learning of both the supervisors and the beginning students seems to be maximized by using this approach. Supplemental reading (e.g., from the "Recommended Reading" sections at the end of the chapters in this book) can be assigned to students as particular topics are focused on in skill-practice sessions. The blending of skill-practice sessions and demonstrations by the teacher, with the students' reading and reflection and with the class lectures and discussion, can produce those exciting moments of illumination when students understand and use a new caring or counseling skill growthfully!

A Holistic Liberation-Growth Model of Pastoral Care and Counseling

Where there is no vision, the people perish.

—PROVERBS 29:18 (KJV)

The image, paradigm,[1] or model that guides one's ministry is crucial to the growthfulness of that ministry. Without an enlivening vision, persons in ministry, like churches and nations, perish, in the sense of losing their inner vitality. What are the defining characteristics of a guiding model of pastoral care and counseling that releases the healing power of these pastoral arts in the new world of the last fifteen years of this millenium? In this chapter I will describe the characteristics of a paradigm that can help enable persons in ministry to respond to the new needs of our rapidly changing world.

To stay relevant to the world of the eighties and nineties, any model of ministry must be open to the future. In our world of continuing change, pastoral care and counseling must be guided by an evolving vision. The growing edges of the field will change as the future unfolds. In this chapter some directions where creative transformations are now occurring are described. My purpose is to delineate a guiding model to help pastoral care and counseling keep growing in ways that are relevant and responsive to the new situation. This statement describes what I see to be the creative trends in the present, and my hopes for the future of the ministry of caring and counseling.

Defining Basic Terms

Pastoral care and counseling involve the utilization by persons in ministry of one-to-one or small group relationships to enable healing empowerment and growth to take place within individuals and their relationships. *Pastoral care* is the broad, inclusive ministry of mutual healing and growth within a congregation and its community, through the life cycle. *Pastoral counseling*, one dimension of pastoral care, is the utilization of a variety of healing (therapeutic) methods to help people handle their problems and crises more growthfully and thus experience healing of their brokenness. Pastoral counseling is a reparative function needed when the growth of persons is seriously jeopardized or blocked by crises. People need pastoral care throughout their lives. They may need pastoral counseling at times of severe crises, usually on a short-term basis. *Pastoral psychotherapy* is the utilization of long-term, reconstructive therapeutic methods when growth is deeply and/or chronically diminished by need-depriving early life experiences or by multiple crises in adult life.

The General Shape of the Model

Here are the major themes in the liberation-growth model:

(1) *The overarching goal of all pastoral care and counseling (and of all ministry) is to liberate, empower, and nurture wholeness centered in Spirit*. Methods of caring and counseling are important dimensions of this wholeness-enabling ministry.

(2) *Spiritual and ethical wholeness is the heart of all human wholeness;* spiritual formation and ethical guidance are core concerns in all pastoral care and counseling rooted in the Judeo-Christian heritage.

(3) *Pastoral care and counseling seek to utilize and integrate both psychological and theological insight regarding the human situation, and the healing of persons*.

(4) *Pastoral care and counseling must be holistic, seeking to enable healing and growth in all dimensions of human wholeness*. The model is systems-oriented, seeing the wholeness of persons as involving interaction among all their significant and interdependent relationships with persons, groups, and institutions. Pastoral care of individuals and pastoral care of groups (e.g., families) and of wider systems (institutions) are equally essential.

(5) *There are special opportunities for nurturing wholeness through pastoral care and counseling at each stage of the life journey*.

(6) *The pastoral care ministry, within the caring community of a congregation, is both the empowering context and the foundation of the reparative ministry of pastoral counseling.*

(7) *Pastoral care is the shared ministry of the pastor and the whole congregation.* Ordained ministers are like player-coaches who have the responsibility of enabling the mutual ministry of lay persons and also doing their own unique and valuable ministry of caring.

(8) *Crises and losses in the lives of individuals and families, and social crises and transitions in the wider society, constitute the occasions within which most caring and counseling opportunities in general ministry occur.* Therefore, short-term crisis intervention methods are indispensible for the effectiveness of this ministry.

(9) *Pastoral care must liberate itself from its dominant middle-class, white, male orientation and become more inclusive in its understanding, concern and methods.* It must become transcultural in its perspective, open to learning new ways of caring from and for the poor and powerless, ethnic minorities, women, and those in non-Western cultures. On a shrinking planet, our circle of consciousness, conscience, and caring must become global.

(10) *Enabling people to increase the constructiveness of their behavior as well as their feelings, attitudes, and values is crucial in the helping process.*

(11) Pastoral care and counseling *should utilize the unique professional identity and role of ministers,* including their positive authority and the socially-defined expectation that they will take the initiative in actively reaching out to offer help to those who need care and counseling.

(12) *Right brain methods of healing and growth* (intuitive, metaphoric, imaging approaches) *should be used more than in the past and integrated with left brain methods (analytical, rational, intentional, problem-solving approaches), if pastoral care and counseling are to become better instruments of whole-person transformation.*

(13) *To become more effective in liberating wholeness, pastoral care and counseling must understand wholeness for both men and women in androgynous ways that encourage growth far beyond traditional sex role stereotypes.* The profound changes occurring

in the identity of women in the last two decades (as reflected in the thought of feminist theologians and therapists), open exciting new possibilities for the liberation of both women and men to their full God-given potentialities. Pastoral care and counseling should be instruments of full human liberation.

(14) *Pastoral counselors and therapists need to strengthen their conceptual base and methodologies by drawing on the newer systems and growth-oriented psychotherapies.*

(15) *Pastoral care can and should occur in all the diverse functions of ministry,* including preaching, worship, and social action.

(16) *To be an effective growth-nurturer, ministers must continue to grow!* To be an enlivener, we must stay alive. To enable healing, we must be vulnerable enough to face and accept our own continuing need for healing. Thus, we become "wounded healers" (Henri Nouwen). In my experience, this is the most challenging, difficult, and exciting part of being in ministry.

Let's explore several of these themes in greater depth now.

The Unifying Goal—Wholeness

In the language of the fourth gospel (John 10:10), human wholeness is described as "life . . . in all its fullness " (NEB). The church's mission in the eighties and nineties is to be *an abundant life center*, a place for liberating, nurturing, and empowering life in all its fullness, in individuals, in intimate relationships, and in society and its institutions. The goal of ministry, and of pastoral care and counseling, as vital dimensions of ministry, is the fullest possible liberation of persons in their total relational and societal contexts. The image of the *life saving station* must be put alongside the image of a *garden* where persons' growth is nurtured, throughout their life journey, and a *training center* where they are equipped and empowered to be agents of wholeness in the lives of other people and in society.

Liberation is the unifying motif of the Christian life-style. The gospel is experienced as good news whenever it frees and empowers people to live out God's dream and intention that they have life in all its fullness. The essence of liberation, in the Hebrew-Christian context, is the freedom to become all that one has the possibilities of becoming. The unifying motif of the diverse liberation movements around the planet is the insistence that all persons have an opportunity to discover and develop their maximum possibilities. As will become evident in these pages, contemporary pastoral care and counseling are power-full instruments for this wholeness-liberating ministry.

Here is a fuller description of the central goal of caring and counseling:

> Facilitating the maximum development of a person's potentialities, at each life stage, in ways that contribute to the growth of others as well and to the development of a society in which all persons will have an opportunity to use their full potentialities. . . . helping people achieve liberation from their prisons of unlived life, unused assets, and wasted strengths. The counselor is a liberator, an enabler of a process by which people free themselves to live life more fully and significantly. Through this freeing experience people discover that happiness is a by-product of actualizing their constructive potentials. Mental-spiritual-relational health is the continuing movement toward living life more fully, joyfully, and productively. Wholeness is a growth journey, not the arrival at a fixed goal. [2]

The holistic approach to pastoral care and counseling sees us human beings as possessing a wealth of undiscovered and undeveloped strengths, assets, and resources. Evidence from the psychological sciences suggests that most of us use no more than a small percent of our potential creativity and intelligence, our capacities to live zestfully, lovingly, and usefully in terms of the needs of our society. [3] Those whose growth is deeply diminished, the emotionally burdened and mentally ill, use even less of their potentialities. The challenge confronting the church in the next two decades is to become a place where this great waste of human life can be reduced drastically as people are awakened to more creative, celebrative, and socially useful living. The effectiveness of churches can be judged by the degree to which people are helped to discover and develop life in all its fullness. This growth in aliveness may someday be measured on an "AQ scale"—an Aliveness Quotient scale.

The Heart of Wholeness

The wholeness, which the church has a mission to liberate and empower, has spiritual wholeness at its center. This means that helping people experience healing and growth in the vertical dimension (Tillich) of their lives is at the heart of all caring and counseling that is truly pastoral. Helping people learn how to increase the power and aliveness of their faith, their values, their here-and-now contact with the loving Spirit of the universe, is an implicit if not an explicit goal of all types of pastoral care and counseling, whatever their other goals.

To facilitate Spirit-centered wholeness requires the continuing integration of resources from the psycho-social sciences and psychotherapy, on the one hand, and from the resources of our theological heritage, on the other. Pastoral counselors are essentially theologically oriented and informed counselors. They are aware, from the wisdom of their theological tradition, of both the amazing resources and the powerful resistances in human beings and in society to realizing these potentialities. These resistances are called "sin" in traditional theological language.

Thus, liberation includes liberation *from*, and liberation *to*, and liberation *for*. It is *to* life in all its fullness—to increasing caring and competence, and creative living. It is *for* life in the Spirit expressed in loving service. (I am indebted to Howard Stone for suggesting the "for" of liberation.) It is *from* those many forces in individuals, relationships, groups, and institutions that limit, constrict, and sometimes strangle the full development of the God-intended possibilities of persons. Many different factors can constrict growth toward wholeness—the lack of an adequate supply of mature love in early life; a traumatic crisis or series of crises (bereavement, divorce, accidents, unemployment, serious illnesses, natural disaster, war); the paralysis caused by inner conflicts, debilitating anxieties, and the accumulated consequences of irresponsible living; the vicious self-perpetuating cycle of a toxic marriage or other close relationships; and societal and institutional growth oppression and injustice. Whatever the causes of blocked growth, persons affected are unable to relate in ways that satisfy their needs for the basic "foods" required for healthy personality growth—the need to receive and give love; the need to be esteemed by oneself and others; the need for security, food, and shelter; the need for inner autonomy and freedom; the need for a sense of meaning; and the need for a growing, trustful relation with God. Such persons seek bread but are able to find only a stone. Their painful hungers of the heart and their stifled growth produce an endless variety of psychological and psychosomatic problems, interpersonal conflicts and destructive behavior, which are damaging to themselves, other people and society. It is this pain and the hope of alleviating it that pushes them into counseling or gives them whatever openness to help they may have when the minister goes to them. This pain *pushes* them while their faint hope of finding a better and more satisfying way *pulls* them toward help.

The Six Dimensions of Wholeness

Pastoral care and counseling seeks to empower growth toward wholeness in all of the six interdependent aspects of a person's life:

—Enlivening one's mind
—Revitalizing one's body
—Renewing and enriching one's intimate relationships
—Deepening one's relationship with nature and the biosphere
—Growth in relation to the significant institutions in one's life
—Deepening and vitalizing one's relationship with God.[4]

We human beings are open systems. Our growth takes place in relationships, the six dimensions of which are listed above. Growth toward greater wholeness in any dimension stimulates and supports growth in the other dimensions. Diminished wholeness in any dimension retards growth in the others. Holistic pastoral care and counseling aim at enabling persons to increase and balance growth in all six aspects of their lives.

Pastoral care and counseling are effective to the extent that they help persons increase their ability to relate in ways that nurture wholeness in themselves and others. To the degree that individuals become able to establish growing, mutually need-satisfying relationships, the following things become possible: They are able to handle their load of problems, losses and responsibilities more constructively. They continue developing their unique personhood centered in an increasingly meaningful relationship with God. They increase their ability to be agents of reconciliation and wholeness in their family, community, and church.

Since wholeness is always relational, self-fulfillment is a psychological impossibility. Growth pursued egocentrically, for its own sake, becomes a *cul-de-sac*. The goal of pastoral care and counseling is self-other-society wholeness. Growth occurs in *covenants-of-wholeness* with others. These are relationships in which there is mutual commitment to nurturing each other's growth toward fulfilling the dream of wholeness that God has for all persons. In such covenants, each person takes responsibility for making her or his side of the relationship growthful to both persons. Self-caring and self-responsibility enable one to enter into such growth-nurturing relationships. A closer look at the six dimensions of human wholeness is now in order.

1. The first dimension—enlivening one's mind—involves developing our rich, partially used personality resources for thinking, feeling, experiencing, envisioning, and creating. The unused capacities of normal human minds are enormous. Enriching our consciousness, releasing our creativity, deepening our insight, sharpening our awareness, expanding our intellectual and artistic horizons—all these are a part of a wholeness-centered approach to pastoral care and counseling (and education).

2. Enlivening one's mind is closely linked to the second dimension revitalizing one's body. This means learning to experience and enjoy one's body more fully, and to use it more effectively and lovingly. Enabling people to overcome their I-it alienation from their bodies and learn how to enjoy body-mind-spirit wholeness is an essential part of liberating counseling. This often involves including a focus in counseling on sound nutrition, exercises, stress-reduction, and other holistic health and body-wellness approaches (see pp. 210-14).

3. Helping people repair, renew, and enrich their network of caring relationships is the third dimension of pastoral care and counseling. Our human personalities are formed, deformed, and transformed in relationships. Healing and growth both depend on the quality of our significant relationships. Relational healing and growth skills are therefore essential for a ministry of wholeness.

4. The fourth dimension of pastoral care and counseling is liberating our relationship with the biosphere by increasing our ecological awareness, communion and caring. People in pastoral care and counseling can become more whole—physically, mentally, and spiritually—when they are helped to develop and cherish a nurturing interaction with our great mother—Mother Nature.

5. The fifth dimension of pastoral care and counseling is institutional-societal liberation, healing, and growth. The weakness of much pastoral care has been its hyperindividualism. Privitized pastoral care and counseling (along with privitized religion in general) ignore the pervasive ways in which racism, sexism, ageism, classism, speciesism, nationalism, militarism, economic exploitation, and political oppression cripple human wholeness on a massive scale in all societies. To correct this myopia, the *pastoral care of groups and institutions* must be seen as the other side of personal and relational healing and growth work. Pastoral care and counseling should include consciousness raising to make people more aware of the societal roots of their individual pain, brokenness, and truncated growth. Caring and counseling should aim at *freeing, motivating, and empowering* people to work with others to make our institutions places where wholeness will be better nurtured in everyone. There can be no full or long-term wholeness for individuals and families in a broken world, a world that destroys wholeness by its systems of injustice, poverty, violence and exploitation.

There is a principle I call the *Gandhi-Day-King-Lee principle,* which can be a corrective for privitized pastoral care and counseling. Mahatma Gandhi, Dorothy Day, Martin Luther King, Jr. and Tai-Young Lee bring together in their life-styles a passion for personal-spiritual growth: with an equal passion for social transformation.[5] *Conscientization,* which increases the awareness of persons receiving care of the societal roots of their individual problems, and *empowerment,* which gives them a sense of their potential strength to work with others to change these societal injustices, are both essential in liberating approaches to care and counseling.

6. The sixth dimension of growth toward wholeness—spiritual growth—intersects the other five and is their unifying bond. The key to human flowering is an open, trustful, nourishing, joy-full relationship with the loving Spirit who is the source of all life, all healing, all growth. Methods of spiritual healing and growth aim at enhancing our meanings, our guiding values, our faith, our moments of transcendence ("peak experiences"—Maslow), and our empowering relationship with the creative Spirit of the universe. Ministers have unique training and resources for enabling spiritual growth. Theological education should equip us

with resources and skills for helping people come alive at their center—their higher Self, which is their inner point of contact with God.[6]

Wholeness at Each Life Stage

Pastoral care and counseling are most effective when they are developmentally-oriented. There is an abundance of opportunities for new growth at each stage of the life journey. Each stage brings new problems, frustrations, losses, and pain. But, fortunately, each stage also brings new strengths, resources, and possibilities. Coping constructively (even creatively) with the new problems of one's present life stage involves discovering and developing the new possibilities of that stage! As a transgenerational social organism, a congregation offers superb opportunities for a life-spanning mutual ministry of healing and growth. A congregation's program of pastoral care should help people use their developmental crises as growth opportunities, responding to the problems and losses of each stage by developing the unique strengths of that stage. Some of a church's caring-sharing groups (growth groups) should be designed to meet the special needs of persons in particular life stages. In such growth-stimulating groups, people may discover the new dimensions of wholeness that can be developed in their present stage. Other growth groups should be available to allow people to form covenants-of-wholeness across generational lines.[7]

The Church as a Caring-Liberating Community

Pastoral care, as understood in the New Testament, is the task of the whole congregation functioning as a caring, healing, growth-enabling community. This general ministry should provide a warm, caring interpersonal environment that becomes crucial when people are going through losses and crises. Being in such a network of mutual nurture can help prevent crises from escalating. It can enhance the healing effects of crisis counseling and therapy. The clergy's task is to train, coach, inspire, and supervise lay persons in their ministry of caring, while also using the rich resources of their training, professional role, and pastoral office in doing their own caring work.

Crises as Growth Opportunities

The vast majority of the opportunities for caring and counseling in the church occur around life crises. There are two kinds of crises—developmental crises that occur around the normal stressful transitions in the life journey (such as marriage, birth, graduation, retirement) and accidental crises that cause unexpected stresses and losses (such as sickness, accidents, surgery, moving, unemployment, natural disasters)—that can come at any life stage. One goal of caring and counseling is to enable people to respond to their crises as growth opportunities. This is done by the use of short-term crisis methods, support-growth groups, and lay caring persons and teams. Every crisis is also a spiritual growth opportunity.

Since the primary focus of pastoral care and counseling in general ministry is on helping people handle their life problems and crises growthfully, the methods used should aim at increasing the constructiveness of behavior as much as feelings and attitudes. Traditional insight-oriented therapy held that changes in behavior often result from changes in feelings and self-perception. This is true, but the opposite is also true. Constructive changes in relationships and behavior often produce significant feeling and attitudinal changes. Pastoral counseling, therefore, aims at helping persons deal constructively with their immediate problems, make decisions, face responsibilities, and make amends for self-other hurting behavior, as well as expressing, experiencing, and eventually resolving growth-blocking feelings, attitudes, and self-perceptions. The part of the personality that copes with reality and with relationships is like a muscle. It grows stronger with exercise and weaker with disuse. Therefore, counseling aims at helping persons exercise and thus develop their potential coping skills. In so doing they usually gain strength, competence, esteem, and hope to cope with future crises.

Using Pastoral Identity and Authority

This model defines the setting and structure of pastoral care and counseling as being more varied and imaginative than simply the structured counseling interview, the "fifty minute hour" in a counselor-therapist's office. My experience in the parish ministry was that the vast majority of fruitful opportunities for crisis caring and counseling occurred in informal settings—e.g., in a parishioner's living room, after a church committee meeting, or standing in a hospital corridor outside the operating room. The structures of formal counseling—appointments, definite time limits, a fee, private meeting place, the agreed upon counseling "contract," and even the label "counseling"—are sometimes possible, but very often are not. A pastor should discover that these features of traditional counseling, though useful in some situations, are not essential to helping people. The structured counseling interview is one effective approach to pastoral healing and growth work. To provide help to the maximum number of hurting people, however, pastors need to apply their counseling skills in a host of informal, often unexpected encounters with persons struggling with staggering loads, complex decisions, and agonizing problems.

One of the most important advantages a minister has is not needing to wait until people ask or come for help. As the professional role of clergy is defined, we are expected to take the initiative in making help available to those who need it but are not ready as yet to ask for help. In contrast to the secular counselor and psychotherapist, pastoral counselors *can* take the initiative by reaching out to those in crises and building bridges of trust with them so that they may be able to accept the help offered.

The constructive use by ministers of their authority in caring and counseling is another unique resource of the pastoral identity. A minister has both the authority of his or her social role as the leader of a faith community and whatever rational authority (Fromm's term) her or his competence gives the person. Both of these forms of authority influence a caring or counseling relationship—often in powerful ways.

Whole Brain Care and Counseling

Research by Roger W. Sperry (for which he was awarded the Nobel Peace Prize) and others has revealed that we human beings have one brain but two minds functioning simultaneously.[8] Although there is instant coordination and considerable overlap in functions, our left-brain hemisphere tends to specialize in speech, reasoning, analysis, evaluation, mathematical and abstract thought. Our right hemisphere tends to specialize in perception, imaging, integration, patterns, and awareness. It is the intuitive, metaphoric, integrating nonanalytic, holistic brain. These discoveries have immense importance for pastoral care and counseling. Following the legacy of Freud, pastoral counseling (and psychotherapy in general) has been primarily left-brain oriented. We now need to use more right-brain methods and to integrate these with the analytical, left-brain approaches. Human transformation is most likely to occur if counseling involves the whole brain of both the counselor (or the teacher) and of the person receiving care and counseling (or education).

Androgynous Understandings of Wholeness

Pastoral care and counseling in the eighties and nineties must be open to the transformation occurring as the increasing impact of the changing identities of women is felt within society. This is the most fundamental of all the profound social changes occurring in our times because it involves a transformation of the way half of humankind define themselves. This is challenging many of us men to become aware of the growth-oppressiveness of our identity as males and our need for liberation. The insights of feminist psychologists, therapists, and theologians should shake the foundations of all our social institutions, including marriage and the church, in the years just ahead. To be relevant to the emerging world—pastoral care and counseling must welcome and integrate the insights and special experiences of women.

Understanding wholeness for both women and men in androgynous terms is one of the most important contributions of feminists to holistic health and healing. "By *androgynous wholeness* I mean a balanced development of one's vulnerable, nurturing, feelingful side (inaccurately labeled the 'feminine' side of the personality by Carl Jung) and one's rational, assertive, analytical side (inaccurately labeled the 'masculine' side). Most of us neglect developing fully one of these two sides of our personalities. Growth Counseling encourages people to nurture and integrate both sides, recognizing that they are complementary, [and] equally valuable aspects of our full humanity as women or men."[9]

Growth-Centered Therapies

To be maximally effective in the next decade, pastoral counseling needs to draw on the insights and methods of a variety of new growth-centered therapies. Our field needs to broaden its conceptual foundation and strengthen its methodologies by being open to these therapies—gestalt, psychosynthesis, transactional analysis, body therapies, behavior-action therapies, feminist therapies, (and other radical therapies), and the systems therapies including conjoint couple and family counseling. Radical therapies offer a conceptual bridge between personal growth and social change, the personal and the prophetic dimensions of ministry.

Pastoral Care and the Other Functions of Ministry

The diagram on the next page depicts the complementary interrelationships of the major dimensions of ministry:

All the functions of ministry have a single unifying goal—increasing human wholeness centered in Spirit. Each function can be an instrument of growth and healing, a channel of pastoral caring. *Person-centered preaching* is one of the minister's most valuable opportunities to enhance wholeness in a congregation by expanding their horizons, shedding the light of biblical wisdom on their down-to-earth problems, and confronting them, in the spirit of love, with their need to grow. *Worship,* a congregation's central group experience, can be a way of helping people renew their basic trust, resolve their guilt, experience the transcendent dimension of life, and have their spiritual hungers nourished. *Education* is a congregation's way of fostering whole-person growth and teaching relevant wisdom from our religious tradition. A congregation's smorgasbord of classes and growth groups can be gardens of mutual caring where the growth of persons and relationships is cultivated. *Congregational leadership and development* is a way of creating and maintaining healthy groups, organizations, and structures, within which wholeness can flourish. Doing church management in a person-valuing way is the heart of organizational development (OD) as applied to a congregation. *Lay enabling* involves releasing the wealth of capacities for mutual ministry in a congregation through a

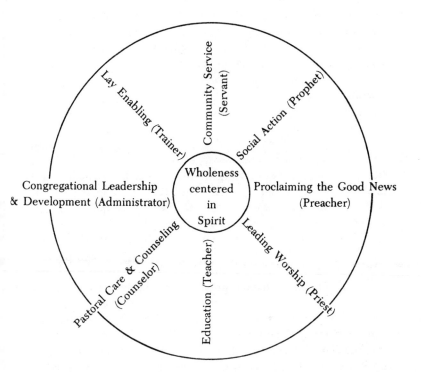

program of lay training. The *prophetic ministry* seeks to change a community and its institutions so that they will support not stifle wholeness in all persons. *Community service* is the ministry of outreach to serve the needs of people in a church's wider community of caring—a community that extends in concentric circles to include the global community. A valuable aspect of the uniqueness of *pastoral* counseling is its being one part of a network of potentially complementary growth-enabling functions. The integrated model of ministry depicted above can help pastors reduce the sense of fragmentation and conflict among their essential functions. [10]

To illustrate some ways two pastoral functions can support and enrich each other, let's look more closely at preaching and counseling. Growthful preaching offers a regular opportunity to communicate the Christian message (the gospel or good news) in a life-affirming, esteem-strengthening, growth-nurturing, and challenging way. It can "speak the truth [that frees] in love" (Eph. 4:15). Person-centered sermons can be, to paraphrase Harry Emerson Fosdick's familiar statement, individual care and counseling on a group scale. By being involved, through pastoral care in the problems and hopes, fears and dreams of their people, preachers can bring the wisdom of the Bible to bear on the real concerns of people. Dialogic preaching can be facilitated by using a variety of pre-sermon and post-sermon small dialogue groups where lay persons have an opportunity to interact with the preacher around the biblical theme or life issue on which she or he is focusing. Preaching often leads to pastoral counseling opportunities. During my years in parish ministry, I learned to evaluate the relevance of my sermons by the opportunities they opened (or didn't open) to the real hurts and hopes of people during the following week.

The Liberation-Growth Model in Light of Our Heritage

It is important that we pastoral counselors see ourselves within the long, rich heritage of pastoral care. When ministers engage in caring and counseling with troubled persons, they are walking in the footsteps of a long line of sensitive, dedicated pastors stretching back through the centuries to a young Jewish carpenter whose words and touch brought healing and growth to troubled persons in the first century. He walked in the footsteps of the "wise guides" of his religious tradition. In the early centuries of the church, pastoral care was called the "cure of souls." Cure (from the Latin *cura*) meant, in some cases "to heal"; more often it meant "to care." Both healing and growth were included in the meaning of this word. [11]

The caring and counseling work of ministers acquires a depth dimension if they sense that they are part of a long heritage, including such great pastors as John Chrysostom (d. A.D. 407), Ambrose of Milan (d. A.D. 397), Martin Luther, Richard Baxter, Horace Bushnell, and Washington Gladden. The heritage also includes a long list of religiously motivated women whose lives were dedicated to those in need, including Elizabeth Anne Seton, Harriet Beecher Stowe, Elizabeth Blackwell, Florence Nightingale, Frances Xavier Cabrini, Jane Addams, and Dorothy Day. With Chrysostom, ministers can think of themselves as "physicians of the soul." They can draw inspiration and energy from knowing that they are part of an ancient caring-helping tradition—the most ancient of any profession.

The contemporary flowering of this ancient ministry should not blind us to our precious heritage. Pastoral care and counseling are a sturdy plant with deep roots in the wisdom of the past. Its flourishing in the last half century has resulted from the convergence of four streams—the clinical pastoral education movement; the new understandings of human beings from the social and behavioral sciences; the flowering of contemporary psychotherapies; and the surging interest in psychology and psychotherapy in America during and after World War II. In the church today, the newer streams have flowed into the century-spanning stream of pastoral care, producing a river of healing and growth like the Mississippi. To change the figure, the ancient plant of pastoral care has been watered by these new streams, producing an unprecedented flowering of caring in our century! Counseling pastors should learn all that they can from contemporary sources, but their self-identity should be molded by their time-tested tradition of shepherding, not by the recent model of the psychotherapist.

The contemporary renaissance in pastoral care started in the the mid-twenties with the pioneering contribution of Richard Cabot, Anton Boisen, Philip Guiles, Russell Dicks, and others who began the clinical pastoral education (CPE) movement.[12] Out of their own illnesses—a psychotic breakdown in Boisen's case and tuberculosis of the bone for Dicks—these two chaplains began to train seminary students and ministers in hospital settings where they ministered with persons in crisis under careful supervision. The treatment settings within which most CPE occurred and the pathology orientation (an emphasis on the diagnosis and treatment of illnesses) of early psychoanalysis, caused pastoral counseling to be heavily pathology-oriented during the forties and fifties. However, the powerful influence of Carl Rogers during this formative period gave this pastoral art something of a balancing growth-centeredness. But it also tended to make the formal psychotherapeutic interview, with intrapsychic insight as its goal, normative in pastoral counseling. My revised model in the 1965 edition of this book aimed at moving the guiding image of pastoral counseling toward a more relational, active, behavioral, and pastoral orientation. The paradigm described in this chapter seeks to continue this process by offering a model that is even more holistic, growth-centered, systems-oriented, nonheirarchical, growth and liberation-oriented, inclusive of the insights of feminism, and deeply rooted in our spiritual heritage and pastoral identity.

In their compendium of pastoral care resources from church history, William A. Clebsch and Charles R. Jaekle lift up four century-spanning pastoral care functions: (1) *Healing*—"a pastoral function that aims to overcome some impairment by restoring the person to wholeness and by leading him to advance beyond his previous condition." (2) *Sustaining*—"Helping a hurting person to endure and to transcend a circumstance in which restoration to his former condition or recuperation from his malady is either impossible or so remote as to seem improbable." (3) *Guiding*— "assisting perplexed persons to make confident choices between alternative courses of thought and action, when such choices are viewed as affecting the present and future state of the soul." (4) *Reconciling*—"seeks to re-establish broken relationships between man [sic] and fellow man and between man and God."[13] Historically, reconciling has employed two modes—forgiveness and discipline.

I would add a fifth essential pastoral care function, which also has been a persistent motif in the history of the church—

Nurturing. The aim of nurturing is to enable people to develop their God-given potentialities, throughout the life journey with all its valleys, peaks, and plateaus. In traditional theological language, this process of growth has been called "sanctification." Although nurturing overlaps and intertwines with the other four interdependent functions, it also is a distinct and crucial pastoral care function. Nurturing and guiding are the pastoral care functions in which education and counseling are most intertwined.

The full development of pastoral care and counseling in the eighties and nineties depends on utilizing all five strands of the pastoral care tradition. It depends on the vigorous interaction and balanced development within a community of faith, of each of these caring functions, applied to the special needs of people in our rapidly-changing society. There is an abundance of both pastoral *care* and pastoral *counseling* opportunities within each of these functional areas. Fortunately, there are modern means of implementing these ancient functions. By emphasizing the contemporary modes of fulfilling these traditional functions, church-related caring and counseling moves away from a predominate medical or psychotherapeutic model to reclaim its pastoral identity. Here, in diagrammatic form, is what I mean:

Pastoral care Function	Historical Expressions	Contemporary Caring and Counseling Expressions
Healing	Anointing, exorcism, saints and relics, charismatic healers	Pastoral psychotherapy, spiritual healing, marriage counseling and therapy
Sustaining	Preserving, consoling, consolidating	Supportive caring and counseling, crisis counseling, bereavement caring and counseling
Guiding	Advice-giving, devil-craft, listening	Educative counseling, short-term decision making, confrontational counseling, spiritual direction
Reconciling	Confession, forgiveness, disciplining	Marriage counseling, existential counseling (reconciliation with God)
Nurturing	Training new members in the Christian life, religious education	Educative counseling, growth groups, marriage and family enrichment, growth enabling care through developmental crises

The Continental Plates Are Shifting

The San Andreas fault passes just a short distance from the cabin in the mountains of Southern California where I go to reflect and write. It boggles my mind when I walk or jog across this fault zone to recall that this is where the huge Pacific plate meets the continental plate that undergirds North America. In his book *New Rules: Searching for Self-Fulfillment in a World Turned Upside Down*, Daniel Yankelovich uses the image of the shifting of vast continental plates (which produce earthquakes, volcanoes, and mountains) to depict what is happening in American society.[14] Profound changes are occurring in the aspirations, dreams, and guiding images of our culture. Much of the turmoil and conflict of our contemporary society is related to these radical, shaking changes.

The search for self-fulfillment or wholeness is no longer confined to youth and the affluent as it mainly was in the sixties and early seventies. Yankelovich reports: "Cross-section studies of Americans show unmistakably that the search for self-fulfillment is instead an outpouring of popular sentiment and experimentation, an authentic grass-roots phenomenon involving, in one way or another, perhaps as many as 80 percent of all adult Americans."[15] He cites, as expressions of this powerful yearning for self-fulfillment, the women's movement; interest in holistic health and physical fitness; the environmental movements; the self-help movements including the hospice movement; the search for new satisfactions in leisure and recreational activities; the greater acceptance of human sexuality; the increasing challenges to the reductionistic, scientific, technological world view; and the new pluralism and freedom of choice that enable many persons to change careers, spouses, residences, faiths and beliefs.

Yankelovich sees a fundamental shift in our culture's values. We are moving away from the old work ethic, which valued responsibility, duty, and success (defined in terms of achieving power, prestige, and property in the competitive struggle). We are moving through the ethic of privitized self-actualization, which glorified freedom, spontaneity, and doing one's own thing (a reaction formation to the lop sidedness of the traditional ethic), and toward a new ethic of commitment, which values mutual responsibility in relationships. What Yankelovich describes is similar to what I call the ethic of commitment-to-wholeness in oneself, others, and society. This guiding ethic prizes the authentic values of the traditional work ethic, but balances them with the healthy values of the actualization ethic. This integrating process can produce a valuing of responsible freedom, creative commitment, playful intentionality, and covenants of growth toward wholeness in relationships.

Rather than being a continuation of the culture of narcissism and the me generation, a commitment-to-wholeness can provide our society with a holistic and liberating vision, desperately needed to help guide the cultural transformation. The wisdom of the Hebrew-Christian heritage has invaluable resources to bring to our culture's understanding of wholeness. A church alive and aware of its changing societal context can become a center of transformation where people can learn how to live the abundant life in this turbulent, exciting moment in history. Amid the convulsions of change chaos, oppression, and violence in our chaotic world, this vision may seem to be a wish-inspired fantasy. But the task of religiously committed persons always has been to dream impossible dreams (in the worst of times) and to work tenaciously to make them a reality! Guided by the wholeness ethic, pastoral care and counseling can become increasingly effective instruments of healing and transformation, and thus participate in the birthing of a new age of human wholeness centered in Spirit on planet earth!

Recommended Reading

Howard Clinebell, *Growth Counseling, Hope-Centered Methods of Actualizing Human Wholeness* (Nashville: Abingdon Press, 1979). Describes more fully the goals, principles, and methods of growth-centered counseling and therapy.

The Mission, Biblical Bases, and Uniqueness of Pastoral Care and Counseling

In our time we have been uprooted from our former homeland, adrift in a mobile and changing society. We are lonely in crowds who seem not to care, pushed to and fro by machines to serve and be served, until we too become mechanical and act like machines. We meet the other persons as strangers, but mostly by external contacts passing by or bouncing away as if we were rubber balls. We . . . do not know the inner life of other persons, and so we give attention mainly to the external appearance. Estranged from them or used by them, we are empty within ourselves, lost souls for whom no one seems to care. The need has never been so urgent for someone to care. How can a pastor care for his people in such a world?

—PAUL E. JOHNSON[1]

Pastoral care is a response to the need that everyone has for warmth, nurture, support, and caring. This need is heightened during times of personal stress and social chaos. Pastoral counseling is a reparative expression of pastoral care, seeking to bring healing to those who are suffering from crisis-induced dysfunction and brokenness. Many who seek a pastor's help are not a part of any church or other caring community. They are the lonely and alienated in our society whose need for caring is acute. Less obvious, but often no less painful, are the needs of those "lost within themselves in our own congregations."[2] Thus a congregation's ministry of care and counseling have both an *inreaching* and an *outreaching* mission to persons, wherever they may be in need. With indices of personal and social disorganization at an all-time high, the need for this ministry has never been greater!

The Crucial Importance of Pastoral Counseling

I recall the vivid awareness that dawned in my mind one Sunday while I was a parish pastor. As I looked over the congregation I saw a man who had admitted his wife to a mental hospital the week before, a young wife deeply depressed by the tragic death of her husband, a couple who recently had learned that their child had leukemia, an alcoholic who was wrestling with his addiction, a couple struggling to overcome the agony of alienation in their marriage, a high school boy whose girl friend was pregnant, an ambulatory paranoid woman who had not responded to psychiatric treatment, a man facing surgery for a condition he suspected was malignant, and another man anticipating with near terror the emptiness that he feared mandatory retirement would bring to his life. I'm sure that other persons in that medium-sized congregation were carrying heavy burdens of which I was not aware.

Such people often trust the very fabric of their lives to the counseling skills of their minister. Frequently the pastor is the only person they allow to enter their private hells. In their desperate need, they open their hearts to the pastor, whether or not he or she deserves that trust. As Wayne Oates points out, pastors (whatever their training) do not enjoy the privilege of deciding whether or not to counsel with people. The "choice is not between counseling and not counseling, but between counseling in a disciplined and skilled way and counseling in an undisciplined and unskilled way."[3] Many people in need see the minister as a competent, trusted shepherd they ask to walk with them through their shadowed valleys. If the pastor lacks the required skills, such persons receive a stone when they ask for bread.

In 1957, an unprecedented study of a cross section of adult Americans was made to discover how many had gone for professional help with a personal problem and to whom.[4] The study was repeated in 1976, the findings reported in *Mental Health in America, Patterns of Help-Seeking from 1957-1976*.[5] The changes over these two decades are impressive. In 1957, only one out of seven Americans (14 percent) reported having sought professional help with a personal problem. In 1976 the ratio was *one of every four Americans* (26 percent). The following chart shows the changes during these two decades in the sources of help people had sought:[6] The increase in the use of mental health professionals (from 27 to 49 percent) probably reflects the establishment of a nationwide network of community mental health centers providing help on an ability-to-pay basis. But, as the authors of the report on the 1976 study observe: "In spite of the

	1957	1976
CLERGY	42%	39%
PHYSICIANS (Nonpsychiatric)	29%	21%
PSYCHIATRISTS & PSYCHOLOGISTS	17%	29%
OTHER MENTAL HEALTH PROFESSIONALS	10%	20%

clear and important shift in 1976 toward the consultation of mental health professionals for personal problems, one cannot fail to be impressed by the continuing critical role that clergy play in assisting many Americans in dealing with personal problems . . . One out of ten Americans in 1976 said that at one time or another they talked to their clergy about a personal problem."[7]

In spite of the increased availability of mental health services, a considerably higher percentage of Americans have sought counseling from clergy than from any other single helping profession. Of those who had sought help, from the clergy, 36 percent were men and 41 percent were women. Among help-seekers in their twenties, 42 percent had sought help from clergy. For those over sixty, the percentage was 45. Among persons who are in church more than once a week, 68 percent had turned to clergy when they sought help.

With what types of problems had people sought help from ministers, according to the 1976 study? As they defined their problems, 35 percent went because of interpersonal problems involving a defect in a relationship, another 19 percent because of a problem involving a defect in another person, and another 16 percent because of a defect in themselves. Because of a crisis such as illness or the death of a loved one, another 16 percent sought help from clergy. Because of practical, non-psychological problems, 8 percent had gone. The importance of ministers having marriage counseling and crisis counseling skills is highlighted by these findings.[8]

What kind of help did persons report they received from clergy? The help that 51 percent received was from "talking and advice"; 18 percent reported they received "comfort and the ability to endure;" 15 percent reported a cure or a change in a relationship. How helpful, from the recipients' viewpoint, was counseling with clergy? Eighty percent reported they were "helped a lot," "helped" or "helped" (in some qualified way)." Only 11 percent reported that counseling with clergy had not been helpful. The helpfulness of clergy, as evaluated by the recipients, was slightly more than that of other helping professionals.[9] This study confirms the strategic role clergypersons fulfill as counselors in our society. It is obvious that we continue to be on the front lines in the struggle to help burdened people.

It is important to obtain the best available supervised training in counseling, both academic and clinical, not only to avoid doing harm but to maximize one's abilities to be an instrument of healing. A competent counselor often has the privilege of guiding other human beings on their inner journey toward wholeness. Sensitivity and skill in counseling allows one to stand on the sacred ground where personality growth and transformation occur. One becomes a catalyst in a healing-growthing process, a pastoral midwife in the rebirth of persons to larger dimensions of their humanity. The minister who has paid the price of the disciplined study and training leading to competence knows at times the wonder, surprise, and joy that come with the realization: "My personhood, with all of its flaws and frailties, has been an instrument by which the Spirit of the love-hearted universe brought healing and growth to another human being!" Whatever theological students or ministers do to enhance their skills in this area will pay rich dividends, throughout their ministry.

Training in caring and counseling also can increase the effectiveness of ministers in the noncounseling aspects of their work. Caring skills are basically skills in communicating and relating in growth-stimulating ways. Since every facet of a pastor's complex job has relationships and communication at its heart, the total ministry can benefit from the sensitivity and skills acquired in counseling training. The same principles of interpersonal dynamics are involved in counseling and in other ministerial functions. Learning to listen empathetically to feelings, for example, has a deepening effect on all pastoral relationships.

Doing Theology Through Pastoral Care and Counseling

The relationship between the practice of pastoral care and counseling and our biblical heritage is like a two-way street. The insights from the heritage illuminate, inform, and guide the practice of these pastoral arts, and this practice brings to life basic biblical truths by allowing them to become incarnate and experienced in human relationships. In counseling, the biblical truths are illuminated by being applied and tested in the arena of human struggles and growth! It is in this sense that pastoral care and counseling are ways of *doing theology!*

In counseling relationships, a pastor and her or his people struggle together with basic theological issues on a deeply personal level. Whether the issues are identified by theological labels or not—and in our secularized culture they often are not—they are the heart of caring and counseling. Sin and salvation, alienation and reconciliation, guilt and forgiveness, judgment and grace, spiritual death and rebirth, despair and hope are interwoven in the fabric of the healing-growthing interaction between pastor and parishioner.

It should not be surprising that truths from the Hebrew-Christian heritage come alive in pastoral counseling relationships. David Roberts, one of my mentors, observes: "Whatever is valid in Christ's disclosure of God is universally operative in human life, and, therefore is verifiable within experience."[10] To the degree that people find release through caring and counseling from the captivity of their inner conflicts and self-oppression, overcome their alienation from others, increase their ability to love and to live life in all its fullness—to that extent the counseling experience has embodied the theological verities that are at the heart of all human life and relationships! An effective caring/counseling relationship thus becomes a part of the continuing incarnation of the Spirit of the creating God in the lives of hurting, hoping people.

I now will describe some biblical images and insights that come alive for me in healing and growth work (with myself and others). These are some of the biblical themes with which persons who do caring and counseling can stay in dialogue to illuminate and energize this ministry. This ongoing dialogue is between a pastor's understanding of the time-tested insights from our religious heritage (informed by critical study of the Bible) and the down-to-earth problems of living with which people wrestle in all counseling.

There are several reasons why it is important to integrate biblical insights with the practice of this ministry. Since the Bible is the wellspring of our Western spiritual tradition, keeping in close touch with it can help keep us rooted in its wholeness-nurturing truths. Second, being in ongoing dialogue with biblical insights can generate attitudes and awareness in the caring person that facilitate both healing and growth. Third, in working with persons from backgrounds, which made biblical images live for them, archetypal images and truths from the Bible can be used as instruments of creative transformation. Living biblical images, stories and metaphors are right brain ways of communicating profound truths about life. They are a sustaining power in the lives of many socially disempowered people who love the Bible. Fourth, *biblical wisdom* about the nature of wholeness is needed to *critique, correct,* and *enrich* contemporary psychological understandings of wholeness. In several important respects, there is a deeper, more realistic understanding of wholeness in the Bible than in humanistic psychology.

Biblical Images of Wholeness

The biblical record emphasizes repeatedly the *remarkable* potentialities of us human beings. The psalmist describes us as being created "little less than God" (Ps. 8:5). The first of the two creation stories in Genesis asserts that we are made in the image or likeness of God (Gen. 1:27). In the anthropology of the Jewish Bible, all aspects of persons, not just their minds or spirits, are seen as created in the divine image.[11] To develop our unique personhood in the likeness of the divine, is the goal of the Christian life. Facilitating this development is the purpose of all ministry including pastoral care and counseling.

As pointed out earlier, the good news according to John describes Jesus' purpose in coming as being so that people could have "life . . . in all its fullness" (John 10:10, NEB). Life in all its fullness (or the "abundant life") is the biblical way of speaking of Spirit-centered holistic health or wholeness-centered-in-Spirit. The life-long task of discovering and developing one's unique possibilities is the means by which the image of God flowers and the abundant life is actualized.

Jesus' parable of the talents (Matt. 25:14-30) is an emphatic statement of the importance of developing one's God-given resources wisely and fully. Paul's second letter to Timothy calls for him "to stir into flame the gift of God which is within you . . . for the spirit that God gave is . . . one to inspire strength, love, and self-discipline " (II Tim. 1:6-7 , NEB).

The biblical understanding of wholeness makes it clear that humans are not God, even though they are made in the divine likeness. Awareness of one's finitude, limitations and brokenness is essential, alongside awareness of one's remarkable potentialities. Without this, one easily falls into self-idolatry and the narcissistic pride that alienates persons from nurturing interaction with other people, the biosphere and God.

Rollo May points out that saying to people that their possibilities are unlimited can be deenergizing and frightening: "It is like putting someone into a canoe and pushing him out into the Atlantic toward England with the cheery comment, 'The sky's the limit.' The canoer is only too aware of the fact that an inescapably real limit is also the bottom of the ocean."[12] (This reminds me of a psychotherapist who said that he is now specializing in "post-actualization depression.") The awareness that we are finite and our growth is limited by the unchangable "givens" of our lives—e.g., our heredity, our socio-cultural context, our historical setting, our age and physical health—can help keep us grounded and constructively humble (from *humus* meaning "earthy"). It can provide a reality-based foundation for our self-esteem and thus reduce the narcissism and pride (defenses against low self-esteem) that undercut wholeness. Accepting our inescapable finitude isn't easy, but it is essential for the lifelong journey called wholeness. The prophet Isaiah puts this well: "A voice says, 'Cry!' And I said, 'What shall I cry?' All flesh is grass, and all its beauty is like the flower of the field. The grass withers, the flower fades, when the breath of the Lord blows upon it; surely the people is grass. The grass, the flower fades; but the word of our God will stand for ever" (Isa. 40:6-8).

Biblical Roots of the Six Dimensions of Wholeness

What are scriptural bases for the sixth dimensions of wholeness set forth in the last chapter? The Hebrew understanding of persons was essentially nondualistic. Wholeness involved the unity of all dimensions of persons—body, mind, and spirit *in community*. Within this holistic view, biblical images depicting the body as the temple of the Holy Spirit and the injunction to "glorify God in your body," (I Cor. 6:19-20), reflect a high view of the physical body. This thrust undergirds the first dimension of wholeness.

The biblical injunction quoted by Jesus (Mark 12:30) to love God with "all your mind" (as well as with all your heart, soul, and strength) underscores the second dimension of wholeness. Put in a modern psychological context, it emphasizes the importance of the cognitive-intellectual as well as the emotional and spiritual aspects of our minds. In contemporary terms, loving God with one's mind could be expressed as the continuing unfolding of one's mental and emotional potentialities through lifelong learning.

Relational wholeness, the third dimension, is a persistent motif in the Bible. Wholeness is seen as nurtured in relationships. A community per se can be healthy (wholeness facilitating) or sick. These views are implicit in the Hebrew concept *shalom* and in the New Testament concept *koinonia*. Shalom, meaning sound, whole, or healthy (as well as peace), is nurtured in a shalom community. In such a Spirit-centered community, the quality of relationships provides an environment within which persons are encouraged to develop their unique personhood.[13] In the New Testament, the Greek word *koinonia* is used to describe the church as a healing, transforming community centered in Spirit. This systemic understanding of mutually nurturing relationships within an integrating religious commitment is communicated in both the "one flesh" concept referring to the marriage bond (Gen. 2:24) and the image of the church as the body of Christ with many members (Rom. 12:5).

Ecological wholeness, the fourth dimension, also has biblical roots. The biblical attitude of respect for and stewardship toward all of creation (the eco-system) is communicated in mythic wisdom of the first of the two creation stories in Genesis. The phrase "And God saw that it was good" is a refrain of affirmation articulated after each stage of the process. These words appear at the close of the story "And God saw everything that he had made, and behold, it was very good" (Gen. 1:31). In the biblical view, we humans do not own the planet, but have it as a trust from God. This is expressed in the words, "The earth is the Lord's" (Exod. 9:29). The nourishing closeness of Jesus and his people, the Jews, to Mother Nature is evident in his persistent use of images from nature—birds of the air and flowers of the field—to communicate truths about our relation to the divine Spirit.

The fifth dimension of wholeness is the ways in which our relation to institutions stimulate or stymie the development of our potentialities. This also is undergirded by the biblical wisdom. A passionate concern about the destructive impact of oppressive institutions is central in the prophetic tradition of the Jewish Bible. Jesus identified his ministry with this thrust when he read, in his hometown synagogue, from the scroll of the prophet Isaiah:

"The spirit of the Lord is upon me . . . he has sent me to announce good news to the poor, to proclaim release for prisoners and recovery of sight for the blind; to let the broken victims go free, to proclaim the year of the Lord's favour" (Luke 4:18-19, NEB). The interrelationship between liberation and healing is obvious in this passage.

Liberation, in its biblical meaning is both personal and societal. Both sin and salvation are communal and social, as well as individual. Here are some New Testament liberation themes, emphasizing the crucial importance of inner liberation of the mind and spirit: "You will know the truth, and the truth will make you free" (John 8:32). "We are not children of the slave but of the free woman . . . stand fast therefore, and do not submit again to a yoke of slavery" (Gal. 4:31-5:1). "For the law of the Spirit of life in Christ Jesus has set me free from the law of sin and death" (Rom. 8:2). The prophetic emphasis on justice underscores God's intention that society and its institutions be liberated so that they will nurture rather than negate human wholeness. Jesus, who shows us God's love in action, identified himself with the oppressed and rejected of his society.

Liberation theology—including Latin American, African, black, and feminist theology—emphasizes that God is understood as *liberator* in both the Old and New Testaments. God's promise of liberation is unfulfilled if only the privileged of the world are free while the social, economic, and political structures of society that cripple the masses are left unliberated. As Martin Luther King, Jr. made clear, we cannot understand God's love separated from his justice. James Cone holds that the image of God in a world of oppression is incarnate in people involved in the liberation struggle against the unjust structures and forces of society.[14] I agree. People who are thus involved become aware of their worth and power in God's sight and of the image of God in which all persons are created and re-created.

Spiritual wholeness—the sixth and integrating dimension—is undergirded by the very core of the biblical view of wholeness. Wholeness like life, is a gift of the creating Spirit of the universe. Throughout the Bible, there is an acute awareness that the fulfillment of our God-given potentialities is supported and energized by the power of the universe. It is as though the gravitational pull of the spiritual universe is drawing us toward becoming what we have the potential to become. J. B. Phillips' paraphrase of Romans 8:19 says: "The whole creation is on tiptoe to see the wonderful sight of the sons [and daughters] of God coming into their own." To say this in modern parlance, we have a lot going *for* us when we seek to facilitate wholeness in ourselves and others! We are never alone when we are engaged in the development of the full image of God within persons.

A counselor's awareness of the gift quality of growth toward wholeness can be both energizing and liberating. It can free us from the weight of inappropriate feeling that growth is entirely dependent on our own efforts. We can be grateful that we need not and, in fact, cannot create either the potential for growth or the élan within people that makes them want to grow. Both are there as gifts of God. As wholeness-oriented counselors, our work is to help people respond to the longing for wholeness that is in them. Paul's words can be both humbling and reassuring to us counselors and educators: "I planted, Apollos watered, but God gave the growth" (I Cor. 3:6). By aligning ourselves and our efforts with the creating Spirit, we become co-creators of wholeness. The counseling relationship becomes a channel for the grace of God, the transforming love that is the source of all salvation and all wholeness (Gal. 2:8; Rom. 3:23-41). The ultimate source of wholeness is identified clearly in Paul's letter to the church at Ephesus: "May your roots go down deep into the soil of God's marvelous love" (Eph. 3:17, Living Bible).

The Nature and Process of Wholeness

From a Christian perspective, Jesus' life shows us the full, rich possibilities of human wholeness. In him we encounter a growing, fully alive, love-filled person. In Jesus, the word became flesh so that God is no longer to be sought out there distanced from our human situation. The unfolding wholeness that God dreams for all persons is seen in him. Jesus' healing, transforming aliveness somehow transcends the centuries. Paul Tillich, one of my teachers, calls this wholeness-nurturing reality the "new being." For Christians, experiencing and participating in this new being means growing into "the full stature of Christ" (Eph. 4:13, NEB) by developing our own unique expression of life in all its fullness.

The growth images of the Bible show unmistakably that wholeness was understood as an ongoing process, not as a static goal to be achieved once and for all. Let this image speak to you: A good person "is like a tree planted by streams of water, that yields its fruit in its season" (Ps. 1:3).

The process by which wholeness is facilitated in relationships is described this way: "Let us speak the truth in love; so shall we fully grow up into Christ" (Eph. 4:15, NEB). Growth occurs in any relationship when one experiences both accepting love and honest confrontation. Movement toward greater wholeness is nurtured in us when someone cares enough to speak the truth in love to us. This enables us to experience something of both the love that does not need to be earned (grace) and caring honesty (judgment) that confronts us with the ways we are hurting ourselves or others. Healing love—the muscular love that brings together caring and confrontation—is essential in all pastoral care and counseling! This principle is what I call the "growth formula."

Jesus' way of relating to persons embodied this formula. He cared deeply but with confronting honesty for all kinds of people, including society's powerless rejects—sinners, psychotics, the sick, the poor. He related to them in terms of what they could become as well as what they were. He saw them through the glasses of growth and thus helped them grow.[15] It is no wonder that ordinary people responded to him in extraordinary, growthful ways. The impact of Jesus' way of perceiving people is well illustrated by his renaming of Simon Bar-Jona (Matt. 16:18). Seeing in him an enormous potential for strength and leadership, Jesus must have said something like this to him: "Simon, my friend, I'm going to give you a new name. I'm going to call you Peter (meaning "rock") to help you see your strength and all that you can become." The fact that Jesus saw and affirmed the potential within Peter, must have helped him develop the character strength and spiritual depth to become a dynamic leader of the early church. As pastoral counselors, we need to put on the glasses of growth, enabling us to see and affirm people's God-given potentialities.

The New Testament clearly indicates that continuing growth toward wholeness involves self-transcendence and self-investment in the growth and healing of others. This principle of growth-through-outreach is enunciated in Matthew 16:25—"For whoever would save his life will lose it, and whoever loses his life for my sake will find it." Put in contemporary terms, if you horde the wholeness you have achieved narcissistically, it will diminish. If you invest yourself in helping others grow, your own wholeness will flower.

Pastoral counselors can learn a vital lesson from their own tradition and from groups like Alcoholics Anonymous—that equipping and empowering people to *serve others* is an essential goal of all religiously motivated counseling. Loving service can stimulate the growth for those who serve, enabling them to form new mutually enlivening relationships, and experience the satisfactions (as well as frustrations) of self-investment in others. The ministering church aims at becoming a supportive community of faith where people will find the motivation, insights, and strength to be healing agents to those in need. Releasing people to use their healing and growth in loving, freely chosen service to people in need is an important goal of pastoral counseling.

The Brokenness of Persons and Society

The biblical wisdom is as aware of the profound alienation and brokenness of human beings as it is of our potential for increasing wholeness. We have a deep need and longing to develop the *imago dei*, yet we persistently resist and sabotage our own growth and the growth of others. The story of the "fall" from the innocency of the garden of Eden (Gen. 3) is a mythic, poetic way of communicating the fact that we are alienated from the image of God, from our potential wholeness. As Tillich puts it, "The state of existence is the state of estrangement. Man [*sic*] is estranged from the ground of his being, from other beings and from himself."[16] The traditional religious word for our alienation and our resultant proclivity to block wholeness in ourselves and others is sin. Sin was understood in the world of the Bible as both individual and societal. To the man who was healed of his paralysis, Jesus said,

"Take heart, my son; your sins are forgiven . . . Take up your bed and go home" (Matt. 9:2, 6). But Jesus also wept over the whole city of Jerusalem because it did not know the things that make for peace based on justice (Luke 19:41-42.) This prophetic awareness recognizes that the sin of society's injustices breeds individual sin and sickness like a stagnant swamp breeds mosquitos.

To minister effectively to the multiple forms of human brokenness encountered in pastoral care and counseling, it is essential to have a tough, realistic understanding of human sin and evil. The biblical view offers a healthy corrective to the superficial optimism that sometimes appears in humanistic psychologies. All of us know the inner conflict expressed by Paul in his letter to the early Church in Rome: "For even though the desire to do good is in me, I am not able to do it. I don't do the good I want to do; instead, I do the evil that I do not want to do" (Rom. 7:18-19, GNB). The Bible is aware that our estrangement from ourselves and others is somehow rooted in our estrangement from God's life-giving love. Freud called the ingenious ways people block their own healing and growth "resistance." But whether it is called resistance or sin, dealing with this recalcitrant reality is crucial in all effective pastoral care and counseling.

Biblical writers were keenly aware of the destructiveness of blocked growth that makes people caricatures of the creative selves they might have been. Demon possession as described in the Bible was, a prescientific misconception that mental illness was caused by the invasion of evil spirits. Although we now know that this view is not literally true, as a metaphor it communicates vividly the demonic destructiveness of deeply distorted growth—e. g., in psychoses or in the collective insanity of institutionalized racism, sexism, or the balance of terror of the nuclear armaments race.

Classical theology's interpretation of the "fall" as describing some deep irreparable flaw in our humanity that irreparably sabotages all our strivings toward wholeness is invalid. But, as a pastoral psychotherapist, I am constantly impressed by the inner crippledness and interpersonal destructiveness that flourish in individuals, in relationships, and in our society. The biblical view of the impact of the "iniquity of the fathers [and mothers]" on their children (Exod. 34:7) parallels contemporary insights from family therapists concerning the ways wholeness-blocking patterns of relating are transmitted from generation to generation in families.

I remember the shock of standing in the crematorium at Buchenwald in the section of East Germany from which my mother's grandfather probably came. That horrible death camp and the homes of Goethe, Luther, and Bach not far away symbolized the psychological proximity of the diabolical destructiveness and the potential grandeur in us human beings! If we underestimate the power of human evil, alienation, and destructiveness, we cannot be effective agents of that reconciliation and healing that are essential to enhancing wholeness through care and counseling.

The biblical awareness of human finitude, sin, and brokenness can keep us in touch with our own limitations as healers and growth-enablers. Our counseling at best produces only partial wholeness. Sometimes it is totally ineffective. At worst it can be harmful. There are many persons in whose lives psychological and spiritual damage is so deep and prolonged that resistances to healing are very powerful. Counseling and therapy methods are imperfect. They are used by us imperfect human beings who live in an imperfect society. However creative and competent a pastoral counselor, the best that can be hoped for in many cases is that people may gain the strength and serenity to accept and live more constructively with whatever cannot be changed in their lives and situations.

Growth as Struggle, Death, and Rebirth

A variety of biblical images make it clear that, though wholeness is a gift of God, it takes effort, intentionality, and often painful struggle to receive this gift by developing our potentials. Images of taking up one's cross (Matt. 16:24); of dying and being born again (John 3:3; Rom. 6:6); of the narrow gate and straight way leading to the new age; of a radical transformation or conversion *(metanoia)*—all communicate this truth.

The early Christians were known as "followers of the way." The Christian life is much more than a way of believing and trusting. It is a way of doing, a way of traveling on one's life journey. Jesus' statements to individuals were full of action imperatives— "Go . . . ! Do . . . ! Arise . . . !" But changing the inner sources of behavior requires much more than intentionality, as important as that is in human growth. The New Testament affirmation that salvation is by grace through faith (Rom. 3:25) is a word of liberation for those of us who are trapped on the workaholic's works-righteousness treadmill, futilely seeking to earn a sense of worth through achievement. The awareness that we can "accept ourselves as being accepted by God" (Tillich) awakens hope and liberates energy for creative change. *This experience* of grace can produce inner transformation, enhancing self-esteem and a sense of aliveness. More responsible and constructive behavior then flows from a life-affirming conscience, transformed by the gift of loving acceptance, not from a guilt-driven conscience that produces controlling moralism and rigid oughts and shoulds. The recognition that the capacity for growth is a gift from God can help save wholeness approaches to ministry from growth-righteousness that sees one's growth entirely as a personal achievement.

The New Testament image of resurrection is a joyful affirmation of the power and possibility of new, authentic human existence. But the process of growth toward this enlivened quality of life often feels like a series of painful deaths and rebirths. The journey of wholeness seems to involve being born again (John 3:3)—and again—and again! The Easter experience of rebirth to greater aliveness and larger dimensions of liberating truth seems possible only after the death of some of one's narcissism and defenses against risking coming alive more fully. The death-rebirth motif in growth is expressed in the fourth gospel: "Unless a grain of wheat falls into the earth and dies, it remains alone; but if it dies, it bears much fruit" (John 12:24). The struggle and eventual joy of the process of human transformation is communicated in this moving image attributed to Jesus: "You will be sorrowful, but your sorrow will turn to joy. When a woman is in travail she has sorrow . . . but when she is delivered of the child, she no longer remembers the anguish, for joy that a child is born into the world" (John 16:20-21).

"The powerful *resistances* to growth are seen, in the biblical heritage, in the context of the more powerful *resources* for growth. Sin is viewed in the wider context of salvation, despair in the context of hope, dying in the context of resurrection, judgment in the context of grace. Seeing the darkness of the human self-other alienation in the context of Light, somehow transforms the darkness."[17]

Healing and Salvation

Healing of sickness and other forms of human brokenness is a central motif in the New Testament. Nearly one-fifth of the four gospels deals with stories of Jesus' healings. His critics probably felt that he spent too much time with the sick, the burdened, and the disturbed. But the importance that he attached to this aspect of his ministry is crystal clear. His parable of the shepherd who left the ninety-nine to find the one lost sheep shows his deep concern for the individual in need (Matt. 18:12-14). His response to those who criticized him for eating with sinners and with the despised tax collectors—"Those who are well have no need of a physician, but those who are sick" (Mark 2:17)—showed the orientation of his ministry. Healings by the disciples (Mark 6:13) and in the early church were commonplace.

As Daniel Day Williams makes clear, the language of salvation and the language of healing are interlaced throughout the Bible, though the two are not identical.[18] He cites H. Wheeler Robinson's observation that of the one hundred and fifty-one uses of the Greek words for salvation (*soteria*, the noun, *sozo*, the verb), sixteen refer to deliverance from disease or demon possession, and more than forty to deliverance from physical death.[19] Williams defines salvation as fulfillment for a person "in a new relationship to God and . . . neighbor in which the threats of death, of meaninglessness, of unrelieved guilt, are overcome. To be saved is to know that one's life belongs with God and has a fulfillment in him for eternity."[20] The most frequently used of the six Greek words related to healing in the New Testament, *therapeuo*, means both "to serve" (a divinity) and "to care for, treat (medically), heal, restore." Salvation is understood in the New Testament as a kind of ultimate healing. It is this healing that makes Spirit-centered wholeness possible!

The New Age of Wholeness

Wholeness in the New Testament is seen in the context of the new age of wholeness called (in the hierarchical language of the first century) the Kingdom of God. This is an age of caring and community, of justice and social transformation based on a new wholeness-making relationship with God. Many of Jesus healings were described as signs of the kingdom. In describing the new age that was coming, Jesus used these growth images:

"The kingdom of heaven is like a grain of mustard seed which a man took and sowed in his field; it is the smallest of all seeds, but when it has grown it is the greatest of shrubs" (Matt. 13:31-32).

"The kingdom of heaven is like leaven which a woman took and hid in three measures of flour, till it was all leavened" (Matt. 13:33).

"A sower went out to sow . . . some seeds fell along the path . . . other seeds fell upon thorns . . . other seeds fell on good soil and brought forth grain, some a hundredfold, some sixty, some thirty" (Matt. 13:3-8).

These parables are invitations to you and me to participate in the process by which the new age of wholeness is coming "on earth as it is in heaven" (Matt. 6:10). Liberation-growth oriented holistic pastoral care and counseling are ways of helping people become participants in the new age now dawning. As Pierre Teilhard de Chardin has made clear, humankind is now confronted by an unprecedented challenge. Because the human psyche has developed self-awareness, we are now able to become co-creators of future directions in humankind's psychological and spiritual evolution. The awareness that we are in a period of "conscious evolution" brings a fresh and exciting dimension to images of the kingdom in the New Testament.[21]

There is in the Hebrew-Christian heritage, an awareness that we are part of one family—the human family—which has a common Parent (see Acts 17:25). The new age must therefore include the community of humankind. The parameters of our concern for liberation, healing, and wholeness encompass the entire human family, with whom we are inextricably related by deep spiritual ties. This is the basis for an emerging and urgently needed whole-earth consciousness, conscience, caring, and community.

A Whole Theology for Pastoral Care

The Bible and traditional theology, and creedal statements through the centuries have been derived almost entirely from the spiritual experiences of men. The rich contribution of women's spirituality has been largely supressed and ignored in the Judeo-Christian heritage. When I am able to hear what feminist theologians of liberation are saying, I become aware of healing insights and images that enrich, complement, and correct the spiritual heritage shaped mainly by males. Recovering the riches of women's spirituality is essential if the churches are to become fully vital places of healing and wholeness in the eighties and nineties. Integrating the best from our biblical tradition, with the empowering contributions of feminist spirituality, can give us a more whole theology for ministry and for pastoral care and counseling in particular. These pastoral arts cannot realize their full possibilities as instruments of healing, liberation, and growth with a lopsided, male-oriented theological foundation. *Nothing is more important than women's spirituality for releasing the enormous healing capabilities of churches in the next two decades!*

Since I have discussed the nature of an inclusive theology elsewhere, let me only summarize some things that need to be done to strengthen the theological foundation of pastoral care.[22] Those of us who value the Judeo-Christian tradition can use its resources more growthfully by doing the following: (1) We can use the ringing affirmation of human equality in Ephesians 3:8 as a freeing vision for pastoral care and counseling. To see that in Christ Jesus there is "neither male nor female" is to become aware that it is our humanity, not our gender, that really matters before God. Unfortunately, this liberation vision has not been implemented in the church dominated by patriarchal images and power. One could give many examples of the way the church's theologians have misused male biblical images (e.g., the second creation story in Genesis 2 and 3) to "keep women in their (inferior) place," thereby crippling their wholeness. As Rosemary Ruether declares: "Traditional theological images of God as Father have been the sanctification of sexism and hierarchicalism . . . allowing ruling class males to identify themselves with this divine fatherhood in such a way as to establish themselves in the same kind of hierarchical relationship to women and lower classes."[23] The sexist uses of the Bible and male-created theology is a tragic illustration of the central thesis of liberation theology—that theological images and interpretations tend to maintain the power and privileges of a society's elite who created that theology. (2) We can recognize that women need feminine images and symbols of divinity—e.g., Spirit, Goddess, wind and fire (as at Pentecost), rebirth—as resources for the growth of full self-esteem and wholeness. Men need these too, to balance and correct the impact on their self-image of the dominant male hierarchical images—lord, king, master. Fortunately there are precious remnants of the earlier heritage of women's spirituality that survived in the Bible—the wisdom literature, the growth images, the strong women in the Old and New Testaments. (3) We can affirm and emulate the liberated wholeness of Jesus' personhood and of his relations with women. He integrated the qualities that our male-oriented society identifies most often with men—courage, strength, leadership, and concern for justice—with ones most often identified with women—caring, compassion, tenderness, and responsiveness to the needs of others. Thus he demonstrated that both sets of qualities are neither masculine nor feminine but *human* capacities, all of which need to be developed by whole persons of either sex. He called God "father" (reflecting his patriarchal times), but many of the attributes of deity in his teachings are those associated most closely (in his culture and ours) with mothers—mercy, compassion, nurture, tender love. Jesus refused to restrict women, as did his culture, to sex roles as servants of men. This is illustrated vividly in the story of Mary and Martha (Mark 10:2ff). In a society that considered it improper to teach women sacred truths, Jesus treated women with the same respect as he did men, sharing his brilliant new understandings of spiritual reality with them freely.[24] In short, Jesus was a remarkably liberated, whole person who was countercultural in his inclusive, egalitarian treatment of women and others regarded as inferior (e.g., Samaritans and tax collectors) in his society. It behooves those of us who do pastoral counseling to emulate him.

Women have much that is precious and unique to bring to the search for spiritual wholeness from their experiences with oppression and with the miracle of new life formed within their bodies. To nourish and enliven the wholeness of women or men, a whole theology must value women's spiritual insights as fully as it does men's. We can rejoice that the feminist theologians and spiritual pioneers of our times are releasing a powerful stream of spiritual energy to feed wholeness in both women and men! We must share their awareness of our society's massive sins against women as reflected, for example, in the epidemic of domestic violence, rape, and economic exploitation of underpaid women (e.g., secretaries).

The Church: Center of Liberating Wholeness

What are the biblical images of the church that can empower its mission as a center for healing, liberation, growth, and empowerment for one's mission to the world? The New Testament vision is of the church as the people of God (II Cor. 6:16)—a caring community united by a covenant with God; the body of Christ (Rom. 12:4-5; I Cor. 10:17)—an organic unity in which each member, each part of the living body, has her or his unique gifts and ministry; and the community of the Holy Spirit (Acts 10:44-47)—a redemptive, healing community through which the living Spirit can work in a very needy world.

A classic study of the church's mission by H. Richard Niebuhr, Daniel Day Williams, and James M. Gustafson concludes that the unifying goal of the church is to increase the love of God and neighbor among persons.[25] This theme is directly relevant to Spirit-centered wholeness. British theologian Norman Pittenger points out that the image of God in the self is the capacity for love, the potential to become more fully shaped into the love that is God's own essence.[26] Daniel Day Williams describes the basis of all care of souls: "Love is the center of Christ's disclosure of our humanity. God has shown his love for us in the action which reveals his purpose, and that action is told in the Christian story of Jesus. To love then, in the New Testament sense, means to participate in this action. Our action is a response—in ways appropriate to our situation—to what God has done for us. Thus Paul enjoins the Christian community, 'Let this mind be in you, which was also in Christ Jesus . . . who took upon him the form of a servant.' (Phil. 2:5ff) And this surely is the foundation of Luther's daring statement that we are to become Christ for one another."[27]

Because we had human, limited parents who had human, limited parents, all of us are limited, to some degree, in our ability to love fully. Many people are severely crippled in their ability to love in growth-nurturing ways. This is the heart of their problem. To say to such a person, "You need to love God and neighbor more," is like shouting to a person floating on a log in mid-ocean, "What you need is dry land!" Nothing could be truer or less helpful. What such a person needs is to know where the land is and how to get there. Counseling and therapy are methods of helping people learn to love themselves, their neighbor, and God more fully and freely. Erich Fromm states: "Analytic therapy is essentially an attempt to help the patient gain or regain his capacity for love. If this aim is not fulfilled, nothing but surface changes can be accomplished."[28] Unearned love (grace) is both the method and the power of tranformation to greater wholeness. For persons whose ability to love is painfully diminished, counseling or therapy can mean the difference between a creative, productive, joyful life and one of inner captivity, stagnation and self-rejection. For such persons, counseling can be an imperfect but effective channel for receiving the gift of God's healing, transforming love.

Traditionally, the church's task has been divided into four functions—*kerygma* (proclaiming the good news of God's love), *didache* (teaching), *koinonia* (the establishing of a caring community with a vertical dimension), and *diakonia* (the expression of the good news in loving service). Although pastoral care and counseling are primarily an expression of *diakonia*, the ministry of service, they also are means of communicating the gospel, teaching life-enabling truth, and establishing *koinonia*. As far as God being a real source of meaning and wholeness, many people consider that God is dead. The word "God" is not a living symbol for them. They are unable to hear the good news. Caring and counseling can be ways of communicating the gospel by helping them open themselves to a healing relationship. Until they have experienced accepting unearned love in a human relationship, it cannot come alive for them. Until they are grasped by caring acceptance (the always limited human counterpart of God's grace) in a life-to-life encounter, the good news of the Christian message cannot become a liberating, experienced reality for them. Helping relationships are places where this limited and fragmentary but transforming incarnation of grace can occur.

Because of their exhausting burden of inner conflicts and pain, many church members cannot contribute to the establishment of a Spirit-centered *koinonia* climate of relationships in a congregation. Their presence is divisive—not uniting, pathogenic—not healing. As Ludwig Binswanger has observed, psychotherapy [and counseling] can help to prepare such persons to become constructive participants in the life of a healing community, *koinonia*. They then can take part in the healing outreach of that congregation to the wider community.[29]

The Uniqueness of Pastoral Counseling

Ministers need to understand their uniqueness as counselors, *vis-à-vis* other professionals who do counseling and therapy, so that they can maximize their special contributions to helping the troubled. *The heart of our uniqueness is our theological and pastoral heritage, orientation, resources, and awareness.* This is our frame of reference and the area of our special expertise. The awareness that the transpersonal Spirit of God that is the core of all reality, should influence profoundly everything we do including our counseling. Dietrich Bonhoeffer's familiar statement, "God is the 'beyond' in the midst of our life," can be used to describe the unique focus of pastoral care and counseling.[30] Wayne Oates aptly calls this awareness "the God-in-Relation-to-Persons Consciousness."[31] This consciousness should help pastors recognize the spiritual dimension present in every counseling situation. This transpersonal awareness is central in all counseling that is truly pastoral.

The unique *training* of pastoral counselors is their dual education in both the theological and the psychological/psychotherapeutic disciplines. Ministers are the only counseling professionals whose usual training includes systematic study of philosophy, theology, ethics, biblical studies, church history, world religions, and—very important in their counseling—psychology of religion. Their knowledge of these theological areas can enable them to be uniquely helpful to persons whose problems and growth-blocks center around ethical dilemmas, religious conflicts, value distortions, and such ultimate concerns as finding a meaning in life and handling the fear of death creatively. Paul Tillich describes pastoral care as a "helping encounter in the dimension of ultimate concern."[32] If ministers have integrated their theological education with their clinical education in counseling, they are prepared to be uniquely helpful in this much-needed ministry of meanings.

The counseling pastor's working premise that *spiritual growth is an essential objective in all caring and counseling* is unique among the helping professions. A minister's area of expertise is in fostering spiritual wholeness as the core of whole-person growth. Enhancing spiritual wholeness should be an explicit goal in the pastor's mind, though it may not be discussed in particular counseling relationships. Whatever counseling does to increase a person's ability to relate openly and authentically to other people may help open him or her for a more vital relation with God. But many of us continue to have immaturities and distortions in our religious lives long after we have outgrown these in other areas. Special help often is needed to nurture spiritual maturing. A growing relationship with God is an indispensable aspect of total wholeness. If this awareness is held in the counselor's mind, it inevitably influences caring and counseling relationships, whether or not explicitly religious topics are discussed. If a person's spiritual life is a primary source of conflicts, guilt, and blocked growth, it must become an explicit focus in counseling.

Another aspect of the uniqueness of pastoral counselors is derived from the fact *they are expected and, hopefully, trained to use the resources of their religious tradition as an integral part of their counseling*. If used in a disciplined and appropriate manner, such resources can be of particular value in several types of counseling including supportive, crisis, bereavement, ethical, existential-religious counseling, and spiritual direction. In addition to resources such as sacraments and prayer, the time-tested wisdom of our tradition (as found in the biblical theological and historical contexts) is a vital resource in a pastor's caring and counseling. Anton T. Boisen puts the matter clearly:

> The priest or minister at his best brings to the task of helping the distressed in mind certain insights. He is versed in the utterances of the great and noble of the race, has traced the adventures of the human spirit both individually and collectively in its quest of the more abundant life. He understands the deep longings of the human heart and the significance of the constructive forces which are manifest alike in the religious conversion experience and in acute mental illness. He recognizes the fundamental need of love, and dark despair of guilt and estrangement from those we love, and the meaning of forgiveness through faith in the Love that rules the universe and in whose eyes no one is condemned who is in the process of becoming better. In such insights lies the important contribution of the competent minister of religion rather than in any particular techniques.[33]

The *setting* and *context* of a pastor's counseling give it uniqueness in profound ways. The setting is the life of a gathered community of faith, a congregation. The context is pastoral care and the other functions of the general ministry through which pastoral care can occur. The fact that ministers counsel within an ecclesial setting, a complex network of relationships where many people know each other and see their pastor in non-counseling situations, influences what happens in counseling significantly. The ongoing, day-to-day relationships with a network of people of all ages, in light and shadow, provides pastors with innumerable opportunities to help. Established, trustful relationships often provide a solid foundation for crises counseling, allowing persons to be helped in much less time than would be required to start from scratch with an unknown counselor. Because ministers often are present at such crises as marriage, childbirth, bereavement, sickness and accidents, they may identify serious problems long before such problems reach advanced stages. (The problems of most people who come to therapists and counseling agencies are usually at an advanced stage.) The natural, continuing contact of pastors with families, the seedbeds where personality is formed and deformed, is an invaluable and unique asset in both preventive pastoral care and crises counseling. Most pastors are aware of numerous emotionally impoverished family systems that breed crises and individual problems. Pastors have direct access to many family systems when they need help. No other helping profession has a comparable supportive community of caring people available year-in, year-out. If the network of small groups in a church is alive and growthful, it can complement and undergird the counseling ministry with burdened persons. Through their counseling, ministers can become bridges by which some of the lonely ones in our depersonalized society discover a caring group.

The fact that pastors are part-time counselors with a variety of other functions that can complement as well as conflict with counseling, is another significant dimension of their uniqueness as counselors. The prophetic function of ministers is a particularly unique dimension of a pastoral counselor's identity.

The unique pastoral care context of pastoral counseling has innumerable possibilities. Through training lay carers and encouraging the development of a variety of caring-sharing groups, pastors can help a whole congregation to become a healing-growthing environment. Through imaginative programs of lay caring, ministers can enable the healing and growth of many more people than they could through their direct caring ministry alone. Between formal, structured pastoral counseling and the general ministry of pastoral care, there is a broad range of informal, short-term crises caring and counseling opportunities.

Pastors are unique among counselors in their social and symbolic role. They are "representative Christian persons"— representatives of the beliefs, values, and life together of a congregation—who "bring Christian meanings to bear on human problems."[34] The perceptions of a pastor's symbolic identity by counselees influence pastoral counseling in subtle but significant ways. Ministers tend to be perceived as religious authority figures, as religious "transference figures." Their presence triggers in some people a variety of early life memories and feelings about such matters as God, parents, heaven, hell, sex, Sunday School, funerals, church, right, wrong, and other clergy they have known. Ministers who are aware of these unfinished spiritual issues from the past have opportunities to help people correct old distortions and acquire more constructive attitudes towards things religious.[35]

The fact that ministers are perceived as representatives of certain ethical values and religious beliefs (whether or not these perceptions are valid) probably prevents some guilt- and doubt-laden people from seeking their help. The fear of being judged causes some persons to avoid clergypersons. Yet ministers who are, in fact, self-accepting and therefore able to be nonjudgmental toward others, communicate acceptance through their total ministry. This tends to diminish, though it does not eliminate, the projection onto them of judgmental images by guilt-ridden people. The fact that parishioners encounter their pastor in a variety of roles makes some of them prefer to take embarrassing problems to another minister or counselor. As one man put it, "I like and respect my minister, but I'd rather not have him know about my affair." But, the fact that ministers are perceived as representatives of the value and belief structures of their religious communities is a tremendous advantage in some counseling.

Pastors usually do not charge for counseling. This has both limitations and advantages. The neurotic meanings of money in our culture (symbolizing the giving and receiving of love and power) are not immediately available for therapeutic scrutiny. Important self-understandings sometimes emerge when paying clients examine their feelings about doing so. Further, a pastor's counselees lack the test of motivation that paying for counseling supplies. Because of this, some people abuse the minister's time in unproductive ways. Ministers should expect that those receiving long-term help will contribute to them or to a designated church fund, especially if they are nonmembers and are not contributing to the support of the church in other ways. Allowing persons to pay for counseling often decreases feelings of dependency and strengthens self-esteem by letting them give, as well as receive in the relationship. For those who do not pay financially for their counseling, it is often constructive to have them pay by some service to persons in need.

That pastors can counsel without charging is also an advantage in that it allows them to see persons, including the very poor, entirely on the basis of need. A troubled person usually can see a minister without waiting several days (or longer), often without an appointment in advance. These are obvious advantages in helping those requiring emergency care and counseling.[36] The pastor's relatively easy accessibility allows persons who are too embarrassed to make appointments for counseling to get help by coming to her or him, ostensibly for less threatening reasons. For persons from non-middle-class backgrounds, for whom structured counseling interviews are foreign to their life-style, the availability of pastors for informal counseling in a variety of settings is a distinct advantage over most mental health services.

The professional role definition of ministers often allow them to take initiative in reaching out to those who need care and counseling (see page 36). This is a unique and valuable professional advantage. As Donald Houts points out, pastoral initiative is a corrective against counselor passivity and uninvolvement. The pastor's willingness to take risks (which models this behavior for the recipient) often builds bridges of help long before people spontaneously seek such help. The ways in which pastoral initiative is exercised should avoid both coercion and paternalism.[37] Pastoral calling is an expression of pastoral initiative, an important means of bringing a ministry of caring to people in their homes, and in so doing, identifying and building relationship bridges to those who need care and counseling.

The Foundation of All Types of Caring and Counseling

Many people are looking for an ear that will listen. They do not find it among Christians, because Christians are talking when they should be listening. He who no longers listens to his brother [or sister] will soon no longer be listening to God either. . . . One who cannot listen long and patiently will presently be talking beside the point and never really speaking to others, albeit he be not conscious of it.[1]

—DIETRICH BONHOEFFER

Bill Shaw phones Kurt Matthews, the minister of a downtown congregation, for an appointment. He had appeared in church three weeks before the call and had not returned. He was not at his room at the local YMCA when the minister attempted to visit him. When he returned, he found the minister's card with a brief, "Sorry to have missed seeing you. It was good to have you in church!" This seemingly unproductive call was what made Bill decide to phone for help. The card, which he carried in his wallet for several days before phoning, communicated the minister's concern as well as his phone number.

Pastoral counseling actually begins when the first contact is made by a person to seek help. Earlier contacts with the minister that may prepare the person to ask for help are called "pre-counseling."[2] Here are fragments of the phone conversation between Bill and the minister:

Bill: Hello, this is Bill Shaw. I found your card. Sorry I wasn't home when you came by. (His voice had a flat, heavy quality.)

Minister: Good to hear from you, Bill. I just stopped by to say "hello" and welcome you to the community. You're new in town?

Bill: Yes, I moved here to the coast from St. Louis last month. Decided I'd try making a new start out here.

Minister: Well, glad to have you among us. How are things going?

Bill: O.K., but it's a little rough getting acquainted in a new place. As a matter of fact, there are a couple of things I'd like to talk with you about. I don't want to take much of your time, but—ah. . . .

Minister: I'll be glad to see you. What's your schedule like? When would it be convenient for you to drop by my office?

Bill: Well, I'm between jobs at the moment, so anytime will be O.K.

Minister: Unfortunately, I was just about to leave for an out-of-town conference. But tell me a little about your situation.

Bill: Well, my wife divorced me three months ago, and I've been lower than a snake's belly ever since. These last few days I've felt like I had to look up to see the bottom. Haven't been able to sleep much.

Minister: It sounds as though things are very rough for you. Would you be free to meet me at the church in twenty minutes?

Bill: Yes, but I don't want to hold up your trip.

Minister: That's all right, I'd *like* to chat with you for a little while before I go. My office is on the Oak Street side of the church. There's an outside entrance. I'll look forward to seeing you at 1:15.

Bill: O.K., see you then.

This brief phone contact accomplished the following: (1) A caring relationship, which began when Bill sensed the minister's warmth during the church service and was strengthened by the pastoral call and the brief message on the card, was continued and strengthened as Kurt communicated his concern. (2) The ice was broken for Bill when he risked talking briefly about his problem with the minister. (3) Kurt obtained a tentative diagnostic impression concerning the nature and seriousness of Bill's problems. (4) Realizing that Bill might be seriously depressed, Kurt made a decision to delay his trip and see Bill briefly. Bill's expressionless voice, the fact that he had experienced a major loss recently, his sleeplessness, and his statement about having to "look up to see bottom" all pointed to severe depression. Kurt knew that the risk of suicide is high among deeply depressed persons, particularly men living alone.

Even if the minister had not been on the verge of a trip, it would have been important to discover, on the phone, something about the nature and urgency of Bill's problem. An open-ended question such as, "What seems to be the difficulty?" or "Tell me a little about your situation" usually opens the door for persons to describe their problems. Because the ice is broken with the minister, it is less likely that Bill will break his appointment because of anticipatory anxiety about opening discussion of a painful problem. This approach allows the minister to distinguish emergency or acute crisis situations from chronic problems in which counseling can be scheduled with much less sense of urgency. It is well, of course, to see any new counselee as soon as is mutually convenient.

The Growth of a Healing Relationship

During the first counseling session, several things should occur. (1) The foundation is laid or strengthened for a growing therapeutic relationship as the person experiences the minister's warmth, understanding, and caring. (2) Through focused listening and empathic reflecting of the parishioner's feelings, the catharsis of painful, bottled-up feelings begins, and (3) the pastor acquires a tentative understanding of the person's "internal frame of reference"—how life looks from within his or her world. This diagnostic impression includes some understanding of how the person defines the problem, the ways where his or her relationships are failing to meet basic needs, and the person's resources and limitations in handling the situation. (4) On the basis of this tentative diagnosis, the minister recommends an approach to obtaining help—such as continuing pastoral counseling and/or referral to some specialized help (e.g., a medical check-up, psychotherapy, or AA). (5) If continuing counseling is agreed upon, an informal counseling contract should be established defining the goals and expectations of that relationship.

Counseling consists of the establishment and subsequent utilization of a relationship; the quality of which can be described as *therapeutic* (healing), *maieutic*[3] (facilitating birth and growth) and *reconciling* (restoring alienated relationships). This is the psychological environment where effective problem-solving, healing, and growth, can best occur. Counseling techniques are helpful only within such a context. Experiencing this quality of relationship is in itself healing and growth stimulating. The most important single objective of the first interview is the beginning of this quality of relating!

A therapeutic relationship grows as the pastor pours herself or himself into being *with* the burdened person. This means concentrating on *listening*, and responding with caring empathy. These activities, important during all phases of counseling, are indispensable during the early stages. Instead of worrying about what one is going to say or do next (as inexperienced counselors tend to do), the counselor should focus energy on being aware of and with the person in an alive human relationship. This is what the existentialists in psychotherapy call "presence." Karl Jaspers declares: "What we are missing! What opportunities of understanding we let pass by because at a single decisive moment we were, with all our knowledge, lacking in the simple virtue of a full human presence!"[4] All of us have known the empty, depersonalizing feelings resulting from conversing with a person who isn't really *present*. The opposite of this experience is required to produce a healing, growthful relationship.

As persons sense, even vaguely, that the minister is really trying to listen deeply and relate fully, a tiny fragile nexus as delicate as a spider web will begin to connect their aloneness with the minister's aloneness. This is the first, vital strand of what will become a sturdy bridge connecting the islands of awareness of two human beings. The bridge is called *rapport*. In a spirit close to that of Martin Buber, Rogers states: "To enter deeply with this man into his confused struggle for selfhood is perhaps the best implementation we now know for indicating the meaning of our basic hypothesis that the individual represents a process which is deeply worthy of respect, both as he is and with regard to his potentialities."[5]

The art of *reflective empathic listening* is essential in all caring and counseling. The pastor attempts to listen to *feelings* (as well as words) including feelings that are between the lines, too painful to trust to words. Now and again he or she responds to these feelings. Dietrich Bonhoeffer's penetrating indictment, quoted at the beginning of this chapter, underlines the importance of learning the lessons of listening and learning it well. A line from Shakespeare's *Henry IV* describes the problem of unawareness, the cause of many failures in pastoral counseling: "It is the disease of not listening, the malady of not marking, that I am troubled withal."[6]

I shall always be grateful to an elderly, dying woman in a mental hospital who many years ago, helped to teach me the crucial importance of listening. She had been in the hospital for over twenty years. We both knew she was dying. Before I tried to comfort her, something told me to ask her how she felt about her dying. Her wonderfully honest reply made what I was planning to say absurdly irrelevant. She responded with intense feeling: "Chaplain, I'll be so glad to get out of this damned place!" I had made the mistake of assuming that I knew how people feel about dying. The reason I was so wrong was that there is no such thing as the way people in general feel about anything!

As counselors listen *in depth*, to the multiple levels of communication, verbal and nonverbal, they reflect back to the person, in paraphrased form, what they hear, particularly the person's big (dominant) feelings. This kind of listening is "disciplined listening"—focusing on what seems to have the most feeling, meaning, energy, and pain.[7] By periodically summarizing significant points and asking occasional questions for clarification, counselors help persons begin to organize their confused inner world, and thus gradually come to understand their problems more clearly.

The process of listening and reflecting in a warm caring way serves several other important functions:

(1) It allows counselors to check the accuracy of their perceptions. If they are not on the counselee's emotional wave length, their reflections provide opportunities for misperceptions to be corrected.

(2) It lets counselees know that the minister is *trying* to understand their inner world of meanings and feelings.

(3) This awareness of the minister's concern and dawning understanding stimulates the growth of the counseling relationship.

(4) In some cases, responding to feelings lances the psychic wound, permitting the poison of powerful pent-up feelings to drain off so that normal healing can occur.

(5) As counseling progresses, the counselor's listening and responding provides the counselee with an opportunity to examine and test the reality of feelings and actions. Helen Flanders Dunbar once compared the listener in therapy to the practice board used by tennis players to perfect their strokes.[8]

The counselor's aim is to achieve the maximum degree of what Rogers calls "empathic understanding" of the person's inner world. Heinz Kohut declares, in effect: Empathy is the accepting, confirming, and understanding human echo evoked by the self. It is an essential psychological nurturant without which human life as we cherish it cannot be sustained.[9]

The research findings of R. D. Quinn are reassuring to new counselors who are worried about not understanding fully or responding with consistent accuracy. Quinn found that it is the counselor's *desire to understand* that communicates caring acceptance to troubled persons, causing them to permit the counselor to establish a beachhead of increasing understanding in their inner world.[10] It is unnecessary for ministers to be highly gifted in the ability to empathize (feel with others) in order to counsel effectively. If they are really *with* persons in a nonjudgmental, accepting way, their attempts to understand and reflect feelings may miss the person's meanings and feelings at times without interfering with the therapeutic relationship.

Several things tend to block a counselor's sensitivity to counselee's feelings—premature attempts to think of solutions to their problems; high anxiety and lack of being "centered" often produces unawareness of feelings (one's own and the counselee's); inner conflicts in the counselor, resulting in blind spots that prevent awareness of similar issues in the client; and too much concern with left-brain counseling theories and techniques. Inexperienced counselors should avoid trying to think of solutions to counselees' problems, and instead concentrate on understanding and being with them caringly in their inner world. The interaction resulting from this quality of presence will tend to increase the counselees' self-understanding and enable whatever solutions are developed, by the counselee or collaboratively, to be reality-oriented and sound.

Empathic listening is active listening demanding an emotional investment in the other and relative openness to one's own feelings. A theological student in a reality-practice counseling session made this discovery:

> In listening to a counselee talk about his situation, the counselor's response is the result of listening to his own feelings. . . . If his feelings are not those of the counselee's, he will

correct him, and the counselor will have another chance on the level of his own feelings to get with it. When I discovered that the voice of my own feelings—what they said about his—were trustworthy, I could relax and reflect spontaneously.[11]

Counselors who cannot feel their own feelings (particularly anger and grief) because of inner blocks are seriously handicapped. They are limited in their ability to experience "resonance," the responsive chord between two persons that makes possible relating in depth, including therapeutic relating.

Motivation, Diagnosis, Intervention, Contracting

Without forgetting the importance of listening and responding warmly to feelings, there are certain questions to which the counselor needs answers, preferably during the first session. If these answers are not acquired in the course of the counselee's discussion, the counselor should ask the questions directly, after rapport has begun to be established: Why did you come for help now? To me? What is the problem as you see it? Are you hurting or did you come mainly because of pressure from another? (In other words, is the person internally or externally motivated?) How do you feel about being here? And, very important, what kind of help do you want and expect from me? These questions are crucially important because they have to do with the key issue of the counselee's motivation. Neglecting them often results in failure to establish a healing relationship. Counselees and counselors often bring very different expectations to a counseling relationship. These must be brought out into the open and discussed if a resolution is to occur.

Returning to the case of Bill Shaw, we find the minister greeting him at his study door and after some initial small talk about the weather, saying, "Tell me some more about your situation." This encourages Bill to focus on his problem *as he perceives it* (the "presenting problem"). There often are deeper problems of which the counselee may not be aware, but the rule of thumb is to *start with the presenting problem*. In the course of Bill's description, Kurt gradually acquires some basic information concerning his troubled life and relationships. He finds that Bill is thirty-seven, had been married for twelve stormy years before the divorce, has two children, and has worked at various jobs, mainly as an auto mechanic. Kurt remembers Bill's words on the phone about "making a new start," suggesting that his previous life adjustment had probably crumbled. As Bill talks, the minister listens for the *big feelings* among the many feelings Bill expresses:

Bill: This divorce hit me like a ton of bricks. Sure, we had our disagreements, and she had threatened to divorce me, but when it happened, I just couldn't believe it. I felt mad, naturally, but mostly I felt like something big was gone.

Minister: You felt crushed and empty; something extremely important in your life was yanked away!

Bill: Yeah, and the empty feeling is worse being so far away. I miss my kids something awful. (Deep sadness in his voice.) My boy started scouts this year, and that's a program where dads are supposed to be in it with their boys.

Minister: The distance makes your loss much more painful since it makes it impossible for you to see him and be really involved in his life.

The minister, at this point, is simply attempting to hear and reflect the man's dominant attitudes and feelings.

Bill: Uh huh, I keep wondering if I made a king-size mistake moving out here. I wanna be a dad to my kids and yet I just felt like I had to get away from the old stomping grounds. I had some bad luck on jobs—gotten in trouble on a couple of them because of my temper. I thought maybe it would be better to make a new start where I didn't have all my old tracks around. I suppose I also wanted to show Jean that I didn't need her—that I could get along without her just fine!

Minister: The pain of both problems—the job and the marriage— made you feel that a move was in order. But now you're having some serious doubts, because of your loneliness for the children.

Bill: (Nods.) There's no hope for the marriage, but I don't want my kids growing up without me!

Minister: You feel pulled powerfully in two directions. Makes it very difficult to decide whether to go back or stay.

Bill: That's right, and the more I mull this over in my mind the worse I feel. Just seem to go around in circles. I lay there on my bed in the Y feeling lousier and lousier—like what's the use? It just didn't seem worth the struggle. Then I remembered your card and decided to give you a call.

> Minister: I'm very glad you phoned. Things are looking very bleak, and hopeless to you.

The minister now has a partial picture of why Bill Shaw asked for help. He knows that he came on his own because of the inner pain of his loneliness and grief and his conflict about returning to St. Louis. Here is a segment later in this interview:

> Minister: You mentioned on the phone that you aren't working at present.

> Bill: That's right. But a fellow at a garage across from the post office said he could use me starting next Monday.

> Minister: It must make you feel better to know you will have a job.

> Bill: Well, I've never had any trouble finding work—I'm a trained auto mechanic. But it will be good to be working again and get away from that room, and I'm nearly broke. I couldn't afford the bus fare to St. Louis now, even if I decided that was the thing to do.

> Minister: I'll be glad to work with you as you decide what's best for you and your boys. I'll be out of town for two days at the conference I mentioned. Would it be convenient for us to get together on Friday at this same time?

> Bill: That'll be O.K.

> Minister: Fine. Let's work together on this.

> Bill: O.K.

> Minister: How are you feeling now—about your situation? (The purpose of this question was to ascertain how depressed and hopeless the man still felt.)

> Bill: Better. It helps to get some of these things off my chest.

> Minister: Would you be open to getting acquainted with one of our men, Sam Turner? Sam's a part of what we call our lay befrienders' team in our church. He's a friendly person and I think you'd enjoy getting to know each other. It's rough being alone in a new city. Would it be O.K. for Sam to call you and arrange to get together?

Bill agreed and the two men met the next day at the coffee shop at the YMCA. They hit it off and Sam proved to be helpful to Bill, as a new friend and as a person trained in listening.

During the interview the minister noted that Bill gradually became more animated. Apparently his depression began to lift and his hope revived a little as a result of the caring relationship and the offer to help. The pastor knew that Bill had two supports during his absence—the availability of a trained lay carer (whose availability to see Bill the minister checked before leaving town) and the security of having a definite appointment with the minister three days hence.

If Bill had come because of pressure by another person, it would have been essential to deal with this by: (1) discovering how Bill sees his problem (if any); (2) finding out if and where he is hurting and therefore might be internally motivated by a need for help; (3) encouraging the expression of anger and resentment about being coerced to see a minister; (4) accepting Bill's right not to continue counseling if he doesn't feel a need for help; and (5) being warmly interested and emotionally available, so that the person may feel free to accept help for his own reasons. Here are some responses illustrating this general approach:

> **Teen-Ager:** My mom thought I needed to have a talk with you. She's got this thing about my making up my mind soon about a career.
>
> **Minister:** It sounds as though your mother has been putting pressure on you to get with it in picking a career, even though you don't feel any hurry about this. It must bug you to be pushed to see me.

There usually is a problem in the relationship between the one who comes and the person applying the pressure. In a situation such as this one, it might be productive to invite the mother and the daughter to come in together to discuss the issues between them, reflected in their conflict about the daughter's career decision. Unlike a secular counselor, the minister has a pastoral care responsibility for the mother as well as the daughter.

The five procedures listed above constitute a method that is often effective in motivating a potential counselee who is coerced and resistant. Unless persons are aware of issues or problems and want the minister's help, there will be no genuine counseling, even though they go through the motions of counseling *ad infinitum*.

During the first interview, the minister forms a tentative diagnostic impression concerning the nature and depth of the person's problems in living. By listening intently he or she may become aware of patterns in the person's feelings, problems, and relationships. These may give clues to the degree of underlying inadequacies in that individual's life-style, personality, and coping resources, of which the presenting problems are only the current manifestations. It may become evident that the person has reasonably adequate coping skills but has been thrown into a temporary tailspin by a severe crisis or series of crises. If so, short-term crises counseling may be all that is needed. Or perhaps the counselee's personality is so conflicted and problems so chronic that a referral for longer-term therapy is essential. This crucial diagnostic decision involves estimating the person's ego strength (see chapter 8).

Because the word "diagnosis" connotes a medical model of counseling, its meaning must be broadened in order to communicate what is meant in a growth-oriented approach. Most counseling, regardless of its orientation, involves a process of understanding and evaluating the person's problems, and then, in the light of this, making decisions about how to intervene and what type of help to offer or recommend. Pastoral diagnosis should include an evaluation of the person's general level of wellness, as well as any pathology. It should also give attention to the health of the person's spiritual life (values, priorities, beliefs, spiritual vitality). As Paul Pruyser observes, our theological-value orientation should inform our evaluative categories.[12]

After forming a tentative diagnosis, the pastor should ask herself/himself: "Is this person likely to benefit from the counseling which my time, training, and skills will enable me to provide? Is there some agency or therapist in the community set up to provide the specialized form of help that this person needs?" On the basis of considerations such as these, the minister comes to a tentative decision concerning whether to offer continuing short-term crisis counseling or to refer the person. In some cases, the effectiveness of short-term counseling can be discovered best by attempting it. If no progress is made or the person is regressing after a few sessions, it is wise to make a referral.

In the case of Bill Shaw, the minister sensed that there were at least two levels to his problem. His painful loneliness, grief, and conflict about returning to St. Louis were aspects of his problem with which the minister felt competent to help Bill deal. But behind these pressing problems the minister sensed what might be some deeper personality problems. He knew that he would learn more about this level as he sought to help Bill with his immediate dilemmas. In the light of what he learned, he could then decide whether or not to refer Bill for help with deeper problems.

If one decides that short-term counseling is likely to help the individual, one should do more than offer it. One should *recommend* it by saying, in effect:

> I believe that it might be helpful for us to work together on these issues for a few sessions. Your situation is very painful and perplexing to you now. Our goal will be to discover some constructive ways of handling these problems, so that you'll not only cope better with them but gain some strengths for handling future problems. How do you feel about getting together three or four times, after which we'll decide whether to continue working together for a few more weeks or perhaps find some specialized help if that is needed?

If persons are resistant to such a recommendation, their resistances should be respected, discussed openly and, if possible, reduced. If they agree to try counseling, contracting should occur whereby an agreement is reached through discussion regarding the purpose and goals of counseling; what each person's expectations and responsibilities are; the time, place, and length of sessions; and a clear statement by the minister concerning the confidential nature of what is communicated in counseling. In this process of contracting, the collaborative nature of counseling should be stressed, particularly if the person has come expecting a magical prescription or easy solution. The doctor-patient model in the minds of some who come for counseling is grossly inadequate because it elicits expectations of external cures that involve the person only minimally. To be effective, *counseling must involve persons actively in mobilizing their own resources* to cope and to grow. Expectations that the minister will perform a miracle must be altered, gently but firmly.

If persons agree to begin counseling, a definite appointment should be made with an understanding that either will phone if there is any change in plans. It is usually best to let persons know that the first few sessions will be approximately an hour long. Most of us cannot listen deeply to another for much longer than that. Briefer sessions (ten to thirty minutes), and contacts by phone, may be all that persons need after they begin to mobilize their own coping resources. It is important to note that establishing a mutually agreed upon counseling contract is what marks movement beyond a pastoral care into an explicit counseling relationship.

Emotional catharsis (also called emotional ventilation and abreaction) is a crucial part of the early phases of nearly all types of counseling. "Certainly one of the significant goals of any counseling experience is to bring into the open those thoughts and attitudes, those feelings and emotionally charged impulses, which center around the problems and conflicts of the individual."[13] The various types of counseling are distinguished mainly by what occurs *after* catharsis.

The accepting quality of a counseling relationship provides a safe environment in which burdensome feelings that most people hide can be revealed and explored. This is a contemporary form of the confessional. In a relationship of trust, counselees can face powerful feelings such as intense guilt, anger, panic, low self-esteem and sexual impulses, and by dealing with them openly, break their stranglehold on their lives. A counseling relationship provides a unique opportunity to unburden one's spirit by discovering, verbalizing, expressing, clarifying, and resolving forbidden feelings, in the presence of an authority figure who does not reject the person for having them, but instead communicates understanding and acceptance. Even if counseling goes no further than the stage of emotional catharsis, it can be healing and growth enabling, helping to remove the inner log jams, which block self-acceptance and coping. Frequently, after pouring out a painful story, a counselee will say, in effect, "I've been carrying this load for fifteen years, afraid to talk about it with anyone. For the first time in years, I feel like I can stand up straight!"

How does the pastor encourage this emotional release? By listening with caring empathy (as described above) and responding to feelings. More specifically, the following approaches tend to facilitate catharsis:

(1) *Avoid asking informational questions* beyond those needed to obtain essential facts. Too many informational questions tend to pull the person away from feelings. (2) *Ask about feelings*—"How did you feel when the chairperson ignored you?" (3) *Respond to feelings rather than just to the intellectual content*. Reflect

feelings, using feeling words in doing so. "You really felt clobbered by what happened!" "This hurts down deep!" "Let's see if I catch what you're feeling here . . . " (4) *Watch for doors* that lead to the feeling level of communication. These include feeling words; emotion in the voice, face, or posture; protesting too much; self-contradictions (indicating inner conflicts); and discussion of need-satisfying relationships such as with parents, spouses, or children. Responding to these often leads to deeper levels of feelings. (5) *Be especially alert for negative feelings*. These are the most frequently repressed and the most in need of being brought into the psychological sunlight of an accepting relationship. (6) *Avoid premature interpretations* of why people function or feel certain ways and *premature advice*. Both of these are tempting traps since they offer the insecure counselor ways of feeling useful and in control, and thus less anxious. Both interpretations and advice tend to block the flow of feelings. It is important to be aware that after a session in which people pour out painful feelings and share intimate aspects of their problems, they may feel embarrassment the next time they see the pastor.

Reducing Premature Terminations

Some counselees terminate before the helping process has had a chance to be effective. Here are some ways of reducing this premature attrition. The counselee's experience of the counselor's warmth, understanding, and acceptance is basic.[14] In addition, terminations can be reduced by:

(1) Expressing *active interest* in working with the person in resolving his/her problem.

(2) Explaining *why* several sessions of counseling are necessary.

(3) Voicing whatever hope is realistic concerning how counseling may help reduce the person's suffering and increase satisfactions.

(4) In addition, it is important to *give the person something definite during the first interview*. This can be an understanding summary of the situation as the pastor sees it, a pamphlet to read, or a "homework assignment" of something to reflect on or do.

(5) Near the close of each session, the counselor should ask, "How do you feel about our discussion during this hour?" If the counselee feels disappointment and does not have an opportunity

to verbalize these feelings, he or she may act out unexpressed feelings by not returning.

(6) If a person seems likely to terminate, the possibility should be discussed openly. This discussion may help to prevent premature termination.

(7) If a counselee's initial expectations about counseling are grossly unrealistic, they should be altered gently and gradually rather than abruptly.

(8) Negotiating a clear contract including an agreement by counselees to come for a specified number of sessions tends to reduce premature termination. Knowing that one has a limited number of sessions also encourages counselees to work hard on their problems from the start.

Mechanics: Publicity, Setting, Records

Some people are not aware of the fact that most ministers have training in counseling. Many who do know this are reluctant to take the pastor's time to discuss their problems. It is well, therefore, for ministers to let their congregations know that providing help with personal and relational problems is one of their normal functions as pastors, and that they are available to discuss whatever is of significant concern to their people.

As pastors' network of meaningful relationships broaden and deepen, in the process of serving a faith community, counseling opportunities tend to increase. The personhood of the pastor, as members of the congregation experience it, either closes or opens doors through which people feel free to come for counseling. Ministers can help to open doors by printing a brief statement such as this in the church bulletin or newsletter:

"All of us occasionally have problems in dealing with the pressures and perplexities of daily life. There are times when we can benefit from talking with a person trained in counseling about the issues we're facing. Our church makes such help available, when it is desired by our members or by others in the community. Your minister is available to talk confidentially with those facing personal or family problems, difficult decisions, crises, spiritual perplexities, or the need for specialized help. Facing one's problems and seeking professional help are signs of strength.

Counseling including spiritual direction is a normal part of any pastor's work. Feel free to call her/him at the church at 611-4342 to arrange for an appointment at a mutually convenient time."

It is easier to do effective counseling if one has a quiet place free from interruptions. If one lacks a secretary who can insure privacy during counseling, a "Pastor Is in Conference" sign on the study door and a phone that will turn off are helpful. It is well to schedule formal counseling sessions with a definite time to begin and end. In situations where counseling emerges unexpectedly, as during a pastoral care contact, simply saying at the outset something like, "We'll have an hour to talk," alerts the person to the time available, and encourages him or her to use the time productively.

Keeping careful records is an essential part of a disciplined approach to pastoral counseling, especially if one does long-term counseling or counsels with a variety of persons so that memory alone is not adequate. Some ministers develop haphazard practices in this matter either because they are "too busy" or because they underestimate its importance. Pastors should be no less disciplined in ministering to people's spirits than doctors are rightly expected to be in ministering to their bodies. Careful records can serve these important purposes: They provide a way of checking and supplementing one's memory. They encourage systematic reflection between sessions, and planning (with relevant reading or consultation in some cases) how best to approach the next session. After several sessions, records may help one become aware of the developing process of a particular relationship. They encourage reflecting on and learning from one's mistakes. They can be useful in making referrals and are valuable for future reference, if persons return for counseling after an extended absence.

Counseling records should be kept confidentially in a locked file. (Before a minister moves, all such records should be destroyed.) A card or manila folder may be maintained for each counselee, couple, or family. Information recorded should include name (or a coded number to protect confidentiality in case anyone else gains access to the records), address, phone, age, interpersonal resources (family members and others), presenting problems, plans for helping, physician's or other helping professionals' names. After each counseling contact, a brief summary of significant developments may be added to the record in a few minutes.

Most counselors find that they can remember and record the vital aspects of an interview if they do so soon after it ends. If one takes notes during sessions, it should be done without sacrificing presence and frequent eye contact. Jotting down a few key words or dates can be done unobtrusively to provide a framework for recall during post-session recording of interview highlights. Before taking notes, it is well to say in a matter-of-fact tone, "I want to jot down a few notes so that I can keep the whole picture in mind. They will be treated confidentially, of course." A similar approach should be used if one wishes to tape record sessions: "I'd like to tape our talks occasionally to reflect between sessions on what was said. We may decide to listen together to a playback of part of a session occasionally. O.K.?"

The Telephone in Pastoral Care and Counseling

The telephone can be a useful, and time-saving instrument in many pastoral care, pre-counseling, informal, and formal counseling situations. It can allow pastors to keep in closer touch with persons in crisis and to become aware more quickly of those needing special care or counseling. In emergency situations, (such as a threatened suicide) where face-to-face communication isn't possible, supportive and stop-gap crisis counseling can be done by phone. Visits by phone can supplement face-to-face pastoral calls on the sick and hospitalized, and on the elderly and homebound. Phoning parishioners on special occasions—birthdays, retirement, or anniversaries—is a thoughtful and efficient way by which a pastor can express caring. The phone is an effective means of giving lay caring team members additional support and coaching when they encounter persons in crises. In extended counseling, the phone can be used occasionally between sessions to increase the frequency of therapeutic contacts and to support persons who are trying new, more constructive behavior.

An experienced and effective pastor (my seminary roommate) reports that he could not begin to handle the pastoral care load of his church without using the phone frequently. He writes:

Surely I don't believe in using the telephone as a substitute for personal contacts. But sometimes the telephone is an excellent supplement. There are times when it can do—and do as effectively—what a personal call could do, and when a personal call is impossible. Much use of the telephone is in the area of administration. However, even as we call on an administrative matter, we must remember that the one to whom we talk is the one whose son we just buried, whose daughter we just married, whose grandson we just baptized, whose daughter's marriage is crumbling, and whose heart is breaking because of it. [15]

Following a discussion of a controversial issue at the church's board, there were several no votes. The next day he phoned those persons and simply inquired, "What were your reactions to the board meeting?" Caring, person-centered administration such as this often leads to counseling opportunities. This minister also uses the phone to supplement his in-person hospital calls now that most patients have bedside phones. He reports that this is deeply appreciated.

Applying the Principles of the Holistic Approach

Several working principles of the holistic or wholeness orientation in counseling should be used throughout counseling to maximize healing and growth. The first of these principles is *to include all six dimensions of wholeness, including physical wholeness, among one's counseling goals*. In counseling with Bill Shaw, Kurt might well have explored Bill's need for a medical exam or for learning better health-maintenance practices. The second principle is *to become as aware as possible of the hidden strengths and potential resources of counselees and to affirm these whenever appropriate*. To develop this awareness requires what was described earlier as "putting on the glasses of growth." This enables one to see persons floundering in crises as created with rich potentialities in the divine likeness, to see persons whose self-esteem is almost nonexistent as precious daughters or sons of God. A corollary of this principle is *to see pathology, brokenness, and sin as truncated, blocked, or distorted growth to a considerable extent*. It is remarkable how much human destructiveness diminishes when people begin to recover hope and grow again.

Here are some illustrations of how the pastor could have implemented this principle in counseling with Bill Shaw. As they were discussing Bill's feelings about needing counseling, Kurt might have said, "I sense that you're feeling very down on yourself. I need to say that it takes real strength for us men to admit to ourselves that we need help and then ask for it." He might have added, "I find that I often pretend that I don't really need other people even when the going gets rough. I feel weak and a failure as a man when I have to ask for help." The first statement affirms the courage it required for Bill to come for help. The second lets Bill know that Kurt was aware of his own humanness and was not pretending to be sitting on a pedestal of wholeness judging Bill for needing help. Such transparent self-disclosure can shake some counselees who feel a need to see the counselor as a "fearless tower of power" (as one such person put it) on whom they can lean. It is important therefore to encourage counselees to express fully their feelings about whatever the counselor has said.

When Kurt was summarizing the highlights of what he had heard from Bill, he might well have said, "I have a hunch that you have more going for you than you're aware of now when you're feeling in the pits—some strengths that you can use to handle your painful situation in a way that will be good for yourself and your kids. For example, you were willing to risk uprooting yourself and moving to a new part of the country to try to make a fresh start. That takes some guts. You may suspect that you were searching for a geographical cure for the situation in St. Louis, and there may be a grain of truth in that. But it still takes courage." After Bill responded, the pastor could mention other present or potential strengths that he sees in him. It is important to be aware that premature affirmation often is not heard by depressed persons. If they do hear it, they may reject it and actually feel worse because they believe that the counselor is not hearing how totally worthless and despairing they feel. If affirmation of genuine strengths is received, it can help reinforce feelings of self-worth and fan the spark of hope. It is essential to find out how counselees feel about affirmation whenever it is given, so that negative responses can be discussed and resolved.

The third working principle is *to use the growth formula—balancing caring and confrontation—throughout counseling*. Until strong rapport is established, the emphasis should be on caring—on hearing the pain and responding with warm empathy and acceptance. Affirmation and confrontation should both be gentle in early stages of counseling. But when gentle confrontation is heard in the context of awareness of the counselor's non-judgmental caring, it can be experienced as an expression of genuine caring. There was a gentle, implicit confrontation in the above affirmation of Bill's strengths. Made explicit, it was, "You have assets that you may need to learn to use in order to pull yourself out of the painful tailspin you're in." As the bond of caring grows stronger, confrontation can become more forthright and explicit.

The fourth working principle is *for the counselor to hold the goal of growth-toward-wholeness in mind throughout the relationship and to articulate this as an expectation and challenge when this is appropriate*. Toward the end of the first session with Bill, Kurt might well have said, "I'm aware that you feel like you're struggling to even stay afloat in the river you're in now. But one of my hopes is that you'll not only learn how to tread water more effectively but that you'll also increase your swimming skills so you can get to where you want to be on the river bank. How do you feel about this hope of mine?" This illustrates the use of a right-brain image, communicating empathy for Bill's feelings that he's about to go under for the third time. It also confronts him with the possibility of using his crisis to learn new skills so he might prevent some future problems and cope more constructively with those that occur. The growth-oriented counselor aims at helping persons do more than simply survive and regain their previous level of adjustment. The aim is to enable the person to learn and thereby grow as a result of coping with the problem.

The fifth working principle is *to relate to counselees in terms of their interpersonal networks and the wider societal context of their problems. These usually play a significant role in both the causes and the treatment of their problems in living*. Bill came alone for help, yet he also brought his significant relationships with him as a part of who he is. The systemic understanding sees persons in their meaningful relationships as the irreducible focus of counseling. In discussing his perception of Bill's resources, Kurt might have pointed out, "It's because your kids are so precious to you that the distance from them is so painful, isn't it? Your love for them and theirs for you is an asset, wherever you are." In describing his perception of Bill's situation, Kurt could say, "You're experiencing a big loss—being uprooted and alone and two thousand miles away from your familiar stamping grounds and the people from whom you formerly got some support. If you decide to stay in this area, rebuilding your support group would seem to be very important." The linking of Bill with Sam Turner was a small step in helping Bill rebuild his support system. Kurt may help him take additional steps in this essential process by encouraging him to join the singles class and later, perhaps, to reach out to other newcomers in the community after taking the befriender team training.

If Kurt's self-disclosure regarding his male programming got a response of recognition from Bill, it might have been helpful for the pastor to have added, "Unfortunately our society seems to teach us to feel miserable as men, when we're not winning and on top of things." The discussion that sometimes follows such a statement helps troubled persons see their personal problems in the broader societal context. This may reduce inappropriate self-blame for what is caused by our culture—e.g., sexist programming of men and women.

The sixth working principle of wholeness-oriented counseling is *to be aware throughout counseling of spiritual and value issues and of the person's need to grow in this central life arena*. As a theologically trained counselor, Kurt was aware that something was seriously amiss in Bill's priorities, values, beliefs, and relationship with God. During the exploration of Bill's motivation and expectations, or in a later session, the pastor might have said, "I'm curious about why you chose to ask a minister for help. Was it only the fact that I had called or was there something special that you hoped I could do as a minister?" Such a question may enable persons to articulate some of the spiritual issues, theological beliefs, and superstitions clustering around and contributing to their problems. If a counseling relationship that goes beyond acute crisis help develops, it might be essential to help Bill explore the dynamics of his values and faith, as resources or impediments to growthful change. Even to handle this immediate crisis constructively may require helping Bill mobilize his spiritual resources.

The Fundamental Counseling Skills

In recent years, the essential helping skills needed by counselors have been identified. Several approaches to learning these one at a time have been developed. Robert R. Carkhuff and his associates have devised a system for teaching and learning these essential skills in sequence. (See Carkhuff and William A. Anthony, *The Skills of Helping*.) The importance of each of the core skills in the helping process has been tested by careful research. Gerald Egan's *The Skilled Helper* offers another method of learning basic counselor skills. A training manual by Egan, to accompany *The Skilled Helper,* is entitled *Exercise in Helping Skills*. Allen E. Ivey has developed an approach called "microtraining" using video feedback to teach the skills in sequence.[16] One or more of these approaches can be used by counselors-in-training to learn the basic skills of the counseling art.

Here is a summary (paraphrased in part from Carkhuff) of the essential helping skills counselors need to learn:

—*Attending and caring behavior,* including frequent eye contact, expressing interest by one's posture (leaning toward the person rather than away) and one's facial expression.

—*Inviting the person to talk* about significant issues by open-ended questions and brief comments or gestures.

—*Careful listening and observing* of non-verbal messages.

—*Following the person's lead,* avoiding switching topics, especially in the early stages of counseling. Staying with the here-and-now flow of the relationship.

—*Empathetic responding* by paraphrasing the main thrust of the significant feelings and issues one has perceived, and their meaning to the person.

—*Clarification* by summarizing the highpoints of what the person has communicated and thus checking out the counselor's understanding of their meanings for the person.

—*Exploring* significant areas that the person has not discussed by asking focusing questions.

—*Confronting* as needed and appropriate, in the context of valuing and affirming the person.

—*Understanding* the meanings, issues, and dynamics of the problem and *making recommendations for help* based on this diagnostic insight.

How these skills relate to the helping process should be evident at least in part, from the case illustration and discussion earlier in this chapter.

Types of Counselor Responses

Psychologist Elias H. Porter, Jr. describes five different attitudes that can be expressed in the responses of counselors:

E—*Evaluative:* Responses indicating counselors have made a judgment concerning the relative goodness, appropriateness, effectiveness, or rightness of clients' feelings or behavior. Such responses say or imply what the client *might* or *ought* to do.

I—*Interpretive:* Responses indicating the counselor's intent is to teach, to impart meaning to the client, or explain why.

S—*Supportive:* Responses indicating the counselor's intent is to reassure and to reduce the client's intensity of feeling.

P—*Probing:* Response indicating the counselor's intent is to query, to seek further information or provoke further discussion along a certain line. Such responses imply that the client might profitably develop or discuss a point further.

U—*Understanding:* Responses indicating the counselors' intention is to respond so as to communicate understanding and in effect to ask the client whether the counselor understands correctly what the client is saying and feeling.[17]

I would add a sixth type of counselor intervention:

A—*Advising:* Responses indicating that counselors' intention is to recommend certain approaches, actions, beliefs or attitudes as helpful. Put in other terms, an *evaluative* response is one that carries the counselor's value judgment; an *interpretive* response is one that intends to teach or explain the dynamics of a person's behavior (the "why"); a *supportive* response is one that seeks to reassure, inspire, or undergird a person; a *probing* response is one that questions; an *understanding* response is one that reflects understanding and empathy for the counselee's feelings and attitudes; an *advising* response is one that offers what the counselor believes to be a constructive suggestion about coping with a problem.

I have found the EISPUA categories useful in helping pastors and students become aware of lopsidedness in their counseling responses. The counseling of many ministers consists almost entirely of P (probing) and S (supportive) and A (advising) responses, without their being aware of it. Moralistic ministers tend to major in E (evaluative) and P (probing) responses. Clergy with some exposure to abnormal psychology and psychodynamic theory often overemphasize I (interpretive) responses, involving theories about why people feel and act as they do. Those whose training has been mainly in Carl Rogers' approach may rely too heavily on U (understanding) responses. Ministers with no training in counseling seldom use U responses.

It is my experience that *all six of these types of responses have a useful place in pastoral counseling*. A minister should be able to use them all with flexible selectivity, depending on the needs of the particular counselee. In the early rapport-building phase of counseling, it is essential to major in U responses. In confrontational counseling, E (evaluative) and I (interpretive in the sense of teaching) and A (advising) responses also are important. In crisis counseling, S (supportive) responses must be used. In short-term educative counseling (premarital, for example), P (probing) and S (supportive) and I (interpretive or teaching) responses are indispensable. In all stages and types of counseling, U (understanding) responses are important. The counseling style of many clergy is weakest in its paucity of U responses.

Let me suggest that you now use the EISPUA system. Try to identify the six responses listed after this statement by a woman, age nineteen:

> I tell you I hate my father. I hate him! I hate him! And there's no reason for it. He is a minister—a good and righteous man. He has never laid a hand on me—but I have this terrific feeling against him—and it makes me feel so terrible because—there is no reason for it. It's a sin to hate your father—especially if you don't have any reason for it. I—it worries me.

(1) Of course you feel guilt about hating him so, especially since you can't put your finger on what he has done to make you

hate him. And then, too, . . . you'll find that underneath it all you have some love for him, and this plays a part in your feelings of guilt.

(2) I guess everyone at some time or another goes through a period when they hate one or both of their parents. It's really not at all uncommon. Most people find they can work out some way of getting along until things settle down.

(3) This is certainly something that you will want to get cleared up. Happy relationships with parents are too constructive a thing. . . . You wouldn't want to jeopardize what that can mean to you.

(4) It worries you that you should hate your father without reason, and you feel sinful for hating him.

(5) Let me recommend that you talk to your father about your feeling—have it out with him.

(6) I think we ought to get at the root of that worry. Tell me about your father—all about him.[18]

The key for scoring this exercise is in footnote 18.

The usefulness of the EISPUA system is enhanced if two types of P responses are distinguished—PI (probing for information) and PF (probing for feelings). The system is a valuable tool for analyzing written verbatim reports or recorded counseling tapes, helping to identify the blindspots in the counselor's responses. In reality-practice sessions, an experienced observer-coach can keep score on the counselor's responses—helping to recognize lopsidedness in his/her pattern of counseling. The EISPUA system can be a mechanical gimmick of little value. But, when used as a self-confrontational device within the context of a dynamic understanding of the counseling relationship, it is a useful tool.

Making Counseling More Inclusive and Transcultural

Like psychotherapeutic theory in general, pastoral counseling has been predominately middle-class in its concepts, methods, and models of healing. To respond effectively to the needs of people in the next fifteen years, those who practice this pastoral art must transcend the Anglo-European, middle-class, white male orientation of these disciplines. In a world of increasing interaction among persons of different cultural and ethnic backgrounds, broadening our horizons as pastoral counselors is increasingly important.

Ministers who serve inner-city or blue-collar congregations soon discover that the goals and the methods of pastoral counseling, as traditionally conceived, are relatively ineffective with many persons from non-middle-class backgrounds. Goals borrowed from insight psychotherapy—growth through self-understanding and personality integration through resolving inner conflicts—are alien to the world of many of these persons. The same is true of the usual psychotherapeutic model—a series of formal, scheduled, one-to-one interviews where persons are expected to talk at deeper and deeper levels about their feelings. A perceptive student of this problem observes: "Many of the poor do not express themselves well. They do not see how 'just talking about it' can resolve their problems . . . Their concerns are immediate, concrete, and pressing. They need to see fast, [even] though limited improvement."[19] Introspective methods of counseling seem like a waste of time to many persons whose culture, unlike the middle-class ethos, does not condition them to look within to find help. This is particularly true if they feel overwhelmed by practical problems. When such persons are seen by ministers who have not transcended their middle-class backgrounds, they often do not return after the first session. It is tempting to believe that such persons are unmotivated. Actually, many are powerfully motivated to find help. They terminate counseling because their understanding of the kind of help they need is utterly different from the counselor's. Disadvantaged persons, as well as those from authority-centered ethnic and culture groups, tend to expect that help will include advice-giving and will be focused on solving, alleviating, or helping them bear their practical problems.

The effective approach with economically disadvantaged persons and those from authority-centered ethnic and cultural groups, focuses on the concrete crises they face. The primary goal is to help such persons discover practical ways of resolving their economic, employment, and health crises. Improvements need not be dramatic or total but they need to occur fairly soon in the helping process.

Clergypersons tend to be seen as authority figures by such persons. The pastor often needs to take the initiative in giving the person useful information (about where to find a job or medical care, for example), suggestions concerning constructive steps to take, and practical support. The willingness to use the pastoral authority one has—the authority of one's social role, pastoral identity, and competence—in growth-enabling rather than authoritarian, growth-stifling ways is important in all pastoral counseling. It is essential in working with persons from authority-centered backgrounds. Unconstructive uses of authority involve manipulating counselees by coercive advice, or taking action and making decisions for them that they could do themselves with the counselor's guidance and support. Growthful uses of counselors' authority aim at gradually diminishing the dependence of persons on this authority. It seeks to help counselees mobilize their own power (through the exercise of their latent coping capacities), which will enable them to handle their problems more constructively, improve their life situation, and do whatever possible to overcome the economic and ethnic discrimination where their problems often root.

Since coming to an office for counseling is foreign to the life-style of many non-middle-class persons, much of the helping must be done in other settings without the formal label "counseling." A study of mental health treatment approaches for low-income groups revealed that "Therapists who play a pastoral type of role are most successful. Those who will leave their offices and relate to their patients informally in their place of work, in the family setting, in informal street visits, etc., soon become trusted members of the patients' community. The poor person welcomes direct intervention during his times of crisis."[20] This study found that informal group counseling was effective with blue-collar workers. Group members, drawn from similar ethnic and language backgrounds, visit and help each other between sessions. Persons who have recovered from problems such as delinquency or drug addiction make excellent role models and group leaders. (The similarity of this approach to AA is striking.) Of special relevance to pastoral counseling is the study's finding that "the psychological difficulties of many low-income patients diminish as they become involved in some meaningful commitment, whether it be religious activity, a hobby, a labor union, or participation in a block committee."[21] It is obvious that pastoral counseling is of the greatest help to the poor when it is most *pastoral* in its methods. Most counseling opportunities with the disadvantaged occur during crisis situations. Charles Kemp's *Pastoral Care of the Poor* is a valuable resource for those who minister to non-middle-class persons.[22]

The black church has a rich and distinctive culture including a corporate inheritance from Africa and from slavery. It also has a rich tradition of pastoral care. Edward P. Wimberly points out that two pastoral functions, *sustaining* and *guiding,* have dominated pastoral care in the black churches. But *healing* also has occurred: "Although the black person's personality was damaged by racism and oppression, wholeness did come for many through the experience of God's love toward them. When the caring resources were brought to bear upon persons suffering from low self-esteem and self-hatred, they experienced themselves as accepted as 'somebody' in the eyes of God and their black brothers and sisters. Healing did exist for some, but for others sustenance was all that could be accomplished . . . for them, God's love as mediated through the resources of the church prevented and lessened the impact of oppression." The symbolic role and authority of black pastors—reflecting the aspirations, dreams, and hopes for liberation of black people—have dynamic functions in their ministry of guiding and sustaining. Futhermore, sustaining is the function of the whole congregation as a caring community, much more so than in most white churches. Black worship and preaching, care groups (prayer meetings and burial societies), rituals such as baptism and funeral, all provided sustaining support for these oppressed people.[23] In short, the mainstream of white pastoral care has much to learn from the corporate ways pastoral care occurs in black churches.

There is significant cross-cultural dimension in counseling of women by male pastors and vice versa. The fact that the majority of pastors are men and the majority of persons they counsel are women, poses serious problems. A study by Inge K. Broverman and others reveals that many counselors and therapists (both male and female) function with unconscious sex-role stereotypes that constrict their effectiveness as growth-enablers with women clients.[24] It is imperative that all counselors get their consciousness raised concerning their own sexism and the oppressive impact of our society's sexism on problems of both women and men. All on sound counseling must include increasing the awareness of counselees of the ways sexist programming has contributed to their constricted wholeness.[25] Male ministers need to recognize that there are inherent limitations to their ability to be facilitators of psychological and spiritual growth in counseling with women. Women counselees, having been socially programmed to be dependent on males, form strong dependency ties with and try to please male religious authority figures. Unless this pattern is challenged by the male counselor, it will work against the woman's developing her full strengths and pursuing her autonomous spiritual search. A male counselor cannot give her the special help she may find in relating to a liberated woman pastoral counselor who knows a woman's experience from the inside and is excited about the unique possibilities that this experience brings to the spiritual search. However liberated from sexism a male counselor is, he has two disadvantages as a wholeness-enabler for women:

> He cannot know the experience of women in a sexist society from the inside, and he cannot serve as a role model, for a woman client, of a strong, competent, caring woman. But if his consciousness has been raised and if he is warm, open, vulnerable, and growing (as well as competent), relating to such a man can be growth-enabling for both women and men.[26]

Until our society is fully liberated from sexism, women counselors will have special advantages in the liberation and growth of women, just as men counselors have advantages in the liberation and growth of men. The same principle applies in counseling with persons from different racial and ethnic backgrounds.

Those of us who do counseling from a one-up position of greater power in a culture (as white males do) have a special problem in this regard. It is probably impossible for those in a one-down position to fully trust those in a one-up power position, or to experience their fullest possible liberation and empowerment in a counseling relationship with them. To meet the need for growth-enablers for women and ethnic minorities, many more persons from those groups must be trained as pastoral counselors.

In her book *Counseling for Liberation*, Charlotte Holt Clinebell (who changed her name to Charlotte Ellen in 1978) gives this description of the characteristics of a liberated and liberating counselor. "Such a counselor: 1. Values being female equally with being male. A woman counselee cannot learn to value herself from a counselor who devalues women. 2. Believes in complete equality between women and men at all levels and in all areas of public and private life, on the job, and at home. 3. Is aware of the fact that deeply imbedded cultural stereotypes are likely to have their influence on him or her at an unconscious level, even though intellectually he or she rejects such stereotypes. 4. Is nondefensive, unpretentious, and nonjudgmental. 5. Holds the basic philosophy that it is his or her job to help the client find out who she or he is and wants to be. This may mean raising the issue of other choices and options for persons who are not raising that issue for themselves. 6. Is constantly aware of his or her limitations in working with persons of the other sex. 7. Is in the process of becoming (and encouraging counselee and client to become) a more fully androgynous person."[27] (Several books on non-sexist counseling will be found in the recommended reading list, chapter 5.)

In working with persons from different ethnic, cultural, or sexual backgrounds, it is essential to be aware of the universal tendency to feel, on some level, that one's own experiences and culture are the norm for all human beings. Each of us judges cultural differences as inferior, according to the degree this tendency operates in us. It may blind us to subtle but significant differences in the ways counselees from other backgrounds perceive, conceptualize, feel, solve problems, and create their world-view. Leading workshops and counseling with persons in some thirty countries, over the last two decades, has increased my awareness of the difficulties involved in transcending one's cultural conditioning. When counseling with a person from a different gender or cultural background, it is helpful to say: "I realize that, much as I would like to understand what you are saying, I won't understand at times because of the differences in our backgrounds. Our work together will be more helpful if you will tell me when you sense I'm not really understanding what you are saying." The new world of global communication and transcultural relationships opens up many problems. It also opens exciting and challenging possibilities for us as pastoral counselors, to learn from each other and thus to transform age-old cultural barriers into bridges.[28]

Reality-Practice Session

Before doing the following skill-building exercise, you may find it helpful to refresh your memory by rereading the description near the end of chapter 1 of how to use the reality-practice approach.

PARISHIONER'S ROLE: Become aware of your own here-and-now feelings and problems. Share whatever you choose of these during this session. Be aware of how the pastor's responses to what you say either increases or diminishes your desire to share more deeply. (Discuss this with the others during the debriefing periods)

PASTOR'S ROLE: Practice active listening and reflecting back (in paraphrased form) the feelings and issues expressed by the parishioner. For this session, do not try to help the person resolve the problems expressed. Instead concentrate on being fully present, listening carefully, and responding accurately and warmly to whatever the parishioner communicates by words, voice tone, or body language. Give only U (understanding) responses. This will allow the parishioner to let you know how accurately you are understanding what is being communicated. Learning to stay with a person by giving accurate U responses is a relationship-building skill that provides a foundation for the use of other helping skills.

OBSERVER-COACH'S ROLE: Be aware of the quality, warmth, and accuracy of the pastor's U responses. Interrupt the flow of the counseling periodically (every 5-10 minutes or so) to share your observations about the interaction between pastor and parishioner, invite feedback, raise issues, and make suggestions for improving the pastor's responses. Call attention to responses that were not U but were E, I, S, P, or A responses. Discuss how the pastor's responses could have communicated more empathic understanding.

After twenty minutes or so of counseling, debrief fully, and then switch roles so that each person has an opportunity to be pastor, parishioner, and observer-coach during the session.

Facilitating Spiritual Wholeness: The Heart of Pastoral Care and Counseling

As you ought not to attempt to cure the eyes without the head, or the head without the body, so neither ought you to attempt to cure the body without the soul . . . for the part can never be well unless the whole is well. . . . And therefore, if the head and body are to be well, you must begin by curing the soul.

—PLATO[1]

Pastors are called to be enablers of spiritual wholeness throughout the life cycle. Their theological education helps equip them with resources and skills to use as teachers, guides, and coaches of the spiritual life in all aspects of their ministry. Enabling spiritual healing and growth is the core task in all pastoral care and counseling. An understanding of humankind's fundamental spiritual needs and the ability to help people learn to satisfy these more growthfully are essential assets in all counseling that is truly pastoral. Exploring the nature and methodologies of enhancing spiritual wholeness is the task of this chapter and the next.

Obvious and explicit theological issues—e.g., problems of belief, doubt, doctrine, the nature and methods of prayer—are the presenting problem in only a small minority of those seeking pastoral help. One study found that only 10 percent of pastoral counseling clients were perceived as having problems primarily in the religious area.[2] This is due in part to the secular climate of our times. Spiritual problems, though epidemic in prevalence, tend not to be understood or described in theological terms. When ministers encounter explicit spiritual problems, they respond by drawing on their theological training, tradition, and personal religious life. In so doing they should utilize the general methods of all sound pastoral counseling (chapter 4) and of educative counseling in particular (chapter 13). In their work as *counseling theologians,* pastors serve the valuable function of helping people fathom and appropriate personally their religious tradition's wisdom about life's meaning. They assist people both in filling traditional symbols and stories with personal meanings and in developing new symbols and stories. As theological counselors—the function of pastors is to nurture the growth of persons toward a more mature (in tune with spiritual reality) faith and a more vitalizing, growthful relationship with God.

When explicit theological issues are presenting problems in counseling, the minister should be aware that they may be surface manifestations of deeper psychological problems. It is usually appropriate to begin by dealing with theological problems as problems in their own right, but to be alert to other problems, which may lurk in the shadows. I recall a middle-aged man who came for help with a distressing loss of vitality in his prayer life. As he puts it, "Prayer has gone dead for me." He asked for the title of a book on prayer. I suggested several but encouraged him to continue talking about his problem by asking: "What has been happening lately? Has anything been heavy on your mind?" This opened the sluice gates. The man poured out his guilt feelings regarding the suicide of a near relative, for whose death he felt an unreasonable but agonizing sense of responsibility. Subsequently, this problem was worked through in a series of counseling sessions and the man's prayer experience "came alive." The inner lumps of icy guilt feelings, which had blocked off his awareness of God, had been melted by the experience of self-forgiveness in counseling.

The onset of psychotic breaks is sometimes attended by sudden, obsessive interest in religion—e.g., in "getting right with God" or in "finding the secret of the universe." This interest may have a paranoid coloration—delusions of grandeur (a messiah complex) or persecution. In one study of mental hospital patients, 20 percent merely clothed their psychoses in religious ideas. Ten percent seemed to use religion as a last straw. Another 17 percent gave evidence of basic religious problems, interwoven with unresolved conflicts with parent figures.[3]

Although religious problems may hide psychological problems, the reverse is also true. Spiritual conflicts and emptiness are significant factors in many neurotic problems. Seward Hiltner writes: "People may get sick emotionally not only because of immediate frustrations but also because they are troubled about their own meaning and destiny." Viktor Frankl's phrase, "value vacuum," describes the emptiness that renders many people vulnerable to anxiety and interpersonal conflicts. In his review of Peter Vierech's *The Unadjusted Man: A New Hero for Americans*, Geoffrey Brunn writes: "Ours is an orphan age, severed from its historic past by the transforming impact of dynamic technology. Today every individual in the 'lonely crowd' is haunted by a sense of desolation and incommunicable singularity." In this "age of longing" (Arthur Koestler), countless millions have found no resources for coping with that common human experience described in Melville's classic line, "a damp, drizzly November in my soul."[4] Like the characters in the play *Waiting for Godot*, they are bored and nauseated by the empty meaninglessness of their existence while they wait for a god who never comes. The purposelessness of our "mislaid generation" provides fertile soil for the seeds of marital pathology, interpersonal conflict, and personality illness.[5]

A strong current in several contemporary psychotherapies challenges the view that all religious problems are merely symptoms of deeper psychological problems. Carl G. Jung, Roberto Assagioli, Erich Fromm, Viktor Frankl, Gordon Allport, Rollo May, and other existentialists in psychotherapy hold this view to be reductionistic and unsupported by clinical evidence. They hold that psychological problems are often rooted in spiritual pathology. Jung regarded "the religious problems which the patient brings . . . as relevant to the neurosis and as possible causes of it." Fromm views neurosis as a secret, private religion. The therapist needs to know what the person's answer to the question of existence is; most of what are considered psychological problems are only secondary consequences of these answers—the secret religion to which all the person's efforts and passions are devoted.[6]

It is easy to miss the hidden spiritual dimensions of the problems a pastor encounters in counseling. If, for whatever reasons, counselors are tuned mainly to the wavelength of psycho-social aspects of human problems, they tend not to hear the profound spiritual longings often present. Such deafness is a serious handicap, particularly when it occurs in a pastor. On the other hand, lopsided attention to the religious dimension may diminish awareness of the complex psycho-social factors that are

always interwoven with spiritual issues. American pastoral care
has properly stressed the dangers of religious reductionism in
viewing human problems, but in so doing has sometimes fallen
into psychological reductionism. To be effective as a *pastoral*
counselor, one must be tuned simultaneously to the psycho-social
and to the spiritual dimensions in every human problem.

A guilt-ridden, bedfast woman, age seventy-eight, said to her
minister: "I'd almost rather die—much as I dread that—than to
have to lie here much longer." Instead of encouraging her to
discuss her feelings of uselessness and her fear of dying, the
minister simply told her he was sorry she felt as she did—an almost
certain way to turn off her expression of feeling. In the next
interview, she again discussed dying.

> **Pastor:** You aren't afraid, are you? [A blocking question.]
>
> **Woman:** Not exactly. No—I wouldn't say that. Maybe. But there are
> so many things I ought to do that I haven't done. I wonder if I'm ready to
> go. Do you think God punishes us for the things we do that are wrong?

The pastor answered that "the Bible teaches that there is a
judgment" and glibly went on to reassure her that she had been a
good woman and had nothing to worry about. The woman's
obvious guilt and fear of death were not taken seriously. Her
profound existential problem—facing death—was missed almost
completely by the pastor, probably because of his own existential
anxiety.[7]

The Spiritual Dimension in All Human Problems

In certain types of problems the religious-existential aspects are
obvious and pressing. According to Erik Erikson, youth in later
adolescence are highly exposed to problems of their basic identity
and, therefore, to existential anxiety. It is no accident that
schizophrenia frequently begins at this time. Spiritual issues are
prominent in the crisis of the middle years, when one's youthful
illusions of physical immortality crumble before the realities of
aging. Psychologist Herman Feifel has discovered that "a primary
subconscious concern of the person over fifty, as revealed through
projective testing, is preoccupation with his own death."[8]
Existential-religious factors are often near the surface in crises

counseling, particularly in counseling with the sick, the dying, and the bereaved. Their crisis experiences crack the defensive shell of pseudo-omnipotence that most of us wear, confronting us with the brevity and vulnerability of our lives, and forcing us to be aware of the clock that relentlessly ticks away, bringing us closer to the grave moment by moment.

Though often not so obvious and in some cases completely hidden, there is an existential-spiritual dimension in *every problem* with which pastor and parishioner struggle in counseling. This is true because awareness of our morality is inherent in every human experience, most often on a subconscious level.

> Anxiety in general is the response of the human organism to anything that is perceived as a threat to what one regards as essential to one's welfare or safety. Pathological (neurotic) anxiety arises when contradictory impulses, desires or needs clamor simultaneously for expression or satisfaction. It is the result of inner conflict. It serves the function of keeping material that is unacceptable to the self-image repressed. In contrast, existential anxiety is nonpathological or normal anxiety. It arises from the very nature of human existence. Human beings are the animals who know they will die. They are trapped by their rootage in nature. They are subject to its forces of sickness, pain, and death, and lacks what Big Daddy, in Tennessee Williams' *Cat on a Hot Tin Roof*, calls the "pig's advantage"—viz., ignorance of his mortality.[9]

As Martin Heidegger observes, our knowledge that we must die is the background music that plays faintly in the distance all during our lives: "At times we may blot it out, but there are other times when it swells in volume and tempo, and we cannot be unaware of it."[10]

Paul Tillich points out that the threat of nonbeing producing existential anxiety has three forms—the threat of fate and death, emptiness and loss of meaning, guilt and condemnation. This anxiety permeates our whole being.[11] It is a part of our "heritage of finitude," the dark shadow touching all other anxieties and giving them their power.

Existential anxiety is the raw material, the prototype, and the wellspring of other anxieties. A woman who knew she was born out of wedlock, unwanted, the result of an accident, lamented to her pastoral counselor, "I feel I have no right to be." She was expressing the haunting sense of rejection and existential anxiety resulting from the precarious circumstances of her coming into being. Tillich summarizes his understanding of existential anxiety and points to the only effective way of handling it.

> Anxiety is the awareness of finitude. Man [*sic*] . . . always lives in the conscious or unconscious anxiety of having to die. Non-being is present in every moment of his being. The vicissitudes of existence threaten him from all sides. Suffering, accidents, disease, loss of relations to nature and man, loneliness, insecurity, weakness, and error are always with him. Finally, the threat of having to die will become the reality of death. All this he must bear, and all this he can bear only in the power of that in which nonbeing is eternally conquered—the power of the divine. It is the function of pastoral care to communicate this power and to mediate the courage to accept finitude.[12]

There are no psychological or psychotherapeutic answers to existential anxiety. It is existential in that it is inherent in our very existence as self-aware creatures. But *its impact on the individual can be either creative or destructive,* depending on how it is handled. Whatever one uses to cope with existential anxiety is, psychologically speaking, one's religion. This may be one of the many forms of idolatry—the deification of possessions, health, success, alcohol, the state, an institution such as a church, one's family, making these matters of "ultimate concern" (Tillich). Neurotic problems can also be understood as defenses against nonbeing, attempts to avoid existential anxiety. Ironically, the use of these defenses inevitably produces precisely what is feared—nonbeing.[13] That is, the neurosis lessens a person's aliveness. Tillich views neurotic anxiety as a way of avoiding the threat of nonbeing by avoiding being (defending oneself against the fear of death by feeling half-dead).

There seems to be a reciprocal relationship between neurotic and existential anxiety. Tillich observes that a high degree of neurotic anxiety renders one vulnerable to the threat of nonbeing and, conversely, "those who are empty of meaning are easy victims of neurotic anxiety."[14] Each form of anxiety tends to reinforce the other.

If one attempts to cope with existential anxiety by pseudo-religious (idolatrous or neurotic) means, the inevitable results are the diminishing of the creativity, awareness, and authenticity of one's life. Existentialist therapist J. F. T. Bugental writes:

Neurotic anxiety is the distress occasioned by our yielding up of our authentic being-in-the-world to illusory hopes of being secure, of avoiding tragedy. It is always accompanied by some reduction of our total being, and for that reason is inevitably a cancerous growth in our lives. . . . We are less real in our living and so our anxiety is renewed, thus requiring greater defensive efforts. Neurotic anxiety tends, thus, to be ever-increasing anxiety.[15]

The only constructive means of handling existential anxiety is an authentic religious life, enabling the actualization of the image of God within the person. In what has become the most quoted passage from *Modern Man in Search of a Soul,* Jung reports: "Among all my patients in the second half of life—that is to say, over thirty-five—there has not been one whose problem in the last resort was not that of finding a religious outlook on life."[16] This is consistent with Tillich's observation that the "power of the divine" is that within which "nonbeing is eternally conquered." Life-enhancing religion enables persons to confront rather than evade their existential anxiety. As Tillich made clear, only as this normal anxiety is confronted and taken into one's self-identity can it enhance instead of cripple life. Within the context of meaning or trust, it becomes, in Kierkegaard's word, a "school." In the very experience of facing anxiety, an individual develops the inner certitude of faith. Anxiety is the teacher who searches one's life thoroughly and roots out the trivial. Thus, existential anxiety becomes the "mother of the drive to know."[17]

Nikos Kazantzakis in *Zorba the Greek* has the bishop express this theory:

There is *some Eternity even in our ephemeral lives, only it is very difficult for us to discover it alone.* Our daily cares lead us astray. A few people only, the flower of humanity, manage to live an eternity even in their transitory lives on this earth. Since all the others would therefore be lost, God had mercy on them and sent them religion—thus the crowd is able to live in eternity, too.[18]

Existential anxiety is transformed to the extent that we are able to live in eternity in the midst of our transitory lives.

The Goal of Counseling on Religious Problems

The goal of the religious dimension of pastoral care and counseling is to help people grow in the depth and vitality of their spiritual life so that it will empower all aspects of their lives. This growth occurs as they learn to relate to God, people (God's children), nature (God's world) and their own inner being in ways that satisfy nine basic spiritual needs—the need for: (1) developing a viable philosophy of life; a belief system and living symbols that give meaning to their lives; (2) developing creative images and values to guide their life-styles constructively; (3) having a growing relationship with and commitment to a loving God that integrates and energizes their lives; (4) developing their higher self (Assagioli) or soul as the center of their whole being; (5) renewing regularly their basic trust (Erikson) to maintain hope in the midst of the losses and tragedies of their lives; (6) discovering ways to move from the alienation of guilt to the reconciliation of forgiveness; (7) developing ways to undergird self-esteem and reduce alienating narcissism (pride) with an awareness of being deeply valued by God; (8) having regular moments of transcendence, mystical "peak experiences" (Maslow) when they experience the eternal in the midst of time; and (9) belonging to a caring community (e.g., a church) that nurtures and sustains them on their spiritual journey.

These needs are not religious in some "churchy" sense. Rather they are *basic human needs* present in all persons including those most secularized and most alienated from institutionalized religions. They are religious needs in the sense that they can be satisfied adequately only in relation to what Tillich called the "vertical dimension," the ultimate spiritual reality, God. Many people have not learned to satisfy their spiritual needs in healthy, growthful ways. Their religion is *pathogenic*—sickness-producing and growth-blocking. Many others satisfy their basic religious needs in relatively *salugenic* ways—ways that nurture healing and wholeness. Pathogenic religion results when people attempt to satisfy their spiritual needs in rigid, authoritarian, reality-denying, idolatrous ways. Salugenic religion results when people satisfy these needs in open, growing, reality-respecting ways that say a resounding Yes! to life. Thus, religion can be crippling or creative—a heavy *weight* on our spirits or *wings* by which we soar and transcend our two-dimensional, space-time bound lives. A central purpose of pastoral care as well as of religious education is to nurture high level spiritual wellness—the key to whole-person wellness. I have discussed these basic spiritual needs in considerable depth elsewhere.[19] Suffice it to say here that enabling spiritual wellness in pastoral care and counseling involves helping people learn more growthful ways of satisfying these needs.

It is crucial to be aware of the spiritual crisis on our planet. This is the context of the spiritual longings, confusion, and emptiness that people bring to the counseling pastor. It is a difficult time to satisfy our deep spiritual hungers constructively. The unprecedented speed of social change has produced a massive collapse of traditional systems of religious beliefs, symbols, meanings, and values for millions on planet earth. Traditional authority-centered ways of handling existential anxiety and satisfying spiritual needs are no longer acceptable or meaningful to them. But they have not yet developed new, more creative ways. This time of radical spiritual transition is saturated with existential anxiety for many people. Some flee from the freedom (and the necessity) to develop more creative spirituality by turning to simplistic, authoritarian religious "solutions" espoused by pseudo-messiahs. In Erich Fromm's term, they "escape from freedom" to reduce the anxiety aroused by our planet's spiritual crisis. A subconscious awareness of this crisis is one factor that brings people to counseling pastors.

When viewed through the glasses of growth, this spiritual crisis confronts humankind with an unprecedented opportunity (and need) for spiritual transformation. When we let go of comfortable answers that no longer satisfy, we are confronted by the necessity to "work out [our] own salvation with fear and trembling" (Phil. 2:12). Those who question authority-validated beliefs and values are confronted by the need to discover beliefs and values that make sense *to them*. The process of putting away childish but comfortable beliefs (see I Cor. 13:11) is painful, but it is an essential part of the process of growing up spiritually. Spiritually-oriented pastoral counseling can provide valuable help to people in their search for spiritual wholeness in our contemporary spiritual crisis.

Pastoral counseling on spiritual issues aims at helping people learn to live in harmony with the basic principles of the psychological-spiritual world, as these are understood in the Judeo-Christian tradition. To align one's life-style with this fundamental spiritual reality is what is meant in religious language by "doing the will of God." Pastoral counseling seeks to help people enjoy an open, growing relationship with God, enabling them to live growthfully amidst the losses, conflicts, and tragedies of life in the world. It seeks to help them become aware of the exciting fact that they are made to be active partners—co-creators with the Spirit of the universe in transforming the world. Pastoral counseling seeks to help persons renew their sense of basic trust by being in touch with the Spirit of love present in this moment, to find healing of those aspects of their brokenness that can only be healed in relationship to this reality. Pastoral counseling aims at helping persons find their vocation—their calling, their cause—into which they can pour their lives with purpose, commitment, and joy.

Pastors should help their counselees discover ways of fulfilling their need for a sense of wonder and transcendence, for "peak experience" in which they become aware of their oneness with humankind, with the biosphere, and with Spirit. In his discussion of self-actualizing persons, Abraham Maslow uses the phrase "oceanic feeling" to describe their experience of oneness with the whole universe. The deep need for a growing relationship with the spiritual center of reality, described by Tolstoy as "a thirst for God," is not easily satisfied in our times. Many persons today experience prayer and worship as pale and anemic, lacking in what Tillich called the "ecstatic moment." For many the prayer of St. Augustine, "Oh! that Thou wouldst enter into my heart and inebriate it,"[20] has wistful overtones. When personal religion loses its sense of the numinous, many people search for transcendence in pseudo-religions. Some try to make a chemical religion out of the overuse of drugs and alcohol. All forms of idolatry eventually betray their worshipers, leaving them in greater spiritual despair.

As persons discover and develop those spiritual capacities that are their transpersonal essence—the higher Self within them—their existential anxiety is gradually transformed into a constructive force in their lives. Persons who treat themselves like machines, who feel they have never lived, whose inner creativity and aliveness are trammeled by neurotic conflicts tend to be most terrified by death. Conversely, persons who have learned to stay open to the loving Spirit of life and thereby come alive within themselves, find that awareness of their finitude is transformed into a stimulus for living more fully and purposefully. The more the image of God is developed within them, the more they can participate in the "celebration of being" (Bugental). Our most basic alienation as human beings is from the transcendent within us. To discover and develop this image of God is the key task of spiritual growth work.

Persons in the mid-years who suddenly realize, "My life is more than half-gone!" experience a wave of existential anxiety. (I remember the first time I was hit by this awareness!) If their lives have a spiritual vacuum, they may feel overwhelmed. If, on the other hand, their sense of meaning is undergirded by a viable faith and a robust spiritual life, they can transcend the shackles of finitude. The process of aging is transformed. Rather than live dying, they will die living! Obviously there are important implications in this for counseling with those in their mid-years and beyond.[21]

The Pastoral Counselor as Spiritual Guide or Director

Many traditions and cultures regard the role of the personal guide of the inner life as crucially important. The shaman in so-called primitive cultures, the guru in Hinduism, the sage-teacher in classical Greek philosophy, the spiritual guides in ancient Judaism (prophets, priests, wise men and women), are all examples. Within Christianity, the tradition of *spiritual direction* was flourishing by the fourth century (in the desert fathers and the Eastern Orthodox tradition). It continued strong in the medieval Roman Catholic Church and subsequently in the Anglican communion. Although the Protestant tradition has not used the term "spiritual direction" until relatively recently, (because of suspicion of anything that seemed to undermine the place of Christ as mediator between persons and God) Luther practiced a ministry of personal direction, Calvin was concerned for the guidance of conscience, and Richard Baxter, in his classic book *The Reformed pastor* (1656), recommended that ministers should not "slightly slubber over" the work of personal counsel, but "do it vigorously."[22] The Wesleyan bands and class meetings were settings for intensive spiritual direction and training in Christian living. Clearly the Christian tradition has regarded spiritual direction as a central dimension of pastoral care. There are important resources within that tradition that need to be recovered and integrated with pastoral counseling, to balance the valuable but often lopsided impact of psychological insights and psychotherapeutic techniques.

The term "director" tends to have hierarchical connotations in our culture, suggesting that the person being directed is a passive recipient from a benevolent authority figure. It is true that the role of spiritual director arose within authority-centered cultures and undoubtedly has been misused on occasion in Parent-Child (in TA terms) ways. But Kenneth Leech declares:

> Max Thurian's definition is a useful starting point. 'Spiritual direction or the cure of souls, is a seeking after the leading of the Holy Spirit in a given psychological and spiritual situation.' Here the stress is on *seeking,* and the seeking is mutual. The director, and he who is being directed, are both seekers: they are both parts of a spiritual direction, a current of spirituality, a divine-human process of relationship. 'Spirituality' and 'spiritual life' are not religious departments, walled-off areas of life. Rather the spiritual life is the life of the whole person directed towards God."[23]

There are salutary emphases in the spiritual direction literature on both the social goal of the process and its nonpathological, growth-toward-wholeness orientation:

> A spiritual guide is thus concerned with the encounter with God, the process by which the human community and the individual human are made one with the divine. The shepherd is involved with the flock, and this social dimension of spirituality is of crucial importance. The Christian is not seeking a solitary walk with God, a private mystical trip, a flight of the alone to the Alone. He is involved in a corporate search for humanity, renewal, the Kingdom of God, the transformed cosmos, the Body of Christ . . . the great masters of the spiritual life in almost all traditions are one in warning of the dangers of the spiritual ego-trip, the search for enlightenment which ignores . . . the human community, the demands of justice and peace.[24]

This thrust in spiritual direction has important implications for pastoral care and counseling. In our culture where privitized salvation-seeking (via religious and secular routes) is epidemic, it is well to remember that the health of our relationship with God is always interrelated with the health of all other facets of our lives—physical, psychological, interpersonal, ecological, and institutional. Spiritual growth is nurtured best in human relationships and groups committed to *mutual* spiritual searching and discovery. Our individual spiritual wholeness is deeply influenced by the quality of the institutional structures of our society and by our relationship with the biosphere. Living in ways that enhance the wholeness of the so-called nonspiritual dimensions of our lives, helps to enrich the quality of our spiritual lives. The nonspiritual turns out to be inextricably intertwined with the spiritual. The creative Spirit moves in all dimensions of our existence.

As Ruth Tiffany Barnhouse points out, there are significant similarities and differences between spiritual direction and secular psychotherapy. They are similar in that both involve inner motivation to change: both involve a more objective person (therapist or director) to help one identify blind spots in one's awareness; both deal with specific and unique issues in peoples' lives; and both involve training in the technique of choice. They are different in the criteria by which the outcome is evaluated— psychotherapy focusing on the changes in the person's inner being and relationships, spiritual direction on the person's relationship with God, and the Christian community. Spiritual direction recognizes the distinction between soul and psyche. It focuses explicitly on the wholeness of one's values and is oriented to issues of religious health: "How does one perceive oneself in relation to time with a capital T, all the time there is, in short, Eternity? What is one's place in the total scene of the universe? Who is one, in relation to all of this? . . . everyone has some sort of answer to these questions, if only negative answers. These answers, whatever they are, constitute a person's religion."[25]

William A. Barry holds that "spiritual direction is a form of pastoral counseling, indeed a form that should be the core from which all other forms of pastoral counseling radiate." He observes:

> People will expect that pastoral counselors will be able to help them not only with their marital problems, their vocational questions, and their grief but also, most especially, with their search for meaning, their search for God. The heart of pastoral care and counseling for people in our times, therefore, may be to help them find their rock, help to hear the rumor of angels and to decide in faith whether the rumor is of angels or not, help to center their lives in the mystery we call God. If pastoral counselors cannot offer

such help, their clients may ultimately feel that they have been offered a stone instead of bread.[26]

Pastoral counseling, to be truly pastoral, must include the perspectives and concerns of spiritual direction. Because of the managerial and hierarchical associations of the word "director," I prefer the term "spiritual guide" to "spiritual director." Effective guides must have both expertise and experience, but they must also walk *with* persons as colleagues and companions on their journey.

A potentially valuable conceptual tool in facilitating spiritual growth is the "Stages of Faith" model of James W. Fowler. He has explored the evolution of the images, beliefs, values, and commitments that guide and give meaning to the lives of individuals. Building on the thinking of Piaget, Kohlberg, and Erikson, Fowler has delineated six stages on the journey of spiritual development—intuitive-projective faith, mythic-literal faith, synthetic-conventional faith, individuative-reflective faith, conjunctive faith, and universalizing faith.[27] The applications of Fowler's understanding of these stages to spiritual direction and the ministry of pastoral care and counseling is one of the challenges facing the field today.

Diagnosing and Treating Spiritual Problems

Facilitating spiritual wholeness in pastoral counseling involves recognizing and understanding the particular spiritual problems of the person, then using appropriate methods to bring healing to that brokenness. When persons talk in counseling about aging and death, the meaning or meaninglessness of their lives, their responses to sickness and crises, their when-the-chips-are-down beliefs, their guilt feelings—usually they are asking for help with spiritual issues. Often the cry for such help is less obvious. It is disguised as dull purposelessness, empty longing, chronic boredom, or simply lack of zest and inner joy in living. The pastor's goal is to lead such persons toward an awareness of the underlying spiritual and value roots of their dilemmas in living. There are two levels in the process of much counseling—helping persons deal with their immediate problems or crises, and then encouraging them to examine the underlying value-spiritual issues of which their current problems are painful symptoms. If ministers help persons handle their immediate problems, they have done only half of their job, though an important half. The other crucial task is to help persons face the deeper problems of inadequate meanings, distorted or destructive values and life-styles that are the hidden sources of many of their problems in living. The spiritual growth opportunities potentially present in the problems that bring persons for counseling are often missed because people are not encouraged to explore the spiritual roots of their crises.

A pastor should not be timid about raising diagnostic questions regarding spiritual issues and the need for spiritual growth. Here are some examples of "opening questions" a counselor can use to invite people to explore spiritual issues:

"How do you understand this decision in light of what's most important in your life?"

"How does this problem with which you're struggling relate to your personal faith, to your relationship with God?"

"What have you learned from this miserable crisis? Has it changed your faith?"

Questions of this type should be asked only after a trustful relationship is established and the pressure of coping with the acute phase of a crisis is reduced. So timed, they may open doors for constructive dialogue about underlying spiritual issues such as unresolved guilt feelings and magical beliefs that persons need to replace with a more reality-respecting faith. Such dialogue can help people find meaningful answers to the big questions—"What does my life mean?" "What is the quality of my relationship with God?" "Is my life-style (and the values it reflects) destroying what's precious to me, including my health?" A man who had suffered a severe health crisis declared, after such a discussion of value and life-style issues, "As long as nobody asks the big questions, you can ignore them and let them be. But once they're asked, you can't put them down until you have an answer." People are more likely to find meaningful answers and to grow spiritually if they have the help of a spiritual guide as they wrestle with such difficult faith issues.

The diagnosis of spiritual pathology and the identification of areas where spiritual growth work is needed can be facilitated by using criteria such as these:

DO THE RELIGIOUS BELIEFS, ATTITUDES, AND PRACTICES OF PERSONS

—give them a meaningful philosophy of life that provides trust and hope in facing the inevitable tragedies of life?

—provide creative values and ethical sensitivities that serve as inner guidelines for behavior that is both personally and socially responsible?

—provide an integrating, energizing, growing relationship with that loving Spirit that religions call God?

—nurture the transcendent dimensions of persons' lives, their higher Self?

—inspire an ecological love of nature and a reverence for all life?

—provide for a regular renewal of basic trust by affirming a deep sense of belonging in the universe?

—bring the inner enrichment and growth that comes from "peak experiences"?

—offer the person a growth-enabling community of caring and meaning (e.g., their church)?

—build bridges rather than barriers between them and persons with differing values and faith systems?

—enhance love and self-acceptance (rather than fear and guilt) in their inner life?

—foster self-esteem and the "owing" and using of their strengths in constructive living?

—stimulate the growth of their inner freedom and autonomy?

—help them develop depth relationships committed to mutual growth?

—encourage the vital energies of sex and assertiveness to be used in affirmative, responsible ways rather than in repressive or people-damaging ways?

—foster realistic hope by encouraging the acceptance rather than the denial of reality?

—provide them with effective means of moving from the alienation of appropriate guilt to healing reconciliation with themselves, other persons, and God?

—encourage creative development in their beliefs and values through the life cycle to keep these congruent with their intellectual growth?

—provide effective means of keeping in touch with the creative resources of the unconscious through living symbols, meaningful rituals, and vital myths?

—encourage them to keep in touch with both the soft, vulnerable, nurturing, receptive, feelingful side *and* the assertive, rational, intentional, ethically demanding side of their personalities and their religion?

—make them aware of person-hurting institutional practices and motivate them to work to change these forces that oppress potentializing on a massive scale?

—give them the trust, hope, and meaing to face their awareness of death and the inevitable losses of life and to allow their awareness to make living more precious?

—keep them aware of the basic wonder and mystery of all life and growth?

—encourage heightened aliveness, joy, celebration of the *good gift of life* and an increasing commitment to living creatively— as an instrument of wholeness in response to this gift?[28]

These criteria have evolved over the years from my observations of the ways personal religion can enhance or diminish human wholeness in all dimensions of people's life. As a working hypothesis, I hold that to the extent that one's religious life meets criteria such as these, it will enhance wholeness-centered-in-Spirit. To the extent that it does not meet such criteria, one's religious life will diminish wholeness. These criteria can be used in self-diagnosis by persons in counseling or in growth groups to help them identify areas where they need to focus their spiritual growth work. The criteria can be presented with the suggestion that they be used to evaluate one's own spiritual health. The criteria all refer to different facets of one reality—the vitality and wholeness of one's spiritual life. They are stated broadly so that they can be applied to the spiritual dimension of any individual's life, whatever her or his religious orientation or traditions.

Changing Pathogenic Beliefs

Religious beliefs that diminish wholeness by reducing self-esteem and increasing guilt and fear are widespread in our society. The cognitive therapies provide counseling pastors with important tools for helping people let go of rigid, destructive beliefs and develop more humane growthful beliefs. Rational-Emotive Therapy (RET), a cognitive therapy developed by Albert Ellis, holds that disturbances in our perceptions, feelings, and actions stem from irrational thoughts and invalid beliefs.[29] Most psychotherapies have underemphasized the role of concepts and beliefs in producing emotional distress and distorted behavior. The cognitive therapies such as RET help to correct this. Ellis holds that our irrational beliefs are the source of the negative, self-depreciating messages we say to ourselves repetitiously.

An illustration of the truth in this assumption is found in the ways religious beliefs diminish or enhance self-esteem, the foundation of the ability to respect and esteem others. Theologies and personal belief systems that foster inappropriate guilt, anxiety, and dependency diminish self-esteem. In contrast, those which provide a sense of loving acceptance by God, give a sturdy theological foundation for self-esteem and interdependence. Helping people transform their wholeness diminishing beliefs is seldom easy. All of us tend to resist this tenaciously because immature, authority-centered beliefs give an illusion of security that comes from avoiding the risk of living out of the freedom of an open, growing faith. Facilitating spiritual self-transformation usually requires all the counseling skills one can muster. In this process, it may be necessary to deal with the pathogenic, growth-inhibiting beliefs directly, to question their validity, and to suggest and model, by one's attitudes and behavior, more growthful beliefs. The following excerpt from a pastoral counseling relationship occurred near the close of the third session, after trust was firmly established:

Pastor: (warmly) As I listen to you putting yourself down, it doesn't seem as if you're treating yourself with much grace—as a precious child of God.

Male parishioner: I guess I don't really believe that I'm worth much—in God's sight or anybody else's for that matter. I keep saying in my head, "I'm no damn good."

Pastor: That feels heavy. For me, it's often hard to believe that God really loves me in spite of the messes in my life. But that's the 'good news' of our faith isn't it? God says yes to us even when we say a loud no! to ourselves.

Parishioner: Yes, but it's damn hard to really believe it deep down.

Pastor: Uh huh. It sure is! My belief that I'm no good is most challenged when I experience acceptance and love I don't deserve and don't have to earn in a human relationship. It's like God speaks to me through that person, challenging my put-downs of myself.

Parishioner: I guess I've felt something like that from you in this counseling.

Pastor: I'm glad you've felt that from me. It often doesn't come through when I'm busy judging myself and others. I do respect and care about you. Glad it shows!

This caring confrontation by the minister (using the growth formula) opened the way to counseling through which the man came to experience himself in a more grace-full, self-valuing way. He gradually internalized something of the pastor's heart-level convictions concerning the value of himself and others as precious children of God. This case illustrates a basic task of much pastoral counseling—repairing self-esteem and then continuing to nurture it through ongoing pastoral care.

Using Religious Resources in Pastoral Care and Counseling

Because spiritual growth is the ultimate aim of pastoral care and counseling, ministers should use theological words, images, concepts, and stories and the religious resources of prayer, scripture, and sacraments with precision and care. Such symbols and practices mean many things to many people. For some they carry heavy, negative, emotional freight. They can be used in rigid, legalistic ways that arouse inappropriate guilt feelings and block creative dialogue and spiritual growth in counseling. William Hulme comments on the destructive uses of these resources:

> Prayer, for example, has been exploited as a way of escaping from the demands of serious dialogue . . . Religious words have also been misused to stifle dialogue. Rather than deal directly with a counselee's resistance, pastors may seek to supress it by taking on the authority role in religion. Retreating to the protected sphere . . . they use 'God-talk'—religiously oriented words associated with the profession—as an attempt to maintain control of the situation. Genuine dialogue, on the other hand, requires the relinquishment of this control, and the dialoguer risks an unpredictable outcome in each encounter.[30]

When religious resources are used appropriately they can be power-full instruments for nurturing spiritual wholeness, unique resources for pastoral care and counseling.

Here are some general guidelines for using religious resources in counseling:

(1) *Use religious words and resources only after one has some awareness of persons' problems and their background, their feelings, and attitudes regarding religion.* Otherwise one is likely to pray or read the Bible in ways that produce irreligious consequences, alienating persons further from a healing relationship with a loving God.

(2) *Before using resources such as prayer or scripture in care or counseling, ask if this would be meaningful.* This shows respect for a person's feelings and beliefs. In some situations, it opens doors for potentially healing discussions of spiritual conflicts and blocks.

(3) *After using a traditional religious resource, give persons an opportunity to discuss the thoughts, feelings, and fantasies they had during the experience.* A focusing question often triggers unexpected and much-needed reflection and discussion of religious issues, hang-ups, confusion, and perplexities.

Pastor: I'm wondering what was going through your mind while I was praying.

Parishioner: I had trouble listening after you mentioned my mother. I felt a wave of sadness and wishing things had been different.

Pastor: Let's talk about that . . . there's a lot of pain there.

(4) *Use religious resources more frequently in supportive, crisis, and bereavement counseling and less frequently in pastoral psychotherapy and insight-oriented counseling.* Using religious symbols and rituals tends to strengthen the authority image of the minister, often arousing guilt and old feelings of compliance, defiance, or powerlessness by activating the counselee's inner Child (in TA terms). This can be useful in insight-oriented counseling if these obsolete feelings are worked through in the process.

(5) *Use these resources in ways that do not diminish a sense of initiative, strength, and responsibility,* especially in dependent people.

(6) *Use prayer and biblical material in ways that facilitate rather than block the owning and catharsis of negative feelings by arousing guilt about them.* Catching up the person's feelings in prayer, (including angry, bitter, or despairing feelings) indicates to that person that God accepts these very human feelings.

(7) *Use religious resources to deepen, enrich, and strengthen a relationship, by giving it a vertical dimension, never as a substitute for relating.*

(8) *Never feel that one has to use religious words or resources.* God is continually active in all relationships, whether or not formal religious words or practices are used. Never use prayer as a tool. Unless the minister who prays, honestly feels prayerful, a counselee will be confused by the incongruence of the minister.

(9) *Inviting people during caring and counseling relationships to pray (if that is meaningful to them) may be helpful in a different way than for the counselor to pray.* Teaching them methods of prayer and meditation may be helpful, as well as a means of awakening awareness of unresolved spiritual issues.

The appropriate use of religious resources can stimulate constructive struggling with spiritual-existential issues in counseling, which may help some persons become aware of the resources of their higher Selves and of the transforming energy of the Spirit of God.

At the close of a meaningful counseling session or series of sessions, a prayer of thanksgiving may be a fitting way to express gratitude for the healing and growth that has occurred. It is helpful to some people to see that the issues at the heart of their counseling—alienation, guilt, anxiety, reconciliation, rebirth, the search for wholeness—are essentially theological issues. With people from church backgrounds, it may be meaningful to state the goals of counseling in theological/biblical language, as well as psychological terms. Skillfully employed, biblical language may express the sense of the ineffable and the deep mystery of the transformation that can occur in counseling.

Using the Bible Growthfully

There are a variety of valuable ways to use the Bible in pastoral care and counseling. The first is *to allow biblical wisdom to inform the process, spirit, and goals of caring/counseling relationships*. In chapter 3, I suggested why pastoral counselors need to stay in continuing dialogue with biblical images and insights. My friend and colleague John B. Cobb, Jr. says: "Pastoral counselors could experience their counseling not simply as in continuity with Christianity in its ultimate purposes but as informed by the Christian heritage in both form and substance." William B. Oglesby, Jr. has shown how biblical motifs can inform the goals and methods of pastoral counseling. He sees one unifying theological theme throughout the Bible—viz., that human beings are sinners needing reconciliation and that God's action enables this reconciliation to occur. Various biblical subthemes—initiative and freedom, fear and faith, conformity and rebellion, death and rebirth, risk and redemption—all throw light on the complexities of the human issues encountered in counseling.[31]

A second and very common use of the Bible in pastoral care and counseling is *to comfort and strengthen people in crises*. Having a sense of the sustaining presence of God, as communicated for example in the familiar words of the twenty-third or the ninetieth Psalm can be a source of great strength for some people in handling shattering losses. They feel empowered as they walk through their shadowed valley, sustained by a sense of God's loving presence. Having such a source of support helps them deal with the new realities they must face, as well as with their agonizing feelings.

A third use of the Bible in counseling relationships is as *a means of diagnosis.* Wayne Oates's *The Bible in Pastoral Care* and Carroll Wise's *Psychiatry and the Bible* show how the Bible can illuminate the inner dynamics and problems of counselees.[32] Paul W. Pruyser in *The Minister as Diagnostician* recommends that basic theological-biblical themes—providence, repentance, faith, grace, vocation, communion, and awareness of the holy—be held in a minister's mind as unique guideposts for understanding theologically the issues in counseling.

A method I have found useful in diagnosing psychological, interpersonal, and spiritual growth issues is to invite clients to tell the Bible story they most like and the one they most dislike. One woman who had struggled with feelings of being trapped for years told the Exodus story as her favorite, adding, "I feel like I've been trying to escape from my own Egypt and, when I do, I end up wandering in the wilderness. It's the hope of finding the freedom of the promised land that keeps me going, I guess." The inner conflicts of church people may be expressed in the biblical characters with whom they identify. For example, many women today feel inwardly torn between the submissive, serving-others Martha side of themselves and the more liberated Mary side, wanting to participate fully as an equal in the "action." Donald Capps observes:

> While there is the danger that the diagnostic use of the Bible in counseling will be thought of as merely a clinical tool, diagnosis can mean using biblical insights to gain a more empathetic understanding of the counselee's struggles and conflicts. It can also mean evaluating the counselee's current difficulties from the perspective of biblical accounts of God's healing activity . . . Jesus' parabolic vision is a particularly valuable biblical resource for this purpose.[33]

A fourth use of the Bible in pastoral care and counseling is *to help heal spiritual pathology and change pathogenic beliefs.* When a pastor senses that the Bible is being used to suppress anger, grief, guilt, or despair, a direct approach to correcting this distorted understanding of the Bible is needed. In dealing with a person who is suppressing anger, one may say, "My understanding is that anger is a gift of God to be valued and used constructively. Jesus seems to have gotten very angry on occasions. It's storing up anger—letting the sun go down on it—that makes it destructive to ourselves and others." Or in responding to repressed grief, "The New Testament says that it's a good thing—a blessed thing—to mourn. The story of Jesus' weeping when his friend died speaks to me when I try to avoid expressing the pain of a loss . . . ." Such statements by a minister may shake and challenge the comfortable but oppressive beliefs of the person. This cognitive dissonance may open such persons to explore in counseling alternative ways of understanding the biblical teachings about feelings.

When people ask questions in counseling about the Bible, it is important to resist the temptation to respond immediately with an answer. As David K. Switzer points out, when a person asks, "What does the Bible say about . . . (divorce, homosexuality, etc.)?," it is crucial to find out why *this person* is asking *this* particular question. "Usually the very simple question, 'Why do you ask?' will open the floodgates of a story that . . . will pour out, accompanied by a variety of emotions. Then we may move very quickly into the same type of pastoral conversation or even counseling that would have been initiated if the person had come and simply laid out a clearly delineated problem before us."[34] In the context of such counseling, the pastor's scholarly knowledge about the Bible can be useful in correcting destructive misunderstandings of biblical texts.

Beyond its use in helping people handle crises and problems, a fifth use of biblical wisdom is as *a key resource in the teaching and growth-nurturing dimension of pastoral care*. There are numerous ways of using the Bible as a growth resource. It can serve in counseling and growth groups to raise consciousness about the Christian vision of life as a gift from God, a calling to serve those in need.[35] Switzer suggests:

> Persons may be taught, individually or in groups, to read selected passages in the Bible imaginatively and in such a manner that in a sense they move back into biblical times and into the life situation of the writer or the person being described, and then move again into their own present life-situation, accompanied by the particular Word they have received from their experience.[36]

Walter Wink's *The Bible in Human Transformation* and Karl A. Olsson's *Find Yourself in the Bible* describe ways to use the Bible for spiritual growth.

The Bible can be misused in wholeness-constricting ways in

pastoral care. It can be quoted in a legalistic way by pastors to buttress their sagging authority, manipulate counselees to conform to rigid moralizing, and justify life-constricting attitudes toward issues such as sex and divorce. An example of the misuse of the Bible in pastoral counseling is the approach of Jay Adams.[37] He begins with a moralistic reductionism (similar to and apparently learned from O. Hobart Mowrer), which reduces the cause of all psychological problems to sin and irresponsible living. Psychological understandings of the human situation and psychotherapeutic methods are rejected as "humanistic" and "nonbiblical." All that a counselor needs, to be "more competent than a psychiatrist," is the Bible. The method is exclusively confrontational—confronting persons with their sin and then pushing them by the use of scripture, to conform to a legalistic and literalistic understanding of the teachings of the Bible.

There are three basic flaws in this approach. It is poor counseling because it does not integrate the biblical wisdom with contemporary wisdom from the human sciences and the psychotherapeutic disciplines. Second, Adams' approach encourages authoritarian advice giving, reinforced by biblical authority. This tends to increase counselees' dependency and block spiritual maturing. Third, the rigid biblicism of this approach tends to prevent people from discovering the Bible as the *living* Word that speaks to their particular situation in transforming ways. Hulme notes:

> In its misuse the Bible is converted into an ultimate authority—and end in itself. Converting a means into an end is basically what is meant by idolatry, and there are no means more susceptible to this distortion than religious symbols. When this happens to the Bible, the flexibility of the Holy Spirit is replaced by the rigidity of the Holy Book. The Bible's value to pastoral care depends on its mediatorial function: it is a means by which the Spirit bears "witness with our spirits that we are the children of God" (Rom. 8:16), that it is "profitable for teaching, for reproof, for correction, and for training in righteousness" (II Tim. 3:16).[38]

Using Prayer and Meditation

Prayer and meditation are complementary devotional disciplines that can enrich each other. Both are direct ways to open oneself to the creative power of God's love. These disciplines have three uses in pastoral care and counseling: They are important resources for the minister's own spiritual preparation for facilitating spiritual growth in counseling; they can be used by the counselor on behalf of the counselee; they are skills that the counselee can be taught for use in self-healing.

For many people in our hectic, secularized culture, prayer has little meaning. Even when they go through the motions of praying, it does not empower them. The inner channels of their spirits are blocked by logjams of guilt, grief and anger (including anger toward God), which prevent them from experiencing the enlivening flow of God's love. Helping such persons in counseling to work through their emotional logjams, and then teaching them effective ways to meditate and pray, can enable them to experience new spiritual aliveness.

There are, of course, many forms of prayer. The type of prayer that the spiritual direction movement seeks to help people develop—contemplative prayer—is useful to teach in pastoral care and counseling. The goal is to develop a heightened awareness of the way God is present and communicating in all experiences, including the most mundane. The spiritual director first discovers what the person finds so absorbing that it allows him or her to move beyond self-absorption.[39] The director then suggests that the person engage in this activity contemplatively, being aware and open to letting God become real in experiences such as looking at the beauty of nature, reading the Bible, listening to music, or walking the streets of a city. The disciplines of looking, listening, and attending to what occurs within oneself when one contemplates in this way, are practiced and discussed with the director. A thrill of joy at a sunset or the stab of inner pain at seeing a child's tears can be, if taken seriously, the beginning of a deeper relationship with the living Spirit. The line from a familiar hymn, "take the dimness of my soul away," comes to mind.

Teaching people in counseling and in spiritual growth groups to meditate and use active imaging can help them enliven their experience of prayer as well as providing valuable skills for self-healing and growth between sessions. To teach them effectively, a counselor must learn and practice these disciplines. This helps deepen and enrich one's own life, which enhances relationships with others including counselees.

"Meditation" is any method of quieting and centering one's consciousness, of getting into a clear, uncluttered space psychologically. Letting one's mental motor idle for even ten minutes each day can quiet one's consciousness, increase awareness of one's body and put one in touch with one's spiritual center. Scientific studies of various meditative and relaxation methods from both the East and West show that they all tend to produce physiological as well as psychological and spiritual benefits. Herbert Benson and Miriam Klipper's *The Relaxation Response* summarizes these findings. Meditation is an integral part of both the Christian and the Jewish heritages.[40] Coaching counselees in meditative techniques should become increasingly used in pastoral counseling in the years ahead.

The use of mental imaging has great potential for pastoral care and counseling. For reasons that are not fully understood, forming certain pictures within one's mind activates the energies of healing and growth. For example, when one is ill, visualizing oneself as well may facilitate the healing process. If persons in crisis counseling can picture themselves as coping constructively with their situation, their insights about what to do and the strength to do this may be mobilized. Research by L. Rebecca Propst demonstrate that the use of religious imagery in cognitive therapy with depressed college students was more effective than similar therapy without religious imagery.[41]

Here is a simple meditation-imaging exercise that can be used to reduce stress and renew inner energies. It can be taught to counselees in a few minutes by leading them through it during a session. I suggest that you try it now:

Find a quiet place where you can be uninterrupted for the next ten to fifteen minutes./(This mark means "Stop reading while you do this.") While standing, tense and relax all your muscles several times stretching and wiggling any part of your body that feels tight./Now, sit in a chair with your lower spine straight./Close your eyes and be aware of your breathing. Allow any tension within you to flow out as you exhale./For the next few minutes, focus only on the inflow and outflow of the air through your nostrils, repeating the word "one" with each exhalation. If a thought, image, sound, or itch enters your consciousness, don't try to get rid of it. Just release it and let it recede as you keep focus on your breathing and continue to repeat "one" over and over. The spaces between your breaths will gradually lengthen and you will feel increasingly clear and quiet within. Let yourself experience this inner serenity for at least ten minutes./ Now, choose the religious symbol that is most meaningful and alive for you (Light, the dove of peace, the cross, the everlasting arms, the burning bush, the Good Shepherd, the water or bread of life, mother Earth, the Star of David, the mandala), and form a picture of this in your mind. Focus on this and let the energy from this picture flow through your whole being—your body, your mind, your relationships, your spirit./[42]

I find that quieting my busy stream-of-consciousness for a few minutes helps me become reenergized and centered, which allows me to be more present with myself and others, particularly when I am feeling "beside myself" or "scattered" by stress. Focusing on a lively religious image while in this quiet inner space can be spiritually enlivening and nurturing. (A variation on this exercise using the image of walking up a mountain to become aware of one's higher Self, is described in *Growth Counseling*, pp. 126-8.)

It is important for the pastoral counselor to stay open to the energy of God's transforming love during counseling sessions. To me the New Testament phrase to "pray without ceasing" (I Thess. 5:17) means seeking to maintain a continuing awareness, in the background of one's consciousness, of the here-and-now presence of the Spirit of love and liberation. It means keeping oneself open to the flow of the inner Light of the divine presence. A right-brain method that can help one be more spiritually open is to imagine a warm healing Light surrouding oneself and the other person in a counseling relationship. Between sessions, it can be helpful for the counselor to picture the troubled counselee, seeing that person enveloped in this Light and handling his or her crisis effectively. This is a form of intercessory prayer.

Prayer, meditation, and imaging are right-brain, experiential resources for spiritual growth. There is a variety of other right-brain resources for enhancing one's spiritual life including music, poetry, art, drama, dance, humor, storytelling. The increased use of such resources as these in pastoral care and counseling can help free the intuitive, imaginative, metaphoric powers of the right hemisphere of the brain, in both the counselor and the counselee.[43]

Using Feminist Insights in Spiritual Growth

As suggested in chapter 3, both women and men need feminine images of divinity if they are to develop their full spiritual potentials. Most women have been conditioned to be dependent on males for their sense of worth, identity, and power. In the church this is reinforced by encouraging dependence on a supreme Father. The Bible and our hymns and rituals are dominated by male words and symbols for deity. The vast majority of ministers are men. The self-concept of many women is so male identified that they are unaware of the profound ways in which this diminishes their wholeness. The frequently heard protest that "my God is neither male nor female" does not change the spirituality constricting impact on women of the constant use of male imagery that excludes them. The maleness of most of our religious images contributes to the spiritual impoverishment of men, too. It helps to alienate us from the so-called "feminine" side of our spirits and from that side of deity, as well as helping to justify our one-up power position in our culture's institutions including the church. The spiritual emptiness and malaise of both men and women in our society is fed by the deep sexism of our religious institutions and the spiritual images they reinforce.

In counseling on spiritual issues, it is essential that ministers, male or female, have a raised consciousness on these issues. Reading and inviting our counselees to read books by feminist theologians and therapists (see references by Mary Daly, Carol Christ, Jean Baker Miller, and Charlotte Holt Clinebell in the "Recommended Reading" in this chapter and chapter 3) can help raise the consciousness of ourselves and our counselees. Furthermore, such reading can open up exciting vistas, which are being illuminated by feminists who are exploring new dimensions of women's spirituality. As discussed earlier (pp. 61-64), in pastoral care and counseling with women and men, it is important to use words and images that communicate our awareness of and appreciation for the neglected "feminine" in divinity rather than the patriarchal words and images that dominate our tradition. In a paper entitled "Why Women Need the Goddess," Carol P. Christ shows how male-oriented religion with a Father God militates against the self-esteem and personal empowerment of women.[44] She holds that as a symbol for the feminine in divinity, the

"Goddess" helps women acknowledge the legitimacy of their female power, affirms the female will and body (both denigrated in our society), and validates bonds among women. The use of images for divinity that include rather than exclude the feminine experience often is resisted by male-identified women and men whose patriarchal power is threatened. But such use can open healing dialogue about issues that are precisely what is preventing women and men from making their spiritual search a more exciting adventure.

The Pastor's Own Spiritual Resources

When ministers counsel in the areas of spiritual crises and confusion, their *living* theology—the way they handle their own existential anxiety—will influence their effectiveness far more than their head-level theology. Their own basic trust, by which they cope with the "ego chill" (Erik Erikson's term for existential anxiety), their own real faith from which they may derive courage to look into the abyss of nonbeing—these will be tested repeatedly—e.g., in relating to a woman dying of cancer or an alcoholic teetering on the brink of meaninglessness and suicide. Their real feelings about their own life and death, and the life and death of those they cherish most, will influence all their counseling, especially that centering in existential issues.

Therefore, our own continuing spiritual growth is essential to our effectiveness as pastoral counselors. Practicing spiritual disciplines, needed to nurture this growth, is not easy in the midst of demanding schedules. But spiritual vitality and health *is* contagious; it is *caught* more than it is *taught*. Keeping the spiritual enlivener alive is the most difficult challenge facing the pastoral counselor.

Fortunately, our effectiveness as spiritual enablers is not entirely dependent on our degree of spiritual maturation. As representative Christian persons we can draw on and share the resources of a rich spiritual tradition—wisdom about life and death—time-tested by many centuries of human struggle. Even at best we are very imperfect transmitters of the wisdom of this heritage. But, surprisingly, God often can use us with all our limitations to carry the spiritual bread of our heritage to feed the deep spiritual hungers of human hearts.

The image that has become increasingly energizing for me in recent years is of an irrigation channel barely two feet wide—flowing within me. Though it is small and imperfect, it carries clear, cool water from an artesian spring flowing from an underground river of unlimited volume. This little channel, to my continuing amazement, often is adequate to carry water that lets some of the parched places in myself and others flower. The sluice gate of my inner irrigation channel often is within my control. But the Source of the flow is from beyond me. A sermon illustration I heard many years ago speaks to me now—"The Gulf Stream can flow through a soda straw if it is pointed in the right direction." At times, I'm glad to report, the water in my inner channel dances and splashes in the sunlight. There are even some toy sailboats on its stream. The dry places in me are also watered by the energy flow from those who care about me in spite of my limitations.

Put in traditional language, it's important in our counseling to pray silently for openness to the presence of the Holy Spirit, the "Great Counselor," working in and through our relationships. This Spirit brings healing *through* our efforts, sometimes more in spite of than because of what we do. The work of an effective pastoral counselor "springs from, and is sustained by, a deep and continuous interior transaction with God."[45] Ultimately, it is the healing energy from our relationship with God that allows us to be used at times as healers in our counseling. Our counseling skills may help remove the blocks to openness in persons—fear, guilt, hatred, self-rejection, and defensive pride—openness to the enlivening energy of God that is the Source of all healing and growth.

Contemporary Therapies

Two streams in contemporary psychotherapy provide particularly rich resources for the pastoral counselor's work with spiritual issues. One is the *existentialist perspective* as reflected in the therapeutic approaches of Rollo May, James F. T. Bugental, and Victor Frankl. The emphases of therapists in this stream on values, creativity, freedom (choice and responsibility), authenticity, existential anxiety (and also existential guilt and joy), being, and meaning all are consistent with much in the Hebrew-Christian view of persons. Their nonreductionistic understanding of persons, in contrast to both behaviorism and psychoanalysis, lifts up the *uniquely human* in us human beings. Bugental says: "Perhaps I can best summarize what existential psychology means to me by using this phrase: 'It restores our divinity.' "[46] The existential perspective in psychotherapy refuses to reduce human beings to mechanisms, even very complex mechanisms like computers. In biblical language, it affirms the *imago dei* as the essence of our humanity and seeks to enable the fullest possible development of this God-like potential.

Psychosynthesis, a therapy developed by Italian psychiatrist Roberto Assagiolo, is a goldmine of insights and methods for the pastoral counselor. It is both growth-centered and spiritually oriented. Many of its methods are useful in facilitating spiritual growth.

Reality-Practice Session

PARISHIONER'S ROLE: 1. Become aware of some area of religious conflicts, doubts, or confusion within yourself, about which you would like some help. Let yourself experience the feelings associated with that area of your life. Go talk with the pastor about this area.

2. (Part to be taken by a woman) You are becoming increasingly frustrated by the constant use of male pronouns and names for God, and the generic "man," by your male pastor in his sermons and newsletter statements. Last Sunday the congregation sang, "Rise Up O Men of God" at the close of the service. You like your minister, but as your consciousness is getting raised, you find that his sexism and the sexism of the worship service is interfering with your finding spiritual nourishment in your church. Go talk with him about your concern.

3. You are a middle-class man, married, with two teen-age daughters. You are a member of a church but repeated surgery has shaken your faith. You feel that God has let you down. Your wife resents the heavy medical expenses and is critical of you for your faltering faith. Things look very dark. You are in the hospital bed recovering from your last surgery when your pastor calls. (Lie down during this reality-practice session.)

PASTOR'S ROLE: Counsel with one of the above persons using insights you learned from this chapter. Be particularly aware of interconnections of the psychological, interpersonal, and spiritual dimensions of the person's problems.

OBSERVER-COACH'S ROLE: Give feedback on the pastor's effectiveness in encouraging the expression of negative feelings and avoiding a defense of God or an intellectualized discussion of theology.

Recommended Reading

Herbert Benson and Miriam Z. Klipper, *The Relaxation Response* (New York: William Morrow & Co., 1975). An introduction to the research on and methods of meditation.

Alastair V. Campbell, *Rediscovering Pastoral Care* (Philadelphia: Westminster Press, 1981). Examines the power of Christian images—the shepherd, the wounded healer, the journey of faith, etc.—for a theologically-centered approach to pastoral care.

Donald Capps, *Biblical Approaches to Pastoral Counseling* (Philadelphia: Westminster Press, 1981). Surveys the literature on the role of the Bible in pastoral counseling and then focuses on the use of the psalms, proverbs, and parables in care and counseling.

Carol P. Christ and Judith Plaskow, eds., *Womanspirit Rising: A Feminist Reader in Religion* (New York: Harper & Row, 1979). Has a section on "Creating New Traditions," which includes Carol Christ's paper, "Why Women Need the Goddess."

Howard Clinebell, "Growth Resources from Existential Therapies" (pp. 103-113) and "Growth Resources in Psychosynthesis" (pp. 263-280) in *Contemporary Growth Therapies*. Describes insights and methods from these therapies for use in facilitating Spirit-centered growth.

Howard Clinebell, "Methods of Spiritual Enrichment and Inner Renewal," chapter 5 in *Growth Counseling for Mid-Years Couples*. (Philadelphia: Fortress Press, 1977). Describes a variety of spiritual growth methods.

Howard Clinebell, "Spiritual Growth—The Key to All Growth," chapter 4 in *Growth Counseling*. Describes a variety of methods for helping people grow spiritually by learning to satisfy their spiritual needs more fully.

John B. Cobb, Jr., *Theology and Pastoral Care* (Philadelphia: Fortress Press, 1977). Discusses the use of process theology in pastoral care and counseling.

Tilden Edwards, *Spiritual Friend* (New York: Paulist Press, 1980). Explores ways of reclaiming the gift of spiritual direction on an individual and group basis.

James W. Fowler, *Stages of Faith: the Psychology of Human Development and the Quest for Meaning* (New York: Harper & Row, 1981). Describes the six stages of the faith journey.

Cecelia H. Foxley, *Non-Sexist Counseling: Helping Women and Men Redefine Their Roles* (Dubuque, Iowa: Kendall/Hunt Publishing Co., 1979). Describes ways of counseling for psychological androgyny and training nonsexist counselors.

Carolyn Gratton, *Guidelines for Spiritual Direction* (Denville, N.J.: Dimension Books, 1980). Explores the relationship between spiritual direction and therapeutic counseling.

William E. Hulme, *Pastoral Care and Counseling: Using the Unique Resources of the Christian Tradition* (Minneapolis: Augsburg Press, 1981). Discusses sound ways of using the Bible, prayer, meditation, and the congregation in pastoral care and counseling.

Morton Kelsey, *The Other Side of Silence* (New York: Paulist Press, 1976). A Christian approach to meditation.

Kenneth Leech, *Soul Friend: The Practice of Christian Spirituality* (London: Sheldon Press, 1977). Relates spiritual direction to counseling and therapy.

Gerald G. May, *Pilgrimage Home: The Conduct of Contemporative Practice in Groups* (New York: Paulist Press, 1979). Reports on the spiritual formation work at Shalem Institute in Washington, D.C.

Gerald G. May, *Care of Mind, Care of Spirit* (San Francisco: Harper & Row, 1982). Psychiatric dimensions of spiritual direction.

H. Newton Malony, ed., *Wholeness and Holiness: Reading in the Psychology/Theology of Mental Health* (Grand Rapids: Baker Book House, 1983). Explores the meaning of health and the process of healing.

Henri J. M. Nouwen, *Creative Ministry* (Garden City, N.Y.: Doubleday, 1971). Infusing the work of preaching, teaching, organizing, celebrating, and pastoral care with creative spirituality.

Wayne Oates, *The Bible in Pastoral Care* (Philadelphia: Westminster Press, 1953). An introduction to using biblical resources in pastoral care.

William B. Oglesby, Jr., *Biblical Themes for Pastoral Care* (Nashville: Abingdon Press, 1980). Discusses guidelines for using the Bible in pastoral care and counseling and then explores major biblical themes as resources in this ministry.

Karl A. Olsson, *Find Yourself in the Bible* (Minneapolis: Augsburg Press, 1974). A guide to relational Bible study in small groups.

Paul W. Pruyser, *The Minister as Diagnostician* (Philadelphia: Westminster Press, 1976). Describes the use of theological categories in pastoral diagnosis.

Ann Wilson Schaef, *Women's Reality: An Emerging Female System in the White Male Society* (Minneapolis: Winston Press, 1981). A psychotherapist shares how our present theology is a product and tool of the white male system and points to the need for a female system theology.

Charlene Spretnak, ed., *The Politics of Women's Spirituality* (Garden City, New York: Anchor Press/Doubleday, 1982). Essays on the rise of spiritual power within the feminist movement.

David K. Switzer, "The Use of the Bible in Pastoral Care," chapter 5 in *Pastor, Preacher, Person: Developing Pastoral Ministry in Depth.*

(Nashville: Abingdon Press, 1979). A case-illustrated discussion of the constructive uses of the Bible in care and counseling.

Edward E. Thornton, *Theology and Pastoral Counseling* (Englewood Cliffs, N.J.: Prentice Hall, 1964). Discusses pastoral care in relation to faith, repentance, salvation, learning, and the community of faith.

Edward P. Wimberly, *Pastoral Counseling and Spiritual Values: A Black Point of View* (Nashville: Abingdon Press, 1982). Explores the moral and spiritual implications of the recovery of soul in pastoral counseling.

Walter Wink, *The Bible in Human Transformation* (Philadelphia: Westminster Press, 1953). Describes how to use the Bible as a resource for spiritual growth.

Daniel Day Williams, *The Minister and the Care of Souls* (New York: Harper & Row, 1977). A theology of pastoral care.

Counseling on Ethical, Value, and Meaning Issues

Speaking the truth in love, we are to grow up in every way into him . . .
—EPHESIANS 4:15

There is a balm in Gilead, to make the wounded whole; there is a balm in Gilead, to heal the sin-sick soul."
—AMERICAN FOLK HYMN (FROM JEREMIAH 8:22)

The difficulty with much of pastoral counseling today is that more time is spent discussing the tools of counseling than in the more challenging process of developing the structure of meanings that should constitute the context of counseling.
—DON S. BROWNING, *THE MORAL CONTEXT OF PASTORAL CARE*[1]

People need sound values and meanings to be healthy. Growth toward Spirit-centered wholeness must include growth in life-guiding values and ethical commitments. The epidemic of moral confusion and value distortions in our society is the seedbed within which are bred many of the psychological, psychosomatic, interpersonal, and spiritual problems that bring people to counseling and therapy. The widespread collapse of old authority-centered and institutionally-validated value systems has left millions of people feeling as though they are drifting in mid-ocean in a small boat without a rudder, a compass, or a chart during a storm. Many who seek pastoral help with personal problems are suffering from distorted, immature, or vacuous · consciences. Often they are unaware of the ethical roots of their pain. In our society, ministers need to develop effective skills as guides to their people on their journey through complex and confusing ethical and value issues. This aspect of pastoral care and counseling is one of the most needed and most often neglected in our times of mind-boggling ethical transition.

Counseling on ethical, value, and meaning issues is not just one special type of pastoral counseling. These issues are present, at some level, in all human dilemmas and problems, often in subtle or implicit form. Frequently these issues are obvious to any value-sensitive person. Helping persons evaluate and revise their values and their life-styles is, in many situations, the heart of the process of helping them cope with their crises and dilemmas in living growthfully.

As Don Browning makes clear, the church is called to be a community of moral inquiry, guidance, and formation. The minister's role is to facilitate this process in the congregation and to help "create, maintain and revise the normative value symbols of his society."[2] It is within this crucial task and within the moral context of the ethical wisdom of the Judeo-Christian heritage, that all truly pastoral care and counseling occurs. Biblical wisdom about ethical values and moral health are much more than the *context* of pastoral care and counseling. They are also an invaluable part of the *content* and resources in the decision-making process of counseling.

In their discussion of the basic functions of pastoral care in a historic context, Clebsch and Jaekle point to the most egregious lack in contemporary pastoral care: "There are many indications that the function of reconciling as a creative and meaningful part of Christian pastoral care has fallen upon evil days. Perhaps more than the other three functions of the cure of souls, reconciling has suffered from misunderstanding and erosion."[3] Clebsch and Jaekle show that in the Christian heritage the ministry of reconciling has enabled persons to renew a right relationship with God and with neighbor by utilizing two interdependent modes— *discipline* (a word of correction, a pastoral admonition, or church discipline) and *forgiveness* (confession, penance, and absolution). Within some mainstream Protestant denominations, this ministry has been underemphasized, as a result of an overreaction to sterile moralism. This neglect has been reinforced by permissive counseling theories. As a result—a considerable segment of Christendom has been virtually deprived of a ministry of pastoral reconciliation "at a time when alienation is at the root of much human woe and anxiety." It is sad but true that "there is no place in the structure and rhythm of the life of modern congregations where a serious discussion concerning the state of one's soul is expected."[4]

A revival of pastoral effectiveness in reconciling is a paramount need in contemporary pastoral counseling. Clebsch and Jaekle declare:

> The reconciling function enjoys an extraordinarily rich heritage in the church and remains a manner of helping for which there is, as yet, no prominent non-pastoral substitute. The burden of guilt under which moderns live—guilt engendered by alienation from fellow man [*sic*] that interprets itself as also alienation from God—is a form of human trouble with which the pastoral ministry has had longer and deeper familiarity than has any other helping profession. Partly by virtue of insisting that broken human relationships involve a breach in man's ultimate relationship with his Creator, pastoral care takes the human need for reconciliation with a seriousness unsurpassed by that of other healing arts.
>
> We foresee in the resuscitation of the reconciling function, synthesized with that of healing, the best hope for a transformed pastoral care that is at once continuous with the history of pastoring, integrated with the church's theological formulations, open to new psychological insights, and able to meet creatively the aspirations and needs of modern men and women.[5]

These authors see a renewal of this dimension of pastoring as offering a sound basis for interprofessional dialogue:

> From the vantage point of a renewed emphasis upon reconciling, the practitioner of the pastoral art may enter more fully into conversations with representatives of the other healing arts, not only as a listener but as an artist able to make significant contributions from accumulated wisdom gained through two millennia of hearing confessions, pronouncing forgiveness, and exercising discipline in an effort to bring to reconciliation countless numbers of men and women in every area of the Western world. Such a renewed emphasis upon reconciling could precipitate the ministry of the cure of souls into a new realization of its therapeutic power for our time.[6]

Many Protestant pastoral counselors have not taken guilt as seriously as its destructive effects warrant. Having appropriately rejected legalistic moralism as destructive and unchristian, we have failed to discover effective methods of resolving guilt and helping people develop constructive consciences. It is imperative that we do so. Psychiatrist Edmund Bergler observes, "A feeling of guilt follows every person like his shadow, whether or not he knows it."[7] Certainly guilt is *the* crucial factor in the problems of many of those who seek pastoral help.

A pastor encounters six types of conscience problems—*consciences with appropriate guilt; consciences troubled by neurotic guilt; self-righteous consciences; underdeveloped or crippled consciences lacking appropriate guilt; underdeveloped consciences lacking in an appropriate sense of social responsibility and guilt;* and *consciences with value and meaning emptiness.*[8] These types often overlap; many people suffer from more than one type. Guilt and its Siamese twin alienation are varied and complex phenomena. To be effective in helping to bring reconciliation and enable ethical growth, counseling methods must take cognizance of the complex diversity of conscience problems.

Appropriate Versus Neurotic Guilt

How guilt should be dealt with in counseling depends on whether it is appropriate or neurotic. All guilt has its objective and subjective sides. Objectively, appropriate guilt stems from any behavior that actually damages or diminishes the wholeness of persons—oneself or others. Subjectively, appropriate guilt is associated with harm to persons resulting from the misuse of whatever degree of inner freedom one possesses in that situation. It is the consequence of intentionally violating the values that the mature side of one's conscience regards as authentic and significant.

In contrast, neurotic guilt is not the result of the real harm one has done intentionally to persons. Psychologically, it is produced by the immature side of one's conscience—the internalized values, behavior, and feelings that were rewarded or punished by one's culture as this was experienced through the values of one's parents and other need-satisfying adults is one's childhood. (This is the way that the initial contents of one's conscience was formed.) This immature side of one's conscience is motivated by fear of punishment and rejection, rather than by a positive striving for what one wholeheartedly affirms as good. Neurotic guilt feelings result mainly from violating internalized parental prohibitions. It often focuses on minor or insignificant ethical issues or on angry feelings, aggressive impulses, sexual fantasies, and impulses. Neurotic guilt feelings and the person-hurting behavior it motivates are compulsive and therefore lacking in the freedom that must be present in any genuine ethical choice. Such persons feel burdened by a chronic sense of their sinfulness. They suffer from punitive consciences, (roughly what Freud meant by the superego).[9] *Guilt*, the inner sense of having violated one's principles, and *shame*, the fear of being caught, exposed, and punished, intermingle in the inner torment such consciences produce in Western cultures.

In many counselees appropriate and neurotic guilt feelings are intertwined. The neurotic elements can be identified by these characteristics: (a) They do not respond to the confession-forgiveness process (described below), but are held onto obsessively. (b) They focus on relatively insignificant ethical issues or on fantasies and feelings. (c) They seldom motivate constructive amends or long-term changes in the guilt-producing behavior. (d) They may produce masochistic satisfactions. As a counselee put it, "I get my kicks from wallowing in my guilt."

The Healing of Appropriate Guilt

The Reality-based, appropriate guilt feelings can be resolved via a five-stage process: *confrontation, confession, forgiveness, restitution (and changing destructive behavior), and reconciliation*. This path, by which forgiveness is actualized, incorporates the time-tested wisdom of the sacrament of reconciliation (formerly called the sacrament of penance in the Roman Catholic Church). It is the path from alienation (from oneself, others, and God) caused by guilt to the reconciliation of completed forgiveness. Let's examine these five steps.

Confrontation is an indispensable skill in much pastoral counseling, involving the sensitive use of the minister's authority—both the authority of his role and the "rational authority" (Fromm) derived from his competence as an ethical guide. The central goal of confronting anyone is to enable *self-confrontation*—i.e., to help them face the behavior that hurts themselves and/or others and to feel guilt that therefore is appropriate. In some counselees, appropriate guilt feelings are like an open wound. Confrontation by another obviously is not needed, since they are already confronting themselves forcefully. But many people are not fully aware of their destructive behavior. If their behavior is to be interrupted and their latent guilt healed, it must be brought out into the open by constructive confrontation. Hidden or denied guilt can easily be overlooked. In vicious marital conflict, for example, the appropriate guilt that the couple should feel (because they are damaging themselves and each other) is often hidden behind the spiral of mutual attack and projection of blame onto the other. (As Lawrence S. Kubie points out, men and women seem to be infinitely ingenious in their ability to find new ways of being unhappy together.[10]) Unless the counselor recognizes the latent guilt and intervenes confrontingly—e.g., "I would think it would make you feel very badly to be hurting each other and yourselves so much"—their guilt may grind on to feed their blind, spiraling mutual attack.

A middle-aged man discussed with his pastor the affair he was having with his secretary. Instead of focusing either on the man's inner conflicts (which undoubtedly contributed to his behavior) or his side of the toxic interpersonal relationship with his wife, the minister first helped him face the destructive consequence of his irresponsible behavior for himself, his children, his wife, and his secretary. This firm confrontation mobilized his appropriate guilt. The pastor then supported the side of the man's ambivalence that wanted to break off the exotic but damaging relationship. He encouraged the man to do so at once and then arranged for him and his wife to enter marriage therapy together to deal with the mutual need deprivation and the protracted deterioriation of their marriage that contributed to the affair.

In couple counseling and marriage enrichment, one effective confrontation technique is for someone else (the counselor or another couple) to role play what is occurring between a couple. This often confronts them with the painfully absurd, self-defeating games they are playing. Tape recording a couple's interaction (with their permission, of course) during a counseling session and then playing it back to them can be powerfully confronting. In marriage enrichment groups and retreats, healthy self-confrontation can be stimulated by couples rereading and reflecting on their wedding vows. A constructive follow-up exercise to this is to rewrite the vows in terms of their current relationship, seeking to make it more mutually-growthful. Healthy self-confrontation can occur when couples discuss the implications for their relationship of this paraphrase of a statement by Erich Fromm: To love a person productively implies caring about and feeling responsible for his or her life, not only for that person's physical well-being, but for the growth and development of all her or his human powers.[11] Such dialogue can bring appropriate guilt feelings to the surface where they can motivate more mutually caring behavior.

Confrontation is most likely to result in self-confrontation when it includes two aspects. These are expressed well in New Testament language as "speaking the truth in love" (Eph. 4:15, referred to earlier as the "growth formula"). Speaking the truth is most effective when it is done in the context of caring love. Honest confrontation, after some trust is established usually strengthens counseling relationships, rather than weakening them. The counselor who speaks the truth, as she or he sees it, without caring, produces only feelings of rejection and defensiveness in the other. Conversely, the counselor who is loving in the shallow sense of always being permissive and accepting is actually depriving the counselee of that tough love that cares enough to risk speaking the truth. Omni-permissive counselors usually are not perceived as authentic or congruent by counselees because they are out-of-touch with the side of themselves that does evaluate and make judgments. Counselors who never confront even when it is appropriate are engaging in "cruel kindness"[12]—like the well-meaning but misguided spouse of an alcoholic who unwittingly helps prevent the addicted person from becoming open to help ("hitting bottom") by overprotecting him or her from the painful consequences of irresponsible drinking. Most people do not begin to change until they experience the pain of their present behavior. Confrontation may help them become aware of this pain. The pain and the appropriate guilt, which is a part of it, may provide motivation to accept help and eventually change their behavior. Reflecting on the contemporary pastoral care scene, Don Browning observes, "The concepts of acceptance, or even forgiveness, may be quite meaningless if a context of moral order and judgment is absent or confused."[13]

Ministers are perceived by many people as bearers of the values of their religious tradition. Some come to them for help precisely because they feel guilty, even though they are not fully conscious of it. If a pastor's acceptance of them as persons is misunderstood as condoning their person-hurting behavior, they may feel confused and let down at the same time they feel relieved of responsibility. In counseling, ministers should never be timid about what they regard as right. The key issue, of course, is *why* and *how* we stand for what we see as right. If we are aware of our own need for forgiveness and have experienced forgiveness in our own lives, it will be easier to stand firm on issues of basic integrity without being moralistic, self-righteous, and rejecting. To the degree that our own guilt is denied or unresolved, we will tend to feel and act judgmentally— deepening the other's pain and alienation.

Self-confrontation leads spontaneously to *confession*, the second step on the forgiveness path. Spontaneous confession often occurs during the early catharsis stage of counseling. It is important to encourage counselees to examine their guilt wound and to pour out their guilt feelings. Experiencing and expressing one's painful guilt feeling is an essential part of the cleansing, healing process. Rather than attempting to make the person feel better, the counselor-confessor should help her or him stay with the guilt in all its facets until it is thoroughly experienced and expressed. The pain of guilt and the cleansing release of confession is expressed by the Psalmist:

> Blessed is he whose transgression is forgiven . . .
> When I declared not my sin, my body wasted away
>   through my groaning all day long.
> For day and night thy hand was heavy upon me;
>   my strength was dried up as by the heat of summer.
> I acknowledged my sin to thee, and I did not hide my iniquity . . .
>   then thou didst forgive the guilt of my sin.
>
>   —PSALM 32:1-5

Hearing confession and serving as a channel of God's forgiveness (as a representative of the church and its heritage) are both pastoral care and priestly functions. The potential value of this priestly dimension is often overlooked by those of us not in the high church traditions. After extended counseling (including depth confession) with a man crippled by guilt from irreparable harm he had done to several people by his excessive drinking, the minister suggested that they go together to the church sanctuary. Wearing her clerical robe, to symbolize her representative, priestly role, she invited the man to pray for acceptance of God's forgiveness as he knelt at the communion railing. Then the minister said a prayer of absolution, followed by a prayer of thanksgiving for the gift of God's forgiveness. After this, the two persons joined in the Lord's prayer together. Priestly acts such as this would not be meaningful for many people. However, in this case, they were bearers of the reconciling symbols of the Good News of the Christian way by which guilt can be transformed into forgiveness and reconciliation (Tillich). They were channels of grace by which cleansing and forgiveness came alive for that man. It should be emphasized that the effectiveness of these priestly acts was built on and integrated with a meaningful counseling experience.

If the experiences of confession, absolution, and forgiveness are to lead to ongoing transformation and reconciliation, they must be followed by *restitution* and *responsible action,* changing the destructive behavior, attitudes, or beliefs that produced the original harm to persons. After the session described above, the counseling continued in the pastor's study for several sessions. The dual focus of these sessions was on what the man would do to make constructive amends to the persons who had been harmed, and on what he had learned from the whole experience that could help him avoid repeating his self-other hurting behavior. As the man implemented his plans, his sense of *reconciliation*—a healed relationship with God, with himself, with some of the people from whom he had been self-alienated (which had dawned in the sanctuary experience) gradually increased. Toward the end of his counseling, he reported that he was feeling "a sense of lightness—like a heavy load has been lifted!"

The inner channel through which the experiences of cleansing and forgiveness flows stays partially blocked until persons do everything possible to repair the harm done to other persons and themselves, and to live in a more caring and responsible way. "Cheap grace" (Bonhoeffer) is never transforming grace. AA's Twelve Step recovery program (in which the man decided he must immerse himself) demonstrates the importance of rigorous ethical self-confrontation. Seven of the twelve steps deal with "a searching and fearless moral inventory," which includes admitting (confessing) "to God, and to another human being the exact nature of our wrongs," making "a list of all the persons we have harmed," and making "direct amends to such persons whenever possible, except when to do so would injure them or others."[14] It is no accident that such an inner cleansing often leads a recovering alcoholic to a spiritual awakening. The pastor should help nonalcoholic counselees be just as rigorous in clearing their lives of accumulated moral debris from sinful, irresponsible living. To do so is the price of inner peace, forgiveness, and restored relationships. The need for Protestant equivalents of the sacrament of reconciliation, integrated with skilled counseling is great in our society where guilt proliferates and corporate ways of moving from guilt to reconciliation (in the confessional phase of public worship, for example) lack healing power for many people.

As persons relate more responsibly and responsively (to others), new sources of need satisfaction are open to them. Glasser declares: "As important as confronting reality is, it is only part of the therapy. The patient must learn to fulfill his needs in the real world [of relationship] . . . and we must teach him how whenever we can."[15] Confrontational counseling aims at facilitating counselees' firsthand encounter with that part of reality which they have defied or ignored (producing the hurt and guilt), and at helping them make the changes in their behavior that will enable them to live more constructively.

Philip Anderson describes his counseling with a recovered alcoholic, Bill, who said he was "just plain not happy":

> My response to this was to say that when I was not happy about myself it usually involved a rather simple mechanism, namely, I had done something which I was not very proud of or happy about or I had not done something I should have done. I went on to illustrate my point by citing a personal experience. . . . When I had not adequately prepared a sermon, I was most unhappy on Sunday morning. So I was prompted to ask Bill what he had been doing lately.[16]

The counselee replied, "Funny you should ask that. The truth is that I have given up drinking but I still waste too much time." They talked about how his irresponsible behavior had allowed his business to deteriorate. Then Anderson asked the counselee about his marriage. Bill began to verbalize his irritation toward his wife.

Anderson: But what are *you* doing, not what is your wife doing, about your marriage?

Bill: Funny you should ask that. I've been having an affair with another woman for about six months, and I'm sick of it.

Anderson: Bill, I'm not surprised that you aren't happy. You are living an irresponsible life which you are hiding from your wife and associates. You don't have any right to be happy.[17]

Bill agreed. Counseling focused on Bill's responsibilities. His wife soon joined the counseling, the marriage problems came under scrutiny, and a reconciliation was achieved in that relationship. As Bill began to act more responsibly, he reported that he was beginning to be happy again.

Anderson's approach is an example of the confrontational thrust in contemporary counseling (also represented by Glasser's reality therapy). It concentrates on current rather than past relationships and on responsible behavior rather than on feelings. Acting more responsible in the here and now, rather than waiting until new feelings produce constructive behavior, is the central emphasis.

Pastoral counseling should learn from the confrontational therapies and be helped thereby to recover our heritage of reconciliation. Most people have greater capacity than they suspect to live responsibly *now*. In most cases they will feel happier with themselves if they do so. Many will activate their potential for responsible living if the counselor firmly expects them to move in this direction. A direct, confrontational, action-oriented counseling approach often enables persons to break out of guilt-paralysis and begin to function more responsibly. When persons are behaving in irresponsible ways that produce spiraling guilt, fear of discovery, lack of self-honesty and honesty in relationships, they are trapped in a vicious cycle. The guiltier they feel, the more they hide, and the more they hide, the greater the buildup of guilt and fear. A caring approach that confronts the guilt and irresponsible behavior directly may help them break out of this self-perpetuating cycle. The tremendous sense of relief and release experienced by many AA members when they do their "moral inventory" fully and make constructive amends illustrates the healing power of this process.

It should be noted that many guilt-laden people need help in both working through their feelings of guilt and in learning to live more responsibly. Some guilt feelings are so deeply repressed that only skilled psychotherapy can enable persons to become aware of and resolve them. If guilt is flowing from unconscious neurotic conflicts, neither the five-step path to reconciliation nor action-oriented therapies will be effective. But in some cases, it is possible to help persons gain clearer access to guilt feelings of which they are vaguely aware by the use of caring confrontation. Bringing such just-below-the-surface guilt into the open makes it accessible to resolution in counseling.

Helping Those with Confused Consciences

Geoffrey Peterson writes:

> Many people reject or ignore traditional systems of values, but find it difficult to replace them. We are surrounded by divergent and frequently changing value systems that compete for our allegiance . . . Confusion or uncertainty about values is thus widespread, and this tends to increase interpersonal conflict and personal insecurity. Unfortunately the church shares in this value confusion and even contributes to it. Within the church as well as within the wider community there are major conflicts about moral issues.[18]

Our culture's moral confusion, conflicts, and pluralism all contribute to the confused conscience problems that pastoral counselors often encounter. In counseling on value problems, it is important to be aware of the ways in which the contemporary crisis in values makes it difficult for many people to find a viable philosophy in life—so alive it bleeds when cut. Millions are uprooted from a sense of community within which sound values flourish and existential anxiety can be handled constructively.[19] They suffer from a social climate of normlessness (a condition that Emile Durkheim called "anomic"). Rollo May articulates the challenge of life in our time of kaleidoscopic change:

> When a culture is caught in the profound convulsions of a transitional period, the individuals in the society understandably suffer spiritual and emotional upheaval; and finding that the accepted mores and ways of thought no longer yield security, they tend either to sink into dogmatism and conformism, giving up awareness, or are forced to strive for a heightened self-consciousness by which to become aware of their existence with new conviction and on new bases.[20]

The frantic (and futile) efforts of authoritarian religious groups to recover the old ethical certainties can be understood as a defensive reaction formation in response to the anxieties and uncertainties of our period of mind-boggling ethical transition.

Peterson describes a constructive response in this situation: "We pastoral counselors cannot attempt to give authoritative answers to all the value problems brought to us. What we can do—and this is more helpful—is to provide a caring and supportive environment in which values may be clarified and strengthened and, when necessary, revised so as to reflect more faithfully the values of Christ."[21] Value clarification and revision have an important place in the church's educational and growth ministry as well as in individual and family counseling. Within relationships of mutual trust, people can be helped to clarify, reevaluate, and revise their confused, conflicted, and destructive values, to attune them to the person-enhancing values embodied in the Judeo-Christian heritage.

The Healing of Neurotic Guilt

Some counselees are crippled—psychologically and spiritually—by neurotic, hairshirted consciences. They feel chronic, inappropriate guilt derived from immature or rigid value systems. Their self-evaluation includes little or no *live grace*. They tend to squander their ethical energies in compulsive self-castigation concerning trivial ethical issues or their "bad" feelings. Consequently, there is little energy left for the important "core moralities" (Ross Snyder). The goals of counseling with such persons is to help them achieve more accepting Christian consciences.

Neurotic guilt feelings are reduced temporarily if a person is "spanked" psychologically. Punishment temporarily lessens guilt. (This explains why guilt-ridden people are attracted to moralistic preachers and counselors.) Regular verbal pummeling functions as a neurotic atonement, thus lessening guilt feelings. In most cases the results do not last, nor do they produce constructive changes in behavior. In many persons with crippling neurotic guilt, long-term pastoral psychotherapy is needed to bring the self-forgiveness that comes with genuine healing of neurotic guilt. In less severe cases, shorter-term pastoral counseling may suffice.

Counselee: You shook me up when you said, after I had gone over and over how guilty I felt about my sexual feelings, "I wonder why it's so difficult for you to treat your own feelings with Christian charity."

In TA terms, neurotic guilt consists of the punishment of the inner Child by the inner Parent, because the prohibitions of the Parent have been broken. The counseling pastor can become a new and more accepting parent figure from whom the person learns something of what Alfred Adler calls "the courage of one's own imperfections." By internalizing aspects of the minister's more positive and life-affirming conscience, the person's inner Parent becomes less punishing of the inner Child. The punitive Parent is reprogrammed (called Re-Parenting in TA) and the person achieves increased self-acceptance and inner freedom from the compulsive moralism that had crippled ethical (choice-making) capacities. The reconciliation of conflicted aspects within the person enables her or him to become reconciled with others.

The counselor encourages persons suffering from immature consciences to exercise their inner Adult's ability to examine competing values and affirm those that are consistent with their own understanding of the good life. This process of letting go of primary dependence on the value structure of one's parents and of finding one's own meanings and values (which usually include some of the parents' values) occurs in normal development during adolescence.[22] In TA terms, this process could be described as letting go of submission of the inner Child to the Inner Parent, and putting one's Adult in the the driver's seat of one's conscience. If this ethical maturing does not occur, neurotic guilt flourishes and long-term counseling may be required to release the person to become an adult ethically. Neurotic guilt feelings often flow from unconscious conflicts requiring psychotherapy for constructive resolution.

Neurotic guilt, particularly about ethical trivia, frequently hides appropriate guilt about unlived life and person-hurting behavior. The neurotic guilt is superimposed on the deeper guilt as a camouflage. On the other hand, what appears to be appropriate guilt may hide deeper neurotic guilt-producing conflicts based on unresolved problems in psychosexual development, such as oedipal attachments.

In pastoral counseling with the guilt-laden, it is wise to begin by dealing with the obvious guilt problem. This may prove to be only a surface manifestation of deeper guilt and conflict. If after extended confessional catharsis and serious efforts at reconstruction of alienated relationships, self-forgiveness does not gradually emerge, a deeper conflict requiring psychotherapy probably is present. If counselees resist making constructive changes in their behavior, it is important to focus on their resistance to acting in a responsible way. Confrontation is not effective if persons receive it in masochistic fashion, using the counselor's confronting words as a form of neurotic atonement. Neurotically guilt-ridden people may defeat confrontation by responding with seemingly endless, compulsive atonement behavior, which allows them to avoid their deeper conflict. The suspected or obvious presence of neurotic guilt should not rule out the use of confrontation. Where the conflict is relatively mild, confrontation may succeed in interrupting a vicious cycle of behavior and feelings, so that the person's constructiveness in living is enhanced without the necessity of resolving underlying conflicts.

A teen-age girl, disturbed about her steadily worsening relationship with her mother, sought the minister's help. A number of sessions were devoted to exploring her ambivalent feelings toward her mother. She expressed her anger and also her positive feelings toward her mother, but there was no improvement in their relationship. Finally, the minister recommended that she try putting her positive feelings into action during the following week. At the next counseling session, she reported: "I was just furious at you for suggesting that I do something to show that I loved my mother. . . . But I found myself setting the table without being asked and enjoying it. I have no idea why. It just happened. We're getting along fine—best we have in five years."

If the girl's inner conflicts regarding her mother had been severe, it is unlikely that the minister's recommendation would have been followed, or if followed, would have produced lasting benefits. What apparently occurred was that the counselor's confronting "push" interrupted the momentum of long-standing negative interaction between the girl and her mother. By doing something helpful, the girl reduced her guilt load and reestablished communication with her mother. The minister's action had enabled her to reestablish a relationship, which could then be helped further by counseling. At a minister's suggestion, the mother and daughter came in for several joint counseling sessions aimed at helping them make their communication more effective and thereby strengthen their relationship.

The Healing of Self-Righteous Consciences

People with self-righteous consciences usually do not seek pastoral help with their own problems.[23] If they come, it is to ask for help in making a family member shape up or to criticize the pastor or someone in the congregation for not measuring up to their perfectionistic standards. The real problems, as self-righteous people see the situation, are the other people with their inferior values. The pain and alienation that self-righteousness generates in marriages and other close relationships are usually what bring this issue to a pastor's attention. As reported in the Synoptic Gospels, Jesus used his strongest confrontation in relating to the self-righteous religious leaders of his day—the Pharisees. People with righteous self-images usually are rigid conformists to conventional morality. They are legalistic and judgmental toward those who disagree with their views of right and wrong. Within religious circles, self-righteous people often misuse the Bible, "proof-texting" to claim divine support for their ethical views.

The familiar line, "Some people don't *have* problems, they *are* problems!" seems to describe self-righteous people Actually they also *have* problems of which their self-righteousness is a symptomatic defense. Self-righteousness is a way of trying to reinforce shaky self-esteem by a sense of moral superiority. Feeling one-up on those perceived as ethically and religiously inferior enables such persons to avoid experiencing their deep feelings of self-rejection and self-judgment. Self-righteousness can also be a way of maintaining a sense of power over others—a spouse or children—and of justifying one's attempts to control them. The need for such feelings of power is as a defense against hidden feelings of powerlessness and fear of not being in control. Self-righteousness enables persons to avoid confronting their neurotic guilt and subconscious conflicts about their own sexual and aggressive impulses. In Carl Jung's terms, self-righteousness is a way of disowning their "shadow" side, the dark, rejected, "inferior" part of the personality.[24] Their idealized self-image, characterized only by light and goodness, is impoverished and threatened by being cut off from the dark, earthy, potentially creative as well as destructive side of themselves.

Helping self-righteous people to soften and humanize their defensive conscience and self-image is nearly impossible until they sense some need for help. If they can let themselves become aware of the exorbitant price they are paying—in the distancing of others and in their own loneliness and lack of joy—self-righteous people become open to counseling help. It is important to remind ourselves that some degree of defensive superiority is in most of us. Ministers and church lay leaders are far from immune. In fact, the pietistic and moralistic thrusts in many church traditions tend to encourage persons to maintain an idealized self-image. This makes it difficult to accept their dark shadow side and integrate it with their "good" side so that the two can balance and enrich each other within their personalities.

Self-righteousness has produced enormous destructiveness in individual lives and in history. Most wars have been fought with self-righteous consciences on both sides. The murders of countless heretics and nonconfronting women as "witches" were done by self-righteous church leaders for reasons they believed ethical and praiseworthy. Even the Nazi leaders claimed to be obeying their consciences in purifying the Aryan race by systematically destroying millions of Jews and other "inferior" persons.[25]

Helping Those With Underdeveloped Consciences

Confrontational methods are essential in counseling with those having weak, underdeveloped consciences. Such persons are characterized by one or more of the following: (a) lack of appropriate guilt, anxiety, and sense of responsibility; (b) ineffective self-control; (c) chronic irresponsible behavior; (d) shallowness of feelings and relationships; (e) a manipulative modus operandi. Freud once observed, in writing to his longtime friend Pastor Oskar Pfister, "Ethics are a kind of highway code for traffic among mankind." Many people have not learned to respect this code. They have not internalized the culture's guiding values and therefore have not learned to control their asocial impulses. Such character problems result from various backgrounds—cold, loveless homes, or homes where parents mistook overpermissiveness for love and did not maintain dependable discipline. As Erik Erikson has shown, virtues such as hope, purpose, competence, fidelity, love, care, and wisdom are vital elements in the ego's strength.[26] Persons who lack these are seriously handicapped. In its extreme form this disorder is called "sociopathic personality." Our culture, with its manipulative "marketing orientation" (Fromm), spawns character problems in all degrees and with great frequency.

A permissive, insight-oriented counseling approach may be effective with guilt and anxiety loaded psychoneurotics, but it usually fails with those who have character problems.

> A girl of seventeen came to her pastor to discuss her sexual activities. Her father was an emotionally nonresident commuter. Although she consciously felt little or no guilt about her activities, she was fearful of "getting caught." If the minister had responded to her reports of promiscuity in a passive or permissive way, she would have interpreted this as more of the weak, detached permissiveness of her father. She needed more acceptance than she was getting at home, but not more permissiveness! On the contrary, what she needed was for the minister to be both an accepting and a firm father-figure from whom she could gain strength in controlling her own behavior and in relation to whom she could establish her own constructive limits. After rapport was well developed, the minister made it clear that from his point of view, certain behavior is harmful to persons and therefore morally wrong. Using accepting confrontation he helped her face rather than avoid the probable consequences of her behavior. Most important, he helped her become aware of and work through her confused, lonely, rebellious feelings which provided the fuel for the behavior. In reflecting on this experience, the minister realized that the girl was, by her behavior, pleading for some adult to set limits. In fact, this is probably why she came to a minister.[27]

Sociologist David Riesman suggests that permissive therapies are useful with counselees who have been exposed to arbitrary power in childhood and for whom a permissive, accepting situation is a new experience: "But many of the college-educated have been brought up permissively both at home and at school and find little that is liberating in a therapist who [only] accepts them."[28]

A pastoral psychotherapist who worked mainly with disturbed adolescents reported that problems of weak consciences predominated among his counselees and that Rogerian and psychoanalytic methods have proved strikingly ineffective with most of them. *Learning-theory or behavioral therapy* has provided the most successful method. The therapist's emphasis is on setting and enforcing limits on the deviant behavior so that constructive patterns may be learned and reinforced through the rewards and punishments of the structure. For example, instead of being lenient and permissive with school truancy, he recommends that the school authorities take immediate disciplinary action. It is essential that the youth involved know that this was his recommendation.[29]

Here are some principles of counseling with weak-conscienced persons, based on a reality-therapy approach:

(1) *Establish rapport*. This often is a difficult step because this type of person tends to distrust and stay distant from authority figures.

(2) *Confront the person with the self-defeating nature of his/her reality-denying behavior*. As Glasser puts it, "The therapist must reject the behavior which is unrealistic but still accept the patient and maintain his involvement with him."[30]

(3) *Seek to block the irresponsible, acting-out behavior*.

(4) *Reward responsible behavior with approval*.

(5) *Help the person learn to satisfy his/her needs in socially constructive, reality-oriented ways*.

(6) *Explore the person's aspirations and help her/him make and implement realistic and satisfying plans for the future*.

Psychiatrist Jerome D. Frank states that persons who have difficulty controlling their impulses need to feel that the therapist has concern for them based on their potentialities: "This concern is best conveyed by a strong attack on the deviant behavior as unworthy of the patient. This type of attack, paradoxically, heightens the patient's self-esteem rather than damages it, because it is obviously based on real concern and respect."[31] Permissiveness, on the other hand, makes such a person feel that the therapist is indifferent or does not expect much of him/her. This hurts already shaky self-esteem further. Consistent firmness is essential in helping such a person. Someone has called this "tough love."

William Glasser's reality therapy assumes that it is impossible to maintain self-esteem if one is living irresponsibly. Glasser declares: "Morals, standards, values, or right and wrong behavior are all intimately related to the fulfillment of our need for self-worth."[32] His therapy aims at teaching persons to credit themselves when they are right and correct themselves when wrong. Self-respect comes through self-discipline and responsible behavior, bringing increased respect from others.

Persons with severe character disorders are very difficult to help, even by a highly trained psychotherapist. But many people with less severe weaknesses of conscience can benefit from skilled pastoral counseling following confrontational, reality-therapy principles. This is particularly true of adolescents whose difficulty often is simply a retardation of conscience maturation. By identifying with the pastor's more mature conscience, a counselee can gradually unlearn destructive patterns and internalize more constructive inner controls.

A future orientation is essential in much pastoral counseling, including confrontational counseling. A favorite question in reality therapy is, "What is your plan?" This stimulates constructive thinking about the future. Glasser writes: "We must open up his life, talk about new horizons, expand his range of interests, make him aware of life beyond his difficulties."[33] Many troubled people do not feel there really is a meaningful future for them. Awakening realistic dreams and making and implementing workable plans to move toward a viable future can be decisive in helping persons break away from the unconstructive patterns of the past. In counseling with persons who have weak inner controls, it is essential to help them discover something about which they can really care. A chaplain who leads group therapy with young adults having a history of behavior problems reports: "I try to find one thing the individual gives a damn about, and then build on that!"

Helping Those with Underdeveloped Social Conscience

Many church people have well-developed consciences on personal and interpersonal issues but a flabby, underdeveloped sense of responsibility and caring on social issues. They have a healthy capacity for appropriate guilt in individual relationships, but a serious hiatus in feeling appropriate guilt for the oppressiveness of the institutions where they have at least some small influence. Such persons have character disorders in the area of social conscience. They do not experience appropriate guilt concerning our individual and collective sins of omission and commission that contribute to the deadly injustices, the growing gap between the rich and poor nations, the squandering of our planet's limited resources on genocidal weapons, the destructive population explosion, the oppression of women and people of color, and the dehumanizing effects of world hunger and poverty. The privitized consciences of many "good church people" keeps them from feeling caring and responsible for human beings beyond their small circles of concern. Those with privitized "tribal" consciences (Fromm) feel responsibility and guilt only for their own in-group, their own small circle of family and friends, or their religious or ethnic group.

Social problems often cause or complicate personal problems. Prophetic confrontation in teaching, preaching, and counseling are essential to help "good people" expand the horizons of their caring and consciences. "Consciousness raising," which helps make the growth-oppressive sins of our institutions and social structures matters of Christian conscience, is essential in counseling for ethical wholeness.

Awakening people in severe crises to wider concerns is usually impossible until the acute phase of their crisis is passed. Then some can reflect on the social injustices and oppression that underlay the crisis. It is the counselor's responsibility to raise these wider contextual issues. Educative counseling and growth groups offer seldom-used opportunities for such awakening, expanding, and empowering of social consciences. The discussion of the social context of particular personal issues, in light of the Judeo-Christian vision, can help to reduce conscience blind spots and lead to social-change action in the community.[34] Other methods of mobilizing the social dimensions of ethical responsibility and caring will be described in the chapter on educative counseling.

Helping Persons with Meaning Vacuums

Many people in our society suffer from zestlessness and a lack of any dynamic meaning or moving purpose in their lives. There is nothing that they value enough to give them a sense of expectation and excitement when they wake up to a new day. Such chronic existential depression stems from what Viktor Frankl describes as a "value vacuum," a frustration of their basic "will to meaning." His "logotherapy" defines the central task of helping persons as that of enabling them to find a sense of meaning. Frankl's basic thesis is that "life is transformed when a mission worth carrying out is uncovered."[35]

Pastoral counselors encounter many people whose root problem is profound emptiness in the area of meanings and values. Their other problems in living are symptoms of this underlying vacuum. Frankl seeks to help persons find a motivating meaning for their lives in one or more of three kinds of values—*creative* values, doing something worthwhile; *experiential* values, derived from experiencing something satisfying such as a sunset, a good marriage, the fragrance of a flower, a precious memory, the smile of a friend; and *attitudinal* values, taking a constructive attitude toward whatever situation one is in, even the worst. In exploring this third type of values, Frankl stresses the "defiant power of the human spirit," the ability to rise above even the diabolic dehumanization of a Nazi death camp by choosing to find some meaning in that situation. The religious person, in his view, is the "one who says 'yes' to life; . . . who, in spite of everything that life brings, still faces existence with a basic conviction of the worthwhileness of life."[36]

Meaning vacuums occur at the intersection of theological and value issues in people's lives. An open, energizing, relationship with God and a dynamic commitment to a cause that is larger than one's circle of self-centered concerns, are complementary, interrelated answers to problems of meaninglessness. Helping counselees find a worthwhile cause that turns them on is important both because it gives them an integrating purpose and because it may help reduce the social sources of individual problems. As Peterson points out, "For members of the Christian community, their mission will be a part of the mission of the church, which is to cooperate with God's saving work in the world. All such healing work may be seen as a part of the creative transformation that Christ is continually effecting in human life."[37]

When life "goes flat," as one client put it, it probably is a signal that one needs to rethink and revise one's priorities and values, and the life-style they create. Here are some questions, designed to help couples discuss and revise their guiding values:

(1) Do my (our) values and priorities, and the life-style they produce, allow me (us) to maintain robust physical-emotional health?

(2) Do my (our) values and life-style allow me (us) time to develop my (our) midyears potential—intellectually and spiritually?

(3) Do my (our) values and life-style allow me (us) time to enjoy the good things of life and to do the creative, worthwhile, and fulfilling things I (we) could do?

(4) Do my (our) present values and life-style leave me (us) enough time with the person or persons I (we) care most about?

(5) Does my (our) life-style reflect the most significant and life-giving values? Maslow calls these "B-Values" (B for Being)—truth, goodness, beauty, wholeness, aliveness, justice, order, simplicity, playfulness, autonomy.

(6) Do my (our) values and life-style allow me (us) time for a significant cause, a challenge beyond my (our) inner circle, that will help others and improve our community?

(7) Are my (our) values and life-style consistent with sound survival values for the whole human family of which I (we) are a part?[38]

Using Confrontation in Other Types of Counseling

Methods of therapeutic confrontation are valuable in a variety of counseling situations not focusing primarily on ethical or meaning issues. James A. Knight writes: "Confrontation as a counseling technique offers the teacher and pastor endless opportunities for creative encounter. When there is awareness, sensitivity, and knowledge, the face-to-face struggle opens new pathways to relatedness between persons and possibilities for growth."[39] Confrontation, he points out, can be particularly useful in helping older adolescents and young adults grow toward maturity: "The young person is in need of face-to-face relationships with authorities who demonstrate their concern for the individual both by support and by judgment. During the tumultuous periods of psychological growth, confrontation at appropriate times will serve to open pathways for growth and to set necessary limits to behavior."[40] A minister met a teen-age parishioner (Sam) loafing at a filling station during school hours.

> **Pastor:** I see you decided not to go back to school.
>
> **Sam:** Yeh, I couldn't seem to cut the mustard.
>
> **Pastor:** What are your plans? Maybe there's something else you should be preparing for.
>
> **Sam:** Don't really know what I want to do. I suppose something will come along.

They talked about the future. The minister stressed the desirability of Sam's choosing a route now that would lead to some work he would find satisfying. Later as counseling continued in the pastor's study, the minister contacted and involved the state employment agency counselor to help the youth make and implement realistic plans. Eventually Sam entered training to become a refrigeration technician. By exercising his pastoral initiative and using confrontative and educative counseling methods, the minister helped Sam interrupt what could have become a chronic failure cycle.

Confrontational methods often are essential in life-threatening crises. A young man reported intense fear that he would harm his woman friend. Knowing of his poorly controlled rage and his previous impulsive behavior toward women, the minister insisted that he commit himself for psychiatric treatment. He confronted the man firmly with the real danger that he might do something irreparably destructive. Rather than resenting the minister's firm stance, (as sometimes happens) the man was relieved and willing to comply. The minister had used the strength of his position and his personality to protect the woman and to protect the man from his own destructiveness. The same kind of strong caring confrontation often is essential in preventing suicides.

Confronting counselees with the way they are relating in a particular session can restore openness in a counseling relationship and provide them with an opportunity to achieve significant insights. It can interrupt futile counselee-counselor games. After two sessions of maneuvering in couple counseling the husband said, "Do you understand what I mean? I'm probably confusing you." The pastor replied: "I think I understand what you're saying right now, but I'm wondering what's going on in our relationship as a whole. I have the feeling we're sort of playing verbal games here—trying to explore the problem and, at the same time, trying to keep it hidden. We seem to have talked around it for two sessions." The startled couple soon centered on what was really troubling them.

When the counselor makes a major error or misses the counselee's wavelength completely, it is well to discuss it openly, as soon as possible.

Pastor: As I thought about our last talk, I realized that I had probably missed what you were trying to tell me at the end. I noticed that you got very quiet. How did you feel when I said . . . ?

The counselor's nonapologetic self-confrontation usually helps repair damaged rapport in such situations. By admitting his fallibility, he strengthens the relationships.

Neo-Moralism—The Danger in Confrontation

Confrontational methods are analogous to a powerful medicine. Used properly they can be a potent means of healing. Yet the dangers of misuse are increased by their potency. James A. Knight observes: "Pastors and teachers have not always understood the meaning of confrontation in counseling. It is often confused with a vertical type of authoritarianism, moralistic preachments, or hostile attacks indulged in under the guise of 'righteous indignation.' "[41]

These principles can provide some protection against the danger of moralism: (a) Confrontation should be used with care and restraint. (b) The emphasis should be on helping persons face reality (self-confrontation) as *they* come to understand it, and discover their own responsibility within it. (c) Counselees should be given full opportunity to respond to confrontation, to discuss it thoroughly, and to disagree with the counselor. In the final analysis, minister's level of maturity will determine whether he/she misuses confrontational methods to manipulate counselee or uses the methods constructively. The crucial variable in all counseling on ethical and value issues is the counselor's own ethical integrity and wholeness.

Psychologist O. Hobart Mowrer has critiqued vigorously the ethical permissiveness of much contemporary psychotherapy including pastoral counseling.[42] He has helped remind us pastoral counselors of the crucial importance of ethical issues in most human problems. But like Jay Adams, his thinking has tended to foster an increase in judgmental moralism, particularly within conservative religious circles. Mowrer's theory, on which his "integrity therapy" is based, has several critical flaws. First, from both the theological and psychological viewpoints, his therapy is a works-righteousness approach. It lacks grace or its psychotherapeutic parallel, caring acceptance by the counselor. Second, his therapy, like most other behavior and action therapies focuses exclusively on making behavior more constructive. Feelings are understood as the simple consequences of behavior. What is lacking in such approaches is a recognition that destructive feelings and attitudes *do* cause destructive behavior, as well as vice versa. Therapy needs to focus on helping people change both their feelings and their behavior.

Mowrer's third error is his reduction of all guilt to appropriate guilt. This is an error with serious consequences for counselors who accept it as valid. Some neurotic guilt is a cover-up for appropriate guilt. But much neurotic guilt is just that and must be so treated in counseling if the person is to be helped!

A fourth and closely related weakness in Mowrer's thought is his oversimplified view that all personality problems are caused by disobeying one's conscience. The correlate of this view is that the single key to helping all disturbed people is to get them to change their behavior so that it will conform to their conscience and value systems. It is true that many people who do this *do* feel better, at least temporarily. But Mowrer's view of the nature of all psychopathology and the blanket treatment derived from this view ignores the crucial cause of many personality problems— distorted, immature, and internally conflicted consciences. A neurotic conscience can produce guilt in response to behavior that is actually constructive. A middle-aged, unmarried man who had spent much of his life meeting the whims of a manipulative mother reported severe guilt feelings when he began to think for himself and act more autonomously. German physicians, whose consciences had been warped by Nazi indoctrination, testified at their war crimes trials, after World War II, that they experienced guilt when they refused to inject deadly viruses into Jews and other "enemies of the state." To bring the behavior of such persons into conformity with their sick consciences, as Mowrer's therapy aims at doing, would have reduced their guilt, and thereby made them feel better. But this therapeutic outcome would have been achieved by violating real ethical integrity. In such people, it is precisely their neurotic values and their warped conscience that need healing!

Nurturing Healthy Consciences

It is important to distinguish between the pastoral *counseling* task of helping to heal distorted, inadequate, and crippled consciences, and the pastoral *care-education* task of helping people develop healthy, maturing consciences, in a community of moral nurture, reflection, and action. Both tasks are vital aspects of ministry, and each complements the other. The task of ethical healing can best be accomplished within the context of the broader work of nurturing ethical sensitivities and action in a congregation. Don Browning declares:

> There is a place in the church for pastoral counseling of all kinds . . . as long as they are placed firmly within a context of a community of moral inquiry. The minister has a clear duty to counsel the ill and dying, but he should first have helped create a community with a religiocultural view of the meaning of illness and death. Certainly the minister should counsel persons with marriage problems, sexual problems, and divorce problems, but he should first have helped to create among his people a positive vision of the normative meaning of marriage, sexuality, and even divorce.[43]

Lawrence Kohlberg's theory of moral development has potentialities for increased use by pastoral counselors. It can be diagnostically useful in understanding ethical problems encountered in counseling. It can provide a structure for moral development work in pastoral care, growth groups, and educational experiences. Donald Capps suggests that the four-step procedure that Kohlberg uses to ascertain an individual's level of moral reasoning can be used in premarital counseling to help couples explore their ethical issues and dilemmas.[44] These steps consist of: (1) *identifying an ethical dilemma* involving a decision to be made; (2) *identifying the norm* used for making or justifying the decision (these are different norms in each of the six stages of moral development); (3) *identifying the modes or strategies of the decision-making* process (e.g., using rules or standards, examining the consequences of a decision, looking at what is fair and just for those involved, considering what a good individual would do with respect to maintaining self-respect, living up to moral principles, or obeying conscience); and (4) *identifying the* social perspective, the understanding of persons, the value of human life, and how people relate to authority, law, and community.

In the six stages of moral reasoning and decision-making, identified by Kohlberg, "right" is determined by: (1) obedience to authority to avoid punishment and gain rewards; (2) instrumental hedonism (what satisfies one's needs) and some reciprocal fairness; (3) conformity to social expectations to gain approval; (4) obeying rules and respecting authority (the law and order stage); (5) respecting universal ethical principles; and (6) responding to one's inner vision of justice, love, and respect for all persons.[45]

Kohlberg's stages (corrected by Gilligan's findings) can help to illuminate the goals of nurturing ethical development through pastoral care and education. Another perspective on such goals is provided by asking what the attributes are of the healthy or mature conscience. Carol Gilligan's significant discoveries of the difference in the moral development of girls and boys reveal the male biases of Kohlberg's theory. Her important insights about the moral development of girls should be incorporated in both pastoral care and education. Geoff Peterson describes six characteristics of such consciences, as understood in light of Christ's life and teachings, pointing out that this is an ideal that no one ever achieves fully.[46]

(1) A healthy conscience *is a positive, liberated conscience*—liberated through the love of God from subservience to rules and the compulsion to conform to legalistic codes or group pressures. Such a conscience is set free for caring, responsible service.

(2) *It is a conscience shaped by participating in Christian community*, particularly in small conscience-nurturing groups through which the call of God is most readily communicated.

(3) *It is continually growing, conscience* awakened to renewal by the confrontation of crises that challenge ethical blind spots and let us discover new areas of human need.

(4) *It is an integrated conscience,* a call toward the wholeness of one's full humanity.

(5) *It is a caring conscience* in the sense of helping other persons grow and accepting help in our own growth.

(6) *It is a socially responsible conscience,* with a global inclusiveness to its caring.

I would add a seventh and eighth characteristic to Peterson's list:

(7) A *healthy, maturing conscience is an androgynous conscience,* equally prizing those *human* capacities that women have had to overdevelop in our culture—nurturing, sensitivity to feelings, caring for relationships—and those *human* capacities that men have had to overdevelop—achievement, rationality, technical skills. Wholeness in one's conscience, and one's life-style as a male or a female, must include valuing and developing both of these sides of our common human capacities. As psychiatrist Jean Baker Miller makes clear, the survival of humankind on planet earth may well depend on society's learning to prize in the public sphere the nurturing, relationship building, cooperative values that our sexist culture has forced women to overdevelop.[47] The shocking fact is that male babies currently have more than eight years less life expectancy than female babies in our society. This suggests that our wholeness as men is diminished and our longevity curtailed by the patriarchal achievement values, which we are socially programmed to overdevelop to the neglect of our nurturing, relating, and cooperative capacities.

(8) *A healthy conscience today must be oriented to give highest priority to survival values for humankind.* "A robust ecological or social conscience is more essential today than ever before in the human story. We're all passengers on a tiny spaceship, planet earth. We cannot possibly continue to have a free, fulfilling life unless we learn to befriend the biosphere and to make the opportunity for a good life the birthright of every person everywhere."[48] Unless those of us in affluent countries alter our greedy life-styles of enormous consumption and waste, the outrageous problem of world hunger will not be solved and the children of the human family will inherit a ravished and impoverished planet.

The ethical issue and value that deserve absolute priority above all other values in a healthy conscience today is that of interrupting the out-of-control nuclear arms race. The probabilities are increasing that the incomprehensive destructiveness of the superpowers' 50,000 nuclear warheads (the equivalent of one million Hiroshima bombs) will be unleashed, by intention or by accident. Both the U.S. and the USSR have enough nuclear warheads to destroy the other country many times, yet we go on building more. If we do not prevent a nuclear holocaust, nothing else we do makes sense. There is a qualitative difference between this threat and all other crucial social issues. In this issue, the survival of humankind on a livable planet is at stake!

In his book *The Fate of the Earth,* Jonathan Schell analyzes the implications of the nuclear madness—pointing out that no other goals or values can compare in significance with the survival of the human community, because all other values presuppose survival for them to exist. [49] As someone has observed, for the leaders of the superpowers, delaying mutual nuclear arms reduction while arguing about who has more destructive power in their nuclear stockpile, is something like two men standing in a basement full of gasoline up to their armpits arguing about who has more matches. There is a collective insanity, a suicidal resignation, in the ways we are willing to go about "business as usual" while thousands of nuclear warheads, many with fifty times the devastating power of the bombs that obliterated Hiroshima and Nagasaki, are pointed at all of us in the major population centers of the United States and the USSR. Our leaders speak insanely of winning limited nuclear wars and of developing more security by building more and more devastating weapons. Scientists with the most expertise in these matters make it crystal clear that *no one* can win a nuclear war and that there is less and less security for everyone in continuing the arms race. Quite apart from survival, it is a tragic social sin to waste over a third of our scientific brains, billions of dollars and irreplaceable resources on defense that only makes us increasingly insecure and vulnerable to obliteration. [50]

To be healthy and in touch with reality today, our consciences must give top priority and commitment to an all-out effort to restore sanity to our planet by interrupting the runaway nuclear arms race. The resources of religious oganizations, national governments, and the United Nations must be mobilized. The insights and skills of all the human disciplines and all dimensions of ministry, including pastoral care and counseling, must bring their resources to help resolve this life-and-death issue for humankind. The biblical vision of the good life is a vision of a new creation for all members of the human family—a new state of consciousness, conscience, caring, and community. This is our calling. This vision is far more than mere survival, but without survival—it will be impossible!

Reality-Practice Session

PARISHIONER'S ROLE: 1. Become aware of an area of ethical conflict or puzzlement within your own thinking and feelings. Discuss this with the pastor. 2. You are a young man who killed several enemy soldiers during the Vietnam war. You come to your minister for help with the agony of your guilt. 3. You are a young woman. Within the last two years you have rebelled against the rigid moral code of your fundamentalist background. You feel intense guilt about your behavior, particularly in the areas of sex and drugs.

PASTOR'S ROLE: Use the counseling approaches described in this chapter as you seek to help one of these persons.

OBSERVER-COACH'S ROLE: Include in your feedback observations on how the pastor's own values influence the way she/he confronts the parishioner on value issues.

(Record and play back the counseling to increase awareness of the interaction during this session.)

Recommended Reading

Don S. Browning, *The Moral Context of Pastoral Care* (Philadelphia: Westminster Press, 1976). Explores the roots and meaning of care in Judaism, early Christianity and Christian history—develops a model of pastoral care to restore its context of meaning.

Howard Clinebell, *Growth Counseling for Mid-Years Couples* (Philadelphia: Fortress Press, 1977). Includes a chapter on revising one's priorities and values.

Mary Daly, *Beyond God the Father: Toward a Philosophy of Women's Liberation* (Boston: Beacon Press, 1973). Describes the oppressiveness of patriarchal ethics and contrasts it with feminist ethical approaches.

Carol Gilligan, *In a Different Voice: Psychological Theory and Women's Development* (Cambridge, Mass.: Harvard University Press,

1982). Reports on her crucial findings concerning the moral development of females as contrasted with that of males in our culture.

William Glasser, *Reality Therapy* (New York: Harper & Row, 1965). Describes the basic theory and methodology of reality therapy.

Roland Duska and Mariellen Whelan, *Moral Development: A Guide to Piaget and Kohlberg* (New York: Paulist Press, 1975). Explores the applications of Piaget's and Kohlberg's theories of moral development to Christian education.

Brian P. Hall, *Value Clarification as Learning Process: A Guidebook for Educators* (New York: Paulist Press, 1974). Three volumes includes exercises that can be used in both counseling and education.

John C. Hoffman, *Ethical Confrontation in Counseling* (Chicago: University of Chicago Press, 1981). Explores the relation between ethics and therapy as the key issue in all psychological healing.

James A. Knight, *Conscience and Guilt* (New York: Appleton-Century-Crofts, 1969). Trained as both a minister and a psychiatrist, the author discusses the destructiveness of guilt from an unhealthy conscience.

Karl Menninger, *Whatever Became of Sin?* (New York: Hawthorn Books, 1973). Criticizes attitudes toward sin in contemporary therapy.

Donald E. Miller, *The Wing-Footed Wanderer: Conscience and Transcendence* (Nashville: Abingdon Press, 1977). Moral development and the nature of conscience from psychological, theological and philosophical perspectives.

Jean Baker Miller, *Toward a New Psychology of Woman* (Boston: Beacon Press, 1976). Critiques the destructiveness of male values and offers a way of integrating women's values into the public sphere.

Brenda Munsey, ed., *Moral Development, Moral Education and Kohlberg* (Birmingham: Religious Education Press, 1980). A collection of papers on moral development by major thinkers in this field.

Geoffrey Peterson, *Conscience and Caring* (Philadelphia: Fortress Press, 1982). A guide to pastoral care and counseling of persons with a variety of types of conscience problems. Comprehensive bibliography included.

Jonathan Schell, *The Fate of the Earth* (New York: Knopf, 1982). Spells out the implications of the nuclear madness including the fact that there is no value that can compare with the survival of human consciousness because all other values presuppose its survival for them to exist and have value.

Edward V. Stein, *Guilt: Theory and Therapy* (Philadelphia: Westminster Press, 1968). Explores the dynamics of guilt and its treatment.

Sidney B. Simon, et. al., *Values Clarification* (New York: Hart Publishing Co., 1972). A handbook of practical strategies for teachers and students.

Edward P. Wimberly, *Pastoral Counseling and Spiritual Values: A Black Point of View* (Nashville: Abingdon Press, 1982). A value and spiritual orientation to pastoral counseling.

CHAPTER 7

Supportive Care and Counseling

The sustaining function of the cure of souls in our day continues to be a crucially important helping ministry. . . . Everywhere today busy pastors are called upon to sustain troubled persons in, through, and beyond a plethora of hurts that brook no direct restoration. . . . Tightly knit communities once furnished friends and neighbors who could stand by in moments of shock, whereas in a society on wheels the tasks of providing such sustenance to urban and suburban people falls heavily upon the clergy.

—WILLIAM A. CLEBSCH AND CHARLES R. JAEKLE[1]

Psychotherapeutic theory and practice draw a distinction between *uncovering, insight-oriented methods* of therapy on the one hand, and *supportive methods* on the other. This distinction is of major importance to the effectiveness of counseling pastors. An understanding of its implications can awaken a new appreciation for the potentialities of supportive pastoral care and counseling and encourage ministers to develop their skill in using supportive methods. These methods lend themselves naturally to the shepherding stance and to pastor-parishioner relationships. By mastering these methods, pastors acquire resources for helping many persons who do not need or cannot respond to uncovering counseling approaches.

In supportive care and counseling, the pastor uses methods that *stabilize, undergird, nurture, motivate, or guide* troubled persons—enabling them to handle their problems and relationships more constructively within whatever limits are imposed by their personality resources and circumstances. The nature of supportive counseling becomes clearer when contrasted with uncovering, insight-oriented approaches to helping (also called pastoral psychotherapy). The latter aim at basic personality

170

changes that occur by means of uncovering and dealing with previously hidden aspects of oneself and one's relationships. Such approaches usually focus on depth factors—unconscious material and early life experiences as well as current relationships. In contrast, supportive counseling does not employ uncovering methods and does not aim at depth insight or radical personality transformation. Instead, the goal is to help persons gain the strength and perspective to use their psychological and interpersonal resources (however limited) more effectively in coping creatively with their life situations. Supportive methods focus on here-and-now problems in living—helping persons to handle or accept these in reality-oriented ways, thus strengthening their ability to cope constructively in the future. Such methods seek to help persons avoid self-hurting or other-hurting patterns, and to increase mutual need satisfaction in relationships. Personality growth often occurs gradually in supportive counseling, *as a result of* persons' increased effectiveness in handling their problems and improving their relationships.

Both insight-oriented and supportive methods depend on a strong, empathic pastor-parishioner relationship. Pastoral psychotherapy uses the relationship as the *foundation* on which uncovering methods are based. The trustful quality of the relationship permits the use of methods aimed at dealing with repressed, threatening feelings, fantasies, and memories. In supportive care and counseling the relationship *per se* is the primary instrument of change. Maintaining a dependable, nurturing relationship is the heart of the process. By relating trustfully to the pastor, such persons are able to draw on the pastor's inner strength. This vicariously acquired ego strength helps persons handle their situation more constructively, thereby strengthening their coping abilities.

The distinction between insight-uncovering and supportive approaches is, in actual practice, usually a matter of emphasis and a choice of *primary* goals, rather than a rigid dichotomy. Most counseling and therapy have a strong supportive dimension. In supportive counseling, this aspect is central. Some increased self-awareness and self-understanding (insight) may result from supportive approaches. In general, supportive methods are more action-oriented and involve a larger degree of counselor activity and careful use of authority than pastoral psycotherapy. In supportive counseling the pastor makes more use of guidance, information, reassurance, inspiration, planning, asking and answering questions, and encouraging or discouraging certain forms of behavior. Supportive methods are used in several other types of pastoral counseling. They play a key role in crisis caring and bereavement counseling.

How does supportive counseling relate to general pastoral care and to the network of sustaining, nurturing relationships that pastors and lay carers have with a congregation? Supportive pastoral relationships are integral to the entire pastoral care ministry. A caring relationship becomes supportive counseling when *counseling methods are employed to help an individual, couple, or family cope with a particular problem or crisis*. Like the reinforcing steel in concrete, these methods are used at stress points to strengthen and enhance the helpfulness of ongoing supportive care-giving.

Methods of Supportive Counseling

Psychiatrist Franz Alexander describes five procedures used in supportive psychotherapy.[2] These are also basic tools in pastoral care and counseling:

(1) *Gratifying dependency needs*. The support giver is a "good parent" figure upon whom the parishioner can lean. There are many forms of dependency gratification including comforting, sustaining, feeding (emotionally or physically), inspiring, guiding, protecting, instructing, and setting dependable limits to prevent self- or other-damaging behavior. Such dependency gratification communicates caring to a troubled person.

(2) *Emotional catharsis*.[3] As Carl Rogers emphasizes, the acceptance of a person's burdensome feelings is one of the most supportive things a counselor can do. Pouring out one's feelings in an understanding relationship drains the poison from the wounds of the spirit. It also helps reduce the paralyzing anxieties that inhibit the use of judgment and problem-solving abilities. To sense that another person *knows* and *cares* about one's inner pain gives troubled persons the strength that comes from having their lives undergirded.

(3) *Objective review of the stress situation*. The supportive relationship allows troubled persons to gain enough objectivity to

view their problem from a somewhat wider perspective and to explore feasible alternatives. This objectivity helps them make wiser decisions concerning what can and should be done.

(4) *Aiding the ego's defenses.* Methodologically, this is the opposite of uncovering, confronting, or probing.

A middle-aged salesman was at the wheel of the car when an accident resulted in the death of his wife. In ministering to him during the bereavement period, the pastor listened as the man went over and over the grim events of the accident. The minister noted that he was minimizing his own responsibility by ignoring the excessive speed at which he was traveling and blaming the driver of the slow-moving truck that his car struck from the rear. The minister respected the man's present need for the ego defenses of *repression* (of the memory of his speeding) and *projection* (of blame). The enormous guilt that awareness of his responsibility in the accident would bring could have overwhelmed the man or precipitated self-destructive atoning behavior. As the acuteness of the crisis began to diminish, the man gradually became able to face his responsibility and guilt and, with the minister's help, to work these through constructively.

(5) *Changing the life situation.* The pastor may either help parishioners make changes or, if this is not possible, arrange to *have* changes made in the circumstances (physical, economic, or interpersonal) that are producing debilitating disturbances in their lives. To illustrate, a minister assisted a distressed family in finding an adequate nursing home for an aged, senile father. She also helpd them face the sadness and resolve their inappropriate guilt feelings regarding this necessary action. The practical help a minister renders as a part of counseling—helping a handicapped person to find a job or arranging for a layperson to drive her or him to a rehabilitation center—has a strong supportive effect.[4]

I would add two other methods of supportive counseling to Franz Alexander's list.

(6) *Encouraging appropriate action.* When persons are stunned or paralyzed by feelings of anxiety, defeat, failure, damaged self-esteem, or tragic loss, it is often helpful for the pastor to prescribe some activity that will keep them functioning and in touch with people. This diminishes the tendency to retreat into depression and to withdraw from relationships.[5] Constructive

activity gives temporary structure to the person's chaotic world as well as providing ways of changing the painful situation.

The prescribed homework should have a bearing on the achievement of the goals that have been agreed on in contracting. Reading assignments relevant to one's problem can be valuable. In fact, the use of bibliotherapy as an adjunct to various types of pastoral counseling has much to commend it.

(7) *Using religious resources*. Prayer, scripture, devotional literature, communion, etc., constitute valuable supportive resources unique to pastoral counseling. When employed appropriately they may give counselees fresh awareness that their lives have meaning transcending the pain and tragedy they face. In moments of spiritual openness, elicited by the meaningful use of these resources, counselor and counselee can become aware of the supportive power of Spirit available to both of them in, through, and beyond the counseling process.

Supportive or Uncovering Counseling?

How does the pastor decide whether a particular person is more apt to be helped by mainly supportive or uncovering methods? This is a crucial issue in selecting counseling approaches and in making referrals. The most useful criterion is *the person's degree of ego strength*. Those with relatively weak, rigid, or defective ego development usually do not respond to uncovering, insight-oriented methods. Supportive methods constitute the approach of choice.

The ego (Adult in TA terms) is the executive branch of the personality. Its function is the integration of one's inner life and coping with the outside world. Its many skills include reasoning, problem-solving, reflection, imagination, and motor activities such as walking and speaking. The ego also includes the sense of personal identity and worth. Persons with sturdy egos have generally firm, positive answers to two questions: "Who am I?" and "What am I worth?" In TA terms, they are persons whose Adult is able to guide and direct their inner Child and Parent and handle their problems and responsibilities effectively.

One or more of these characteristics may indicate ego weakness:

(1) *Inability to handle ordinary adult responsibilities and everyday relationships constructively*. The fact that a person has

been chronically unable to hold a job or maintain ongoing relationships often indicates ego weakness. Conversely, the fact that a person has held a job or remained married to the same person for a considerable time may indicate inner strengths upon which counseling can build. (Societal factors such as de facto discrimination against women and minorities must be taken into account in evaluating chronic unemployment and other factors as indicators of ego weakness.)

(2) *Inability to tolerate frustration and control impulses.* Weak-egoed persons tend to be pushed about by their impulses. Their frustration tolerance and willingness to postpone gratifications in the interest of long-range goals are limited.

(3) *A low degree of ability to organize one's life, plan ahead realistically, or learn from experience.* Weak-egoed persons often suffer from chronic economic chaos, repetitive mistakes, and general disorganization. Their "executive department" is no match for the demands of economic reality or interpersonal relations. They suffer from what Roger Price calls "copelessness."

(4) *Pronounced and chronic dependency.* They tend to form parasitic relationships with anyone who will take care of them, or give them a vicarious sense of importance or strength.

(5) *Perceptual distortion.* Since perception is an ego function, the degree to which persons' perceiving apparatus distorts reality is an indication of the ego's relative strength. Distortions result from inner pressures and conflicts. The accuracy with which counselees see the counselor is a reliable index of their ego strength. Do they, for example, see the pastor as a stern judge or magical protector when, in fact, she or he is neither? If, under ordinary life stresses, a person regresses to a severe denial of reality, faulty ego functioning is present. The psychotic individual suffers from extreme ego weakness and perceptual distortion.

(6) *Personality rigidity.* A lack of resiliency in the ways persons relate can often be sensed by the pastor. Rigid theological or political views, held with a kind of drowning-person-clutching-straw tenacity, are frequently present. Persons who hold obsessively to a cult or peace-of-mind ideology may be using this repressive mechanism to hold off inner chaos. Efforts to alter the views of such persons by rational, logical means are usually futile. The only humane approach is to respect persons' needs for such magical beliefs until they are able to relinquish them and grow

beyond them. A magical, manipulative theology may be a person's only source of certainty and safety in a chaotic inner world of frightening fantasies and impulses.

People have ego defenses because they need them.[6] Defenses function automatically to protect people from unbearable threats to their self-image and self-esteem stemming from societal, interpersonal, or intrapsychic sources. In a relatively healthy person, defenses operate with certain flexibility. For example, students who fail exams often defend their sense of self-worth by the temporary use of *rationalization* ("It's because I'm a well-rounded person and not a bookworm that I flunked"), *projection* ("It was the teacher's fault for giving such a hard exam"), or *denial* ("Passing exams isn't really important"). But as their self-esteem gradually recovers, they usually become aware of what they contributed to their failure and take appropriate action to better their situation. In contrast, weak-egoed persons' defenses tend to operate inflexibly, limiting their capacity for creative change, insight, or problem-solving. The goal of caring and counseling with such persons is to give them support and esteem-enhancing experiences (little successes) to *lessen their need* for heavy defenses such as projection and denial of reality.

(7) *Inability to benefit from an insight-oriented counseling approach* may indicate limitations of ego strength in middle-class people. Some people lack the ability to engage in the prolonged self-scrutiny leading to self-understanding and the modification of basic attitudes. Their capacity to order life, control impulses, and learn from experience by reflecting on it is so limited as to vitiate the effectiveness of insight-uncovering methods. When counselees do not respond to a pastor's attempt to use an insight-oriented approach, it is usually wise to shift to more supportive approaches. It must be noted that insight-oriented methods are oriented to middle-class values and ways of communicating. The ineffectiveness of such methods with non-middle-class persons therefore is usually not a sign of ego weakness. It should be noted that everyone's ego strength changes continually, to some degree, depending on many factors—e.g., inner pressures and outer circumstances.

Insight-uncovering therapy is more apt to benefit persons who use neurotic rather than acting out or psychotic ways of attempting to handle their inner problems.[7] Unlike the acting-out type (character problem or sociopathic personality), the neurotic person experiences a painful degree of guilt and anxiety. Neurotic individuals have considerable ego strength, but their defenses are very heavy and costly, producing painful symptoms including exhaustion by their inefficiency. Because of their motivating guilt and anxiety and their relative strength, such persons often profit from insight-oriented psychotherapy.

In most cases the minister is dealing with a considerable degree of ego weakness when counseling with chronic alcoholics; drug addicts; the overtly or borderline psychotic; the chronically depressed, delinquent or dependent; and those with chronic multiple psychosomatic problems. In working with such persons, a supportive approach is most likely to be helpful. Many factors in our society contribute to the current proliferation of ego weaknesses—the breakdown of family and community stability, ethical and theological confusion, extreme mobility, and the depersonalization of technology and urbanization.

Varieties of Supportive Counseling

There are at least four types of supportive care and counseling: *crisis, stopgap, sustaining,* and *growth.* Supportive crisis counseling constitutes a major pastoral opportunity (see chapter 8). Stopgap supportive counseling consists of the use of supportive methods with disturbed persons until they can be referred.

Sustaining counseling uses supportive methods periodically, within a long-term pastoral care relationship. The goal is to help persons *continue to function at their own optimal level,* however limited, in spite of their difficult and unchangeable life situations. Some older adults and many chronically ill or emotionally crippled persons are able to remain functional because of the help of a minister and/or the members of a caring congregation.[8]

The heart of this approach is the ongoing supportive relationship that such persons establish with a pastor and congregation.[9] Year after year this network of meaningful relationships sustains the person. Within this context, *occasional brief counseling contacts* that use supportive methods can have a helping effect that far outweighs the limited amount of time invested. In many cases little can be done to change their life situations. But the fact that they can discuss their problems with their minister or a member of the congregation's caring team occasionally, gives them strength to bear loads that would otherwise be crushing. Periodically the pastor may check with such persons by phone or face-to-face to be brought up to date on their situations and to let them reexperience concern for them on an individual basis. This occasional informal chat may be much more helpful to them than a formal session with another counselor. Because of the minister's symbolic role and continuing pastoral care relationship, brief counseling contracts can be very helpful.

Most pastors have a network of such sustaining relationships. By being nurturing parent figures, pastors can help make such persons' lives bearable, giving them resources for carrying inescapable loads. During periods of particular stress, such persons often come for brief counseling to clarify their problems or get practical assistance in meeting immediate needs.

In supportive counseling it is often important to help parishioners achieve an attitude of acceptance toward the unchangeable aspects of their problems. When acceptance replaces an attitude of brooding bitterness or self-pity, remarkable changes occur in persons' ability to live constructively within the "givenness" of their situation. The psychic energy that had been invested in resentment or self-pity becomes available for carrying their load.

Supportive growth counseling is a valuable approach in pastoral work. Many people can utilize a supportive counseling relationship, not merely to continue functioning but as *the psychological environment in which gradual personal growth occurs*. The growth takes place in persons' ability to handle life situations constructively by making better use of their personality resources and relationships, rather than in a fundamental reorientation of their personalities. Supportive growth counseling shows that persons' coping abilities gain strength as they are used. Short-term supportive relationships enable some people to use their own strength much more effectively.

The recovery of alcoholics in AA is a clear illustration of a supportive growth process. As long as alcoholics are drinking, their inner resources tend to be immobilized. They are like a car with its engine racing but out of gear. The drinking alcoholics' ego resources are out of gear. They are unavailable for handling such adult roles as marriage, parenthood, and employment constructively. In TA terms, the Adult is largely decommissioned, while the demanding, frightened Child and punitive Parent battle.

AA provides a key supportive relationship (a sponsor) and gradually a network of supportive relationships (the AA group). The *sponsor functions in a supportive guiding role* that, in relation to the group is comparable to the relation between a counseling pastor and the pastoral care function of an effective congregation. Sponsors backed by the group help new persons interrupt the self-perpetuating vicious cycle of compulsive addictive drinking. Then, without bothering about the underlying causes of alcoholism, AA provides supportive, accepting relationships that become a growth environment within which the alcoholic's floundering ego regains its ability to function constructively. Thus AA helps alcoholics get their personality motor back in gear, acquiring strength by identifying with and seeking advice from their sponsor and other stable AA members. They begin to substitute person-centered for alcohol-centered ways of dealing with problems. They discover that they *can* face their fears and guilt feelings. As they face and resolve these (in the moral inventory), their emotional load lessens and their inner strength grows. The experience of getting and holding a job, making workable plans, and forming friendships, strengthens their self-esteem and coping abilities. Their previously weakened, paralyzed egos gradually recover the ability to cope with adult responsibilities and relationships. Usually without any depth therapy, their personalities and life-styles grow in this mutually caring and supportive growth environment. Throughout the process there is considerable informal supportive counseling in which more experienced members help the newer members. The great majority of successful AA members achieve their recoveries entirely on an ego-adaptive level through the supportive growth approach of AA.[10]

A minister has many opportunities to do supportive growth counseling. Jack is a lonely fourteen-year-old. Shyness, rooted in low self-esteem and guilt feelings about his sexual impulses, caused him to withdraw from his peer group. The more he withdrew, the further behind he fell in acquiring the social skills that other teen-agers were learning in their peer interaction. The more learning experiences he missed, the more awkward he felt, *and actually was,* in teen-age relationships. If this vicious cycle had continued, it would have become increasingly difficult for him to become reintegrated into his peer group without professional counseling or therapy.

The original cause of Jack's withdrawal was a common adolescent personality struggle. However, the longer the withdrawal continued, the more his fears grew and the more the withdrawal became *a problem in its own right*, requiring direct help. Fortunately, Jack's underlying fears were not so intense nor his withdrawal from peer relationships so extended as to render a supportive-growth approach ineffective. The help he got enabled him to get a foothold in a peer group. This was accomplished by a double strategy. The minister enlisted the help of a more secure boy about Jack's age, who was well accepted in the youth group. A friendship developed between them that served as a bridge to group affiliation for Jack. Both boys were also included in a growth group for teen-agers—a setting in which Jack had an opportunity to learn peer-relationship skills under the leadership of an adult who liked adolescents and was trained in group counseling. This helped Jack pull out of his tailspin of fear and withdrawal and begin to grow in his ability to relate. If a supportive growth approach had not accomplished this, individual or group psychotherapy probably would have been required to help Jack interrupt his vicious cycle of guilt and withdrawal from peer relationships.

Supportive-growth counseling often has a permanently beneficial effect because, as in the case cited above, it interrupts what psychiatrist Harry M. Tiebout aptly calls a "runaway symptom." What begins as a symptom of some underlying problem becomes a self-perpetuating pathological process in its own right that must be interrupted. If it is interrupted, it often is unnecessary to treat the original source of anxiety.[11] Persons with runaway symptoms are encountered frequently in pastoral counseling.

Dangers in Supportive Counseling

A supportive counseling relationship is like an orthopedic device that has two valid uses—to provide temporary support while a broken bone heals and as a brace to allow permanently crippled persons to function. There is a danger that supportive relationships may be used as crutches, in the negative connotations of the word—blocking growth by continued dependency.[12] This occurs when a minister does things for counselees that they could do for themselves, thus allowing them to avoid the personality exercise required to develop the strengths and skills needed to cope with their situation. It is important therefore to be alert to the development of unconstructive dependencies in supportive counseling so that the counselee can be gradually but firmly weaned.

How can ministers protect their mental health, creative edge, and family relationships from the exorbitant demands of a host of dependent people, as they function in supportive caring and counseling? Highly dependent people are plentiful in our society. They attach themselves leech-like to available parent figures. Ministers can reduce this hazard by: (a) being aware of and resisting any neurotic needs they may have to "collect" dependent relationships, (b) learning how to say no when necessary and appropriate, and (c) distributing the dependencies of such persons to supportive church groups and lay pastoral care team members.[13] Fortunately, pastors who train key lay persons in caring skills have a network of co-pastors to help dependent and needy people.

Reality-Practice Session

PARISHIONER'S ROLE: You are Mrs. V., a widow aged eighty-one, bedfast as a result of a fall that resulted in a fractured wrist and collarbone. You live with your son and his wife. Your faith has been severely tested by your accident. You cannot understand why God seems so far away. Many of your friends have died and you feel extremely lonesome. You know that you may not live much longer. (Lie down to take this role.)

PASTOR'S ROLE: You are Mrs. V's pastor. She is the oldest member of your church. You have a strong pastoral relationship with her, but prior to this visit, she has never discussed her deeper feelings with you. As she talks during this visit, you sense the opportunity to do supportive counseling as a part of your pastoral care ministry with her. As you talk, be aware of her feelings and let her know that you are aware by reflecting what you think she is saying and feeling. Experiment with supportive methods described in this chapter as these are appropriate. Be sensitive to the possible presence of tension among the family members.

OBSERVER-COACH'S ROLE: Your function is to help Mrs. V. and the minister increase their awareness of what is occurring between them and the feeling tone of the counseling relationship. Feel free to interrupt the counseling occasionally to make suggestions concerning how it might become more helpful. Be candid. As an observer you will perceive important things that they may not see.

Experiment with a tape recorder, playing back segments of this reality-practice session.

Recommended Reading

Howard J. Clinebell, Jr., "Ego Psychology and Pastoral Counseling," *Pastoral Psychology*, February 1963, pp. 26-36. Shows how ego psychology provides a foundation for supportive counseling.

Howard J. Parad, ed., *Ego Psychology and Dynamic Casework* (New York: Family Service Association of America, 1958). Applies ego psychology to a variety of types of counseling.

Lewis R. Wolberg in "Supportive Psychotherapy" in *The Technique of Psychotherapy* (New York: Grune and Stratton, 1954), pp. 170-75, 523-47.

CHAPTER 8

Crisis Care and Counseling

The pastor moves from one crisis to another with those whom he [*sic*] shepherds. . . . Two thousand years of Christian ministry have conditioned Christians to expect their pastors to be with them at these times of crises. Therefore, the Christian pastor comes to his task in the strength of a great heritage. Even though he feels a sense of awe in the presence of the mysterious and tremendous crises of life, he also feels a sense of security in the fact that his people both want and expect him to be present at their times of testing.

—WAYNE E. OATES[1]

Through the centuries pastors have given care, support, and guidance during personal crises and losses. In our day of proliferating personal and social crises, ministers have an unprecedented opportunity to give both care and counseling to persons struggling in the riptides of chaotic crises. Pastors are *natural crisis counselors* because of the inherent advantages of their position and role—their network of ongoing relationships with their people; their entree to many family systems; the trust that many people have in ministers; their accessibility; and their presence during many of the developmental and accidental (unexpected) crises in people's lives, including illness, death, and bereavement. In the eyes of many who are experiencing crises and loss, the minister's image and identity have a supportive and nurturing meaning. It is within these natural advantages that pastors do crisis work, including the rituals with which our religious heritage has surrounded the major human crises of birth and growth, living and dying.

A national study of where Americans turn when they seek help revealed that 39 percent of those who had sought professional help for a personal or family crisis had gone to ministers. For help with crises related to the death of someone close, 54 percent had turned to ministers.[2] This study confirms the strategic role of ministers in facilitating healing and growth in crises. The twin skills of crisis and grief counseling are among the most frequently used helping tools of persons in general ministries, including parish pastors.

As one who symbolizes the dimension of ultimate meanings and who is the spiritual leader of a religious community with a rich spiritual tradition, the minister has many resources for crisis ministry. In crises and losses people often confront their spiritual hungers, the emptiness of their lives, and the poverty of their values and relationships. Reflecting on his death camp experience Viktor Frankl declares, "Woe to him who saw no more sense in his life, no aim, no purpose . . . He was soon lost."[3] In the crisis ministry the role of pastors as *awakeners of meaning and realistic hope* is crucially important. Their unique function, as spiritual growth-enablers, is to help crisis-stricken people discover the ultimate meaningfulness of life lived in relationship with God whose steadfast love is always available, even in the midst of terrible tragedy.

Crisis Care and Crisis Counseling

A minister's help to those in crises and losses has four aspects—the general ministry of pastoral care; informal crisis counseling; short-term (one to five sessions) formal crisis counseling; and longer-term counseling and therapy to help persons repair the psychological causes and/or consequences of severe crises. It is important to distinguish crisis care from crisis counseling, even though the two frequently overlap in practice. People in crisis often move back and forth between needing supportive care and needing the skills of crisis counseling as they make difficult decisions. Everyone needs increased care and nurture when they are going through deep water. Only a small percentage need formal counseling, and an even smaller percentage require reparative therapy. The general ministry of pastoral caring is a ministry of presence, listening, warmth, and practical support. Trained lay carers can and should share responsibility with the pastor for this important and demanding ministry. Short-term crisis counseling, informal or formal, is needed by persons who could mobilize their coping resources more quickly, and handle their crises more constructively with some help in reality-testing and in planning effective approaches to the new situation created by the crisis. Formal longer-term counseling are needed by those who are so traumatized and immobilized by overwhelming losses or multiple crises that they are unable to mobilize their coping resources without therapeutic help. It is often well to refer persons whose lives have been so shattered to psychotherapists (pastoral or secular) who have the time and training to do the reconstructive psychotherapy needed.

Because crisis counseling and grief counseling overlap and are so interrelated, I will discuss them in this chapter and the next. Modern approaches to crisis and grief counseling are derived from the pioneering work of Erich Lindemann in his 1943 study of bereavement among survivors and relatives of those who died in the tragic Coconut Grove fire in Boston.[4] In the years since that study, crisis intervention methods have been perfected as they have been used by counselors to help persons cope with a wide variety of crises, changes, and losses. The core experience in both crises and grief is that of loss. A loss or the threat of a loss is always involved in crises. Feelings of grief are a part of all major life changes, transitions and crises. In most crises and losses, there is separation anxiety, feelings of identity confusion, and the necessity of developing new ways to meet one's basic emotional needs.

The Nature and Dynamics of Crises

Psychiatrist Gerald Caplan has provided all the helping professions with valuable conceptual tools for understanding the psychodynamics of crises. In his *Principles of Preventive Psychiatry,* he points out that everyone is constantly faced with situations demanding problem-solving activity.[5] Ordinarily the disequilibrium (tension) caused by problems is reduced quickly through the use of familiar skills. A crisis occurs *within persons* when their usual problem-solving activities are ineffective, allowing the stress of unmet need to rise unabated. The stress stems from the deprivation of the satisfaction of some fundamental physical or psychological needs. Caplan delineates four characteristic phases in the development of a personal crisis:

(1) The problem (stimulus) causes tension in the organism that mobilizes the person's habitual problem-solving responses.

(2) Failure of these responses and the continuing unmet need produce inner disturbances including feelings of anxiety, confusion, guilt, ineffectuality, and some degree of disorganization of functioning.

(3) When the tension of the seemingly insoluble problem passes a certain threshold, it becomes a powerful stimulus to the mobilization of additional crisis-meeting resources:

> The individual calls on his reserves of strength and of emergency problem-solving mechanisms. He uses novel methods to attack the problem. . . . He may gradually define the problem in a new way, so that it comes within the range of previous experience. Aspects of the problem which were neglected may now be brought into awareness, with the consequent linking with capacities and accessory problem-solving techniques which were previously neglected as irrelevant. . . . There may be active resignation and giving up of certain aspects of goals as unattainable. He may explore by trial and error, either in action or in abstract thought, which avenues are open and which closed.[6]

Thus the problem may be solved or avoided by resignation. Crisis counseling aims at helping persons in this third stage by encouraging them to mobilize their latent coping resources.

(4) If the problem is not resolved, the inner stress of unmet needs mounts until it reaches another threshold—the breaking point where major personality disorganization (psychological, psychosomatic, interpersonal, or spiritual illness) occurs.

Caplan distinguishes two categories of crises: *developmental and accidental*. Human growth is the result of meeting a series of developmental crises successfully. As Erik Erikson shows, the development of personality occurs through a series of growth stages, each of which has a challenging task for the ego, and builds on the accomplishment of these tasks in earlier phases. Transitions between stages are periods of heightened anxiety and crisis when persons are both pushed forward by inner maturational forces and pulled backwards by the security of the familiar stage.[7]

Developmental crises are normal in the sense that they happen as an integral part of all or many people's growth. Among these are birth, weaning, toilet training, the oedipal conflict, going to school, adolescence, leaving home, completing school, entering a vocation, engagement, marriage adjustment (or the adjustment of singlehood), pregnancy, parenthood, the middle-age crisis, loss of parents, menopause, retirement, death of spouse, death of friends, and eventually one's own dying. These stressful experiences are the occasions of crises for an individual to the extent that they pose problems for which her or his previous coping abilities are inadequate. Each developmental stage and crisis is the occasion for a variety of caring and counseling opportunities.

Accidental crises can ocur at any age, precipitated by unexpected losses of what one regards as essential sources of need satisfaction. Precipitating experiences include all the life events listed on the Holmes-Rahe scale below, plus many others—e.g., loss of status and respect; an accident or surgical operation; mental illness or alcoholism; a physical handicap; an unwanted pregnancy; a natural disaster such as a flood or earthquake; or a massive social calamity such as a war or economic depression. Crises can be triggered by seemingly positive changes such as a job promotion or graduation from college. All these events produce *emotionally hazardous situations*. Crises happen *in* people rather than *to* them, but they tend to occur in high-stress, emotionally hazardous situations. So frequent are both developmental and accidental crises that a minister may spend many hours in a single week in crisis-related care and counseling.

A crisis is more than simply a time of danger, pain, and stress to be endured. It is important for the counselor to see that it is a turning point, a growth opportunity where persons move toward or away from greater personality strength and wholeness. This makes crisis counseling a strategic helping opportunity. Caplan writes of the persons in crisis:

> His new equilibriums may be better or worse than in the past, in that the realignment of forces both inside his personality and in relationships with meaningful people . . . may lead to more or less satisfaction of his needs. He may deal with the crisis problems by developing new socially acceptable, reality-based problem-solving techniques *which add to his capacity to deal in a healthy way with future difficulties*. Alternatively, he may, during the crisis, work out new coping responses which are socially unacceptable and which deal with difficulties by evasion, irrational fantasy manipulations, or regression and alienation—all of which increase the likelihood that he will also deal maladaptively with future

difficulties. In other words, the new pattern of coping that he works out in dealing with the crisis becomes thence forward an integral part of his repertoire of problem-solving responses and increases the chance that he will deal more or less realistically with future hazards.[8]

Short-term crisis counseling frequently can be of major help to persons simply by steering them away from maladaptive responses and toward constructive facing of their crises. Relatively rapid results often are possible because forces within the person are teetering in the balance. Thus a relatively minor influence by the pastor can have a major effect in helping the person cope constructively. If the individual who is coping with a crisis in an unhealthy manner can be helped to face the problem and cope with it in a healthy way, there is usually no need to attempt the difficult, time-consuming process of searching for the underlying reasons for the initial maladaptive response.

Crises and Losses Are Culmative

The particular crisis or loss that motivates a person to seek pastoral help often is only the last straw, the most recent in a series of stressful changes and losses. Such a series, within a limited time period has a cumulative effect in which one plus one produces more than two units of stress in the person. It is well to ask persons who are floundering in crises what other significant changes, transitions, or losses they have had in recent months. A series of crises intensifies the need for pastoral care and nurture.

Thomas H. Holmes and R. H. Rahe, professors of psychiatry at the University of Washington, have developed a stress scale of common life experiences. They assigned the death of a spouse a stress score of 100; then they measured the relative stress in the lives of the people they studied, caused by other changes and losses. Their scale is useful in pastoral crisis counseling.

All these life events produce some stress and grief. Holmes and Rahe discovered that approximately 50 percent of persons with a cumulative stress score (within one year) of between 150 and 299 became sick—physically, psychologically, or psychosomatically. Some 80 percent of those with stress levels over 300, got sick. This scale can alert pastoral counselors and lay crises carers to the importance of searching for clusters of life changes from which

THE SOCIAL READJUSTMENT RATING SCALE[9]

Life Event   Mean Stress Value

1. Death of Spouse..100
2. Divorce...73
3. Marital separation from mate...................................65
4. Detention in jail or other institution........................63
5. Death of a close family member..............................63
6. Major personal injury or illness...............................53
7. Marriage...50
8. Being fired at work..47
9. Marital reconciliation with mate..............................45
10. Retirement from work..45
11. Major change in the health or behavior of a family member....44
12. Pregnancy..40
13. Sexual difficulties..39
14. Gaining a new family member (through birth, adoption, oldster moving in, etc.)..39
15. Major business readjustment (merger, reorganization, bankruptcy, etc.)...39
16. Major change in financial state (a lot worse off or a lot better off than usual)..38
17. Death of a close friend..37
18. Changing to a different line of work......................36
19. Major change in the number of arguments with spouse (either a lot more or a lot less than usual regarding childrearing, personal habits, etc.)............................35
20. Taking out a mortgage or loan for a major purchase............31
21. Foreclosure on a mortgage or loan.......................30
22. Major change in responsibilities at work (promotion, demotion, lateral transfer)...................................29
23. Son or daughter leaving home (marriage, attending college, etc.)..29
24. Trouble with in-laws..29
25. Outstanding personal achievement........................28
26. Wife beginning or ceasing work outside the home............26
27. Beginning or ceasing formal schooling..................26
28. Major change in living conditions (building a new home, remodeling, deterioration of home or neighborhood)............25
29. Revision of personal habits (dress, manners, association, etc.)....24
30. Troubles with the boss...23
31. Major change in working hours or conditions...........20

32. Change in residence.. 20
33. Changing to a new school.. 20
34. Major change in usual type and/or amount of recreation......... 19
35. Major change in church activities (a lot more or a lot
    less than usual)... 19
36. Major change in social activities (clubs, dancing,
    movies, visiting, etc.).. 18
37. Taking out a mortgage or loan for a lesser purchase (for a
    car, TV, freezer, etc.).. 17
38. Major change in sleeping habits (a lot more or a lot less sleep,
    or change in part of day when asleep)............................... 16
39. Major change in number of family get-togethers................... 15
40. Major change in eating habits (a lot more or a lot less food
    intake, or very different meal hours or surroundings)............. 15
41. Vacation... 13
42. Christmas... 12
43. Minor violations of the law (e.g., traffic tickets)................... 11

people are suffering cumulative stress overloads. It is important to note that other major life stresses are not included in this scale—changing female/male roles; spouse and child battering; rape; the loss of one's dreams, faith, idealism, and values; hunger; poverty; discrimination; environmental pollution; sexism; racism; and the awful threat of a nuclear holocaust. Factors such as these add significantly to the cumulative stress in many people's lives.

Informal Crisis Counseling

The position and role of pastors allows them to take the initiative in reaching out to many persons *who will not come for formal counseling*. To utilize this strategic advantage fully, ministers must learn to recognize and respond to the host of often quiet cries for help that occur in the normal course of calling, group contacts, educational and administrative duties. Much of the counseling done by pastors takes place in informal settings without being called counseling. Some occurs in the minister's office or home when people drop by for a chat, without an appointment. By allowing the sensitivites and skills of counseling to permeate their many informal and chance encounters, ministers can help many times the number of people they could reach through formal counseling alone. To keep a creative edge on one's ministry and to protect oneself from pastoral care overload, it is essential to have times when one's privacy (to study, reflect, meditate, relax, and play) is protected from drop-in counselees. But it is also important to have parishioners know that their pastor ordinarily is available when severe crises strike unexpectedly.

As ministers learn to recognize and utilize the pastoral care opportunities potentially present in many interpersonal contacts, this becomes a natural pastoral reflex. They discover frequent opportunities to do informal one-session crisis counseling during the ordinary encounters of parish life. Occasionally these will become formal and multiple-session counseling relationships.

Informal counseling is informal in one or more of these ways—setting, set, structure, sequence. The setting may be anywhere—a street corner, a grocery store, a hospital room, the church lounge, a parishioner's office or living room, an AA meeting, on a plane or bus, or at the community swimming pool. The counseling happens in the context of a relationship not identified as counseling—a chance encounter or a pastoral call, perhaps following a meeting or Sunday service. The person's mind-set reflects this informal atmosphere. He/she probably thinks of what occurs as "talking over a problem with the pastor" rather than counseling. The structure and sequence of formal counseling interviews—appointments, stated time limits, and an agreed–upon series of sessions—are usually lacking. Such brief informal counseling can be very helpful to some people.

Informal crisis counseling opportunities occur frequently during a pastor's home and hospital visits. Much of what is done during such calls is general pastoral care. It becomes counseling when two factors—the *sine qua non* of counseling—are present: (a) some degree of awareness of a problem on the parishioner's part, and (b) a desire for the pastor's help with the problem. Awareness of the nature of the problem may be vague, the desire for help minimal. All human motivation is mixed, including that which causes people to seek and/or accept help. The pain of a problem and the fear of telling another about it offsets each other in some people—blocking action. Motivation is like a teeter-totter. Until the pain of a problem and the hope of getting help outweigh the fear of self-disclosure and the neurotic satisfactions accruing from the situation, persons usually will not seek help. But this motivational teeter-totter often tips back and forth for a considerable time before persons actively seek help. They may be open to help long before they take the initiative to get help. Such persons often are receptive to informal counseling long before they enter formal counseling. Some people have great difficulty making a formal appointment for counseling, even when wrestling with very painful problems. They feel that to do so would be to admit failure, which would increase their feelings of low self-esteem and powerlessness. This is why the ability of pastors to go to *people, make themselves emotionally available, offer help, and establish informal counseling relationships* is a *priceless* professional asset, which should be used to the full!

How can ministers create opportunities, during their pastoral contacts, for care-giving conversations, informal and formal counseling?[10] First, they can *maintain a confidential, up-to-date "Special Help List,"* including the names of persons they know *or suspect* are in particular need of pastoral care—the bereaved, the sick, the unemployed, the depressed, the hospitalized, the disgruntled, those in psychotherapy (and those who should be but aren't), newlyweds, new parents, the recently retired, the handicapped, alcoholics and their families, the lonely, those with disturbed or handicapped children, and those who face painful crises and perplexing decisions. An alert pastor often senses intuitively that a certain family is under extreme pressure. Such "pastoral care suspects" should go on the Special Help List. By devoting extra pastoral visitation time to these persons, ministers can build strong relationship bridges with them. Such relationship can bring pastoral care and informal counseling help to the troubled, and also make it easier for them to seek formal counseling. The building of relationship bridges with those who are likely to need help but are not yet motivated to seek it, is described by Seward Hiltner as "precounseling."[11] The many interpersonal contacts of pastors contribute to this objective if people feel they are warm, nonjudgmental, caring, competent, shockproof, not "too busy," and human—aware of their own humanity.

Second, a pastor's *sensitivity to the subtle signs of distress* is an asset in spotting potential counseling opportunities. Many ministers walk by on the other side of their parishioners' Jericho Roads simply because they lack awareness.[12] The pastor's emotional radar antennas should be tuned to the wavelength of people in order to pick up subtle cries for help and coded "mayday" signals. Here are some typical distress signals:

(1) Embarrassment at the minister's call.
(2) A frantic attempt to keep the conversation on the surface, avoiding all depth encounter.
(3) Depression—including such symptoms as sleeplessness; loss of interest in one's usual pleasures; anxious agitation or heavy sluggishness; feelings of worthlessness, emptiness/meaninglessness or helplessness; a phony-fixed smile.
(4) Veiled antagonism between spouses, sometimes hidden behind saccharine-sweet surface behavior.
(5) Emotionally disturbed children including those with behavior problems, (which often reflect hidden marital unhappiness).
(6) Frequent intoxication, particularly at inappropriate times.
(7) A radical change in usual behavior, including church attendance.
(8) Irrational or frantically compulsive behavior.
(9) Guilty avoidance of the pastor.
(10) Affiliating with extremist political or religious groups.

When such distress signals are identified, pastors should make every effort to be emotionally accessible to the persons and to offer help in a way that respects their right to refuse it.

A third way to open up informal and formal counseling opportunities is the *judicious use of "openers"*—questions or statements designed to interrupt superficial conversation and provide an opening for people to discuss their real feelings and issues if they choose. Here are some samples: "How are things going for you in this difficult situation?" "What you're saying feels very heavy." "How are things going with you really?" "You seem to be feeling very discouraged (upset, angry, remorseful)." "I get the feeling you have a burden on your mind." Although such openers may startle people initially, they express the pastor's concern and by implication, offer help. A well-chosen question, asked with warmth and empathy, can help free people to talk about their burdens. A question about one's spiritual health is as appropriate from a minister as is a question about one's physical health from a family doctor.

Fourth, *listening and responding to feelings,* during pastoral encounters help carry a conversation to the level of a person's real needs. In this way a pastoral conversation can move into informal counseling in a natural, unthreatening way.

When people sense that a minister is emotionally aware and available, informal counseling opportunities will occur during many pastoral contacts. While making a routine hospital call on a man convalescing from surgery, a minister ran into a heated family conflict centering on whether or not the man's daughter should marry:

> **Father:** Dorothy, why don't you tell Reverend Macom what we were discussing? Maybe he can help us out.
>
> **Daughter:** (Dorothy) Well, yes, maybe you can help us, though I hesitate to bother you with my problem. I'm feeling so mixed up and confused.
>
> **Pastor:** If you will tell me, I'll try to help.
>
> **Daughter:** (with halting speech and great uneasiness) Well, I hardly know where to begin. (Pause) I—well—for some reason I don't think I want to go through with my marriage. All of a sudden I have a feeling I don't love Ed anymore.[13]

As the pastor listened, the girl's confusion and the father's domineering became evident. The minister sensed that he should try to prevent the father from pushing his daughter into marriage, without jeopardizing the father's recovery from surgery, and that he should see the girl individually to help her make her own decision. This illustrates the type of informal counseling in which an ongoing, formal counseling relationship should be established or a referral made to a trained family therapist. Hospital calls should have high priority in a minister's schedule, because they bring the pastor into contact with people in crisis. They offer frequent opportunities for both pastoral care and informal counseling. Home visits help a minister establish strong bonds with people by relating to the family in their natural setting. Furthermore, it is often helpful in understanding family dynamics to observe their interaction at home. Occasional home visits can be a valuable part of marriage and family counseling, as family therapists are discovering. There are also relationship-building values in informal contacts with parishioners by phone, at their work, and at community functions.

The Transition from Informal to Formal Counseling

Following a commitment service at a summer youth institute, a minister noticed a sobbing girl and offered his help. She poured out her guilt feelings (apparently aroused by the service) about her hatred of her stepfather. Emotional catharsis and the minister's acceptance helped her to reduce her guilt load. Although this brief, informal counseling was helpful, the minister failed at a crucial point. He did not attempt to refer the girl to her own minister for continued counseling to deal with her complex, conflicted family problem. He should have sought her permission to contact her pastor and/or encouraged her to do so as soon as she returned home.[14]

A woman lingered in the church narthex after the Sunday service to inform the minister that she had decided to leave her husband. This was the minister's first knowledge of their trouble. The pastor responded, "Let's go to my study where we can talk without being interrupted." The woman indicated that an urgent obligation would prevent an adequate discussion then, so an appointment was made for three o'clock that afternoon. People often will move from informal to formal counseling, if they are encouraged to do so and are offered a definite appointment.

The Goals of Short-term Crisis Counseling

Most of the counseling a pastor does is short-term, often one or two, and seldom more than four or five sessions. For this reason, a minister needs to develop the sensitivity and skills required to give significant help in relatively brief contact. Sizing up a problem quickly and recognizing the key issues requires a considerable degree of counseling expertise. It is erroneous to assume that because most of a pastor's counseling is short-term, he or she needs relatively little training. It often takes considerable skill to move quickly and effectively in brief counseling.

The short-term nature of most counseling by pastors does not mean that its results are necessarily superficial. If judged by its own goals and not those of long-term counseling and psycho-therapy, it is clear that significant help *can* be given in many cases. Here are some *realistic goals of short-term counseling;* not all apply in every situation:

(1) Provide a supportive, empathetic relationship.

(2) Help restore functioning by reducing the pressure of pent-up, blocking feelings through emotional catharsis.

(3) Help persons deal directly and responsibly with a specific decision or concrete problem.

(4) Help persons mobilize and use their latent resources for coping.

(5) Assist persons to achieve a broader and more constructive perspective on their situation by an objective review of it.

(6) Interrupt panic reactions and regressive snowballing by helping persons face and deal with immediate, here-and-now problems.

(7) Help persons clarify the issues and explore the alternative approaches to their problem.

(8) After alternatives have been explored, help them choose the most promising plan of action and then take steps toward implementing that plan.

(9) Provide guidance in the form of useful ideas, information, and tentative suggestions. These can become useful tools that the person employs between sessions and after counseling terminates.

(10) Stimulate the person's self-reliance and functional competence by suggesting a limited number of sessions.

(11) Establish a warm, accepting relationship that will make it easy for the person to return for additional counseling later. As Wayne Oates says, "The door of the relationship should always be left ajar so persons can feel free to come back again if they choose to do so."[15]

(12) Ascertain whether persons are deeply disturbed or for other reasons are in need of medical, psychiatric, or other specialized help. Make a referral if this appears to be the case.

Counselors who *expect* to give genuine help in brief counseling are most likely to do so. Psychoanalysts Franz Alexander and Thomas Morton French report: "Both the theoretical survey of the psychodynamics of therapy and the impressive evidence gained from actual observation require us to abandon the old belief that permanent changes of the ego cannot be accomplished through shorter and more intensive methods."[16]

Many people come to a pastor for help with specific decisions or concrete problems. When these are solved, or are discovered to be insolvable, such persons often have no further desire for counseling. One to three sessions will often suffice in such cases. Some counselees can "turn the corner," to use Seward Hiltner's phrase, in a few sessions:

> Turning the corner means that the direction has been changed. Many of the problems that come to the pastor's attention are life-situation problems. . . . They are . . . made worse because the point of view, which the person assumes is the only one he can take toward the situation, is narrow and inadequate. If he can turn the corner, clarify the conflicting forces involved, gain a bit of insight into why he feels as he does, then he has a new point of view or a new place on which to stand. Even brief counseling can often do just enough to bring a slightly new perspective, hence altering the approach to the situation and giving a chance for spontaneous successful handling of it by the parishioner.[17]

As John Dewey showed clearly, serious thinking often occurs at the fork in the road in one's life when it is unclear which way leads to one's desired goal. *Fork-of-the-road counseling* is often both short-term and fruitful. A bright young man, as a result of brief vocational guidance by his pastor, decided to go to college, in spite of his parents' indifference. By helping this lad choose the path that led to the fulfillment of more of his potentialities, the minister, in three sessions, had a long-range constructive influence on the youth's life. This case, and many others like it, recall the sign at one end of a muddy dirt road: "Choose your track carefully. You'll be in it a long time." Some decisions are like that. Having wise guidance at such times can be invaluable. Guiding of this sort is a time-honored part of our pastoral tradition.[18]

The Process of Crisis Counseling Short-Term
(Formal and Informal)

What approaches are most helpful in one-to-five-interview counseling? These elements are usually part of such a process:

(1) *Listen intensively and reflect feelings* with caring (U responses). The pressure of time in short-term counseling tempts ministers to spend too little time listening. If they yield to this temptation, they deprive persons of the salutary effects of emotional catharsis and deprive themselves of an essential understanding of persons' internal frames of reference. In most one-interview counseling, the pastor should spend at least half of the session listening.

(2) *Use questions carefully to focus on conflict areas rapidly* (P responses). After giving persons an initial opportunity to describe their problems, a few key questions can fill in the major gaps in essential information. Such questions can also encourage persons to explore neglected dimensions of problems and look in new directions for solutions. The use of selected questions permits *focused listening* in crucial problem areas. Mrs. D., a woman in her mid-forties, consulted her minister for help in deciding whether or not to leave her alcoholic husband. Through disciplined listening, the pastor began to grasp the broad outlines of the situation—many years of excessive drinking by the husband, a series of job losses, and repeated broken promises to stop drinking excessively. To be of help as a *pastoral guide*, the minister had to know whether the man had any awareness of his need for help, the nature of the marital interaction, and the dynamic role of other members of the family. The most efficient way to acquire this knowledge was to ask the woman and eventually to ask her husband questions aimed at these key issues.

(3) Help persons *review the total problem*. This enables them to gain a clearer perspective and helps prepare them to make wise decisions. It also helps them mobilize their inner resources. Under protracted stress persons often become confused about the real nature of their problem and lose sight of their own strengths for coping. They bog down in the swamp of their own hopelessness, neglecting the very things that they need to do to meet the problems constructively. Mrs. D had become so obsessed with her husband's drinking that she had neglected her friendships in the church, which she now needed desperately. As a result of her pastor's guidance, she began to rebuild this support system.

(4) *Provide useful information*. By explaining certain well-

established facts about the nature and treatment of alcoholism, the minister helped Mrs. D. abandon her futile attempts to shame her husband into controlled drinking. This knowledge helped her turn the corner and function more realistically and constructively in her relationship with him. Such educative elements in brief counseling can provide persons with information and ideas they can use to improve their situation during and after counseling.

(5) *Focus on the persons's major conflicts, problems, and decisions with the aim of clarifying the viable alternatives*. The minister asked Mrs. D., "What do you see as the real options that are open to you now?" He then helped the woman explore the consequences of each alternative. If she left her husband, he might intensify his drinking or even commit suicide. Could she face these possibilities? On the other hand, the shock of her leaving might confront him with the painful consequences of his drinking, which could open him to help. What would be the probable destructive effects on the children if she didn't leave and he continued drinking? Without leaving, could she release him emotionally in order to insulate herself and the children from the full impact of his destructive behavior? Before counseling she had, in her words, "muddled around in the problem," never really thinking clearly about the probable consequences of her options.

(6) *Help the person decide on the next step and take it*. Getting persons to act constructively, even if decisions and actions are on minor matters, helps break the paralysis of chronic indecision. In Mrs. D.'s case, the minister helped her plan the steps she would take *the next day* to discover job possibilities and sources of temporary financial support. She needed to do this before she could make her larger decision. As described previously, the human personality is like a muscle. Using it in constructive thinking and action tends to strengthen its coping abilities. Taking even small steps begins to enhance self-confidence, hope, and competence, enabling a person then to take progressively larger steps.

(7) *Provide practical guidance when it is needed*. The minister urged Mrs. D. to do several things, including attending the local Al-Anon group regularly and obtaining psychotherapy for their disturbed adolescent son. These suggestions were based on the minister's general knowledge about alcoholism and his increasing awareness of the dynamics of the D. family. The minister made his

recommendations in a form that would allow her to reject them *without rejecting him*. He respected Mrs. D.'s right not to implement them and encouraged her to express her reactions to them. All this is radically different from dispensing facile, off-the-cuff advice. Implicit in the careful use of suggestions is the view that the role of the counseling pastor is modeled more on the image of the *guide* and the *coach* than on the long-term *psychotherapist*. The use of the minister's knowledge and authority is often essential in brief counseling.

(8) *Give the person emotional support and inspiration*. The familiar line, "Walk softly, for every person you meet is carrying a cross," is poignantly and repeatedly illustrated in a counselor's experience. Many crosses are hidden. If persons come for counseling, it is safe to assume that their cross is a heavy one from their perspective. They need someone to walk with them and temporarily put a shoulder under the load. The most vital support offered in counseling is the relationship, *per se*. But, within the relationship, it often is appropriate to give persons verbal affirmation—e.g., for their courage in carrying their burden, their efforts and successes in developing better ways to cope. The careful use of religious instruments—prayer, scripture, sacraments—can deepen brief crisis counseling by strengthening contact with divine resources beyond human relationship. Pastoral counselors *confront*, but they also *comfort!* They *challenge*, but they also *care*. It is the bringing together of these two paradoxical dimensions (judgment and grace) that produces growth in counseling.

(9) Move into longer-term counseling if brief counseling does not prove adequate. This may involve continued counseling with the pastor or a referral.

The Use of Supportive Methods in Crisis Counseling

Mr. P., fifty-five, burdened with tensions, anxiety, and depression, seeks the help of his pastor. He is so distraught that he has been unable to work for several weeks. As he tells about his situation, it becomes evident to the minister that the onset of his present difficulties followed his job advancement to a position of foreman. Up until that time he had functioned well under a strong, paternalistic foreman. Now *he* is the foreman, responsible for the production record of his group, in competition with other groups within the plant. His new position demands leadership and assertiveness.

The pastor senses the strong dependency with which Mr. P. relates to him. The pastor-parishioner relationship provides a clue to P.'s general relationships with authority figures. The pastor begins to realize that P. is terribly afraid of the very things his new position demands—competitiveness, aggressiveness, and being in a position of having others depend upon him. Mr. P. is trapped between his need to remain dependent on a parent-like foreman and the demand of the job that *he* become a parent figure.

An insight-oriented counseling approach would aim at helping the man become aware of and change his paralyzing feelings by uncovering their roots in his early life and relationships. But the counselor senses that such goals are unrealistic because of the man's rigidity and lack of ego strength. As he has opportunity to ventilate and experience the acceptance of his feelings, P. begins to see that the new position, as he puts it, is "not for me," that he needs the satisfaction of working on a lathe himself, and that it bugs him to have to make decisions for those under him. Any deeper insight as to *why* it bothers him seems to be beyond his grasp.

The pastor helps P. explore other possibilities of employment on the job. He then encourages him to transfer to another department where he would be able to use his skill at the lathe in the development of new products under the direction of a strong department head.

The pastor continues to see the man several times in a supportive relationship as he adjusts to the new department. Being in a work environment where his skill as a lathesman is used and valued, and where his fear of aggressiveness does not present a problem, his anxiety and depression subside. He can now grow in his ability to handle life constructively.[19]

Most crisis counseling utilizes the basic methods of supportive counseling described in chapter 7. In P.'s case, leaning on the minister *gratified his dependency needs and reduced his anxiety,* which helped to free his reasoning abilities for use in solving his problems. His minimal self-understanding (resulting in his decision to transfer back to lathe work) followed the *emotional catharsis* that reduced the paralyzing pain of his negative feelings.

The counseling relationship allowed him to gain enough emotional distance from his swirling subjectivity to be able to *review his stressful situation* with some objectivity and to examine the probable consequences of various ways of dealing with his problem. His strong dependency needs and fear of aggressiveness were unacceptable to his self-image and were therefore held out of his awareness by repression. The pastor *aided his ego defenses* by not pushing him (except in a gentle, exploratory way) to become aware of these threatening feelings, and by accepting his valid conscious level and less threatening reason for not liking his new position. The minister helped P. *change his life situation* by encouraging him to go back to work on the lathe. *Action therapy* was involved throughout the minister's approach to helping him. During the first interview, he encouraged P. to *do* something about his situation. When P. talked of the possibility of changing jobs, the minister responded: "Wouldn't it be a good idea to check with the personnel manager at the plant to see if a transfer might be possible, in case you decide that that would be the best thing to do?" As counseling progressed, the pastor helped P. take the action P. had decided was possible and wise. At the close of each session, the minister said a prayer in which he gathered up the major feelings of the session and asked for increased awareness of God's sustaining care. The use of *religious resources* gave the helping process a vertical dimension; it reminded P. of his relationship with God who is a "refuge and strength, a very present help in trouble" (Ps. 46:1).

The minister's help in a few sessions enabled P. to pull out of his emotional tailspin. If P. had used the defenses of denial and withdrawal when his crisis hit—if he had not been open to help—he probably would have become trapped in a self-feeding, vicious cycle of anxiety, failure, and withdrawal from interpersonal relationships. His paralyzing anxiety would have caused him to fail as foreman, and this failure would have shattered his already shaky self-confidence, making failure on his next job almost certain. Spiraling failure and withdrawal would have increasingly magnified the very anxiety that produced them initially. His maladaptive responses might have become an ongoing part of his faulty equipment for meeting future crises. Turning to the minister was a reality-oriented response, enabling him to avoid this vicious cycle.[20]

More specifically, what are the nonconstructive responses to crises that lead into emotional tailspins and increase vulnerability to future failure and personality problems?

(1) Denial that a problem exists.
(2) Evasion of the problem (via alcohol or drugs, for example).
(3) Refusal to seek or accept help.
(4) Inability to express or master negative feelings.
(5) Failure to explore the nature of the crisis and alternative solutions.
(6) Projection onto others of major responsibility for causing and/or curing the crisis.
(7) Turning away from friends, family, and other potentially helpful persons.

The crisis counselor should be alert to the presence of these malignant responses in order to help the person move away from them and toward the following healthy ways of coping:

(1) Facing the problem.
(2) Enlarging one's understanding of it.
(3) Expressing and working through negative feelings such as resentment, anxiety, and guilt.
(4) Accepting responsibility for coping with the problem.
(5) Exloring alternative ways of handling it.
(6) Separating the changeable from the unchangeable in the situation, and avoiding wasting precious energy by trying to change the unchangeable.
(7) Surrendering grandiose, burdensome aspects of one's self-expectations.
(8) Opening channels of communication with helpful people among relatives, friends, and professional persons.
(9) Taking steps, however small, to handle the problem constructively.

The growing body of experience in crisis centers is providing valuable insights concerning the methodology of crisis counseling. Here are some of the techniques used in Los Angeles at the Benjamin Rush Center for Problems in Living:

There are several techniques which are utilized here. One is to desribe to the consultee the problem as you see it, integrating the present crisis into the perspective of his life pattern, still without losing the here-and-now orientation of the treatment. Another is to help him to gain a cognitive grasp of the issues at hand, at the same time bringing into the open his present feelings to which he may not have access. A third technique is to bring into play previously learned behavior patterns not being employed at present. A fourth is to explore with him the alternative mechanisms of coping with the problem, and different ways in which the problem may be seen and defined. A fifth is to consider re-peopling his social world and re-distributing the role relationships within the group. A sixth is to clarify and re-emphasize the individual's responsibility for his own behavior, decisions and way of life. . . . As time passes and the hoped-for reduction of anxiety and increased ability to cope occur, a summary is made of the changes which have occurred, thereby reinforcing the adaptive behaviors which are developing. Help is given to the consultee in making realistic plans for the future. . . . Also explored with him are specific ways of warding off future crises with the new coping tools which he has gained during the consultation.[21]

A TA Approach to Crisis Counseling

Eric Berne's therapeutic approach is useful in understanding crises and doing crisis counseling. For instance, with persons in a crisis marked by feelings of panic, it is often helpful to ask (after explaining Berne's Parent-Adult-Child system), "What part of you is afraid?" Being aware that one's inner Child, not his total self, is frightened releases the person from the paralysis of panic. The effect of this awareness is to help one's Adult regain control. In TA counseling—the Adult is strengthened by freeing it from the dominance of the Child and by *exercising* the Adult. Berne writes:

> Actionism is an essential feature of structural analysis. The Adult is regarded in the same light as a muscle, which increases in strength with exercise. Once the preliminary phases of decontamination and clarification are well under way, the patient is expected to practice Adult control. He must learn to keep the Adult running the show for relatively long periods. . . . What the Adult acquires is not exclusive dominance, but increasing *option*. It is he, and not the Child, who decides more and more effectively when the Child shall take over.[22]

Crisis counseling, in TA terms, consists of reducing the fear and guilt of the inner Child by allowing him or her to draw strength from the counselor's nurturing Parent temporarily, and, at the same time, activating and strengthening the Adult by encouraging the person to face reality and move into action. The counselor's Adult allies itself with the counselee's Adult in a joint strategy aimed at bringing the Child under control and releasing the Adult for coping with the problem in a reality-oriented way.

A firm, Adult approach helps a counselee control his or her inner Child. The counselor may say, in effect, "You have an Adult who can learn to exercise control." A firm stance helps frightened, disorganized persons to pull themselves together and mobilize their Adult coping abilities.

The ABCD Training Model

Here is a model I have found very useful in introducing seminarians, pastors, and trainees for lay caring teams to the basic steps in the process of helping people in crisis. The "A-B-C Method" of crisis helping was developed by psychiatrist Warren Jones for training the lay staff of a community crisis center in Pasadena, California.[23] His approach utilizes the essence of crisis intervention theory. This model incorporates my additions and interpretations of his original approach. (An illustration of how the model can be used in lay training is given in chapter 16.)

Hope-Action Counseling: How to Help a Person in Crisis

This method of crisis help consists of doing four things:

A. ACHIEVING A RELATIONSHIP (OF TRUST AND CARING)

—Listen nonjudgmentally and with caring to what the person is feeling and experiencing ("listening love"). Check out what you understand the person to be saying to see if you're on her or his wavelength.

—Let the person experience your warmth and concern by your attending, listening, and empathetic responses.

—Ask the person to tell you about the crisis—when it started, how it developed, how he or she feels about it now.

—Let the person know you'd like to work together in finding something that she or he can do to make the situation better.

—Affirm the person whenever possible—point out that you are aware of the strength it takes to carry the burden of the crisis, and to ask for help.

—See the person as having the ability to cope with the crisis and to learn and grow from handling it constructively, and let the person know you see him or her in this way.

B. BOIL DOWN THE PROBLEM (TO ITS MAJOR PARTS)

—As the person explores the crisis, help her or him sort out the pieces of the problem, separating those parts that he or she can do something about from those about which nothing can be done. (No use wasting energy on the latter.)

—Help the person choose one part of the problem on which to work first.

—Encourage the individual to describe previous efforts at a solution to that part of the problem. (No use repeating things that haven't worked.)

—Encourage the person to think of other possible solutions— perhaps suggest approaches for the person to consider.

—Help her or him examine each approach in terms of probable consequences—"what will probably happen if you . . . ?"

—Help the person decide which alternatives he or she wants to try *now*.

—Discuss all the person's resources—the "things you have going for you"—inner strengths, friends, family, spiritual resources, to help in coping.

—Keep affirming the person's efforts to deal with his or her crisis, expressing appreciation for the small step the person takes in coping responsibly.

C. CHALLENGE THE INDIVIDUAL TO TAKE CONSTRUCTIVE ACTION (ON SOME PART OF THE PROBLEM)

—Encourage the person to plan how to approach that part of the problem on which she or he has decided to focus; the plan should be realistic, with small achievable goals.

—Encourage commitment to implementing the action plan, beginning soon and on a realistic, agreed-upon time schedule.

—If the person resists acting on the problem, help him or her explore and resolve these resistances.

—Assure the individual that you will be available as a caring, concerned person as the struggle to implement her or his plan occurs.

—Support the person in crisis with realistic hope. Use religious resources such as prayer to strengthen the person's sense of responsibility, strength, and support by other people and by God.

—Don't agree to do anything that the individual can do himself or herself.

—Point out that as one begins to do something, however small, to improve the situation, one's feelings probably will improve—one will feel less depressed, more hopeful, and more self-esteem.

—Have the person phone you between sessions to let you know how the action plan worked; make a date to see her or him again soon.

—Encourage the individual to actively mobilize his or her resources for dealing with the crisis—spiritual, interpersonal, inner, practical, resources.

—Keep affirming the person by expressing appreciation for whatever she or he does to handle the crisis responsibly.

—Discuss the growth possibilities in coping successfully.

—Set a time to get together again soon.

D. DEVELOP AN ONGOING GROWTH-ACTION PLAN

—In the next meeting(s), ask the person to describe what happened in implementing the action plan, affirming successes (however small).

—Help the person develop further action goals for coping with other parts of the crisis. (What's the next step?) Repeat those parts of B and C that are necessary to help the person continue effective action.

—Tell the person that the more one copes effectively, the easier it becomes because one's coping muscles gain strength. Realistic hope based on the person's potentials and successes increases as one's coping strength is used and grows stronger.

—Encourage the person to reach out to help and be helped by others going through similar crises.

—Help the person become a part of an ongoing support and outreach group (a grief group, A.A., a prayer-support group, etc.).

—Help the person recognize growth as it occurs through constructive coping.

—After the heat of the crisis diminishes, encourage the person to reflect on and learn from the crisis experience.

—Help the person put the crisis in the context of his or her faith, and thus grow spiritually.

Care and Counseling in Developmental Crises

An understanding of the problems and possibilities of each life stage is an invaluable asset in doing pastoral care and counseling programs that are responsive to the changing issues of people at different phases of the life journey:

> When one puts on the glasses of hope and growth, each life stage, from birth to death, offers a fresh set of emerging strengths and possibilities that did not exist in previous stages. This awareness is the source of an unfolding hope. Each stage also has within it a new set of problems, limitations, frustrations, and losses. These painful realities bring many people to counseling. The strategy . . . is to help people deal with the problems and losses by developing the new strengths and possibilities of their particular life stage. The developmental orientation also implies a strategy of positive prevention that involves providing an abundance of easily available growth groups to help people develop the special treasures of each life stage.[24]

As a cognitive map for understanding the life stages, I use an expanded version of Eric Erikson's familiar stages of growth, augmented by recent studies of adult development and corrected by the insights of feminist developmental psychologists. Such a conceptual scheme can help a pastor and a congregation evaluate their present pastoral care program and strengthen it by developing new caring groups and programs to respond to the needs of those in particular developmental crises—e.g., new parents, empty-nest couples, recent retirees. I have discussed the care and counseling opportunities of the life stages elsewhere.[25]

In thinking about the nature and potentialities of crises, I am reminded that the Chinese word for "crisis" is actually two characters—one means "danger," the other "opportunity." How true of crises generally, but particularly of developmental crises! At each life stage one stands at a new fork in the path of one's life journey—one direction leads toward greater wholeness, the other toward diminished wholeness. Pastoral care aims at helping people choose to develop the unique possibilities of each stage and thus handle the new challenges, frustrations, and losses that stage brings. Crises and losses are a part of the very fabric of everyone's life. How we deal with them determines whether we stagnate or grow!

The church needs an innovative strategy for enabling people in the mid-years and beyond to discover and develop life in all its fullness during the second half of their lives. Unfortunately many people fit the description of the man whose tombstone should have carried the inscription: "Died at forty, buried at seventy." The growth perspective on the whole life cycle becomes more difficult but also increasingly vital to wholeness in the mid-years and beyond. Persons between forty and sixty-five already constitute a new majority in the United States. The median age of our population is rising each year.[26] To respond to the needs of the increasing numbers of older people, all our people-serving institutions must develop more imaginative programs of continuing education, growth groups, and community service aimed at enabling people in these age groups to develop more of their unused assets.

Churches have an unrivaled opportunity to develop exciting new programs of mutual care, learning, and outreach, because they have so many persons in the mid-years and retirement years among their members. Without neglecting the important care needs of children, youth, and young adults, congregations who define their mission as being lifelong wholeness centers, are now challenged to minister in more creative ways to those in the second half of life. In a church's program of outreach to the needs of its community, those over forty represent a gold mine of barely tapped knowledge, skills, influence, and wisdom gained from living. The lay caring team and the service and social action task force in a congregation should draw heavily on the expertise of these mature women and men.

Holistic Health and the Crises of Sickness

The renewed interest in holistic health and healing in the contemporary church has deep roots in the biblical heritage.[27] In the New Testament, the search for salvation is intertwined with the search for healing. In Jesus' great commission he sent his followers to heal as well as to baptize and preach the good news (Mark 16:18). Jesus has been called the "great physician" since the early centuries of the Christian era. The writings of the early church include specific instruction for healing the sick (James 5:13). A strong emphasis on spiritual healing of physical illness continued through medieval times. Unfortunately, this aspect of ministry has been relatively neglected in recent centuries in most mainstream churches. The focus of the modern pastoral counseling movement on psychotherapeutic methodologies and on the findings of the psychological sciences has been a major source of the movement's vitality. But it also has contributed to the continued neglect of the heritage of spiritual healing. It is well to remind ourselves that the words health, heal, hale, whole, and holy are all derived from the same or closely-related Old English root words. One of the exciting challenges of the future is to recover the riches of this heritage and integrate these with the new resources of contemporary counseling, psychotherapy, and holistic health.

During the time I served as a hospital chaplain, I often felt frustrated by some hospital personnel who perceived my role as exclusively that of bringing religious resources, anxiety-reduction, and comfort to patients—especially when medical treatment had done all it could and failed. Although I regarded those traditional functions as valuable, I sensed that a minister's role with the sick also had another significant dimension—to help enable healing. Experience in recent years has increased my appreciation of the great importance of this second aspect of the minister's role with the sick. The skillful use of listening, caring, and counseling methods with those who are ill can help them become more open to the God-given healing resources within their bodies, minds, spirits, and relationships. When those counseling skills have a vertical dimension and use religious resources appropriately, they can be particularly helpful in enabling people to help people open themselves to experience the healing energies of the ever-present love of God—the ultimate source of all healing.

The holistic health movement, a flourishing development that is influencing more and more health professionals, throws new light on the nature and importance of the clergyperson's role, as an essential part of any whole-person approach to healing. This movement has the potential of accelerating the process of recovering and enlarging the vision of the Christian heritage of healing. Four key principles are foundational in holistic health thinking and practice:

(1) *Health is much more than the absence of illness; it is the presence of "high level wellness,"* a concept akin to "life . . . in all its fullness" (John 10:10, NEB). There are as many degrees of wellness as there are of sickness. (2) *High level wellness involves wholeness in all six interdependent dimensions of persons' lives*—physical, psychological, interpersonal, environmental, institutional, and spiritual. (3) *The two major determinants of levels* of wellness or sickness are one's life-style and the level of chronic stress in one's life. (4) *The two keys to maintaining high level wellness are wellness awareness and understanding* (achieved through education) and *self-responsibility,* meaning accepting primary responsibility for living in ways that enhance one's wellness.[28]

To become more effective centers for nurturing lifelong wholeness centered in Spirit, churches must recover their heritage of healing and enable it to flower by integrating it with the insights and methods of the holistic health movement. Counseling pastors can have a strategic role in this exciting development. Here are some of the health-nurturing things that wholeness-oriented ministers can do and teach key lay persons to do in holistic pastoral care and counseling, education, and growth groups. *They can teach people to:*

—Take primary responsibility for their own wellness rather than continuing to project responsibility onto medical practitioners.

—Make friends with their bodies, learning to respect and care for this aspect of themselves lovingly as good mothers-fathers to themselves.

—Practice eating-for-wellness by learning health-nurturing nutrition.

—Do vigorous exercise they *enjoy* several times a week—walking, biking, jogging, swimming—to keep their body-mind-spirit tuned up.

—Evaluate their life-style and the values it reflects, and revise it so that it will foster wellness, not sickness.

—Learn one or more whole-body relaxation techniques to enable them to reduce stress and center in their "serenity zone" for a time every day.

—Live in an ecologically sound, environmentally aware and caring way, so as to help protect and enhance the biosphere for themselves and their children and the whole human family.

—Experience regularly the healing energy of play and laughter (*at* themselves and the absurdity of life, and *with* others).

—Revitalize their body-mind-spirit-relationships by opening themselves through prayer and meditation to the energies of God's here-and-now love and thus renewing the sense of meaning and mission in their lives.

—Share with others (including their children and friends) their insights and experiences of healing and wellness. Wellness is contagious. It increases as we share the wellness we have at that moment.

—Use creative imaging regularly for activating the self-healing energies and immune systems of the body, thus participating in their own recovery from illness and in the positive prevention of illness.

Here is a summary of an imaging approach developed by physician O. Carl Simonton and psychologist Stephanie Matthews-Simonton in their work with cancer patients. This method can be used by people to help activate the healing resources of their bodies in any type of major or minor illness. It is designed to complement and supplement, not replace conventional medical treatment. I have added a *spiritual* healing thrust to the Simontons' approach: (step 5)

(1) (Full body relaxation) Go to a quiet room with soft lighting. Shut the door, sit in a comfortable chair, feet flat on the floor . . . ["/" means stop reading and close your eyes while you do this.] Become aware of your breathing. Take in a few deep breaths, and as you let out each breath, mentally say the word, "relax."/ . . . Tense the muscles of your face and

around your eyes, squeezing tightly, then relax them and feel the relaxation spreading through you body./ Move slowly down your body [tensing and releasing]—jaw, neck, shoulders, back, upper and lower arms, hands, chest, abdomen, thighs, calves, ankles—feel—until every part of your body is more relaxed. For each part of the body, mentally picture the tension, then picture the tension melting away, allowing relaxation./ Now picture yourself in pleasant, natural surroundings—whatever feels comfortable for you. Mentally fill in the details of color, sound, texture./

(2) Create a mental picture of any ailment or pain that you have now, visualizing it in a form that makes sense to you. [Hold this and subsequent pictures in your mind for at least a minute or two]/

(3) Picture any treatment you are receiving and see if either eliminating the source of the ailment or pain or strengthening your body's ability to heal itself./

(4) Picture your body's natural defenses and natural [healing] processes eliminating the source of the ailment or pain [e.g., picture the millions of white blood cells as tiny vacuum sweepers or pac men cleansing your body of the infection or tension or other causes of your pain/.]

(5) Picture a soft Light, a little above your head and just in front of you, the healing energy of God's love./ Picture this Light flowing into your whole body—bathing, cleansing, and healing every cell, particularly in the area of your ailment or pain./

(6) Imagine yourself healthy and free of the ailment or pain, [full of energy and enjoying life.]

(7) Give yourself a mental pat on the back for participating in your recovery. See yourself doing this relaxation-mental imagery exercise three times a day, staying awake and alert as you do it.[29]

Some people find it helpful to record these instructions with appropriate time intervals between each step, so that they can keep their eyes closed while doing the exercise.

An imaging exercise such as this can also be used helpfully with some psychological and interpersonal problems. Before attempting to teach this method to persons with physical or psychophysiological illnesses, it is essential to read and digest *Getting Well Again*. The approach can be presented by describing to the person (briefly) how the regular use of this method by them *may* enhance their self-healing, physically and/or psychological, and then asking them if they would like to try it. In major, life-threatening illnesses such as cancer, it is important to talk with the person's physician to discover if she or he sees any problem in the use of this form of healing ministry with this particular patient.

The fact that this approach seems to be effective in enhancing the healing processes in some people is another indication of the enormous influence of one's mind and spirit on one's physical wellness. The implications for ministry, of imaging approaches such as this are profound indeed! Such methods can be integrated with ancient rites of healing in the Christian tradition such as intercessory prayer for the sick and the laying on of hands. Ministers who are skilled in counseling *and* in traditional and contemporary healing methods can contribute in unique ways to the self-healing of persons. The holistic health movement can provide new bridges of communication and collaboration among those in the healing professions, including the ministry. It can lead to an increased awareness of the centrality of spiritual health in whole-person wellness, and the importance of well-trained ministers in that dimension of healing.

Reality-Practice Session

PARISHIONER'S ROLE: Recall a significant crisis in your own life and let youself relive that now. Seek the minister's help in dealing with your unfinished feelings, making the decisions and taking the action needed to resolve this crisis fully. Or, role play someone you know well who is going through a painful crisis. Get inside that person's situation and feelings, so that you can *be* that person as empathetically as possible. You may find it helpful to role play someone you have been attempting to help with less than overwhelming success.

PASTOR'S ROLE: Use the ABCD approach to crisis help as you are counseling with this person. Be aware of the ways in which your own experiences of crises and losses influence your counseling, positively or negatively.

OBSERVER-COACH'S ROLE: Help the pastor use the ABCD method effectively.

Recommended Reading

Crisis Counseling

Ernest Bruder, *Ministering to Deeply Troubled People* (Englewood Cliffs, N.J.: Prentice-Hall, 1974). Insights from his long experience as a mental hospital chaplain.

Gerald Caplan, *Principles of Preventive Psychiatry* (New York: Basic Books, 1964). Describes the basic methods of crisis intervention.

Lowell G. Colston, *Pastoral Care with Handicapped Persons* (Philadelphia: Fortress Press, 1978). Based on his own experience with a major handicap.

Charles V. Gerkin, *Crisis Experience in Modern Life: Theory and Theology for Pastoral Care* (Nashville: Abingdon Press, 1979). Reviews the meaning and nature of crises from a theological perspective and draws implications for pastoral responses.

Edgar N. Jackson, *Coping with the Crises in Your Life* (New York: Hawthorn Books, 1974). Discusses both developmental and accidental crises in terms of therapy and growth possibilities.

Eugene Kennedy, *Crisis Counseling* (New York: Continuum Publishing Corp., 1981). A guide for nonprofessional counselors.

David Lester and Gene W. Brockopp, eds., *Crisis Intervention and Counseling by Telephone* (Springfield, Ill.: Charles C. Thomas, 1973). Reviews some of the ways the telephone is used by suicide prevention centers, teen-age hotlines, psychotherapists, etc.

Howard N. Stone, *Crisis Counseling* (Philadelphia: Fortress Press, 1976). An introduction to the theory and practice of crisis counseling.

David K. Switzer, *The Minister as Crisis Counselor* (Nashville: Abingdon Press, 1974). A thorough review of crisis counseling methods in pastoral ministry.

Developmental Crises: Mid-Years and Retirement Years

Robert N. Butler, *Why Survive? Being Old in America* (New York: Harper & Row, 1975). A challenging confrontation of the inhumanities of aging.

Robert N. Butler and Myrna Lewis, *Aging and Mental Health: Positive Psychosocial Approaches* (St. Louis: C. V. Mosby, 1973).

William M. Clements, ed., *Care and Counseling of the Aging* (Philadelphia: Fortress Press, 1979). A guide to creative ministry with the aging. Annotated bibliography.

_____, ed., *Ministry with the Aging* (San Francisco: Harper & Row, 1981). Explores the context, foundations, new challenges, and designs of this ministry.

James E. Birren and K. Warner Schaie, eds., *Handbook of the Psychology of Aging* (New York: Van Nostrand Reinhold Co., 1977). Papers on the psychology of the later years.

Howard Clinebell, *Growth Counseling for Mid-Years Couples* (Philadelphia: Fortress Press, 1977). An autobiographically oriented discussion of ways to make the most of the mid-years, individually and as a couple. Annotated bibliography.

Seward Hiltner, ed. *Toward a Theology of Aging* (New York: Human Sciences Press, 1975). Papers on the theological issues and challenges of aging.

Bernice Hunt and Morton Hunt, *Prime Time: A Guide to the Pleasures and Opportunities of the New Middle Age.* (New York: Stein and Day, 1975). A personal and practical discussion of the new possibilities of the mid-years.

Henri J. M. Nouwen and Walter J. Gaffnew, *Aging: The Fulfillment of Life* (New York: Image Books, 1976). A discussion of aging and ministry in poetic prose.

Eda J. LaShan, *The Wonderful Crisis of Middle Age* (New York: David McKay, 1973). Suggestions for self-actualization in the mid-years.

Carol LeFevre and Perry LeFevre, *Aging and the Human Spirit* (Chicago: Exploration Press, 1981). Readings in religion and gerontology.

Bernice L. Neugarten, ed., *Middle Age and Aging* (Chicago: University of Chicago Press, 1968). A reader in the social psychology of aging.

Paul Tournier, *Learning to Grow Old* (New York: Harper & Row, 1972). A practical, spiritually-oriented guide by a holistic physician.

Holistic Healing and Health

Donald B. Ardell, *High Level Wellness: An Alternative to Doctors, Drugs and Disease* (Emmaus, Pa.: Rodale Press, 1977). An overview of the principles of holistic health. Bibliography with depth annotation.

Howard Clinebell, "Growth Resources in Holistic Health, Biofeedback, and Body Therapies," chapter 8 in *Contemporary Growth Therapies* (Nashville: Abingdon Press, 1981). An overview of healing insights and methods.

Norman Cousins, *Anatomy of an Illness, Reflections on Healing and Regeneration* (New York: W. W. Norton, 1979). Describes his self-healing by means of laughter.

Morton T. Kelsey, *Healing and Christianity* (New York: Harper & Row, 1973). A study of healing in the Jewish and Christian traditions.

Kenneth R. Pelletier, *Mind as Healer, Mind as Slayer* (New York: Delta Books, 1977). Documents the power of the mind to heal or hurt the body.

Anne Kent Rush, *Getting Clear Body Work for Women* (New York: Random House, 1973). Health-nurturing exercises for women (and men).

John A. Sanford, *Healing and Wholeness* (New York: Paulist Press, 1977). Jungian and biblical approaches to healing.

O. Carl Simonton, Stephanie Matthews-Simonton, and James Creighton, *Getting Well Again* (Los Angeles: J. P. Tarcher, 1978). Describes their use of imaging with cancer patients.

Granger E. Westberg, *Theological Roots of Wholistic Health Care* (Hinsdale: Ill.: Wholistic Health Center, 1979). Discusses the biblical foundation of healing and the Westberg model of wholistic centers.

Bereavement
Care and Counseling

Blessed are those who mourn, for they shall be comforted.

—MATTHEW 5:4

He comforts us in all our troubles, so that we in turn may be able to comfort others in any trouble of theirs.

—II CORINTHIANS 1:4 (NEB)

In the midst of winter, I finally learned that there was in me an invincible summer.

—ALBERT CAMUS[1]

Bereavement is the universal human crisis, striking everyone sooner or later. Clergy are the key professionals in helping people with this crisis. Wayne Oates observes:

> Through the centuries the pastor has been the primary person responsible for dealing with the bereaved . . . Whether or not the pastor has accepted these responsibilities, carried them out with skill and wisdom, or even appreciated the weight of the expectations placed upon him or her, nevertheless the pastor is the one to whom people still look for the care of the bereaved.[2]

Ministers are the only professional persons with training in counseling who have automatic entrée to the world of most sorrowing people. This gives clergy an unparalleled opportunity and responsibility to be effective guides and companions of the bereaved as they walk through their shadowed valley of loss. Obviously it behooves pastors to develop a high degree of competence in bereavement care and counseling.

There is no dimension of the pastoral care ministry in which the stakes are higher in terms of human wholeness. Psychiatrist Erich Lindemann, a pioneer in grief research, reports:

Studies show that many people become sick following the death of a loved person. A great many more hospital patients have had a recent bereavement than people in the general population. And in psychiatric hospitals, about six times as many are recently bereaved than in the general population. . . . Furthermore, in a great many conditions, both physical and psychological, the mechanics of grieving play a significant role.[3]

Grief is involved in all significant changes, losses, and life transitions, not just in the death of a loved person. Every life event on the Holmes-Rahe stress scale involves some loss and therefore grieving. There is evidence that many psychophysiological (psychosomatic) illnesses are related to unhealed grief. The same is true of much alcoholism and other addictive illnesses (including food addiction). Several years ago, the staff of the pastoral counseling and growth center of which I am a clinical director, decided to ask all persons who came for help if they had experienced major changes or losses within the preceding two years. More than a third of our clients could identify a painful loss or cluster or losses. In many cases, a major loss was correlated with the onset or dramatic worsening of the painful symptoms that brought them for help. Included were persons with a wide range of presenting problems—depression, marriage and family crises, sexual problems, job difficulties, substance abuse, psychophysiological illnesses, and religious problems. Also included were persons with general spiritual malaise—boredom, zestlessness, feelings of deadness, lack of creative energy and purpose in life.

Blocked, unfinished grief takes a heavy toll, sapping one's creative juices. The longer the healing is delayed, the more costly the protracted grief is to the person's wholeness. The death of my younger sister, Ruth, on her first birthday when I was four and a half, cast a dark shadow over our family. We all paid a high price for not knowing how to experience healing of our grief. More than thirty years of reduced aliveness, chronic drivenness, and periodic depression in my life followed Ruth's death before my infected but hidden grief wound was eventually lanced in my therapy so that healing could occur. If our pastor had known how to help our family express and work through our devastating feelings of loss and guilt, we all could have been spared years of unnecessary suffering and diminished wholeness.

There is a virtual epidemic of unhealed and largely unrecognized grief wounds in most congregations and communities, particularly those with a sizable group of older persons. Life is a continuing series of separations and losses, small and large. Handling bereavement is an indispensable part of human growth. Many losses are potential opportunities for personal and spiritual growth. The frequency of losses accelerate with the passing years. For this reason, learning to handle losses without being crippled by them is an essential skill of creative aging. The decline of community support and of corporate rites of passage and mourning in our society has made it more difficult to recover from grief. The uprootedness of the lonely crowd in megapolis has deprived millions of people of a community of caring. Personal crises and tragedies are exacerbated by the loneliness and social crises in our world.

In the last decade, I have asked many adult groups, both lay and professional, "How many of you have had painful changes or losses within the last few years?" In most groups, depending on their ages, from 35 to 50 percent raise their hands. Since most of us are adept at hiding our wounds (even from ourselves), my hunch is that the percentage of those with grief wounds may actually have been higher. A new strategy is needed to help those with unhealed grief experience healing. Congregations and their pastors must have a central role in devising and implementing such a strategy.

The loss of someone who has been a significant part of one's world of meanings and satisfactions is a psychological amputation. How traumatic it is depends on the nature and importance of the relationship in one's life. The responses people employ in coping with major bereavements are the same ones they have learned in coping with previous deprivations, frustrations, or losses—small or large. These are the coping skills they learned from their culture, as filtered through the responses to loss by their parents. If the individual has learned constructive, reality-oriented coping skills, his/her psyche will follow a somewhat predictable process of working through the mixture of powerful feelings resulting from the bereavement and making the adjustments required to live without what has been lost. Lindemann calls this process by which the grief wound heals, "grief work." The work is by the grieving person's own psyche.[4]

Healing the Grief Wound

The following chart lists the five tasks of this process and the type of help that facilitates the completion of each task.[5]

Grief Work Task	*Help Needed*
1. Experiencing shock, numbness, denial and gradually accepting the reality of the loss.	A ministry of caring and presence, practical help, and spiritual comfort.
2. Experiencing, expressing and working through painful feelings—e.g., guilt, remorse, apathy, anger, resentment, yearning, despair, anxiety, emptiness, depression, loneliness, panic, disorientation, loss of clear identity, physical symptoms, etc.	A ministry of caring, and responsive listening to encourage full cartharsis.
3. Gradual acceptance of the loss and putting one's life back together minus what was lost, making decisions and coping with the new reality; unlearning old ways of satisfying one's needs and learning new ways to satisfy these needs. Saying "goodbye" and reinvesting one's life energy in other relationships.	A ministry of crisis care and counseling, facilitating reality testing, and support in the difficult tasks of rebuilding one's life (the ABCD approach).
4. Putting one's loss in a wider context of meaning and faith; learning from the loss.	A ministry of facilitating spiritual growth.
5. Reaching out to others experiencing similar losses for mutual help.	A ministry of enabling outreach to others.

Except for the first two, these grief work tasks do not necessarily occur in lineal sequence. For example, coping with the new reality brought by the loss (task 3) begins almost immediately after the loss and continues throughout the other tasks. (These tasks will be discussed now in terms of the death of a loved person; the tasks in other severe losses are similar.)

When death or any severe loss strikes, the usual response is feelings of psychological numbness and shock (nature's anesthesia) mixed with feelings of unreality—of being in a nightmare from which one expects to awaken. The mind cannot yet accept the overwhelming pain—the reality that the person is really gone. Accepting the full reality of the loss must eventually occur or the healing will be incomplete. This acceptance must occur gradually, usually over a period of months.

The minister's role in facilitating normal grief is to cooperate with the psyche's inner process of recovery. During this shock phase, effective caring includes using supportive care methods, including gratifying dependency needs. Severe losses activate the inner Child (in TA terms), often bringing painful feelings of anxiety, deprivation, and abandonment. The need to be comforted is intense. I remember nothing the minister said at my mother's funeral, but I recall with appreciation that he put his hand on my shoulder as he left the funeral parlor after the service. Acts of ministry, including familiar scripture, prayers, hymns, and rituals often bring quiet comfort to the bereaved. Both physical touch and gifts of food are symbolic nonverbal ways of communicating caring and nurture. A congregation's lay caring or grief recovery team should surround the grieving individual and family with the supportive caring they need. The meal after the funeral affirms the ongoingness of life in spite of the loss. Eating together becomes a kind of communion meal—a way of saying, "we can and must go on, together."

In seeking to understand why some people's grief wounds healed relatively soon, some very slowly, and some not at all, after the 1942 Coconut Grove nightclub fire in the Boston area, Lindemann made a striking discovery—*experiencing and expressing the agonizing feelings fully is an indispensable part of the healing process!* Blocked feelings = delayed healing. Thus, the second grief work task is facilitated by responsive listening, which enables the full catharsis of whatever feelings the loss has triggered in the person. These can include any feeling from total despair to relief and joy. Often the feelings are ambivalent and conflicted. The catharsis task begins intermittently as the numbness and denial gradually diminish, and the stark reality of the loss is allowed to enter awareness. In major losses, the working through of feelings occurs on many different levels and usually takes at least a year. Several years are often required in severe loss such as the death of a spouse or child. My father has been dead for nearly seven years. Most of my feelings about his death have been worked through and released. Yet, recently I experienced a wave of sadness and nostalgia when I saw a corner full of fishing tackle in the room of an elderly man I was visiting. (My dad loved to fish.)

To help people do the healing catharsis of their grief work, one must go against the cultural tendency to avoid painful feelings. During the visit immediately after the death, as the funeral is being planned, the minister should encourage the bereaved family to talk together about their loved one—the circumstances of the death, and the memories and attributes they most cherish about that person. (These cherished memories can well be incorporated in the memorial message during the funeral.)

One purpose of the funeral is to facilitate the emotional releases of grief feelings. What is said during the service should be straight and clear about the painful reality of the loss, so far as this life is concerned, and the appropriateness of mourning. Nothing should be said implying that stoicism in the face of grief is a sign of real strength or Christian virtue, or that one whose faith is genuine will not experience agonizing grief. The funeral should include familiar hymns, prayers, and scripture that bring enspirited comfort and also help release dammed-up feelings. A grief-enabling meditation on a text such as "Jesus wept" (John 11:35) or "Blessed are those who mourn" (Matt. 5:4) can help to give permission to grieve to those who need this. (The Greek word for "mourn" in the latter text refers to the most open and demonstrative type of grieving and lamentation.) The funeral is also a service of thanksgiving for the deceased person, a service of mutual support of the bereaved by the Christian community, and an affirmation of the beliefs of this community that helps the bereaved put the loss in the larger context of a life-affirming faith. The pastor can help the family and friends mourn by expressing her or his own feeling of grief and loss, and by creating appropriate rituals of participation such as inviting everyone to put a flower on the casket as they leave the gravesite.

It is crucial that caring support of the family continue during the weeks and months following the funeral. Many people are unaware that the bereaved continue to need special support during the extended process of working through the loss.

Catharsis of feelings can be encouraged by asking questions such as these during post-funeral visits with the family: "What have you been feeling since the funeral?" "What sort of memories keep coming back?" "How often have you let yourself cry?" "Have you had trouble keeping going?" "Would you tell me more about the way he/she died?"[6] The two feelings that most often infect the grief wound are unresolved *guilt* (remorse, shame) and *anger* (resentment, rage). It is important therefore to ask questions such as, "If you had your relationship to live over, what would you do differently?," "Do you feel much anger or resentment?," and "Have you been able to express these feelings?" These questions should only be asked when the pastor is willing to help the person express, talk through, and begin to release and resolve the intense feelings they may elicit.

The way people respond to losses varies greatly depending on their own resources, the quality and length of the relationship, the timeliness of the loss, whether the death was expected, and the nature of the death. The more dependent and ambivalent the relationship, the longer and more complicated the recovery process. Grieving following the untimely deaths of children or young people is usually exceedingly difficult. Sudden, unexpected or violent deaths usually are followed by more extended and difficult grief than slow, expected deaths. There are several reasons for this—there has been no anticipatory grief work before the death; there is greater shock and often greater anger; there are more unfinished aspects of the relationship, producing greater guilt; the vacant social roles of the deceased have not been gradually filled. Deaths where the body is lost or terribly mutilated (so that the casket is left closed) often result in protracted recovery because the bereaved persons are not able to accept the reality of the loss and deal with the dead person's body image. Since our own identity and that of others is integrally related to body images, having an opportunity to deal with feelings about the body is often essential for the grief wound to heal fully. The traditional wake or visitation time before the funeral, when the body is visible, can be a grief-enabling experience for many mourners.

The difficult grief task of rebuilding one's life without the lost person involves unlearning countless habitual responses, learning new behavior to meet needs formerly met by the deceased, and making countless decisions about how to cope with the new problems the loss brings. Church members in general and the lay caring team in particular should be guided in functioning as a substitute extended family for those who lack a support system, offering whatever practical help and emotional support is needed. Such support can take many forms—e.g., a widow who has never handled her finances or a widower who has never cooked for himself need help in learning these skills. Both emotional support and reality-testing are needed as bereaved persons make decisions and begin to venture out into new relationships and experiences— e.g., going to social gatherings without the lost person, dating, beginning a new job. Two signs that persons are moving toward the completion of the recovery process are "saying good-bye" (emotionally) to the lost person and reinvesting some of that energy in other relationships. The grief wound cannot heal fully until one has *accepted the reality* of the loss, *surrendered* one's emotional tie to the lost person, and begun to form other relationships to provide new sources of interpersonal satisfaction.

Religious resources have much more than a supportive-comforting function in bereavement. The death of another confronts us with our own mortality. Existential anxiety (about nonbeing) can be handled constructively only within the context of a vital faith. The symbols and affirmations of one's religious tradition can touch deep levels of the psyche, gradually renewing the feelings of basic trust that alone can enable persons to handle existential anxiety creatively. Therefore, the minister's teaching and priestly roles are important in helping the bereaved put their loss in the context of faith. A pastor's skills in facilitating spiritual growth may help grieving people enlarge their faith and revitalize their relationship with God.

In crisis and bereavement counseling, the original root of the word "religion"—*religio*, to bind together—has dynamic significance. When shattering loss fragments one's life, vital religion may help bind it together, restoring some sense of coherence and meaning. The crisis of death confronts some people with the poverty or obsolescence of their beliefs and values. This awareness can open them to the growth process of revising and renewing their spiritual lives. A renewed faith usually develops only after one has finished much of one's painful grief work and is able to reflect on and learn from the painful loss.

In working with the bereaved (as with the permanently handicapped), it is crucial to help the person learn to distinguish what can and what cannot be changed in the situation. AA's familiar "Serenity Prayer" (authored by Reinhold Niebuhr) may be useful in such counseling:

> Grant me the serenity to accept the things I cannot change,
> The courage to change the things I can,
> And the wisdom to know the difference.

In discussing crisis therapy Gerald Caplan states:

> Not all problems are capable of solution by removal of the threat to need satisfaction; but in these cases, too, a "healthy" type of activity, consisting of *an act of resignation* of this avenue of need satisfaction and *its replacement by alternatives,* can be differentiated from "unhealthy" problem avoidance in which no decision is made and no conflict resolved. Thus, in the crisis of bereavement . . . the sufferer must actively resign himself to the impossibility of ever again satisfying his needs through interaction with the deceased. He must psychologically "bury the dead"; only after this has been done will he be free to seek gratification of these needs from alternative persons. Those who cope maladaptively with bereavement may pretend that the loved one is not dead, or they may magically introject his image by taking his chracteristics into their own personality, and they will thus evade the painful act of resignation. This is likely to result in their energies remaining bound up with the deceased, so that they are not free to love others.[7]

The Grief Wound that Does Not Heal

In normal recovering from grief, persons gradually deal with those ambivalent feelings that are present in all close relationships. If, instead, persons continue to overidealize the deceased, they are utilizing the defenses of denial and repression. These defenses enable them to avoid the agony of the loss, but they also prevent the grief wound from healing. The wound is infected and cannot heal until the person deals with the repressed feelings.

Here are some danger signs that may indicate pathological grief if they persist over several months or longer: increased withdrawal from relationships and normal activities; the absence of mourning; undiminished mourning; severe depression that does not lift;

severe psychosomatic problems; disorientation; personality changes; severe, undiminishing guilt, anger, phobias, or loss of interest in life; continuing escape by means of drugs or alcohol; feelings of inner deadness. Skillful bereavement counseling in the early phases of such maladaptive responses, may help heal some pathological grief. When ministers encounter what appears to be blocked grief work, they should encourage the person to talk about and express feelings about their relationship with the deceased, and to continue to do so until these feelings are faced and talked through. By responding acceptingly to tentative expressions of mixed or negative feelings, further catharsis is facilitated. Along with resentment and/or anger (toward the lost person, God, relatives, physicians, etc.) there is usually a load of guilt about these feelings that must also be worked through. The grief wound must heal from the inside. Healing cannot be forced, but the counseling relationship can help facilitate the process. If pathological grief symptoms persist after several months in spite of the minister's efforts, referral to a competent psychotherapist is imperative. The longer grief work is delayed, the more painful and costly to a person's mental and spiritual health the grief will be, and the more psychotherapeutic skills will be required for healing.

It is important to emphasize that grief *per se* is not an illness. It is a normal human healing process for which most people have adequate resources—resources that they can be helped to mobilize by pastoral caring. Only when a grief wound is infected does it become a pathological process requiring counseling or psychotherapy. In our death-denying culture, many grief wounds become infected. Most of these infections are relatively minor and will respond to the helping skills of a counseling pastor.

Setting Up and Leading a Grief Healing Group

The new strategy needed to enable a congregation to minister more effectively to the bereaved, has three parts. The first is to inform members of the congregation, through sermons and adult education programs, about the nature and importance of grief work, and how they can enable this healing in themselves, their families, and friends. The second part of a strategy is to train a carefully selected lay-caring team to carry much of the load of supportive caring of persons with normal grief in the congregation (see chapter 16). There are too many persons going through a variety of crises, losses and transitions in a typical congregation, and the process of full recovery is too extended (at least a year and often much more) for a pastor working alone to respond fully to these multiple pastoral care needs.

The pastor of a downtown church in Minneapolis discovered that ministering to the bereaved was requiring more of his time than anything else. As he became aware of the many widows and widowers in his congregation, he realized that he had a rich pastoral care resource at his fingertips:

> He invited these widowed people to meet with him to plan a lay ministry to the bereaved . . . Each year there is a training period of six weeks for new recruits to this ministry. When someone dies, the pastor selects a grief minister from this group and introduces him or her to the bereaved. This grief minister commits him or herself to minister to the bereaved person or family for a year, making regular contacts that complement the pastor's ministry.[8]

This lay ministry has continued for fifteen years, helping that congregation become a healing community for many bereaved persons.

The third part of a strategy for helping the bereaved is for the pastor to set up and lead (or co-lead) a grief healing group periodically. Such a group is both an efficient way of deepening the grief ministry of a congregation and a means of beginning the training of a lay crisis and grief team. Participating in such a group can help one both finish one's own grief work and learn to help other grieving persons. I cannot think of any one thing that a pastor or congregation could do that would have greater healing impact than providing regular opportunities for grieving people to participate in such a grief group.

The capacity of human beings to turn miserable minuses into at least partial pluses—to use crises and losses as challenges to grow—is one of the great things about being human. But to use bereavement in this way requires two things—being in relationships of mutual caring and finding spiritual meaning in the loss. Grief healing groups are settings within which these two transformational experiences often occur.

Grief groups are relatively easy to set up and lead.[9] In a congregation, a group can be drawn together simply by the minister's inviting all those who have experienced losses within the last two or three years to attend. Personal invitations by phone and a general invitation in the church bulletin or newsletter to reach others is all that is usually necessary to assemble a group. Persons with a variety of types of losses can be included in the same group, although it is helpful to have at least two persons with similar losses (e.g., divorce, death, retirement) in a group to give each other the special empathy that comes from persons who know each other's loss from the inside.

Several grief group formats have been used effectively in churches. The most common model is a series of weekly one and a half or two hour meetings, for four to eight weeks. Such groups often recontract at the end of the agreed-upon time to extend the length of the group to deal with unfinished issues.

A second format is to meet for a longer time on a single day or a weekend retreat. Bob Kemper, pastor of a church near Chicago, reports that a three hour grief sharing session in his church was remarkably effective. Twenty-six people attended the session.

> The name of the group was 'Alone/Together' and so I spoke of the loneliness we feel in coping with a loss and the power of fellowship in helping us cope with losses. Then I spoke of the anxieties we all have in facing a new experience, suggested that most of us did not want to be here . . . I suggested that they had already done the hardest part of the day, namely, just coming to the gathering . . . Finally, I announced the ground rules, explaining that each was free to respond as they were moved to do so. Here it would not be necessary to play the part of the brave widow, or the one who always had their feelings in check. Here it would be all right to cry or even to laugh if that is what their feelings required.[10]

After this introduction, the pastor led a brief worship service in the church's chapel, including the singing of hymns, appropriate scripture and a short meditation on the promises of God. Then the group returned to the church parlor for Bible study of I Corinthians 15. Following this, each person was invited to write a letter to a friend beginning, "Last week at church we studied St. Paul's writings and the new insight that came to me was _____." A few of the letters were shared with the group. Next Kemper presented the stages of grief as outlined in Granger Westberg's book *Good Grief*. He paused between each stage for a reality check, asking if something like that had been a part of their experience. This offered opportunity for dialogue, shared tears, and mutual support to develop within the group.

Lunch together was a time of rich informal sharing around the tables. When the dishes were cleared, Kemper invited the group to describe resources—books, people, activities—they had found helpful or disappointing. At the close, the group decided to meet again and agreed upon a time. The session was closed by joining hands around the table for shared prayers for each other and thanksgiving for their experiences together. In describing the group, the pastor declares: "Of all the many activities I have participated in this year, none has given me more personal satisfaction or made me feel as useful or more like a minister than the establishment of a grief growth group in our congregation."[11] This model demonstrates that healing *can* occur even in a relatively large group that meets for a relatively brief time.

Pastoral Care of the Dying and Their Families

Ministering to the terminally ill and their families is a vitally important pastoral care opportunity. I remember vividly the pain and the richness of being with individuals and families as their pastor, during the last weeks, days, and hours of a terminal illness. Their heartfelt appreciation was a clear indication of how much they needed supportive pastoral care. Frequent brief calls in the hospital or (if the dying person is fortunate) in the home or hospice facility, are needed. If possible, it is important to stay with a family who desires the minister's presence during the final hours of the person's dying.

Since writing the first edition of this book, I have learned much about the experience of dying. My teachers have been five dying persons—my parents and Charlotte's parents, and a dear friend, Lois, who died in her mid-years after a long struggle with cancer. Shortly before her death, I asked Lois if she would be willing to talk in detail about her experience, so that I could learn from her and share her insights about dying with others (as I am doing here). She was glad to do so.[12] In our conversation, she spoke of the intense need she felt to have people *really* listen to her swirling and changing feelings as her malignancy gradually spread. She described how let down she felt when some of her friends and one of her doctors changed the subject or tried to give her superficial reassurances, because of their own discomfort with her feelings. She said that among her many feelings, the five identified in terminally ill persons by Elisabeth Kübler-Ross (denial, anger, bargaining, depression, acceptance) would come and go, not following a particular sequence.[13] Lois told of experiencing fresh anger at each new stage of her progressive illness and of the help of a friend who hugged her (after she had been told that the cancer had spread to her vital organs) and exclaimed, "Damn! Damn! Damn!," thus sharing her anger. She described her multiple grief at "losing everything," and how this made experiences such as touching her children, talking with friends, and looking at the beautiful mountains both urgent and very special. The preciousness of being alive made little things very important, she said. Lois talked of her fear of the possible pain and loss of control she might experience during her dying and her feelings of jealousy when she saw an old couple walking together (and her embarrassment about these feelings). She spoke of the importance of not postponing dealing with issues between herself and others. I shared my perception that she had in recent months become even more vital and alive than she had been before. She responded that when you know your future here will probably be short, it makes the present more important. As we concluded our conversation, she said it had been very meaningful to her to talk about her experiences so fully. I told her how deeply I had been touched by all that she had shared. Louis helped me see more clearly that the process of dying *can be*, for some, an important stage of their continuing growth as persons!

Each person's dying is as unique as his or her living. But five things seem to help some people use their dying to gain wider perspectives, mobilize new strengths, and thus die well: (1) *Having a small caring community* of persons who will listen and give warm support. Dying is both a very private and an intensely interpersonal experience. In our lonely society, the richness of one's interpersonal network makes a tremendous difference in the quality of one's dying. (2) *Completing as many of the unfinished issues* as possible in their lives, especially in their close relationships (e.g., expressing love or asking and receiving another's forgiveness). Ted Rosenthal points out, "I don't think people are afraid of death. What they are afraid of is the incompleteness of their life."[14] (3) *Doing the complex grief work of dying* so that they can reach the experience of acceptance (Kübler-Ross). (4) *Having a faith system, a sense of trust and at-homeness in the universe* that gives some meaning that transcends the multiple losses of dying. (5) *Having a setting where one can die with dignity.* The hospice movement is the most humanizing development in recent years so far as dying is concerned. A Christian physician, Cicely Sanders, who started the first modern hospice St. Christopher's Hospice, in a suburb of London in 1967, states: "A modern hospice, whether it is a separate unit or a ward, or home care or hospital team, aims to enable a patient to live to the limit of his potential in physical strength, mental and emotional capacity and social relationships."[15]

Hospice programs enable some terminally ill people to die in their homes surrounded by family members rather than in the impersonal atmosphere typical of many hospitals. They do this by attending carefully to the control of pain and by frequent visits by a trained volunteer to give both the dying and their fmily support and caring. The hospice volunteer continues to stay in touch with the family as they do their grief work after the death.

The pastoral care program of a congregation should learn from and cooperate fully with the hospice program in its community, or take the initiative in helping to launch such a program if none exists. Pastors should encourage members of their congregation to take hospice training and participate in its program. The people close to a dying person are simultaneously struggling with severe anticipatory grief and bearing the enormous emotional and often physical load of caring for the dying person. They need the pastor's caring expertise as well as massive support from a lay caring team and/or from a community hospice program.

The Crisis and Grief of Divorce

Divorce is one of the most widespread grief experiences in Western societies. In the United States, for example, over one million couples terminate their marriages each year. This means that nearly three million people (including children) are directly involved in the trauma of the death of a marriage and the rupturing of a family system. If current trends continue, over 40 percent of all marriages will end in divorce. A study of the similarities and differences between the experiences of divorced and widowed women revealed that the divorced felt significantly less social support and more sense of restriction and isolation than did widows. They also suffered from more physical and mental health disturbances than the widows. Yet, our society has few organized resources for helping divorcing women and men do their grief work, learn and grow from their painful experiences. Churches have a strategic opportunity to develop innovative pastoral care programs to help divorcing people use their losses as occasions for emotional, spiritual and interpersonal growth, including helping step-parents learn the difficult but essential skills of co-parenting a reconstituted family.[16]

To be effective in establishing a healing ministry to divorcing people, clergy who have not been through divorce must develop heart understanding of the experience. Divorce is usually an ego insult, an experience that diminishes self-esteem. Women are programmed to feel especially responsible for the success of interpersonal relationships including marriage. Thus their sense of failure and guilt is often intense. Both men and women feel the painful wound of being rejected by their ex-spouse, particularly if they did not initiate or want the divorce. Feelings of failure and rejection are reinforced by the judgmental attitudes of some church people. Unresolved anger, bitterness, resentment, loneliness, self-doubt, and depression swirl together producing the infected grief wounds that frequently result from divorce. Even if the individual wanted and needed to be freed from a miserable, mutually destructive relationship, there is usually pain and grief intermingled with the sense of relief and release.

The ministry of pastoral care and counseling with divorced persons should aim at accomplishing three closely related objectives. The first is to help *them work through and resolve the grief and the pain*. If people remarry before their grief work from an earlier marriage is completed, the new relationship is almost certain to be complicated by unresolved feelings and conflicts from the earlier relationship. Some people are not open to pastoral divorce counseling because they fear that they will be judged or at least not understood by ministers. When a couple in marriage counseling decides to divorce, it is important to encourage them each to continue in individual counseling aimed at helping reduce the emotional damage of splitting a family.

The second closely related objective is *to help divorcing people learn and grow from the experience*. To do this is the best preparation for either remarriage (which five out of six divorced men and three out of four divorced women in the U.S. do) or creative singlehood. Helping persons identify and change whatever they contributed to the death of their marriage and coaching them as they learn new communication and conflict-resolution skills are two essential parts of this learnng-growth process. The scores of new decisions a divorcing person must make are likely to be more constructive if she or he has an opportunity for reality-oriented crisis counseling around these complicated issues. Participating in a creative divorce retreat or group, or in a grief growth group can be a valuable experience for those going through separation and divorce. The third objective of divorce counseling—*to reduce emotional damage to children to a minimum*—will be discussed in chapter 13. The decision to end a destructive marriage is often a first and essential step toward a new, more constructive life. The possibilities that it will be so can be increased with the aid of a skilled pastoral counselor and/or an effective growth group.

The minister of a church in North Carolina contacted each of the divorced members of his congregation to explore the possibilities of their helping each other cope with the problems and issues of divorce.[17] The response of those he called was an enthusiastic yes. The first meeting was held at the parsonage. After a brief statement by the minister concerning the purpose of the meeting, sharing began spontaneously and continued for over two hours. A strong *espirit de corps* developed almost immediately. The group decided to meet twice a month. Subsequent meetings dealt with topics chosen by the members, including child rearing, jobs, sex, personal growth, finances, and legal problems. The group has provided mutual support and a place to share feelings and problems with others who understand. The minister reports, "The group continues to meet after 17 months because it has been *koinonia* for these people." Among the books used for discussion starters are Krantzler's *Creative Divorce* and Nouwen's *Reaching Out*.[18]

Numerous churches have developed creative responses to the largely unmet needs of divorcing people for mutual support, caring, and encouragement to not waste the growth possibilities of their painful experience. Divorce and remarriage are becoming an increasingly common pattern in Western societies. It is appropriate that more and more churches take the initiative in reaching out in healing ways to a group of people who have often felt kept at a distance and judged by the church.

Suicidal Crises and Grief

Suicidal persons are more likely to turn to clergy than any other profession except physicians. Yet, many ministers are less able to recognize suicidal lethality than are those in other helping professions.[19] It is crucial for ministers to know how to respond in suicidal crises. The pastor's role in such crises has four facets: (1) recognizing suicidal persons; (2) providing emergency help until a referral to an appropriate mental health professional or suicide prevention center can be made; (3) continuing pastoral care and counseling of the person and the family to help them deal with the underlying causes of the suicidal behavior within the individual and in the family system; and (4) helping the family deal with the destructive consequences of an incomplete or a completed suicide.

Suicide is seldom a sudden, unpremeditated act. Before attempting suicide, most people send out cries for help.[20] These distress signals include: *Obvious suicidal threats*—The old belief that "People who talk about suicide don't kill themselves" dies much more slowly than the countless people who demonstrate its falsity. The only safe axiom to follow is this: *All* suicidal threats must be taken very seriously! Even if persons are only trying to manipulate others, with no intention of self-destruction, the fact that they use such a deadly threat indicates that they and their relationships are profoundly disturbed. *Covert suicidal threats*— Those who articulate feelings that life is empty and meaningless, who believe they are no longer valued or needed by others, who wish they could go to sleep and not wake up, or who feel trapped and powerless in a no-exit situation, often are expressing pre-suicidal feelings. *Depression*—Psychiatrist Karl A. Menninger declares, "All deeply depressed people are potential suicides!"[21] Psychodynamically much depression is rage turned inward on the self. Depression has many faces including marked retardation in speaking and moving; severe agitation; feeling that there is "a ton of lead on my mind"; severe feelings of hopelessness and worthlessness; chronic insomnia; loss of appetite or interest in other previously enjoyed activities; severe apathy and chronic exhaustion; withdrawal from relationships; a brittle facade of chronic cheerfulness. *Crushing losses and pathological grief*— Shattering blows to self-esteem and other traumatic losses may produce suicidal behavior during the reactive depression that follows. The greater the anger and frustrated dependency, the more likely is a suicidal response. *Psychological disturbances and chronic illnesses*—Some mentally ill persons are suicidal, but most suicidal persons are not mentally ill, though they experience agonizing inner disturbance. Anyone in a disorganized, chaotic mental state who feels rejected and/or hopeless, should be regarded as a suicidal risk. Those in chronic pain and/or those suffering from incurable illnesses may become suicidal, especially if they have intense fear of dependency, helplessness, or financial disaster.

In counseling with persons who are known or suspected to be suicidal, it is crucial to ask about suicidal impulses, fantasies, or intentions. The fear that by asking about it, one will suggest suicide to persons who are not considering it is largely unfounded. The suicide prevention center where I had some clinical training, gives these instructions to its counselors:

> Your own openness and willingness to confront the patient directly with the problem of suicide is very helpful in reducing the patient's anxiety. Inquire about the suicidal aspects of the behavior matter-of-factly. Ask about prior attempts and when they occurred; whether he is presently planning an attempt, and, if so, specifically what his plans are; and whether he has the means available to carry out his plans.[22]

One reason for asking such questions is to get information to evaluate the degree of danger involved in suicide threats. The presence of any of the following factors increases the statistical probability that persons will actually destroy themselves: *male*—men attempt suicide less frequently but succeed more often than women; *older age*—older persons who threaten suicide are more apt to attempt it than younger persons; (However, suicide *is* the second highest cause of death among teen-agers.) *a specific suicide plan; the means necessary to implement the plan* (e.g., a gun or sleeping pills); *prior suicidal behavior; recent severe losses or medical problems; depression; alcoholism; lack of a strong support system; mental illness; poor communication with significant people; and defensive reactions by family members.*

The higher the lethality probability, the greater the need for the pastor to use whatever approach is necessary to prevent suicidal action. In a caring and accepting but a very firm manner, the minister should use persuasion, theological arguments, staying with the person, driving her or him to a physician or hospital emergency room, or—if nothing else works—phoning the police and using physical restraint. An appeal to at least postpone suicide is sometimes effective. *Minister:* "Killing yourself may seem to you in your present despair, to be the only way out. But I'm sure we can find a better way. If you end your life, you'll deprive yourself of any possibilities of our finding a better solution to your situation. At least wait until we've tried!"

During the first conversation with suicidal persons, obtain the names and phone numbers of close relatives, friends, and physician, and explain why it is necessary to let them know that he or she needs extra emotional support during this crisis. The family should be told not to leave persons alone during their acutely suicidal phase. Involving the family physician as soon as possible is also important, in case antidepressant medication or temporary hospitalization is needed. An evaluation by a psychiatrist of persons making a suicide threat can be helpful in deciding whether hospitalization and psychiatric treatment are needed. The methods of crisis counseling described earlier are relevant in working with suicidal people.

Most suicidal persons need three forms of help once they are beyond the acute suicidal crisis. First, they need ongoing, supportive pastoral care; second, psychotherapy and/or family counseling to resolve the underlying intrapsychic problems (e.g., pathological guilt) and the interpersonal pathology that fed the suicidal behavior; and third, help with the spiritual and value problems at the root of their sense of meaninglessness and despair. At its deepest level, the suicidal person's problem is a theological problem. As one with some expertise in spiritual growth, the minister has a unique and indispensable contribution to make to the longer-term healing of suicidal persons and their families.

In working with suicidal persons, it is helpful to remember that only a small portion of those who threaten suicide actually attempt it, and that of those, only a fraction actually kill themselves. It is also important to remember that the ultimate decision and responsibility for suicide remains with the person. If they have decided *unequivocally* to end their lives, (which 5 percent or less of suicidal persons actually have), they will probably do so, no matter how competent the persons who attempt to prevent it.

Suicide is often the tip of the iceberg of deep problems in a family system. The whole family needs pastoral care and often conjoint family therapy. Following an incompleted suicide attempt, it is important for the whole family to receive help in opening up their communication and resolving destructive interaction that probably contributed to the suicidal behavior. The family of a completed suicide almost always needs extended pastoral care and counseling to deal with the swirling feelings of unhealed shame, guilt, and rage toward the dead person. Their grief wounds are almost always infected. The family's shame, denial, and self-protective hiding often prevent them from being open to help. Patient, persistent pastoral initiative is essential to help them lower their defenses and gradually become open to the help they desperately need. If they will join, a grief group experience can be especially helpful for family members after a suicide.

Counseling with suicidal pesons often is threatening and demanding. It confronts us with the ultimate issues of life and death, and with our own suicidal tendencies (included protracted suicide such as killing ourselves by chronic overwork and self-stressing). Our effectiveness in dealing with the existential issues with which the suicidal person is struggling will depend on how we deal with these issues ourselves and whether we have found meanings in our own lives that enable us to transcend and transform, to some degree, the pain and tragedies of our existence.

The Pastor's Own Losses and Crises

Go back in memory, now, and recall a painful personal failure, rejection, defeat, or loss of someone (or something) you felt you couldn't live without—or some awful crisis where you felt as if the rug had been pulled out from under your life. Take a few minutes to *relive* that awful experience, letting yourself experience again the agonizing feelings you felt when it happened./ Now, reflect on what you have just relived; become aware of what is still unfinished about that experience; what you learned from it; and how it altered your faith, your real beliefs, and your relation to God, what was and was not helpful to you./

You may have just gotten in touch with your most valuable potential asset in pastoral care and counseling with people in severe crises and grief. Whatever your crisis counseling and bereavement skills, their ultimate usefulness will depend on how you cope with your own crises and losses, and what you learn about yourself, life, people, and God from those unwelcome intruders. People who feel shattered need your supportive strength, but they also need to sense that you know something about how it feels to be shattered. They need your faith and hope, but they may also need to sense that you have known doubt and despair firsthand. In short, they need to experience the strength in you that comes from admitting your weaknesses and failures, from accepting your vulnerability and your deep need for others.

During the past decade, life has brought me a series of heavy losses and wrenching changes. Henri Nouwen's apt phrase "the wounded healer" has acquired fresh meaning for me. In working with people in crises, I've noticed that I often feel more connected with their inner world than I have in the past. The image that best communicates what I hope for myself and for you (when you deal with your crises and losses) is of the sharp blade of a painful loss as a plough that cuts a deep furrow in our souls, becoming a channel through which a healing stream of understanding and caring flows into the broken lives of others going through crises and losses.

Reality-Practice Session

PARISHIONER'S ROLE: If you have had a painful loss in your life (perhaps the one you relived above), go to the minister for help.

Or: Attempt to get inside the feelings of someone you know well who is in the process of dealing with a severe loss. Role play that person seeking the minister's help.

Or: You are Jane Carey, a woman in her mid-forties whose husband Dick died unexpectedly two months ago from a heart attack. You feel the loss intensely and find it almost impossible to go into social situations, especially to the church where you were active as a couple. You feel very depressed and would like to hide from people.

PASTOR'S ROLE: Use what you have learned from this chapter about facilitating grief work as you counsel with one of these parishioners. Be aware of the person's need for help with particular grief work tasks.

OBSERVER-COACH'S ROLE: Interrupt the session periodically to give the pastor feedback on her/his effectiveness in facilitating the grief work process—especially the pouring out of unfinished feelings.

Recommended Reading

Counseling the Dying and the Bereaved

Howard Clinebell, "Growing Through Loss," (Nashville: United Methodist Communication, 1983). A video-cassette series showing six sessions of a grief healing group led by Clinebell, for use in learning how to lead such groups.
_____ "Helping and Being Helped by the Dying." Cassete Training Course II A in *Growth Counseling, Part II: Coping Constructively with Crises* (Nashville: Abingdon, 1974). Includes an interview with Lois, a dying woman.
Glen W. Davidson, *Living with Dying* (Minneapolis: Augsburg, 1975). Insights about the various meanings of dying.
Paul M. DuBois, *The Hospice Way of Death* (New York: Human Sciences Press, 1979). Describes a more humanizing approach to dying.
Edgar N. Jackson, *Understanding Grief, Its Roots, Dynamics and Treatment* (Nashville: Abingdon Press, 1957). A comprehensive discussion of grief and methods of helping the bereaved.
Elisabeth Kübler-Ross, *On Death and Dying* (New York: Macmillan Publishing Co., 1969). Can be used as a resource in grief groups for the dying and their families.
Kübler-Ross, ed., *Death: The Final Stage of Growth* (Englewood Cliffs, N.J.: Prentice Hall, 1975). A variety of papers on the growth possibilities of dying and growth.
C. S. Lewis, *A Grief Observed* (New York: Seabury Press, 1961). A moving account of his self-observations following his wife's death.
Wayne E. Oates, *Pastoral Care and Counseling in Grief and Separation* (Philadelphia: Fortress Press, 1976). Describes the pastor's

crucial role and suggests new approaches to both separation and grief.

E. Mansell Pattison, ed., *The Experience of Dying* (Englewood Cliffs, N.J.: Prentice Hall, 1977). Explores the experience of dying at the various life stages.

Granger Westberg, *Good Grief* (Rock Island, Ill.: Augustana, 1962). Summarizes insights about the stages of healing of grief; useful in grief groups.

Colin Murray Parkes, *Bereavement: Studies of Grief in Adult Life* (New York: International Universities Press, 1972). Reviews the evidence of the detrimental effects of grief on physical and mental health; describes the author's understanding of grief and its treatment.

Ronald W. Ramsey and Rene Noorberger, *Living with Loss* (New York: William Morrow & Co., 1981). Describes "guided confrontation therapy," a behavioral method utilizing the full reliving of the painful feelings related to a variety of losses (including divorce, death, and unemployment).

Bernard Schoenberg and Irwin Gerber, eds., *Bereavement: Its Psychosocial Aspects* (New York: Columbia University Press, 1975). Thirty papers on the basic concepts, process, and treatment of bereavement and the bereaved family.

Jack M. Zimmerman, *Hospice: Complete Care of the Terminally Ill* (Baltimore-Munich: Urban and Schwarzenberg, 1981). A description of the major dimensions of hospice care.

Divorce Counseling

Russell J. Becker, *When Marriage Ends* (Philadelphia: Fortress Press, 1971). Pastoral care and counseling approaches to divorce.

Howard Clinebell, "The Crisis of Divorce: Growth Opportunities," Cassette Training Course III B in *Growth Counseling, Part II: Coping Constructively with Crises,* (Nashville: Abingdon Press, 1974). Includes segments from a divorce growth group.

Journal of Divorce, published by Haworth Press, 149 Fifth Ave., New York N.Y. 10010. Reports on research concerning the causes of and responses to divorce, and on counseling approaches.

Jim Egleson and Janet F. Egleson, *Parents Without Partners* (New York: Dulton, 1961). A guide for divorced, widowed, and separated parents.

Esther O. Fisher, *Divorce: the New Freedom* (New York: Harper & Row, 1974). A guide to divorcing and divorce counseling.

Richard A. Gardner, *Parents Book About Divorce* (New York: Doubleday & Co., 1977). Guidance for parents in helping children deal with divorce; *The Boys and Girls Book About Divorce* (New York: Bantam Books, 1971). Deals with children's feelings about divorce, custody, visitation, and remarriage of parents.

Myrna and Robert Kysar, *The Asundered* (Atlanta: John Knox Press, 1978). Biblical teachings on divorce and remarriage.

Mary Ann Singleton, *Life After Marriage* (New York: Stein and Day,

1974). A guide for building a different and better life after divorce.

Jim Smoke, *Growing Through Divorce* (Irvine, Calif.: Harvest House Publishers, 1976). A helpful book for divorcing people on growing and not just surviving divorce.

Emily B. Visher and John S. Visher, *Stepfamilies* (Syracuse, N.J.: Lyle Stuart, 1980). A guide to working with stepparents and stepchildren.

Women in Transition, *A Feminist Handbook on Separation and Divorce* (New York: Charles Scribner's Sons, 1975). Gives help from the feminist perspective.

Counseling Suicidal Persons

Howard Clinebell, "The Suicidal Emergency," in *First Aid in Counseling*, C. L. Milton, ed., (Edinburgh: T. and T. Clark, 1968), pp. 148-159.

Norman L. Farberow and Edwin S. Shreidman, eds., *The Cry for Help* (New York: McGraw-Hill Book Co., 1961). A classic in the field of helping suicidal persons.

Doman Lum, *Responding to Suicidal Crises* (Grand Rapids: William B. Eerdmans Publishing Co., 1974). A guide to handling suicides in the church and community.

Paul W. Pretzel, *Understanding and Counseling the Suicidal Person* (Nashville: Abingdon Press, 1972). A guide to helping suicidal individuals and their families.

Howard W. Stone, *Suicide and Grief* (Philadelphia: Fortress Press, 1972). Explores the interrelation between grief and suicide.

Marriage Enrichment and Marriage Crisis Counseling

Marriage represents for most people a central life adjustment area. . . . Being married or not married is an all-pervasive life condition which sets up . . . certain channels for the gratification of important human needs, and certain inevitable blocks to these needs. Furthermore, the marriage role can . . . set the pace for other important life roles—friendship, parenthood, work.

—*AMERICANS VIEW THEIR MENTAL HEALTH*[1]

Marriage is not a dying institution. It is a changing one. Today more people marry at some time in their lives than ever before. Today more people divorce than ever before, too, not just because divorce is easier now but because they expect much more of a marriage—Intimacy only thrives when the commitment is unconditional and long-range . . . and intimacy is only possible when two persons are equals.

—JEAN STAPLETON AND RICHARD BRIGHT, *EQUAL MARRIAGE*[2]

Marriage and family enrichment and marriage crisis counseling are among the pastor's most important helping skills. A reasonable degree of expertise in all types of care and counseling is important. But in the area of family life, as in crises and grief, the minister's opportunities are so frequent and crucial that a high degree of competence is required. (This chapter and the next are tandem chapters focusing on couple and family issues respectively.)

Four interrelated factors make it imperative that pastors develop skills in marriage and family care and counseling. *First*, ministers are in a more strategic position to do family care and counseling than any other profession. The contexts within which they function as leaders of congregations provide frequent and natural entrées to many family systems. Their professional role gives them continuing contacts with couples and families in the successive stages and stress-points of the family life cycle. In youth and church school work, in preparation for marriage and in

243

weddings, in calling in the homes of families, and in participating in many of the joyful and sorrowful events of the intergenerational cycle of families, ministers have countless caring and counseling opportunities.

Furthermore, the role of ministers as educators enables them to teach relationship-nurturing insights from our religious tradition as well as contemporary communication and conflict-resolution skills. Such teaching can help prevent family problems. It also plants seeds that may flower in counseling opportunities when family crises strike. In my experience, an insightful, caring sermon or talk on marriage and family life frequently produces counseling opportunities. The importance of marriage and family skills is underlined by the fact that nearly six out of ten people who seek pastoral counseling do so for help with marriage crises, parent-child issues, or other family problems.[3]

A *second* factor that makes it essential for ministers to develop competence in this area are the precious and long-range human values often at stake. A loving, mutually nurturing family is like a cold spring on a hot, dusty journey. It is a place of emotional nourishment and spiritual renewal—an interpersonal garden were mutual growth is nurtured. A healthy growing marriage, with moments of joy and ecstasy as well as conflict and pain, may be as close to heaven on earth as many of us finite human beings come. Conversely, a fractured family resulting from a mutually-destructive marriage can be a close approximation of hell on earth. In marriage and family care and counseling, the stakes are indeed high!

A good marriage or a good family is one where there is mutual caring about and support of each other's continuing growth toward fulfillment of each person's God-given potentialities. In no other area of ministry are long-range personality values more centrally involved. Through marriage and family enrichment, and counseling, a pastor can contribute to the long-range mental, physical, and spiritual health of marital partners, their children, and their children's children, *ad infinitum*. The family is the garden of human personality—the primary place where persons are formed, deformed, and (hopefully) transformed. Parents are "architects of the family."[4] Thus, marriage counseling and enrichment can focus a healing, growthing light on the very roots of personality health and illness. As such—these pastoral skills constitute a much-needed form of positive prevention of mental and spiritual pathology whose impact can continue into the unborn future.

A *third* factor that make family skills crucial is the contemporary crisis in marriage and family life. The institution of marriage is being challenged today as never before in human history. Soaring rates of divorce, family desertion, wife battering, child abuse, youth delinquency, suicide, and general marital boredom, pain, and unhappiness are overwhelming evidence that marriage, as traditionally defined and practiced, is all too often a person-damaging experience. In the last century, the divorce rate in America has increased fifteen fold. In one decade between 1968-78, it doubled. Sociological evidence shows that many traditional marriages are destructive to the health of women.[5]

A *fourth* factor, intimately related to the third, is the profound changes that have occurred in women-men roles, relationships, and identities within the last decade—changes that continue at an accelerating pace. These changes shake and often shatter the foundations of increasing numbers of traditional marriages. The rising consciousness and appropriate insistence of more and more women that they have fair, equal opportunities to develop and use their God-given potentialities (in careers *and* in home making), and participate equally in the decision making of a family, threaten many men.

Charlotte Ellen, feminist therapist and marriage counselor predicts:

> It is likely that we have thus far seen only the tip of the iceberg in the upheaval in relationships between women and men. Marriage relationships are especially vulnerable and responsive to changing roles and identities. More and more marriages will feel the pain and the excitement of change. It may be that the divorce rate will rise even higher as couples struggle unsuccessfully to develop more satisfying marriage styles. At the same time many couples will succeed in discovering the gains in more egalitarian and companionable marriages. Counselors of all disciplines can have a positive role in helping to redefine the institution of marriage and in helping couples to develop creative and growth-producing relationships.[6]

The complexities and pressures of two-career marriages are being faced by more and more couples. In only one-third of American families is the husband the only wage earner. Because of economic necessity and/or the desire to have a fulfilling career, the majority of women now work for pay outside the home. From our personal experience, Charlotte Ellen and I can attest to the fact that an egalitarian marriage is potentially more fulfilling, both for the woman and for the man, but such a relationship is also more complicated and conflict-prone than a traditional marriage. This is especially true for couples who lack role models in their parents from which they could learn how to make an egalitarian relationship work. The widespread search by couples for more flexible and creative ways to be married and the rejection of rigidly defined sex roles will increase both marital conflict and the need for marriage care and counseling in the eighties and nineties. Remarriage and step-parenting are becoming major American life-styles. Approximately one-fourth of all marriages involve at least one formerly married person. Major changes have occurred in attitudes and practices regarding sexual freedom and cohabitation, with more than a million couples living together in more-or-less committed relationships. The pill and the demand for equality by women have drastically reduced and eventually may eradicate the male-female dual standard of sexual freedom. In addition, there is a continuing decline in the support available to couples and nuclear families from their extended families. This makes them more vulnerable during crises.

One study produced evidence that a new more demanding marriage style has emerged among young adult couples—*the mutual potentializing marriage*. The study discovered that many such couples chose marriage mainly because of the expectation that it would provide a satisfying relationship, meaningful communication, and personal growth.[7] When such couples enter marriage without the relationship-building (communication) skills required to fulfill these expectations, disillusionment is almost inevitable. This disappointment, plus the increased willingness of couples to end unsatisfying marriages, feeds the rising incidence of marital separation, desertion, and divorce.

All marriages and all families have problems, of course. Psychiatrist Harry Stack Sullivan expresses this with a touch of humor:

> I have yet to find a marriage which has only satisfactions and only securities. . . . If a person tells me his home-life is perfect, I take off

my glasses, which means I can't see him, and gaze at him, and say, "Extra-ordinary!" I then pass on to some other topic but I return to this later.[8]

Marriage enrichment and education can increase the growthfulness of many reasonably adequate marriages. Marriage crisis counseling can help some couples face their problems and resolve them in growthful ways. In deeply disturbed marriages, marital therapy is essential.

Family life offers many people opportunities for "covenants of intimacy" in our lonely culture, and it is important that the Good News come alive in the dailyness of family relationships. A healthy growing marriage is one of the most psychologically intimate of all relationships. This makes it both one of the most rewarding and one of the most demanding of human relationships. In short, marriages and families are places where people can "live their religion" (Regina Westcott).

A New Strategy for Marriage

To help people respond creatively to the stress and changes in marriage and family life, churches need to develop innovative programs. Such program should have two thrusts—a *pastoral care-education* dimension consisting of a variety of attractive marriage enrichment and family-strengthening events (including classes, workshops, retreats, and camps); and a *pastoral counseling* dimension consisting of growth-centered marriage and family counseling for those going through periods of storm and stress. Each of these thrusts can undergird and complement the other. A marriage enrichment program will enable some couples needing marital counseling or therapy to seek this help sooner. It does this by making them more aware of the painful inadequacies of their current relationship and the possibilities that their marriage can become less frustrating and more mutually satisfying. The long-term effects of marriage counseling can be enhanced significantly by referring couples who complete counseling to a marriage growth group or to regular enrichment events that will support their continuing growth.

With all the chaos and problems in marriages today, there are also greater possibilities and strivings for depth relationships than ever before in human history. The increasing liberation of women and men from the growth-limiting bonds of traditional one-up and one-down roles opens new possibilities for deeper closeness and love. If a church is to be a human wholeness center, it must include a robust emphasis on helping couples learn how to develop this quality of liberated and liberating love. In no other area does the use of the wholeness model of ministry have more exciting and satisfying possibilities. The challenge is to help people learn practical methods for nurturing their own and each others' wholeness in their intimate communities of caring.

The common goal of wholeness-oriented marriage counseling and enrichment (including premarital training) is to *help each couple co-create a relationship where both partners are enabled to discover and develop their maximum gifts as individuals in mutually enhancing ways*. Each couple creates its own unique variations on this theme. Liberating love in any relationship can be defined as *caring about and commitment to each other's full becoming*. This is a working definition that can be used by couples and by counselors to discover how liberating and mutually growth-producing what is called "love" in a particular relationship really is.

Making Marriage Enrichment and Counseling Liberating

The deepest intimacy, including the most satisfying sex that couples are capable of, is psychologically possible only within a relationship of genuine equality.[9]

> The distance and anger (whether hot or frozen) that builds up in a one-up/one-down marriage in which one or both persons feels 'used', blocks depth communication and . . . impedes liberated sex. The awareness that we men also are exploited—by the present 'success' system—and that we're also depriving ourselves of much of our personhood (by the male rat race) makes it obvious that the basic issue is *human* liberation. The goal is to create relationships and institutions (including marriages) in which both women and men will have the greatest freedom and encouragement to use their full intelligence, creativity and productive energies. We who are married, and we who do marriage enrichment and counseling, should help overcome sexism, a central cause of diminished and destructive marriages, which blocks human becoming of both

women and men on a massive scale. We can do this by struggling and bearing the pain it often requires, to create and help others create equal and mutually-liberating relationships.[10]

Every committed relationship is based on an understanding (usually implicit) of what each person's privileges and rights, obligations and duties are within that relationship. In marriage, this is called the marital contract or covenant. Often there are major differences in the two partners' implicit understanding of their working contract. This discrepancy is a hidden source of conflict between them. Marriage enrichment and counseling sometimes enables couples merely to adjust to their existing contract more comfortably without evaluating and changing its unfair and unequal aspects. Such an approach is inherently unliberating and will in the long run prevent them from strengthening their relationship in a continuing way.

What are the characteristics of a liberated and liberating marriage?

> Responsiveness to meeting each other's needs; open and caring communication; closeness *and* respect for individual privacy needs; autonomy (each a person in his/her own right) *and* interdepenence; genuine fairness and equality; commitment to each other's growth; no rigid or satellite roles; continued change and growth through the years; the ability to use conflict to deepen intimacy and resolve differences by negotiating (rather than deadlocking and distancing); deepening sexual pleasure integrated with love; increasing intimacy in the areas of meaning and faith; strengthening of the marriage identity (the "two becoming one"); positive fidelity (based on a valuing of the relationship rather than on guilt and fear).[11]

The ideal toward which couples should be helped to grow is two autonomous, growing individuals who *choose* to develop loving *interdependency* rather than the symbiotic dependency of two half-persons.

To be genuinely liberating and growth-producing (rather than merely sugar-coating an unjust relationship), marriage counseling and enrichment should always include consciousness-raising. This means increasing couples' awareness of the ways in which the unequal allocation of power, decision-making, and opportunities for growth are root causes of marital anger, unhappiness and conflict. Consciousness raising should increase couple's understanding of how their sexist social programming as women and men diminishes mutual growth in marriage. (For methods of consciousness raising, see Charlotte Holt Clinebell's *Counseling for Liberation*.) Marriage counseling and enrichment should challenge and teach couples how to revise their contracts to make their relationship as just and equal as possible. The principle that the *only solid foundation for love is justice* should be implemented in all marriage counseling and enrichment.

Sexism is a central cause of both diminished and destructive marriages. Therefore, pastoral counselors cannot nurture the mutual growth of married persons fully unless they actively help couples grow mutually liberating and equal, as well as intimate marriages. The institutional male chauvinism of most churches and theologies militates against such liberating marriage counseling and enrichment. We must take seriously the freeing insight of Paul that in Christ there is neither male nor female (Gal. 3:28), that one's *humanity*, not one's gender, is what really matters. The most important implication of all that is that pastoral marriage counselors and enrichers must have a raised consciousness in the area of both women's and men's liberation.[12]

A Church's Marriage Enrichment Program

Marriage enrichment programs are designed to help couples make reasonably well-functioning relationships even more mutually fulfilling. Such programs focus mainly on helping them identify and develop their unused strengths; enhance their communication, sexual relationships, spiritual intimacy; establish their own growth goals, and then implement workable plans for moving toward those goals.

Because I have described marriage enrichment methods and programs in detail elsewhere (see Recommended Reading), I will only highlight some essentials of a church's program here. A church should create a smorgasbord of enrichment and growth experiences designed to respond to the needs of the maximum number of couples at all the stages of family life. (A checklist of marriage and family enrichment groups and suggestions for setting up a church program to enhance family life is described in chapter 11.) An exciting challenge facing a church today is to become a wholeness center for both single and married people in all their basic relationships.

The publicity for marriage enrichment events (and other growth events) should spell out their nature, purposes, and goals in a positive, growth-oriented way. It should describe what is expected of participants and give a brief theological rationale for the event, which serves both to relate it to the church's spiritual heritage and reduce inappropriate anxieties that may cause some who could profit from the event to stay away. Here is an announcement for use in recruiting couples for an enrichment event:

An Invitation to Couples

Our church is sponsoring a marriage enrichment group on the theme, "Making Good Marriages Better." The group will meet in the church lounge on Tuesday evenings from 7 to 9, for five weeks beginning October 7. (The second meeting on October 14 will be an extended session beginning at 6:00 P.M. with a potluck supper and ending at 10:00 P.M.) The Christian life centers on love—of ourselves, each other, God, and God's world. This group seeks to increase love in these four relationships by helping couples discover the unused strengths in their relationship, deepen their communication, resolve conflicts more constructively, and nurture their love together. All couples—newly married, considering or planning marriage, and longer-married—are welcome. The group will be co-led by our pastor and her husband. Contact the pastor if you would like to register or would like more information about this event.

Five types of activities can be used in enrichment groups, classes, retreats, or workshops: (1) *Whole group awareness, communication,* and relationship-*strengthening exercises* led by the facilitator-couple and debriefed as individual couples; (2) *brief whole-group input sessions* where the facilitator-couple or members of the group share practical ideas that have worked for them (e.g., about conflict-resolution, spiritual sharing, or sex); (3) *relationship-strengthening exercises done as couples*—the IMM (Intentional Marriage Method) is one of the most helpful; (4) *small, usually leaderless sharing groups* of three or four couples into which a larger group or workshop divides periodically; (5) *relaxed times,* structured and unstructured, to allow for fun and playfulness between partners and among couples.

Here are the basic themes that I often include in relationship enrichment events (which are emphasized depending upon on the group's interests and the available time). Each theme is approached experientially:

> *Getting Connected as a Couple and as a Group:* This includes discussion of the hopes, expectations, and needs of couples and the leaders: On the basis of this discussion, a group agreement (contract) on the topics to be emphasized is evolved.
>
> *Strengthening Our Communication Skills:* This includes self-awareness and responsive listening exercises.
>
> *The Intentional Marriage Method:* This can well be the heart of marriage enrichment events (described below).
>
> *Resolving Unproductive Anger and Conflict:* Role-playing of conflict situations and TA are used in this experience.
>
> *The Pain and Possibilities of Changing Women's/Men's Roles:* This is a time for a consciousness raising and for sharing ways of discovering the positive potentialities of more equal and mutually fulfilling marriages.
>
> *Evaluating Our Priorities, Values, and Life-style:* This involves helping couples become more aware of their values and make changes to increase the quality of their lives together.
>
> *Enhancing Our Sexual Enjoyment:* The goal is to help couples communicate openly about what they enjoy and learn nondemand pleasuring—i.e., mutual pleasuring done for its own enjoyment and not for any other goal, expectation, or achievement. Free time is scheduled for couples to practice full-body massages privately.
>
> *Coping with the Crises in Our Family:* This includes practicing crisis skills that couples can use.
>
> *Enriching Parent-Child and Parent-Youth Relations:* Exploring how parenting can diminish or enhance the quality of our marriage, and vice versa.
>
> *Deepening Our Spiritual Intimacy:* This segment focuses on resolving religious conflicts, increasing shared peak experiences, and deepening enjoyment of the Spirit of life and love in marriages.

The Growth Possibilities of Our Marriage Stage: Helping couples cope with the problems by developing the new possibilities of their present age and stage of marriage.

Developing Intimacy through Shared Outreach: Near the close of an enrichment group or event, couples are challenged and invited to plan ways of reaching out to others in the church or community to share the growth they have experienced.

Planning for Continuing Growth: Before the end of an enrichment event, couples should have an opportunity to work out their own growth covenants consisting of concrete plans for taking next steps on their growth journey, individually and as couples. The group as a whole should make plans for follow-up reunions to give mutual support to each other's growth.

Evaluating the Experience: Midway through an enrichment event and at the close, it is important to give everyone a chance to indicate what has been most helpful and least helpful about the experience, their overall evaluation, and, at the end, their suggestions for future events.

Closing Celebration: A worship time of thanksgiving for the growth that has occurred and recommitment to each other's continuing wholeness, helps people celebrate their experiences and become aware of God's love that undergirds and feeds their love for each other. A love-feast where partners feed each other bread and affirm their new growth covenants, is a meaningful way to close.

To be liberating, marriage enrichment events and groups should have male-female co-leaders with raised consciousnesses on the issue of sexism. The woman and man should have balanced and equal roles in the leadership. Initiative in leading should be alternated. Co-leaders should model an egalitarian way of relating and be free to disagree and still be friends. Such a leadership team models what is being taught and brings the differing perspectives of two individuals who know women's and men's experiences respectively from the inside.

A variety of suggested formats and schedules, communication exercises and relationship-enhancing skills are described in the books with an asterisk before them in the Recommended Reading section.

Guidelines for Enriching Relationships

Here are some recommendations for strengthening a marriage, a family, or a committed relationship between singles:

(1) Set aside regular time to communicate about what really matters to each of you; communication is to a relationship what oxygen is to your bodies.

(2) Recognize and affirm the strengths and assets in each other and in your relationship—warmly, caringly, and regularly.

(3) Keep the wall of unresolved anger, hurt, and resentment from growing between you by discussing disagreements, negotiating fair compromises, resolving conflicts, and revising your basic covenant *regularly* to keep it fair, current, and just.

(4) Provide equal opportunities for each person to discover and develop her/his unused strengths, and possibilities.

(5) Let your Child sides play regularly together; learn to chuckle *at* yourself and *with* each other; give yourselves a mini-vacation each day (at least a few minutes of relaxation and fun).

(6) Enrich your inner life, spiritually, and intellectually, by reading and by the spiritual disciplines you enjoy; you'll have more to give in close relationships if you do.

(7) Develop your support group—individually and as a couple.

(8) Increase your self-nurture and your autonomy to give you healthy spaces in your togetherness.

(9) Find a shared cause bigger than your relationship—a way of responding to the need of your community and world.

(10) Develop and implement an intentional growth plan for your relationship; choose growth goals that will improve your relationship in the ways you both want, and commit yourselves to concrete action plans, designed to help create your own better future.

P.S. If you don't have time to do things like these, you may need to check and revise your priorities. If do-it-yourself methods don't work, it's a sign of your strength to seek the help of a counselor-therapist trained in relationship-strengthening methods. [13]

This list can be used by couples during or between sessions of enrichment events to identify areas where they need to do growth work together to nurture their love. Invite them to improve the list for themselves by adding other items that articulate their particular needs and dreams.

The Intentional Relationship Method

The communication exercise that many couples in enrichment events have found most helpful as a do-it-ourselves enrichment tool is called the Intentional Marriage (or Intentional Relationship) Method. It consists of four steps. Here are the instructions:

Step 1: *Identify and affirm the strengths in your relationship* by one of you completing the sentence, "I appreciate in you . . . " as many times as you can. The listener's assignment is to hear and to receive these gifts./(This step increases a couple's awareness of the strengths and assets in their marriage or friendship and gives them a warm glow of mutual affirmation.) After both of you have completed telling the other what you appreciate, take time to jot down the two lists in your growth journals for future reference./

Step 2: *Identify the growing edge of your relationship* by one of you completing the sentence, "I need from you . . . ," as many times as you wish. State your unmet or partially met needs-wants in terms of behavior you would like from the other./ After one person has completed the list, the other should repeat what she or he has heard, to make sure the needs-wants have been understood accurately./ After both of you have stated your needs and the other's perception of what you have said has been checked out, take time to list each person's needs in your growth journals. (This step enables a couple to reflect on and state explicitly the unmet needs, which are areas of potential growth in relationship.) In using this step in enrichment or counseling, it is important to do some consciousness raising regarding needs—couples may not be aware of what needs should be met to make their marital contract more fair and just.

Step 3: *Intentionally increase the mutual satisfaction of your relationship, and thus nurture your love, by choosing one of each person's needs (or a shared need) which you will meet.* Work out a concrete, workable plan, with a time schedule, to meet these needs./ Write out your plan in your growth journals./ (In this step the couple is intentionally revising or adding a clause to their working contract, through discussion and negotiation.)

Step 4: *Implement your change plan./ Then choose another pair of needs—devising and implementing a plan to meet these intentionally./* It is well to repeat step 1 regularly as you work together to make your relationship more need-satisfying. Keep track of your progress in your growth journals./ (This step is the pay-off. The process becomes self-reinforcing as the positive satisfactions increase for both partners. If a change plan doesn't work for some reason, a couple should devise a better plan.)[14]

This exercise is really a communication paradigm that can be used productively in any close relationship—a family, friendship, colleague, or staff relationship—to increase mutual need-satisfaction, and thus decrease frustration and conflict. Its use in marriage counseling will be described below.

The Nature of Marital Interaction and Conflict

Two persons meet, begin to relate, and eventually marry. Their interaction before and during the course of their marriage results in the creation of a new psychological entity—*their relationship*. This new entity, called the "identity of the marital pair" by family therapy pioneer Nathan A. Ackerman, includes what each brought to the relationship—the needs, problems, personality patterns and resources, expectations and hopes—but much more.[15] The more is *their interaction*—what each becomes in the process of responding to what the other becomes in the process of interacting, and so on. Out of the intricacies of relating on many levels emerges an unique creation—their marriage relationship. We are dealing here with what Martin Buber describes, in discussing the potentiality that exists when two people meet, as the "dimension of the between."[16] Every human relationship that is mutually need-satisfying creates something of this "between-ness." The longer and the more intense the interaction, the stronger the shared identity of the relationship.

Marriage enrichment, counseling, and therapy focus mainly on enhancing the marriage relationship, not (as in most individual psychotherapy) on resolving intrapsychic personality conflicts. Addressing psychotherapists in training, Harry Stack Sullivan once declared: "If you are to correctly understand your patient's problems, you must understand him in the major characteristics of his dealing with people.[17] It is true that disturbed relationships reflect *inner* conflicts and unhappiness. But the distortions in the relationships perpetuate, intensify, and produce new layers of inner psychological disturbance. In relationship counseling and therapy, the disturbed relationship *per se* becomes the object of treatment. It is the "client." As a relationship becomes more constructive, the individuals who compose it become freer to change. (This is the opposite of the way a relationship in conventional psychotherapy is changed—by first changing each of the individuals.)

A man and a woman are attracted to each other because each hopes that the relationship will satisfy a variety of their needs. Each brings a unique pattern of personality needs to the marriage. These needs must receive at least minimal satisfaction if the person is to be capable of satisfying the partner's and the children's needs. A happy marriage is one where there is a relatively high degree of mutual need satisfaction. Conversely, an unhappy marriage has a high degree of mutual need deprivation. If a relationship produces chronic, unmet emotional hungers, it will diminish the self-esteem of those involved, resulting in rejection, anger, and aggression. The particular need-pattern that one brings to marriage depends on the personality-molding experiences with need-satisfying adults in one's early life. Marital conflict is fundamentally the conflict of two need systems—the needs of one person colliding with the needs of the other. For example, Joan and Larry, married three years, each have an incompatible need to "parentify" the other. Each wants to be the child in a child-parent dependency relationship. Their needs are mutually contradictory.

Because of severe early life need deprivation, many people bring *neurotic needs* (as contrasted with normal needs) to their marriages. A neurotic need has two characteristics: (a) It is an *exaggeration* of a normal need—so much so that no one could possibly satisfy it. (b) It is *ambivalent* or conflicted. On a conscious level the person desires one thing; on a nonconscious level just the opposite! This inner contradiction makes interpersonal conflict inevitable. The person is always frustrated because it's impossible to eat one's cake and have it too. The counselor's awareness of such self-contradictory need patterns may help couples understand and interrupt their eventually painful marital battles.

Carl was raised by a cold, nongiving mother and an emotionally distant father who could not feed their children's personality hungers. As a result, Carl, now in his late twenties, has an insatiable craving for reassurance, warmth, and emotional feeding. To him, normal amounts of affection from his wife, Patricia, provide an inadequate emotional diet. Unfortunately Patricia finds it difficult to give Carl even moderate amounts of emotional food. In spite of a warm exterior, she is remarkably like his mother in her underlying personality. Why was Carl attracted to a person who could not meet his needs? Because he has other, conflicting needs. He needs to be dependent, but he also needs to feel super-manly. His powerful dependency needs make him feel weak and unmasculine. To protect himself from these intolerable feelings, he must deny his dependence and strive for an exaggerated self-made-man independence. His fear of his dependency prevented him from marrying someone who could give him generous nurturing. On an unconscious level, Patricia has a parallel conflicted need system that drew her to Carl. As Lawrence S. Kubie states: "No one has ever married himself out of a neurosis. Instead, when two people are drawn into marriage by the lure of the other's illness, one will add the weight of his own neurotic infirmity to that of the other, with growing pain and resentment."[18] Most of us have some neurotic needs intermingled with our appropriate needs.

For the generalist in ministry (parish pastors, chaplains, seminary teachers, etc.), it is important to distinguish between couples and families who can be helped by brief relational crisis counseling and those who require long-term marriage or family therapy. Many couples with reasonably functional relationships can be thrown off keel (like a sturdy ship in a typhoon) by a severe crisis—a serious illness, the loss of a job by a sole or primary breadwinner, or the tragic death of a family member. Extreme need frustration leads to verbal attacks, diminished communication, counterattacks, and spiraling resentments and distancing. A few counseling sessions may help such functional couples pull out of their relational tailspin and mobilize their resources for working together to handle the crisis more constructively.

In contrast, couples and families with chronically disrupted relationships dominated by neurotic interaction need more than short-term crisis counseling. To be helped, they require marriage and/or family therapy to enable them to renegotiate their basic contract and thus rebuild their relationships on a stronger foundation. In addition, some who seek marriage counseling are so disturbed in their personalities that they must have individual psychotherapy before or concurrently with relational therapy. The task of those in general ministries is to assist such persons in finding competent help from specialists trained in the particular therapies they need. Referral to a clinical member of the American Association of Pastoral Counselors (9508a Lee Highway, Fairfax, Virginia 22031, Phone 703-385-6967) or the American Association of Marriage and Family Therapists (1717 K St., N.W., #407, Washington, D.C. 20006, Phone 202-429-1825) is appropriate in such cases.

Even pastors with advanced training in marriage counseling and therapy must face the fact that helping chronically disturbed marriages and families requires more time than most generalists in ministry can afford. The quality of marriages and families in one's congregation can be enhanced much more by investing time in group enrichment programs and short-term couple crisis help, than in spending many hours helping a few disturbed persons or families. Marriage is a complex human relationship. Many couples with severe relational problems are extremely difficult to help, even if one has the skills acquired by advanced training in the field.

The Goals of Marriage Crisis Counseling

The overall goal of marriage crisis counseling and also marriage therapy is to help couples learn how to make their relationship more mutually need-satisfying and therefore more growth-nurturing. To help them accomplish this, certain operational goals should be in the counselor's mind during the process. In short-term marriage crisis counseling, the counselor seeks to help the couple:

(1) Reopen their blocked communication lines and learn more effective communication skills (which are essential for accomplishing the other goals).

(2) Interrupt the escalating, self-perpetuating cycle of mutual

attack and retaliation, triggered by their severe frustration of mutual need-satisfactions; and become aware of the futility and self-sabotaging consequences of their own behavior, including their efforts to reform each other.

(3) Become aware of the strengths and unused assets in themselves and their relationship which they can use to make constructive changes in themselves and their marriage.

(4) Identify specific areas where change-growth must occur in each person's own behavior to interrupt their crisis and make their marriage more mutually need-fulfilling.

(5) Negotiate and then implement workable and just change plans in which each person takes responsibility for changing her/his side of the interaction between them. This is a renegotiation of their marriage covenant. In this process, they will mobilize some latent coping resources, learn new problem-solving skills, (e.g., constructive conflict resolution) and raise the level of mutual-satisfaction in the relationship.

(6) Experience the reawakening of the energy-for-change in realistic hope. Realistic hope is generated in three ways in counseling. It is first caught empathetically from the counselor's expectation that the couple has the capacity to change and grow. Hope is then nourished by increased awareness of their strengths and assets with which they can rebuild malfunctioning aspects of their relationship. Hope is strengthened and reinforced as they actually change self-hurting behavior in and between themselves. Constructive change generates realistic hope, and hope generates further change.

Marriage crisis counseling and marriage therapy are actually on a continuum. Marriage therapy shares the above goals, but in addition seeks to help couples:

(7) Discover, explore, and to some degree, exorcise the subconscious or unconscious roots of conflicted role image and neurotic (exaggerated and conflicted) needs learned primarily from their parents; deal with relationship-diminising fantasies, fears and rage. Individual psychotherapeutic sessions may be needed concurrently with joint couple sessions, to facilitate this individual growth.

(8) Renegotiate and revise major aspects of the marital contract that are unjust and/or unworkable. Marriage therapy is longer-term than marriage crisis counseling because it involves a greater

degree of learning of relationship-building skills and a more basic reconstruction of the relationship. (For a detailed description of methods used in marital therapy relationships, see chapter 3 in *Growth Counseling*. Many of these methods can also be used in shorter-term marriage counseling.)

The Initial Session in Marriage Counseling

What occurs during the first interview in marriage counseling or therapy determines whether or not the foundation is laid for an ongoing, workable therapeutic relationship. During the first session, the pastor should:

(1) Communicate warmth, caring, and a willingness to help, and affirm the couple for seeking help.

(2) Find out how each feels about being there; why each person came *now;* what each wants, fears, expects, and hopes for from counseling; discover how much motivation each person has to improve their side of the relationship.

(3) Help motivate the less-motivated partner by building rapport with that person and awakening realistic hope for more satisfaction and less pain in the marriage.

(4) Discover how long the crisis or problems have been going on. Is the alienation chronic and protracted, or does the couple have periods of connectedness between crises?

(5) Provide comparable opportunity for each person to describe the problems, express their feelings, and say what changes must occur (usually in the other) to make the marriage workable for them, (i.e., which clauses of the marriage contract are unfair and unsatisfying and therefore must be revised?).

(6) After their anger and hurt are expressed and reduced, find out what each person still values about the marriage and about each other, and affirm whatever strengths and potential resources they have with which to strengthen their marriage through counseling.

(7) Make a tentative decision (based on what is discovered in 2 and 4) concerning whether to try short-term marriage crisis counseling or refer the couple to a marital therapist. If, after three to five sessions of crisis counseling, the couple has made little or no constructive movement, they probably need longer-term marital and/or individual therapy.

(8) If short-term counseling seems likely to help, ask the couple to agree to come for three or four additional sessions with the expectation that at the end of that series, they and the counselor will decide what is needed. If in the initial session referral obviously is needed, the pastor should explain why and assure the couple that she or he will assist them in finding the specialized help they need.

(9) Help the couple decide on and commit themselves to some between-sessions at-home assignment—some small, constructive action they will take to help make their relating more mutually satisfying as soon as possible.

(10) Near the close of the first session (and other sessions) ask them how they feel about what has occurred—drawing out and accepting any negative feelings they may have.

(11) Use prayer or other religious resources only if clearly appropriate with that couple.

(12) After the interview, reflect on what was learned, and make tentative plans for helping the couple; check with a consultant or colleague (peer consultant) if the situation is complicated or confusing.

Methods of Marriage Crisis Counseling

These goals will become clearer when viewed operationally in the following account of crisis counseling with Joan and Bill Sheldon. (This is a composite case based on several similar experiences of marriage crisis counseling.)

Joan Sheldon phoned the Reverend Sally Marks to ask if she would see her about a marital problem. Joan (34) and Bill (36) are members of Sally's church. They have been married eight years and have two children, ages 5 and 1½. Sally responded: "Yes, of course I'll be glad to be of whatever help I can, Joan. Tell me a little about what's happening." (This question was aimed at finding out how acute the crisis was and enough about its nature to decide whether to begin with individual or couple counseling.) Joan described a marital problem of several years duration, centering on Bill's excessive drinking. Their marital conflict had skyrocketed since he had been terminated three months ago from his position as an engineer with a nearby aerospace company.

> **Joan:** He's unbearable! So discouraged about not finding another job he often just sits in front of the tube and drinks beer most of the day.

Yells at me when I ask him why he isn't out looking for a job. I should find a job again—his unemployment compensation will run out soon. But I'm afraid to leave our kids with him—he's so upset and half drunk much of the time, shouts at them when they make any noise. I suspect his heavy drinking is one reason he was let go!

Pastor: Sounds as though you've about had it! Things are really rough! How would Bill feel about the three of us getting together to talk? Since the problem is at least partly in your relationship, it would be helpful if I could hear how both of you see it.

Joan: He's very upset about the mess we're in and what's going on between us, but he feels our main problem is his being out of work.

Pastor: That certainly *is* a major problem, but from what you say, it seems that the suffering for all of you is made worse by what this is doing to your relationships as a family. Do you suppose he would be willing to come at least once so that I could hear both of your viewpoints about the crisis you're in and what you can do to make things better?

Joan said he probably would and a tentative appointment was made for the next day, to be confirmed after she had talked with Bill.

When the Sheldons came to the pastor's study, she greeted them warmly and asked them to have a seat in a small cluster of three comfortable chairs away from the desk.

Pastor: I appreciate your accepting my invitation to come, Bill. I can understand how you might be feeling some resistance since it wasn't your idea to talk to me. As I explained to Joan when she phoned, I think I can be more helpful if I know how each of you sees and feels about your situation.

Bill: Things have been going down hill since I lost my job. I'm willing to talk if it might help.

Pastor: Joan told me a little about the problems on the phone, but I suspect that you may have some different views on the situation. How do you see the problem, Bill?

Bill: Well, I lost my job and with the economy being in the miserable shape it's in I haven't been able to find a comparable position in my field. It's been damn discouraging and I guess I've been kinda hard to live with. But her nagging me hasn't exactly helped!

Pastor: The whole job situation must be very rough on you, Bill! I realize that finding another job has to be your biggest concern right now and talking with me won't be of direct help on that. But it sounds as if the conflict between the two of you are making being out of work even harder for both of you. Perhaps we can discover some ways that the two of you can make things better in that area.

The lines of meaningful communication were gradually reopened as the pastor encouraged Bill and Joan to describe their perceptions of their crisis. This produced heated disagreement, especially about the role of Bill's drinking in his firing. Sally watched their pattern of communication carefully, noting that they talked to each other only through her. This suggested that their communication, except for circular arguing, mutual attack, and accusation (stemming from their anger and suffering) had become constricted and ineffective as a means of problem-solving. Effective communication, including all the verbal and nonverbal ways people exchange ideas, attitudes, meanings, desires, hopes, angers, fears, warmth, and caring, is what nurtures love in a relationship by feeding the basic psychological hungers and satisfying the basic human will-to-relate. The pathology of the Sheldons' communication system was both a cause and an effect of their increasing alienation. (Marriages where there has been little if any effective communication for years are not a rarity. The need-starvation in such relationships produces intense suffering, with consequent anger and mutual attack.)

As Joan and Bill poured out their feelings and described their escalating marital crisis, the pastor became more aware of their interaction pattern. She focused her attention back and forth between them, giving each person comparable opportunities to express their differing perceptions and feelings on the issues they raised. During this hour, the pastor concentrated some extra attention on Bill, drawing him out and responding with warmth and understanding to his expressions of pain. The counseling principle being utilized was that of *focusing on the less motivated or resistant spouse in order to establish a bond of rapport and increase the motivation of that person to continue counseling*. This must be done without neglecting the more strongly motivated person.

The presence of the minister allowed the Sheldons to talk more effectively about the issues that caused their suffering. Their marital diad, paralyzed by mutual attack, became a three-person group with the pastor taking the role of mediator and communication-facilitator.

As in a deadlocked labor-management dispute, a neutral third party changed the dynamics and interaction of the Sheldons' "group," enabling the couple gradually to reopen communication.

The presence of the pastor as a person outside the marriage system also helped interrupt the escalating cycle of mutual retaliation in which they were caught. Speaking from the perspective of their long experience in marriage counseling, Emily H. Mudd and Hilda M. Goodwin observe: "When the marital relationship does not afford an acceptable degree of satisfactions for each spouse's needs, or if conflict develops, several processes are set in motion which undermine personal identity and promote failure of each partner to alleviate the anxiety of the other"[19] These processes include spiraling resentment, feelings of rejection, and the progressive breakdown of problem-solving communication. The more each person's self-esteem is undermined—the faster the rejection-anger spiral whirls, the stronger the momentum of the vicious cycle, and the more difficult it is for the couple to interrupt it unassisted.

Basic to interrupting this vicious cycle is draining off the intense feelings of hurt, resentment, anger, and rejection that feed it. The pastor does this by encouraging emotional catharsis, sometimes in individual sessions (one or more) with each party. Individual sessions are needed if the rage is very intense, or if the pastor suspects there may be something crucial, such as a secret affair, that will not be brought out in a joint session. The reduction of the explosive emotional head of steam in both persons must be accomplished *before* healing communication can occur in couple counseling.

During the first session, the pastor encouraged the Sheldons to give a brief chronological overview of their relationship since they met. They both agreed that, although they had had their share of pain and conflicts, their marriage had been relatively good until the last few years.

> **Pastor:** It's hopeful that you both have some good memories and that you both know that you have the capacity to make things much better between you. You can draw on this when you're feeling in the pits in this crisis.

> **Bill:** Yeah, but as she'll be glad to tell you, she's been bugging me for some time to cut down on my drinking.

> **Joan:** (heatedly) Would you believe for four years!

> **Pastor:** Sounds like that's been a big bone of contention between you long before the present job crisis. Do you think you need to cut down on your drinking, Bill? Is it a problem as you see it?

> **Bill:** (defensively) Just a way of relaxing after a heavy day and living with her constant nagging.

> **Joan:** But you said your supervisor at work warned you a couple of times about not being with it after you'd had several martinis at lunch.

After a heated interchange, Bill's defensiveness declined enough to allow him to admit his drinking probably had hurt his job rating and contributed to his being cut soon after his company began to reduce its engineering staff due to economic difficulties. He eventually admitted that his doctor had recommended that he reduce his drinking.

> **Pastor:** Have you tried to reduce your drinking, Bill?

> **Bill:** Yes, I tried on my own and even went to a few AA meetings about a year ago, but that didn't seem to be what I needed.

After further exploration of this issue, the pastor said:

> You mentioned, Bill, that you drink partly to make bearable Joan's nagging you to cut down on your drinking. There seems to be a mutually sabotaging cycle going on between you. You nag because you're worried about Bill's health and about the family finances, Joan, which gives you more reason to drink, Bill, which gives you more reason to keep after him, Joan. (The couple both nodded in agreement.) It seems as though what each of you is doing is producing the opposite of what you really want from the other; it doesn't seem to be working. (This confrontation led into a discussion of what they might do to interrupt this self-defeating cycle. During subsequent sessions, Bill and Joan became more aware of other ways that they were sabotaging themselves and their relationship by such negative cycles of interaction.)

Midway through the first session the pastor summarized what she had heard (pausing occasionally for their response):

> Each of you is suffering a lot because of at least three things in your situation. A central one is the fiscal worries and problems caused by the cutting off of your major income and having to dip into your savings more and more, plus the big disruption of many of your

familiar routines, schedules, and satisfactions by having Bill out of work. You lost a job but also a lot more. The anxieties and tensions are a lot worse because the prospects aren't good for finding another job soon. You've both had a many-sided loss with a lot of grief. (Both Joan and Bill agreed, commenting that they hadn't thought of what they were experiencing as grief.) The second cause of pain you're both feeling is what's going on between you. Your anxieties and frustration about the job loss has triggered the self-defeating cycle of blaming each other and pushing each other away just when you need to pull together to handle the practical difficulties you're facing. The third issue, your use of alcohol, Bill, seems to be complicating the other two. The big blow to your self-esteem of losing a job you liked, and the discouragement of not being able to find another yet, has made it easy to drink more. And you feel that this is interferring with his job hunting, Joan. Because of Bill's depression and drinking, you're reluctant to return to the nursing job you had before your second child was born, Joan. Does this sort out the major problems to which you need to find some solutions?

After the couple responded, the pastor said: "It's clear that there are a lot of things you find annoying and frustrating with each other. I'm wondering, what do you still like about each other or about your marriage?" This question (step 1 in the IRM) enables some couples to become aware of and hear what each person still values in the relationship. Joan responded first, affirming a number of things about Bill and their relationship that she still liked. Bill seemed very surprised by Joan's affirmation. He mentioned a variety of things he appreciated in her. The energy of the mutual caring still present in their relationship was clearly evident at this point in the session. Realistic hope was beginning to be awakened.

Pastor: It's obvious from what just happened that you two still have a lot of caring and warmth between you. In spite of your painful problems and the crisis you're in, you two have got a lot going *for* you.

This simple exercise is also a useful diagnostic tool. The fact that Bill and Joan still valued so much in each other and were able to become aware of these assets so early in counseling indicated to the pastor that they would probably be able to use short-term marital crisis counseling productively. When this type of question is asked in counseling and couples can think of little or nothing they appreciate, it is either a sign that the marriage is almost dead (and they haven't buried it yet by a divorce) or the question has been raised prematurely, before the anger has been expressed and reduced enough to allow them to be aware of what they still like.

Later in the session the minister asked: "What do you each want or need from the other in order to make your relationship more supportive and satisfying to you?" This adaptation of the second step in the IRM gave Bill and Joan an opportunity to clarify in their own minds and tell the other the particular changes of behavior they needed and/or wanted in the other to cope with the three facets of their problem.

After they had each described the major needs, the pastor said:

> I would be glad to work together with you to help you develop some workable plans to meet more of each other's needs. Of course it isn't realistic to expect that anyone can meet *all* of anyone else's needs. But my experience has been that couples who still care about each other as you do can learn to meet more of each other's needs and wants. If you do this, the satisfactions in your marriage will increase and the frustrations and conflict will decrease. Bill, would you be willing to meet weekly for four more times to see what the three of us can do together to help you work with rather than against each other in handling the crisis you're in? (The less motivated person was intentionally asked first.)

Bill responded that although he still needed most to find a job, he would like to try to improve things in their marriage. As expected, Joan accepted the pastor's offer.

> **Pastor:** Good, I'll look forward to working with the two of you. Among the things you each said that need to be changed to make things better, is there something you can begin doing within the next few days, before we get together again? It will help you feel better, if you begin soon to improve your situation.

After agreeing that alleviating their financial and job worries must have priority, they worked out a plan with the minister's help that was aimed at this goal. Joan would take a part-time nursing position at the local hospital where she knew there was an opening; Bill would follow up a job lead he had seen in a professional journal but had put aside because of his depression. He also agreed not to drink, except in the evenings, and to be responsible for childcare and meals on the days she worked. The minister affirmed their willingness to take concrete steps to cope with their crisis and suggested that they would debrief how their plans worked when they met at the agreed upon time the next week.

At the close of the session, the minister asked: "How do you each feel about our discussion today?"

> **Bill:** I feel a hell of a lot better than when I came in. Also a little surprised, I guess, since I expected to only come once.

> **Joan:** I feel much more hopeful, like there's really a way out of the mess we're in.

> **Pastor:** The way you used this session is a good sign—a sign that you both have important resources you can use in straightening out the mess so that things will be better for you and the kids. I hope things go well as you do the things you agreed on.

When they returned the next week, Bill and Joan reported a serious problem in implementing their plans. Bill was remorseful. Both were very discouraged. Bill had discovered that the job announced in the journal was already taken. When Joan returned from her job the second day, he had been drinking heavily. Their meal was not prepared and the children were crying. A fight ensued. Bill drank until he passed out. The minister helped them look carefully at this incident.

> **Pastor:** If you have a fight and don't learn something from it, you've wasted a fight.

In the discussion that followed, Bill admitted that he had taken a drink that morning, (in spite of his strong intentions not to drink) and that as on many earlier occasions, one drink led to getting drunk. In an individual session with the minister following the second joint session, Bill faced the fact that his drinking *had* cost him his job and that his loss of control over alcohol was hurting his family and interfering with his recovery from his job crisis. He agreed with the pastor's recommendation that he attend AA again on a regular basis. In her individual session, Joan explored the way her responses to Bill's excessive drinking were actually exacerbating his drinking. She agreed to attend a local Alanon meeting regularly to get help with her side of this problem. They accepted the pastor's offer to put them in touch with seasoned members of AA and Alanon (who were also members of that church), who could help them feel at home in those groups. In addition to her Al-Anon meetings, Joan also began attending the open AA meeting with Bill, one of the two he attended each week. Bill apparently had hit bottom, facing the fact that he must stop drinking if he was to avoid more serious damage to his family and his vocational future.

During the subsequent couple counseling sessions, the pastor helped Joan and Bill focus on the major unmet needs in their relationship. The three steps in the IRM became the basic structure of the counseling. For example, they negotiated and agreed upon a plan to make the division of the house work and childcare fairer to Joan. In this way they gradually modified their marriage contract making it more fair and satisfying to both of them.

By the end of the fifth week, when they all evaluated what they had done together in the counseling, it was clear that the couple had used the pastor's help well (which she affirmed warmly to them). Communication was more open and joint problem solving skills improved. There were numerous unresolved issues in their relationship but they were acquiring skills to work effectively on these and on new problems as they emerged. Except for one brief slip, Bill had not had a drink since he had returned to AA. He had not yet found a job, but was carefully following up what meager leads there were in a depressed aerospace industry. Joan was supporting him in this frustrating process and in exploring steps that would be necessary to prepare for a job in related areas of his profession. Joan's work was going relatively well. The satisfactions she was getting made her realize that she needed, for her own development, to continue her career in nursing on a full-time basis, as soon as they could afford a day-care center. Bill's relationship with their children also had improved with his sobriety.

By mutual agreement the couple agreed to meet every other week for a month and then on a monthly basis for a while, as they continued to struggle with unsolved issues and consolidated their newly learned ways of relating. As they left the fifth session, Bill and Joan expressed their heartfelt thanks for all the help Sally had given them. The three joined hands as they prayed the AA serenity prayer, followed by a prayer by the minister celebrating their growth and the gift of the new life they had received.

Many of the couples who seek counseling from ministers are much more difficult to help than were the Sheldons. Often one of the partners is resistant or closed to receiving help. When only one person seeks help with a marriage problem, the pastor should take whatever initiative is needed to involve the other in the helping process. In many cases, an invitation by phone will get the person to come for one or two sessions aimed at establishing rapport and reducing that person's resistances to continuing counseling. If only one person will come for counseling, it is essential to focus on what that person can do to improve her or his side of the relationship, including how to release the other emotionally so as to interrupt the neurotic interaction.[20]

As indicated earlier, the neurotic interaction of many couples is so deep and complex that short-term counseling is not enough. Some couples come to ministers after their relationship has disintegrated beyond repair. Seeing a minister is a kind of last resort, a way of pacifying their consciences by going through the motions of having counseling. When things have moved far along toward a divorce, it is important to ask for a moratorium, a postponement of further legal procedures until serious marriage therapy can be tried. It is usually futile to attempt marriage counseling or therapy in the midst of legal maneuvering.

In marriage counseling (and therapy) it is not the counselor's function "to save all marriages," but rather to help couples discover if their destructive relationships can be reconstructed by them with a more just, satisfying and growthful contract. Some marriages are so irreversibly destructive to the couple and their children that a divorce is the only hope of salvaging anything constructive. Divorce represents the failure of a relationship, but there is no reason to compound the harm by staying together in person-damaging interaction (which often is a marriage in name only) after serious marriage therapy has failed to heal the marriage pathology. To facilitate merciful release from such mutually strangling marriages is a constructive and essential ministry!

The Counselor's Role

It is evident that the minister took an active role in working with the Sheldons. I agree with the view that "if joint interviews are to be constructive, the counselor must assume responsibility for establishing limits, structure, balance, and focus during the interview."[21] The pastor was, in Sullivan's phrase, a "participant observer," but also an "observant participant." She was a *referee* who saw that both persons had a fair chance to express their views and participate equally in decisions affecting them both. The minister was also a *coach* who helped them learn how to play the game of marriage more creatively, a *teacher* who suggested or recommended actions for them to consider. She was a *communications-facilitator* who helped them practice the art of getting messages through to the other effectively. She was an *accepting authority figure* with some expertise in relationships. As such she was not shy about confronting them (caringly) with the hurtful consequences of their immature behavior or affirming them when they responded to each other more constructively. By her sensitivity to what was happening in their interaction, the minister was an *awareness stimulator*. She was a *reality-tester* for them, allowing them to check their perceptions of the realities of their relationships against hers. She was a *guide* who encouraged them to explore some of the dynamics of their relationships. The pastor was also a *role-model*, particularly for Joan, of a strong, competent, caring woman. She shared some of her learnings from her own marriage. She was a *pastor* who symbolized and sought to be a channel for the healing love of God to flow into the lives and the marriage of this couple. Most of all, Sally Marks was a *warm human being* who reached *out*, not *down*, to help Joan and Bill.

Being actively involved as a counselor does *not* mean making decisions for counselees, doing for them what they could do for themselves, or pushing them toward solutions chosen by the counselor. To illustrate, if persons ask, "Should I get a divorce?" it is important to accept their feeling of desiring (ambivalently in most cases) authoritative advice, but then (gently but firmly) make it plain that this is too complex and personal a decision for *anyone* else to make for them. The counselor's role, as it is then interpreted, is to help the counselee examine alternatives, face the consequences of various paths, deal with inner resistances (to leaving a destructive marriage), and gain a greater degree of freedom and objectivity so that she or he can make a wise decision.

Sexual Enrichment and Counseling

An important dimension of both marriage enrichment and counseling is helping couples liberate their potential to enjoy sex (one of God's best gifts) more fully. Contemporary sex therapies, pioneered by Virginia E. Johnson and William H. Masters, offers insights and methods often useful for sexual enhancement, in marriage enrichment events, *and* for helping couples with sexual problems, in marriage counseling and therapy. Much of the treatment in sex therapy is not therapy in the usual sense. Rather it consists of helping couples learn more sex-affirmative attitudes and feelings, and through practice, learn nondemand pleasuring skills. Performance and fear-of-failure anxieties are gradually diminished by practicing arousal exercises for their own inherent pleasure, with no other goal. The effectiveness of sex therapy techniques is increased when they are integrated with marriage counseling and therapy resources (see the books by Helen Singer Kaplan in Recommended Reading).

It is possible for many couples with functional marriages to improve their sex life. Here are some guidelines for enhancing sexual enjoyment:

(1) *Liberate your attitudes toward sex.* We human beings are the most highly sexed of all the animal species. Contrary to old dual-standard stereotypes, women have at least as rich a potential for sexual responsiveness as men. God would not have equipped us with such capacities for sexual satisfaction, without also intending that we enjoy sex! Sexual responsiveness begins in our heads rather than our genitals, so that's the place to begin enhancing sex. Many couples find it freeing to read together a book that describes and shows illustrations of ways to introduce more imagination and playfulness into sexual relationships—e.g., the books by Alex Comfort and James McGary in the Recommended Reading.

(2) *Keep your total relationship growing and sex will tend to improve.* Sex for human beings is a powerful form of communication. Whatever enhances your communication, caring, and companionship in other aspects of your marriage will tend to make sex better. Feed each other's heart-hungers for appreciation, touching, and affirmation regularly, and sexual responsiveness will usually increase. Virginia Johnson declares: "Nothing good is going to happen in bed between a husband and a wife unless good things have been happening between them before they got into bed. There is no way for a good sexual technique to remedy a poor emotional relationship."[22]

(3) *Resolve accumulated hurts, resentments, and anger by*

talking them through before you try to make love. Unfaced negative feelings build up into a wall (of hot or frozen anger). This wall will gradually diminish the flow of the loving and sensuous feelings that cause sexual arousal. Eliminating the injustices and inequalities in your marriage reduces the causes of much of the anger. Sex between two liberated, growing, equal individuals with a loving bond of mutual caring tends to be rich, whole-person sex.

(4) *Discover and enjoy the special romance of your present marriage stage*. Studies have shown that lusty, full-bodied sexual enjoyment usually can continue almost indefinitely into the latter years if a couple's general relationship has been nurtured. The popular fallacy that sexual pleasure is mainly for the young ignores the fact that sex can improve with experience and as a relationship grows richer with the struggles and satisfactions of passing years.

(5) *Use your imagination to create new ways to let your Child sides play together*. Set aside an hour or two once a week for a mutual pleasuring session. Introduce variety and adventure into the places, positions, and surroundings of love-making. Take the telephone off the hook, add a childproof flip-lock on your bedroom door, put some music on the stereo, light a few candles, and let your inner Child sides frolic. Dinner out, an afternoon at the beach or walking in the woods, a shower together, a night at a motel—these are but a few ways to give yourself a mini-vacation to let yourselves forget your adult responsibilities for a time and just play! Sex can be a revitalizing form of lovingly shared recreation. Enjoy!

(6) *Discover what you each enjoy most sexually, and coach each other on how to maximize your pleasure*. Explore and experiment to discover your own pleasure preferences. Find out what scents, words, flowers, pictures, jokes, caresses, approaches, positions, music, and drinks help you have the most luxurious feelings of body arousal. Then coach your partner in how to include these in your sexual play.

(7) *Learn and enjoy sessions of leisurely nondemand mutual pleasuring*. Many couples have discovered that this is the key to increasing sexual zest in marriages when sex becomes flat, dull, or boring. Forget the we try harder approach to sex. It's a dead-end street. Give each other a full-body massage using a warm body lotion with a sensuous aroma. Relax and enjoy giving and receiving mutual pleasure, with no other goal or agenda. Just flow with the natural pleasures of your bodies. Wherever the flow takes you will probably

be very good. Let yourself enjoy whatever the two of you both like.

(8) *Don't judge yourself because you have occasional sexual response problems*. In our culture most people have some inhibitions or hang-ups about sex. Within a relationship of mutual caring, patient and playful loving, old inhibiting attitudes may be unlearned. Many men experience occasional episodes of temporary impotence, often when they are tired or have had too much to drink. Shifting to nondemand mutual pleasuring for a while, to reduce anxiety about failure and self-imposed pressure to succeed, usually helps to restore the ability to have intercourse.

(9) *Avoid the triple traps of hurry, fatigue, and too much alcohol*. These often interfere with fully satisfying sex, especially in the mid-years and beyond. Loving takes time. Don't always put off sex until everything else is finished and you are both exhausted.

(10) *If do-it-yourself methods such as these don't improve your sex life, get the help of a qualified sex therapist who is also trained in marriage counseling*.[23]

Counseling Those with Alternative Life-styles

Many people, especially young adults, are experimenting with alternatives to traditional sexually-exclusive, lifetime-committed marriages. These alternative life-styles include cohabitation (living together), trial marriages, group marriages and communes, gay marriages, open marriages, and swinging. People are drawn to alternative styles for a variety of reasons. The majority have some degree of commitment and continuity in their relationship contracts, although usually not of a "till-death-do-us-part" duration. Many cohabiting couples have what are really trial or mini-marriages. Some are searching responsibly for ways that are more humanizing than traditional marriages often are. They are seeking fresh ways to satisfy the universal human needs for closeness, mutual caring, and sex. Many are searching for relationships where love and freedom can exist together more fully than they do in most marriages. Many young people are reacting against the hypocrisy, sterility, or emotional dishonesty of their parents' conventional marriages.

All close relationships involve conflict and problems. It is not surprising that some persons in such alternative relationships have the same types of interpersonal conflicts and pain as do some in traditional marriages. For those in relationships that are still stigmatized by our society, such as gay couples, there is the added burden of hiding or of social prejudice and discrimination.

Persons living in alternative types of relationships probably do not seek counseling help from clergy in as great a proportion as traditionally married couples. This is the result of their expectation (sometimes justified) that ministers will not understand or will judge them because of their life-styles. But pastors who become known in their communities as being warm, open, accepting human beings, *do* have opportunities to counsel with such persons. If churches are to become healing and wholeness centers for human brokenness in our world, they should seek to become so for persons in the variegated life-styles of our society, not just for those in traditional marriages.

Many couples who are living together need the same kinds of relationship enrichment, care, and counseling as do couples in traditional marriages. Unfortunately it is a rare church where they would feel accepted if they came for a marriage enrichment event.

Fortunately the basic principles of marriage enrichment and counseling can be applied in working with any close, committed relationships. In counseling with gay couples, it is important to help them identify and deal with the dynamics of their own interpersonal conflicts, as distinguished from the burden of hiding or social rejection, prejudice and discrimination that complicate their problems. In this sense, counseling persons with different sexual preferences or alternative life-styles involves issues similar to those confronted in working with persons from any minority—religious, ethnic, national, or racial—who suffer from a one-down position in their society. In such counseling, it is important for pastors to feel and create a climate of genuine respect for differentness. People who have been rejected by others quickly sense subtle condescension and disguised judgmentalism in the counselor. It is possible to accept the right of others to be different without abandoning one's own real values and standards.

Pastoral Care of Singles

In our society the norm is being married. This means that some forty million singles in America (one out of every three adults) are by definition abnormal. Those who are unmarried, by choice or by circumstances, often feel like a fifth wheel in church programs that have a strong emphasis on marriages and family life, but a neglect of singles. It is crucial that a church's program of care and counseling be structured so as to also minister to persons who are separated, divorced, widowed, or never married. Many of these persons are in great need of care and counseling. The challenge is to devise a strategy to make churches family-like environments for persons from the whole broad spectrum of relationships—single and unsingle. Churches should be supportive, *extended* family for everyone who wishes this, including those who live alone and those who are married or live in other committed relationships. Everyone needs a support system to nurture their wholeness. Many single people have to work hard to build and maintain a viable support system of need-nurturing relationships. Churches, through their pastoral care, education, and growth group programs, should be an oases for singles, offering nonexploitative alternatives to singles bars.

Without weakening family programs, churches should model positive attitudes and develop programs that help make singlehood a genuine option, a fully legitimate life-style. As people become freer to choose singlehood in our churches and our society, they will also be freer to choose marriage, if that is feasible and their preference. Fewer people will marry for the inadequate reasons of seeking to escape from singlehood or conform to the societal norm of being coupled.

John Landraf declares: "It is not only tolerable to be single . . . it can even be good! Singleness is a legitimate choice, for the long run as well as the short. It is not necessarily a better choice than being unsingle, or married; but neither is it necessarily worse. The married state can be wonderfully fulfilling; so can the nonmarried state. Spousehood can be hellish; so can singlehood."[24]

Church leaders should support and work with their single members to develop a variety of sharing and growth groups for singles—widows-to-widows support groups (and other grief healing groups), single-parent groups, and events such as creative singlehood retreats, classes, or workshops. (It is important to avoid thinking of singles programs as matchmaking opportunities, though that is one legitimate function for some singles.) Most singles do not like to feel welcome only in singles groups. Unmarried persons should be invited to and made to feel welcome in the whole range of sharing and learning groups in the life of a wholeness-oriented church.

Some people remain single, not because that is their real preference, but because they lack interpersonal skills or are afraid of being hurt in close relationships. Such persons often have an intense need for closeness yet cannot risk it. A combination of personal therapy and experience in a counseling or growth group may be helpful to them in overcoming their blocks to intimacy. A creative singlehood growth group can help young adults who suffer from such blocks to learn relationship skills and practice them in a relatively safe environment. Overcoming blocks to emotional closeness at this life stage can prevent the person from adopting a distancing loner stance as a permanent, defensive but impoverished life-style—freeing them to develop intimate relationships that are essential for human wholeness, for both the single and unsingle person. The philosopher Schopenhauer once told a fable about two porcupines who alternately huddled together to avoid freezing and were pushed away by the pain from each other's quills. It is noteworthy that many married couples also suffer from what might be called the freezing porcupines' dilemma.

Some older unmarried women have special needs for pastoral care and counseling. They suffer from both the pressure of the "coupleness" norm of our society, and in addition, the social prejudices and stereotyping of older unmarried women. Helping to make singlehood a genuine option and erasing the cruel, inaccurate stereotypes that make many older unmarrieds feel themselves to be social failures—these are dual challenges to be faced in pastoral care and education programs. Older unmarried men also encounter alienating social attitudes that assume they must have mother attachments or other deep neurotic hang-ups. The support and growth work occurring in creative singlehood groups and events can help singles—young and old—repair some of the self-esteem damage inflicted by our society and its institutions, including churches.

The growth perspective in pastoral care and counseling can help singles see the unique potentialities of being single:

> One of these is the opportunity to use the enormous time and energy, which most couples invest in childrearing, in other forms of satisfying, socially useful and generative ways. (Childless couples also have this opportunity of course.) Another is the freedom and

the motivation to develop new more creative models of relating. There's no logical or psychological reason why one lifestyle—marriage—should be regarded as superior to all others for everyone. Singles can develop a variety of other fulfilling options. A third positive thrust in singleness is inescapable motivation to keep growing as a person. Many married persons can avoid facing their emotional immaturity because it's protected by a neurotic marriage. This protection carries the high price of mutual stifling of personal growth. It's much harder for a single person to avoid the challenge to continue personal development.[25]

Learning to affirm and develop one's own singleness is as essential for creative marriage as it is for creative singlehood. John Landgraf observes: "Individuals with mutually satisfying marriages . . . have either carried a healthy singlehood into their marriage relationships, or have painstakingly developed their capacity for a high level of autonomy within their marriages." In his apt phrase, they are "well married to themselves."[26]

Sexuality is complicated enough for married persons. It is often doubly problematic for singles. Abstinence and sublimation are the only options recognized by traditional morality and most churches as not ethically off-limits for singles. There is something dehumanizing about a society that simultaneously glamorizes sex and offiially seeks to deny it to over forty million adults. The majority of singles ignore society's limits, but often they do so at a price of guilt and inner conflicts. Because of this, single sex (probably more frequently than sex in marriage) is often separated from relationships of trust, commitment, mutual respect, and caring—the context in which sexuality flowers. Many people (single and married) hurt themselves and others by rebelling against old straitjacket sexual morality, rather than struggling to discover new sexual values that are *both* liberating and person-respecting. Many singles feel pressured by the swinging singles image. They feel social pressure to perform sexually in casual relationships when they would prefer to reserve sexual involvement for a committed relationship. Our culture's values about sex are in a state of transition, conflict, and confusion. Many persons, single and unsingle, are searching for sound guidance and direction in this area. Counseling pastors need to be open to helping such persons work through their ethical conflicts, confusions and pain about sex, to discover what con-

Reality-Practice Session

stitutes life-affirming and person-enhancing sexuality for them.

With your spouse, or (if you are single) with a close friend, do the four steps of the Intentional Relationship Method (IRM) described earlier in this chapter. This is the most effective way to learn to use it with others and a means of enriching your own relationship.

PARISHIONER'S ROLE: (Requires two people.) As a couple, you are experiencing painful conflict and frustration in your relationship. (Use a relationship with which one of you is very familiar to define the dynamics of the roles.) Seek your pastor's help.

PASTOR'S ROLE: Use what you have learned in reading and reflecting on this chapter as you counsel with this couple. Try the adaptation for counseling of the IRM described in the case.

OBSERVER-COACH'S ROLE: Give feedback to the pastor on how much she/he focuses on the couple's interaction as the primary orientation of couple counseling.

Recommended Reading

Marriage Enrichment

(Books with asterisk include experiential exercises for use in marriage enrichment.)

David W. Augsburger, *Anger and Assertiveness in Pastoral Care* (Philadelphia: Fortress Press, 1979). Useful in helping couples deal with their anger constructively and become more healthily assertive.

Jessie Bernard, *The Future of Marriage* (New York: Bantam Books, 1972). Reveals the destructiveness of traditional marriage for women.

Beryl and Noam Chernick, *In Touch: Putting Sex Back Into Love and Marriage.* (Toronto: Macmillan of Canada, 1977). Uses a hypothetical couple to show the interrelationship between communication and sexuality.

*Charlotte Holt Clinebell, *Counseling for Liberation* (Philadelphia: Fortress Press, 1976). Discusses the interrelationship of pastoral counseling and consciousness raising in the church context.

*Howard Clinebell, *Growth Counseling for Marriage Enrichment, Pre-Marriage and the Early Years* (Philadelphia: Fortress Press, 1975). Describes basic resources for marriage enrichment and offers a new model of preparation for marriage and enriching new marriages.

*_____. *Growth Counseling for Mid-Years Couples* (Philadelphia: Fortress Press, 1977). Marriage enrichment approaches to the mid-years, including spiritual and value enrichment.

*_____ *Growth Counseling: New Tools for Clergy and Laity, Part I, Marriage and Family Life* (Nashville: Abingdon Press, 1973). Seven audio-cassette courses with users guide, including course IB, "Leading a Marriage Growth Group," II A and B, "Highlights of a Marriage Enrichment Workshop," III A, "Using Marriage Problems for Growth."

_____ *Growth Groups* (Nashville: Abingdon Press, 1977). Methods of leading growth groups, including marriage enrichment (chapter 4) and women's and men's Liberation (chapter 5).

*Howard Clinebell and Charlotte H. Clinebell, *The Intimate Marriage* (New York: Harper & Row, 1970). Explores the many facets of creative closeness.

Alex Comfort, ed., *More Joy: A Companion to the Joy of Sex* (New York: Crown, 1974). Includes drawings of a couple making love imaginatively.

John Gagnon, *Human Sexualities* (New York: Scott, Foresman & Co., 1977). An introduction to contemporary understanding of sexuality.

Bernard Gunther, *What To Do Till the Messiah Comes* (New York: Collier Books, 1971). Includes photographs and a description of how to give a full-body massage.

Robert Leslie, *Sharing Groups in the Church* (Nashville: Abingdon Press, 1971). Chapter 4 describes a marriage enrichment group.

Robert Leslie and Margaret G. Alter, *Sustaining Intimacy* (Nashville: Abingdon Press, 1978). A guide for couples.

Richard L. Lessor, *Love, and Marriage and Trading Stamps* (Chicago: Argus Communications, 1971). A TA and Gestalt approach to marriage.

William H. Masters and Virginia A. Johnson, *The Pleasure Bond: A New Look at Sexuality and Commitment* (Boston: Little, Brown & Co., 1974). Explores the interrelationship of commitment and sexuality.

James L. McCary, *Freedom and Growth in Marriage* (Santa Barbara, Calif.: Hamilton, 1975). Explores creative marriage, sexuality, and alternatives forms of marriage.

*Sherod Miller et. al. *Alive and Aware: Improving Communication in Relationships* (Minneapolis: Interpersonal Communication Program, 1975). The Minnesota Couples Communication Program detailed; book includes *Couple Workbook* for increasing awareness and communication skills.

*Herbert A. Otto, ed., *Marriage and Family Enrichment: New Perspectives and Programs* (Nashville: Abingdon Press, 1976). Twenty-one chapters describe the major family-centered and marriage-centered (including marriage encounter) programs of enrichment.

Letty M. Russell, *The Future of Partnership* (Philadelphia: Westminster Press, 1979). Explores partnership from the standpoint of a Christian feminist.

Jean Stapleton and Richard Bright, *Equal Marriage* (Nashville: Abingdon, 1976). Explores the problems and exciting possibilties of equality in marriage, sexuality, and child rearing.

Marriage Counseling and Therapy

George R. Bach and Peter Wyden, *The Intimate Enemy: How to Fight Fair in Love and Marriage* (New York: William Morrow & Co.,

1969). Methods of handling conflict and anger in intimacy increasing ways.

*Howard Clinebell, *Growth Counseling: Hope-Centered Methods of Actualizing Human Wholeness* (Nashville: Abingdon Press, 1979). Chapter 3 describes methods of growth-oriented marriage counseling and therapy.

_____ *Understanding and Counseling the Alcoholic* (Nashville: Abingdon Press, 1968). Chapter 11 deals with "Helping the Family of the Alcoholic."

Alan S. Gurman and David G. Rice, eds., *Couples in Conflict: New Directions in Marital Therapy* (New York: Jason Aronson, 1975). Describes a variety of approaches to marital therapy.

Journal of Marital and Family Therapy, published by the American Association of Marriage and Family Therapists. (Address on page 259.)

Helen Singer Kaplan, *The Illustrated Manual of Sex Therapy* (New York: Quadrangle, 1975) and *The New Sex Therapy* (New York: Brunner, 1974). Integrates sex therapy with psychodynamically-oriented marriage therapy.

David Knox, *Marriage Happiness: Behavioral Approach to Counseling* (Champaign, Ill.: Research Press, 1972). An application of behavior (learning theory) methods to marriage counseling and therapy.

William J. Lederer and Don D. Jackson, *The Mirages of Marriage* (New York: W. W. Norton, 1968). A guide to improving marriages by recontracting.

Robert F. Stahmann and William J. Heibert, eds., *Klemer's Counseling in Marital and Sexual Problems,* 2nd ed. (Baltimore: Williams and Wilkins, 1977). Articles on marriage, sexual and premarital counseling.

Paul G. Shurman, *Money Problems and Pastoral Care* (Philadelphia: Fortress Press, 1982). Explores the relation between money problems and family dynamics for clergy and laity.

Creative Singlehood

Margaret Adams, *Single Blessedness: Observations on the Single Status in a Married Society* (New York: Basic Books, 1976). Explores singlehood by choice as a healthy option.

Buff Bradley, Murray Suid, and Roberta Suid, *Single* (Reading, Mass.: Addison-Wesley Publishing Co., 1977). Resources on the joys of singlehood that can be used in programs for singles.

John R. Landgraf, *Creative Singlehood and Pastoral Care* (Philadelphia: Fortress Press, 1982). A guide to the psychology, care, and growth of persons single by death, divorce, default, and choice; describes launching a singles ministry.

Clark E. Moustakas, *Loneliness* (Englewood Cliffs, N.J.: Prentice-Hall, 1961). Explores the positive values of solitude, contrasted with loneliness.

Robert S. Weiss, *Going it Alone: The Family Life and Social Situation of the Single Parent* (New York: Basic Books, 1979). A helpful resource on single parenting.

Family Enrichment and Counseling

Where there is a breakdown in family life it is important to have some way of knowing what has gone wrong, and to help parents, children and youth regain problem-solving abilities and some sense of equilibrium in their life together. Religious tradition and values are not to be thrown out but reevaluated and made contemporary for each family member. The church should not be at the periphery of this struggle but at its heart, and involved in supportive, caring, and strengthening ways. . . . So learning methods of family counseling, analyzing family problems, and seeing the whole family picture in the emerging world of the last decades of this century becomes an important task.

—CHARLES W. STEWART, *THE MINISTER
AS FAMILY COUNSELOR*[1]

By "family" I mean the social system of primary relationships from which individuals derive their major sources of psychological and spiritual nurture. There are many types of families in modern society and in churches—traditional two-parent families, single-parent families, couples without children (and with no intention or possibilities of having children), three-generation families, and a variety of intentional committed relationships that are the families of many unmarried adults. Most people who live alone also have a support-nurture system of friends, constituting their family. This chapter focuses on understanding and helping families that include children, but many of the insights and methods can be used with all types of families.

A church as a family of families (of many types) is in an unrivaled and strategic position to become a family wellness center. The basic methods and approaches of conjoint couple enrichment and counseling, described in the preceding chapter, are equally useful, in doing counseling and enrichment with whole families.

Families As Social Systems

The family is a social organism, or system. Family therapy pioneer Nathan Ackerman suggests that the term "organism" connotes the biological core of the family, its qualities of living process and functional unity, and its natural life history—"a period of germination, a birth, a growth and development, a capacity to adapt to change and crisis, a slow decline, and finally, dissolution of the old family into the new."[2] Whatever affects one part of the family organism automatically affects all parts, just as an infected, injured, or well-functioning hand influences the entire body.

> The family is the strategic center for understanding of emotional disturbances and also for intervention on those psychic forces in human relations that have to do both with health and illness. In other words, the family group can make or break mental health. It has this power, insofar as it influences every aspect of human development, and of human relations.[3]

> A family system, like other social organisms, is composed of several interdependent subsystems. It is important for family counselors and therapists to be aware of the patterns of interaction within and among these subsystems—husband-wife, mother-children, father-children, child-child, grandparents-parents, grandparents-children, child-pet, and so on.[4]

As an organism a family has its unique psychological identity. The marital pair identity becomes the core for the expanding family identity as children are added.

> It is the interaction, merging, and redifferentiation of the individualities of the partners of this marital pair that mold the identity of the new family. Just as a child's personality internalizes something of each parent and also evolves something new, so too the identity of a new family incorporates something of the self-image of each marital partner and the image of their respective families-of-origin and also develops something unique and new. . . . The psychological identity of the marital pair shapes the child, but the child also shapes the parental pair to his needs.[5]

> The behavior, attitudes, values, and pattern of relating of individual family members are shaped by the family structure— that is, by the unconscious family rules, expectations, values, taboos, beliefs, patterns of communication, and distribution of power among its members. The dynamic family structure can frustrate or facilitate the potentializing of all its members.[6]

The personality health or disturbance of individuals is to a considerable extent an expression of the emotional climate of their families or other need-satisfying network of relationships. An individual's symptoms can be understood as the product of that person's interaction with a total family organism that is not meeting the personality needs of its members. As Virginia Satir observes, the pain of the "identified patient" (the one who is labeled "sick," "neurotic," "delinquent") is an overt expression of the covert pain that the whole family is suffering in its relationships.[7] The "negative complementarity" of a disturbed family organism has been observed by many therapists. Psychoanalyst Martin Grotjahn describes the complementary neuroses that often exist among members of a family, producing mutual reinforcement of neurotic behavior.[8] Apparently all members in a disturbed family derive some emotional gains from the identified patient's sickness. The interpersonal balance in such families appears to be based on this unconscious family contract: "We all agree that this one of us will be 'sick' ('delinquent,' 'alcoholic') so that the rest of us can continue to function." These are cases in point—the alcoholic's spouse who becomes disturbed when her or his mate achieves sobriety; the "good" family that has chosen, unconsciously, a deviant member to act out the family's forbidden impulses; and the schizophrenic's family where the relative adequacy of the other members' functioning is contingent on the sick member staying sick. These are examples of extreme negative family complementarity. Negative complementarity exists in all disturbed families, to some degree, even though it may appear that only one member is disturbed. Families usually seek outside help only when the member who bears their conflicts disturbs persons outside the family or disrupts the precarious functioning of the "well" family members.

Since families function as organisms or social systems, it is logical to enhance healthy families and treat unhealthy families as units. This is precisely what family enrichment and therapy do. Pastors who grasp the profound implications of the family systems' perspective find that it makes dramatic differences in all dimensions of their work with marriages and families.

In all counseling we are actually dealing with interlocking networks of persons, whether or not we are aware of this fact. In individual counseling one has direct access to only one part of that individual's total interpersonal network. The limitations of this are roughly analogous to those that phsycians would face if they attempted to help ill persons by examining and treating only their arm. In spite of the limitations of this analogy (the person obviously has more functional autonomy and ability to form new relationships than does an arm), it communicates a fundamental truth—the *essential* interdependence of persons. Couple and family enrichment and counseling are methods that intervene directly in total family systems, enabling help to be given to all the persons involved. Family enrichment and counseling aim at helping whole family systems improve their interdependent network of need-satisfying relationships, so that all will be freer to move toward wholeness.

A Church's Marriage and Family Program

There are four steps in developing a more effective care and counseling program in marriage and family living:

Step 1. *Assigning Responsibilities:* A congregation should have a "Marriage and Family Wholeness Committee" that works in partnership with the pastor to plan and develop marriage-family programs, following the four steps listed below. It is wise to include persons with decision making positions in related committees and boards—e.g., the education, pastoral care, and program planning committees. Such overlapping membership makes for better coordination in developing new programs.

Step 2. *Sizing up and Prioritizing the Needs:* The following checklist is a vehicle for helping to identify unmet needs:

Types of Needs and Examples of Groups Designed To Meet Them	*Our Church Meets This Need Adequately*	*We Should Develop New Programs*
Long-range Preparation for Marriage		
—A youth growth group, relationship skills group, or a "Sex and the Whole Person" group for youth.	____	____
Enrichment for Older Teens and Single Young Adults		
—Retreats, workshops, classes and growth groups to help them increase		

their capacity for growthful relationships, as preparation for marriage or creative singlehood.

    _____   _____

Premarriage Preparation (six months to a year before the wedding)

—A "Preparing for a Good Marriage" group or workshop, plus a minimum of three growth oriented sessions with each couple.

    _____   _____

Mutual Support and Enrichment for New Marriages

—Post-wedding growth sessions with each couple at six months and one year.
—A neo-marriage enrichment retreat or workshop.

    _____   _____

Training and Enrichment for Young Parents

—Parenting skills workshop for expectant and new parents.
—Class for parents to prepare them for infant baptism or dedication.

    _____   _____

Enrichment for Mid-Years' Marriages

—Parents-of-teens enrichment group.
—Emptying nest couple enrichment retreat.

    _____   _____

Enrichment for Creative Retirement

—A group or retreat to help couples make the most of these new years.

    _____   _____

Transgenerational Marriage and Family Enrichment

—A family camp or work-playshop.
—A parents-teens communication workshop.

Annual all-church enrichment retreat for couples of all marriage stages.

_____   _____

Single Parent Support and Enrichment

—Growth events for divorced, widowed, and unmarried parents.

_____   _____

Spiritual and Values Enhancement for Marriages and Families

—A Bible study or spiritual discovery group for couples.
—A spiritual nurture retreat for families.

_____   _____

Enhancing Sexuality

—A separate class or workshop or one important emphasis in all marriage and premarriage training events.

_____   _____

Coping with Changing Women/Men Roles.

—A separate consciousness-raising event; or an essential part of all marriage enrichment.
—A workshop on raising nonsexist children.

Training Lay Marriage and Family Enrichment Facilitators

—A training workshop for couples with special interest in and aptitudes to help support couples and families in crises, and newlyweds, especially teen couples.

_____   _____

Coping with Marriage and Family Crises

—Crisis care and counseling for couples.
—A grief group for the widowed and divorced.
—A grief growth workshop or class for families with major losses.

—A support group for parents of seriously handicapped or terminally ill children.

—A growth group for families who have recently moved to the community.

—A support-growth group for families with a dying child, parent, or grandparent.

Empowering Families for Outreach to the Community

—Training events to equip couples and families with the skills needed to respond to the needs of individuals and families within and outside the church, and empowerment for both social service and social change work.

The group and services listed above under the needs in the left hand column are illustrative of some of the rich variety of marriage and family resources that wholeness-oriented churches are developing. No church needs all of these groups since several of the needs can be met well in a single group or event—e.g., enriching marriages, parenting skills training, changing roles, and sexual enhancement. But every church should devote major leadership to developing a smorgasbord of such family enhancement experiences to respond to the needs of their congregation and community. Arranging the unmet needs in order of importance and urgency is essential in deciding the sequence in which new family events and groups will be developed.

Step 3. *Devising Goals, Strategies, and a Workable Plan to Respond to Unmet Needs:*

The Marriage and Family Wholeness Committee may delegate responsibility, to an *ad hoc* task group, for particular family life projects. In devising plans it is well to remember that creating new groups may not be essential in order to meet certain needs more fully. Existing couples clubs, adult church school couples classes, and men's and women's groups should be encouraged to include in their programs marriage and family enrichment retreats and events at least once a year.

Step 4. *Implementing the Plan, Evaluating and Deciding on*

Next Steps To Meet Other Needs of Couples and Families:
Everyone who attends an event should have an opportunity to
evaluate it in writing. Some who were invited but did not attend
should also be contacted. To illustrate, a retreat for young
marrieds at a camp away from a local community was poorly
attended. Feedback from several couples who did not attend made
it clear that cost and the child-sitting problems were major reasons
for the sparse attendance. Later the planning group decided to
sponsor a low-budget enrichment series at the church, with
child-care services provided.

Family Pastoral Care and Enrichment

Charles Stewart suggests that there are three basic dimensions
to a church's strategy for strengthening families:

> (1) The church should develop a network of caring and express
> its family concerns through visiting the sick, the grief-stricken, and
> those who are homebound. Intercessory prayer for those
> undergoing crisis may become a regular part of the church's order
> of service . . . the congregation is the primary agent of pastoral care
> with its pastors serving as enablers and consultants as well as
> visitors.
> (2) The church should develop a family ministry through its
> educational program. This ministry may be effected through
> intergenerational classes (in the summer when other classes are
> slack); intergenerational retreats for the entire church membership
> including single, widowed, and divorced persons—these are ways
> in which groups may study together and develop the family support
> bonds which such inclusive study generates.
> (3) The church should focus finally on family enrichment and
> counseling. Most family members can be helped to cope with the
> developmental passage points and accidental crisis periods through
> enrichment experiences. . . . Family counseling should be avail-
> able to those families for whom group interaction and support are
> not enough to help them through a critical period. The pastor will
> need to be aware of those who are under stress . . . and who require
> more counseling help than an enrichment group can provide.[9]

Douglas Anderson describes a variety of "Family Growth
Groups"—an approach he defines as "a program involving three to
five families who meet together regularly and frequently for
mutual care and support and for the development of family

potential."[10] He sees such programs as having these unique advantages as family-strengthening approaches:

(1) The family growth group goes beyond most traditional family life education programs by involving the whole family together as a unit in the experience . . . (2) The family growth group provides a supportive network of families to strengthen the family unit. In a society that fragments the family and that isolates families from extended kin and other families in the community, there is increasing need for programs that give families a sense of community and belonging . . . (3) The family growth group facilitates family change and growth by focusing upon the development of family potential. Family potential can be understood as those latent resources within every family for changing and growing, loving and caring, communicating, resolving conflicts, adventuring, creating and experiencing joy. The family growth group, focusing more upon growth than upon problems, provides opportunities for families to increase their awareness of their unique strengths and resources and then to actualize these dormant capacities in family living.[11]

Margaret Sawin has developed a model of family education and nurture called "Family Clusters." A cluster is composed of four or five families at various stages of family life, plus several single people. Clusters usually involve twenty to twenty-five persons. They commit themselves to meet weekly for two and one-half hours for a series of successive ten-week learning experiences. Sawin summarizes the goals of these clusters:

(1) To provide an intergenerational group of family units where children can relate easily to adults and adults to children;
(2) To provide a group which can grow in support and mutuality for its members;
(3) To provide a group where parents can gain perspective about their own children through contact with other children and other adult's perception of their children; likewise, where children can gain perspective about their own parent through contact with other parents and other children's perception of their parents;
(4) To provide an opportunity for families to consider experiences seriously related to themselves as individuals, as family members, as group members, and as members of a faith community;
(5) To provide a group wherein there is opportunity for families to model for each other aspects of their family systems in

communication, decision making, disciplining, interrelating, problem solving, etc.;

(6) To provide a joint experience between generations where adults can share their concerns regarding the meaning of life's experiences for them amidst a time of rapid social changes and aberration of traditional values; children can deal existentially with their real world experiences, using the group as a place to check out their experiences amidst its support and value system;

(7) To help families discover and develop their strengths through increased loving, caring, joy, and creating;

(8) To provide an opportunity for positive intervention into family systems so as to facilitate their living and growing together more productively. [12]

Family cluster sessions often include pre-session activities such as records, free play, and socializing (15 min.); a sandwich meal (with one family bringing the dessert for the group) (30 min.); singing, games, and fun (20 min.); a structured experiential educational period (45 min.) on an issue or theme chosen by the cluster; and evaluation and closing (10 min.). Issues explored by clusters include communication, family histories, interpersonal relations, beliefs and values, sexuality, conflict resolution, family strengths, world hunger, creative problem solving, ecology, freedom and responsibility, dreams and hopes, self-worth, careers and vocations, prayer and meditation, and TA. When families in clusters encounter crises or celebrate family milestones, they are supported spontaneously by their cluster. Family clusters and other types of family growth groups are exciting ways to enhance and strengthen family life through multiple-family, intergenerational education and caring.

Family enrichment retreats offer another productive method of family pastoral care. Charles and Alma Stewart co-led such a weekend at a church camp for sixteen families from a suburban church. The theme was: "Communicating the Christian Faith Across the Generations." The purpose was spelled out as follows: "To enrich family living by bettering communication between family members, by working through current levels of family conflict, by increasing coping skills and management of family problems, and by providing family members with models of intergenerational living." [13] The activities of the weekend included:

Friday evening—a light supper followed by a get-acquainted session, singing and refreshments.

Saturday morning—session of youth and adults (with children's activities in a separate group) led by Charles on how family members can work through blocks to communication; Alma then led a session on "getting in touch with our family story"; she also suggested children's literature that can be read together and discussed by families.

Saturday afternoon—family recreation.

Saturday evening—each family made and shared with a small group a "family tree" on which they pasted pictures of their immediate family. This was followed by a bonfire, hymn-sing communion service, and finally refreshments.

Sunday morning—Charles led a group discussion on how we learn faith differently at each age and stage. Each family was given time to discuss their family traditions, which to keep and which needed rethinking. In the closing worship couples were helped to share what they hoped to pass on to their families about their faith. "Sabbath Song" from *Fiddler on the Roof* was learned and sung by the group as a closing theme.[14]

One important goal in all family education and parent training should be to help parents raise children who are free from sexism. An experienced child therapist writes:

It's not easy to be a child of either sex. Children are hurt very early by many things. Some are crippled for life by poverty, ignorance, fear and emotional or physical pain. Our rigid expectations of what's okay for boys and what's okay for girls is crippling too. It shows in homes, classrooms, and on playgrounds as well as in play therapy rooms. An image that comes to me now is the tiny bound feet of a Chinese baby. Though that practice has disappeared, most cultures still bind the spirits of children in many ways. Girls are bound tighter than boys, particularly when it comes to passivity and aggressiveness and life choices. Very early, girls know that they are to be compliant and submissive and to behave so as to please others.[15]

Teachers—public and church school—have significant roles in liberating children from life-constricting sexism and racism. But parents are the key figures in this liberation. Children acquire their basic attitudes and feeling about racial differences and about men and women by observing their parents. As Charlotte Holt Clinebell (now Charlotte Ellen) points out, "Children raised by liberated parents in equalitarian marriages will be liberated themselves. Their inner freedom will make it possible for them to cope with the cultural [sex role] boxes which change so slowly."[16] (For a description of what parents can do to raise nonsexist, liberated children, see the books by Letty Cottin Pogrebin and Carrie Carmichael in the Recommended Reading section at the end of the chapter.

Conjoint Family Therapy

Family group therapy—the simultaneous treatment of an entire family—is one of the most productive developments among current methods of helping troubled persons. During the last twenty-five years, there has been a surge of interest in this approach, broadening the focus of many counselors and therapists from individual intrapsychic therapies to include family-organism therapies. A variety of distinctive styles of family therapy have been developed.[17]

Family therapist Jay Haley declares:

> The family therapist would seem to be arguing thus: psycho-pathology in the individual is a product of the way he deals with intimate relations, the way they deal with him, and the way other family members involve him in their relations with each other. Further, the appearance of symptomatic behavior in an individual is necessary for the continued functioning of a particular family system. Therefore, changes in the individual can only occur if the family system changes, and resistance to change in an individual centers in the influence of the family as a group. Most techniques of Family Therapy center in shifting the focus from the identified patient to the family and then resolving the problems in family relationships. At that point the individuals in the family undergo change.[18]

The common assumption of the family therapies is that the most effective way to help a troubled family member is to help the whole family change their ways of relating and communicating. All these therapies start with the systems perspective described above. Their shared goal is to enhance relationships within families so that they will become better environments of healing and growth for all their members. Family therapist Virginia Satir has identified these characteristics of families where growth flourishes: people feel and support each other's self-worth; they communicate in clear, direct, and honest ways; they accept each other's differences and tolerate each other's mistakes; the implicit rules within the family are fair and flexible; they are *open* systems that interact in mutually supportive ways with other people, families, and institutions.[19]

Here is a summary of the major goals of family systems therapy. Family therapists meet with the entire family, and occasionally with a subsystem within the family, to help the family learn:

(1) To communicate their feelings (both positive and negative), needs, desires, values, and hopes more openly, clearly, and congruently. The therapist is a "coach" of effective, relationship-strengthening communication skills. (2) To shift from focusing mainly on the "identified patient" and to deal with the hidden pain, conflict, and blocked growth in all family members that cause the individual's problems. This may involve a number of marriage therapy sessions with the wife-husband subsystem. (3) To interrupt their mutually damaging hurt-anger-attack cycles sooner and to gradually substitute self-feeding cycles of mutual need satisfaction among family members. (4) To mutually nourish rather than starve self-esteem in all family members. (5) To become aware of their family's contract—its implicit rules, roles, values, expectations, and beliefs—and then to renegotiate a more growthful working agreement that distributes satisfactions and responsibilities, power, and growth opportunities fairly. (6) To see the positive but abortive growth strivings in much of the frustrating behavior of family members and to learn how to encourage the expression of these strivings in more self-actualizing ways. (7) To resolve more constructively the inevitable conflicts of living together, recognizing that growth often can be activated precisely at the points of conflict. (8) To develop a healthier balance between their need for togetherness and their need for autonomy, giving more room for the latter. (9) To experiment with new behaviors and ways of relating that are more responsive to the real needs of all family members. This often involves doing family "homework" assignments between sessions. (10) To make the interaction within and among their subsystem more growth-engendering. (11) To open up their family system by developing more supportive relationships with other people, families, and institutions outside the family. (12) To create an interpersonal climate of high-level wellness within the family, thus making it a better growth environment for all its members.[20]

Virginia M. Satir's conjoint family therapy approach emphasizes the marital relationship as the axis around which all other family relationships are formed. The identified patient—e.g., a disturbed child or adolescent—is the family member who is most obviously affected by the pained marital relationship. But there is a circular relationship among all the persons within the family system—the disturbed child's behavior disturbs the parents' relationship, and vice versa. The distorted communication patterns of a family reveal the nature of its underlying problems. Dysfunctional persons did not learn in childhood to communicate effectively because of low self-esteem and distorted parent-child communication. Dysfunctional parenting produces dysfunctional families, which perpetuate distorted communication patterns.

Family therapists help families improve communication, about both feelings and family problems; take the risk of looking at themselves and their interactions, often for the first time; rebuild their self-esteem; and renegotiate their implicit family rules and contract to make these more fair and need-satisfying for all family members. Family therapists may help families unscramble garbled and "double-bind" or conflicted messages, complete gaps in messages, recognize the hurt behind anger and the control behind silence, and make sure no one continues to speak for another. A family therapist is a teacher of conflict-resolving, and need-nurturing communication—a coach of constructive interpersonal relating.

The Pastor's Uses of Family Therapy

Effective family therapy with troubled families, like individual psychotherapy, requires considerable therapeutic skill and understanding of individual and interpersonal dynamics.[21] Most clergy in generalist ministries have not had and do not need the training nor do they have time to do family therapy with dysfunctional families. As indicated earlier, a pastor's crucial function with such families is to help them find a well-trained family therapist.

But many of the insights and methods of family therapy can be utilized in enrichment work with healthy families, and in short-term crisis counseling with functional families. The family systems perspective (the conceptual foundation of family therapy) can function as a valuable new set of glasses for a pastor. These glasses enable one to see and understand families in fresh illuminating ways. It is invaluable for example, to become aware of the interpersonal atmosphere or emotional climate of a family, when making a pastoral call in their home or seeing them for counseling during a family crisis. Otherwise enigmatic behavior is clarified when understood in light of the family's general pattern and implicit rules of relating. The family systems perspective affirms the fact that we are "members of each other," that both our brokenness and wholeness reflect the quality of our network of need-satisfying relationships. This perspective tends to reduce unproductive blaming, since everyone in the family is involved in helping to maintain the family pattern of which much individual behavior is a manifestation, to a considerable degree.

"Healthy Family Enrichment Sessions," with individual families or with several families in a family camp, workshop or cluster represent an adaptation of family therapy aimed at helping functional families develop more of their potentials and thus discover the latent family in every actual family.[22] The wholeness of families can be enhanced significantly by their participation in a family growth booster once a year.

Seeing a person in individual counseling through the family systems perspective helps a pastor be aware that the person's childhood family and current family are *actually present* in the session within the individual being counseled. All of us carry within us the family system where our personalities were uniquely shaped and the current support system that enables us to maintain some measure of humanity. These inner families influence our present behavior, thinking, feeling, and relating in pervasive ways. In short-term family crisis counseling, it is sometimes helpful for counselees to become aware of the roots in their childhood families of their inappropriate responses in the crisis. In conjoint marriage counseling, a session or two that include the couple's children and/or parents, often brings to light otherwise hidden aspects of their marital interaction. This can prove helpful to them in altering their unconstructive patterns of relating. Individual pastoral therapy seeks to help people claim the strengths and grow beyond the limitations of their internalized family-of-origin, including withdrawing the projection of obsolete roles, attitudes, and expectations from that family onto current family and other close relationships. Growth following individual crisis counseling or therapy is more likely to continue if the person's significant others are involved at some point in the therapeutic process.

The systemic perspective offers a variety of resources for enhancing spiritual and value growth. Family therapy and family crisis counseling are ways of helping families whose guiding values and priorities are not functioning growthfully, to revise their values and priorities. A family's basic philosophy and theology of life, their values and spiritual orientation are "caught" by young children (more than they are "taught") as they absorb the meaning and value orientation of that family. Continuing spiritual development throughout adulthood is best nurtured in family-like caring groups in which spiritual values are *experienced* in relationships.

A vital dimension of an open, growing family system is its openness to the wider spiritual reality whom we call God. This openness provides a transpersonal and transfamilial context of meaning and spiritual support. The wholeness of family members can be profoundly nurtured by their awareness of their bond and basic oneness with other persons and with humankind, with the biosphere, and with the love-hearted Spirit of the universe.[23]

Family Crisis Counseling

Many family crises with which a minister's help is sought involves parent-child, parent-adolescent, child-parent-grandparent, in-law, and sibling relationships. The goal and methods of crisis counseling and of couple counseling described earlier are directly applicable in such family crisis counseling. But resources from these approaches need to be integrated with the family systems perspective and augmented by methods from conjoint family therapy.

All human crises are essentially interpersonal events. Both the causes and the potential resources for constructive coping are derived, to a considerable degree, from one's interpersonal support system. People who live alone and lack robust support systems, and nuclear families who do not have close relationships with their extended family (or its psychological equivalent in a network of close friends) are acutely vulnerable to crises of all types. It behooves the pastor, therefore, to use the family systems perspective in approachig all crisis counseling, especially family crises.

When the lives of individuals are hit by trauma, their entire family network is impacted. It is important to provide pastoral care and, in some cases, counseling for the whole family. All probably are hurting, some more obviously than others. To help families use their problems for growth, it is essential to intervene pastorally in the whole family. Charles Stewart states:

> When the family approaches a counselor for help its members have reached an impasse in their relationships, are not coping with their problems, and are in overt or covert conflict with one another . . . The counselor does not set out *to solve* their problems but rather hopes to open up communication between family members, to help them understand their actions and interactions which produce the conflicts, and to enable them to try new forms of behavior and role relationships which will be more satisfying to all and more productive of family harmony.[24]

When ministers are contacted by one individual (usually a parent) about a family crisis, it is important to talk with that person to establish rapport and then to involve the whole family in a conjoint counseling session. In contacting other family members by phone the pastor may say: "When one member of a family is hurting, others usually are feeling some pain, in my experience. It might be helpful to all of you if your whole family could discuss the situation you all face and what to do about it. Each of you probably has some valuable ideas that could help make things better for all of you." Family meetings may take place in their home (if interruptions such as phone calls and TV can be kept at a minimum) or in the minister's study. Somewhat different aspects of family's interaction will be evident in each setting.

The most difficult transition in moving into whole-family counseling is helping family members change their definition of the problem from the one who is obviously disturbed, to the whole family system. But only to the degree that this occurs will other family members accept the fact that *they* have some responsibility to change their behavior in the family. Unless this happens, family counseling will not be effective.

The ABCD approach to crisis counseling can be integrated with the Intentional Family Method. The IFM is the IRM applied to families in helping families cope with and grow from their crises.[25] In the A and B steps it is important to establish a trustful relationship with each member of the family. Each should have an opportunity to articulate perceptions and feelings regarding the family problem, and thoughts about constructive solutions. "Boiling down" a family's problem (identifying its separate aspects) is best done with all family members contributing their perspectives. Using the second step of the IFM ("What I want or need from this family is . . .") can be a valuable part of the diagnostic, boiling-down process. When young children are involved in family counseling sessions, the second step of the IFM can be paraphrased, "If I had a magic wand and could use it to make things better in our family, I would . . ." The steps of the IFM can often be done by a series of family "go-round," beginning with the least assertive and verbal member.

When the unmet needs that have caused and/or resulted from the crisis are out on the table for family discussion, the pastor can help the family negotiate a change plan enabling them to meet more of each person's needs. In this step, each family member identifies the "growth points" at which they can enhance their relationships by responding more fully and intentionally to each others' needs. Helping the family develop and act on a workable change plan is step 3 in both the ABCD crisis help approach and in the IFM. Relatively functional families often can, with a pastor's help, decide within a few sessions on ways of making constructive changes in their basic family contract. Before the end of the first session, but after their hurt and anger have been expressed and reduced, it is important to give each member an opportunity to tell the others what she or he appreciates about the family and the individuals within it (step 1 in the IFM). It can be remarkably healing to families bogged down in cycles of mutual hurting to hear the mutual affirmations in this exercise. I recall being deeply touched when a long-alienated father and adolescent son began to be reconciled during a conjoint family session as they told each other what they still liked about the other. Mutual family affirmation can well be repeated occasionally during the process of family counseling as a way of making them aware of positive changes they are accomplishing.

Family recontracting, using the IFM, often can help functional families improve their interaction in a few sessions. In negotiating a family change plan it is essential to work out an agreement about precisely what each person will do—what each will give and get as the plan is implemented. In this way, a family can revise their family contract to make it fairer and more effective in coping with the family's crisis.

The minister needs to be able to recognize seriously hurting children and youth.

> The majority of parents who seek help for a child do so because the child's behavior worries them or someone outside the family, often the school authorities or law enforcement officers. Here are some signs of serious behavior problems: Aggressive and destructive behavior; lying and stealing; severe learning problems. Children who are disturbed or unhappy do not always act in ways that upset adults. Quiet, shy children are sometimes simply that—there's nothing wrong with being quiet or shy. But if this quietness seems excessive, it may mean there are serious problems. Problems which are expressed within children (rather than directed outward in destructive behavior) include withdrawal from peer relationships; exaggerated fears, phobias and terrifying nightmares; serious speech problems; bizarre behavior; and severe or multiple psychosomatic problems such as asthma, colitis, frequent stomach aches and headaches, rashes and other physiological problems rooted in emotional conflict within the child and interpersonal conflict in the family.[26]

To assist parents in identifying serious problems with which the help of a child therapist is needed, it is important to raise several questions: Is the behavior you're worried about age-appropriate for your child? How severe is the problem and how long has it been occurring? Does the behavior represent a sharp change? Is the child's behavior related to major stresses and crises in the family? Children often respond in disturbed as well as disturbing ways after major grief experiences such as an uprooting move, the hospitalization and/or death of a family member, or the divorce of parents.

Unless it is clear that a child is seriously disturbed, it is appropriate for a pastor with some training in family crisis counseling to discover if that will help the family. When young children are in family sessions (counseling or enhancement), I usually provide them with simple play therapy materials such as crayons and paper. Using these materials during the session provides something expressive and satisfying for children to do; it often also involves them in the therapeutic interaction of the family on their own level. Several times the pictures that children have drawn, when shared by them during the session with other family members, threw light on family issues.

Parents of families going through crises such as a natural disaster, an auto accident, or a major move can help prevent disturbances in their young children by using do-it-yourself play therapy methods. Clark Moustakas suggests that there be a particular place or corner in the child's room for this special play.[27] This corner should be stocked with a variety of play materials such as paints and paper; puppets or doll families for fantasy play; clay for making and squashing things; a pan of water and a sand tray for messing; toys for encouraging constructive release of pent-up frustration, anger, and aggressiveness—e.g., pounding boards, punching devices, and things for throwing without hurting.

Sensitive teachers in church school and public school sometimes can use such play-therapy methods to help children play through and resolve feelings from family crises and losses.

> The adult's role in play therapy is to encourage free expression, to be available to relate as children reach out, and to enforce (if necessary) the ground rules—"Here we can do anything we like except hurt ourselves or others, or destroy property." Communication and expression by children should be spontaneous and free—through play, fantasy, words, paintings, acting with dolls, and expressing aggressiveness. Activities may be pursued individually or in spontaneous subgroupings of children. The facilitator doesn't pressure the children to discuss what they are doing, but welcomes and encourages spontaneous communication by listening attentively and responding warmly.
>
> Such a play-growth group encourages children to play out so-called negative feelings (anger, jealousy, fear, guilt, destructiveness) so that these will not be expressed in self-hurting or other-hurting behavior, nor will they block positive feelings (joy, love, pleasure, self-esteem), nor distort relationships. Play-growth groups . . . encourage children to use their imaginations in healing and growthful ways. Finally, they provide an experience of relating to adults (parents, teachers or counselors) who really value feelings, imagination and play in children and in themselves.[28]

Play therapy-growth experiences can help children grow in their self-esteem, their all-important "it's good to be me" feelings.

Right-Brain Methods for Marriage and Family Care and Counseling

As indicated in chapter 2, recent research on the functioning of the human brain, by Roger Sperry and others, has revealed that the two hemispheres tend to specialize in different and complementary functions. In our rational, analytical, verbal, technological society, education, counseling, and general socialization encourage the lopsided development of left-brain capacities to the neglect of the balancing right-brain potentialities—the inituitive, metaphoric, relational, and holistic functions. This imbalance often is more prominent in males than in females.

Healing and wholeness for many people involves discovering and developing their neglected right-brain capabilities. The most skilled counselors and therapists are those who are in touch with and able to integrate their own left-brain's rational, analytical skills with their right-brain's intuitive, imaging, integrating abilities, and to help their clients do the same. Facilitating religious wholeness often involves integrating left and right brains' spiritual resources and functions. Healthy, whole-brain religion balances left-brain elements—belief systems, creeds, theologies, ethical codes, intentionality, responsibility—with equally vital right-brain elements—myths, rites, liturgies, parables, art, drama, dance, experiences of nature, religious experience, and life commitments. The spiritual truths and riches of the Bible are frequently expressed in metaphoric word and images:

> Throughout its pages we read imagistic, dreamlike language: "streams of living water," "valley of the shadow of death," "the wolf shall dwell with the lamb," "the light shines in the darkness," "tongues as of fire," and . . . "his voice was like the sound of many waters." Jesus spoke of "bread from heaven" and used as his chief teaching medium the parable, a powerful vehicle for communicating with the metaphoric mind.[29]

Here are some types of right-brain approaches that can help facilitate growth in marriage and family enrichment and counseling. (I am indebted to Douglas Anderson for spelling out and exploring most of these categories of right-brain methods in his book *New Approaches to Family Pastoral Care*.) The statements following each category illustrate some alternative ways a counselor can lead a couple into that type of experience:

(1) *Active imagination:* "Picture yourself and your relationship whole—the way you would like it to be." "Imagine yourself inside each other's skin." "Surround your partner with caring energy, seeing it in your mind as a warm, healing light around him [or her]."

(2) *Stories and Parables:* "I knew a couple once who . . ."; "This happened in our marriage . . ." (sharing vignettes of your own struggles, with your partner's permission); "A familiar Bible story that your relationship reminds me of is . . ."

(3) *Dreams (both daydreams and night dreams):* "Describe of our dream"what happened in your dreams as though it is happening now." "In your imagination, be the various parts of your dream" (two approaches to dream work from gestalt therapy). "Tell us a daydream where your conflict is healed."

(4) *Reframing a problem:* "Do you see any positive message to you in your spouse's nagging?" "What have you learned from your family crisis?"

(5) *Reliving Creative Memories:* "Go back in your memory and let yourself relive . . . the first time you met"; or ". . . . a crisis like this which you survived and even grew a little stronger"; or, ". . . a time when you really felt close and loving"; or ". . . a beautiful experience you shared."

(6) *Aphorisms, Jokes, and Paradoxes:* "Instead of trying harder (to maintain an erection), let yourself relax and enjoy the closeness. Don't try to have an erection. Just flow with the pleasure, wherever it takes you" (example of a paradoxical technique).

(7) *Free drawing and painting:* "Draw a symbol or a picture of the way you feel now about your marriage (or family)." "Now draw the way you'd like to feel about it." "Using circles to indicate the power and distance-from-others of each person, draw a picture of your childhood family." "Now draw your present family."

(8) *Play:* "Will the two of you reenact that argument you had last night so we can all see what happened?" "Plan together a mini-vacation—a day when you do things each of your Child sides really enjoys; then have the vacation you planned."

(9) *Action Imperatives:* "Plan and then do something to improve things in your marriage a little this week; if you do, you'll probably feel more hope." "To help interrupt the vicious cycle that's going on between you, I recommend that you each do one small thing the other person will like this week, even if you don't feel much like it yet" (this should be followed by concrete planning of what each will do).

(10) *Affirmations:* "It takes strength to admit you need help and then get it." "It takes a lot of guts to have survived what you two

have been through!" "Take turns now telling each other what you still like about the other, or what you still appreciate about being married."

(11) *Body Enhancement:* "Give each other at least three hugs a day this week, OK?"(or a back or foot massage).

(12) *Centering:* "Go inside yourself and become aware of the place where you feel centered. Stay in that place for a little while. Now talk with each other from that center."

Right-brain approaches can be used growthfully in all types of pastoral care and counseling (and in all aspects of ministry) to balance the dominant left-brain approaches. Rational, intentional, analytical teaching, preaching, and counseling methods need to be balanced and blended with metaphoric, playful, intuitive, parabolic approaches to enable these arts of ministry to maximize human wholeness.

Counseling in Family Violence and Rape

Domestic violence—spousal homicide, spouse beating, child battering, and sexual molestation, and rape—have reached epidemic proportions in our culture.[30] These traumatic, shattering, often hidden experiences occur in all socio-economic-educational classes. Pastors need to know how to respond. Churches should include domestic violence and rape among the social problems they inform their people about. They also should support both preventive and therapeutic programs in their communities.

Violence against women—physical, sexual, spiritual, and psychological—is the psychological consequence of our society's socialization of men and women. Men are trained to feel strong and successful only if they are in positions of power over others. But since power is defined hierarchically, only a few—those on top—can really *be* powerful. Therefore, most men live with some feelings of failure, powerlessness, and rage. The targets at whom men are conditioned to vent this frustration and rage are those who are weaker (children) or who are socially defined as less significant and powerful (women). In other words, violence against women is a consequence of the unequal distribution of social status and of economic, political, and legal power between women and men. It also is the consequence of the learned powerlessness and passivity that many women feel when they relate to men.[31] Furthermore, it is the result of the fact that most men, in patriarchal cultures, learn to define women as "other" and to feel masculine only to the degree that they are different from women. The long-range solution to violence against women is the full liberation of women from their one-down position in society and from their alienation from their real strengths, and the full liberation of men from the destructive self-image that equates "masculinity" with male aggression (in sports, hunting, the competitive marketplace, in war, and in relations with women and children) and "success" defined as dominance.

In our society, the odds are great that a chronic wife- (or cohabiting woman-) beater will never be arrested or taken to court. The odds are even greater that if tried, he will not be convicted. Many police are reluctant to interfere in family fights unless the neighbors complain or the violence becomes extreme. Women who desperately need to flee from violent relationships often have no safe place to go, are without funds, and cannot qualify for welfare because of their violent husband's salary.

Here are some suggestions for helping women who are in violent relationships:

(1) If the violence has been chronic and the man is unmotivated to change (most batterers are not motivated), it is crucial to encourage and help the woman and her children move to a place where they will be safe—with relatives or to a shelter for battered women—and to initiate legal separation proceedings. As long as a violent culture reinforces their violent pattern, and the police and courts do not intervene effectively, batterers have little reason to change their violent behavior.

(2) Pastors should put victims of male violence in touch with hot lines or counseling programs staffed by women volunteers trained in working with women who have survived battering or rape. This is crucially important if a pastor is male.

(3) Couple counseling or individual psychotherapy *may* be helpful in relationships in which there are constructive dimensions and infrequent violent behavior—if both partners are motivated to interrupt their spirals of escalating frustration, rage, and attack.

(4) In order to empower women to stop accepting violence from men, it is essential for them to unlearn their learned helplessness

and take back the power they have been giving away to men. A consciousness raising group of women can be invaluable in raising the consciousness and empowering battered women.

Here are some guidelines for helping rape victims:

(1) Put the woman in touch immediately with a rape hotline or center staffed by women who understand her terrible trauma, know the community resources she may need, and can help protect her from the accusatory attitudes of some medical personnel and police.

(2) Encourage her to notify the police. Have a volunteer from a rape hotline or center with her when she is questioned by police.

(3) Get the woman to a doctor or the emergency room of a hospital immediately to receive whatever medical treatment she needs *and* get the evidence that will be required to press legal charges. A woman from the rape program should accompany her when she goes for medical help.

(4) Encourage the woman to press charges if her assailant is caught, and help her find a lawyer (preferably a liberated woman) who is known to be competent in handling rape and domestic violence issues.

(5) Get the woman into individual therapy with a woman therapist or into a rape or battered women's group to help heal the severe psychological wounds that usually result from being the victim of sexual violence. If the woman is coupled with a man, joint counseling may be needed to help the male deal with the trauma of rape to intimate relationships.

When child battering or sexual abuse occurs in families, it may be necessary for the courts to intervene either to remove the abusive or molesting parent or other relative from the home, or place the child in a healthy foster home. Wife battering and child abuse often occur in the same families. Battered children who do not receive effective therapeutic help often grow up to be spouse and/or child batterers.

Reality-Practice Session

PARISHIONER'S ROLE: If three or four people are available for this session, take the roles of a family with whose dynamics and problems one of you is thoroughly familiar. That person should help the others get into their roles.

PASTOR'S ROLE: Counsel with the whole family, helping them communicate more openly. Use the steps of the Intentional Family Method discussed in this chapter, as the structure of your counseling approach.

OBSERVER-COACH'S ROLE: Help the pastor be more effective in giving each person an opportunity to be heard by the other family members, and in helping the family become aware of their strengths as well as their problems. Be aware of the family's dynamics.

Recommended Reading

Nathan W. Ackerman, *The Psychodynamics of Family Life* (New York: Basic Books, 1958) A classic by a pioneer in family therapy.

Douglas A. Anderson, *New Approaches to Family Pastoral Care* (Philadelphia: Fortress Press, 1980). Discusses the use of right-brain metaphoric communication in marriage, family enrichment, and counseling programs.

Robert W. Beavers, *Psychotherapy and Growth: A Family Systems Perspective* (New York: Brunner/Maxel, 1977). A growth-oriented description of family systems theory and therapy, reports research findings on the healthy family.

Carrie Carmichael, *Non-Sexist Childraising* (Boston: Beacon Press, 1977). A guide to raising liberated children.

Charlotte Holt Clinebell, "Liberated Childhood," chapter 6 in *Meet Me in the Middle: On Becoming Human Together* (New York: Harper & Row, 1973). The why and how of raising nonsexist children.

Charlotte H. and Howard J. Clinebell, *Crisis and Growth: Helping Your Troubled Child* (Philadelphia: Fortress Press, 1971). A guide for parents in helping children with disturbing crises.

Howard Clinebell,, "Growth Resources in Family Systems Therapies," in *Contemporary Growth Therapies*, chapter 9. Overviews four types of systems therapies and then discusses the generic goals of family therapies.

_____ "Growth Groups for Children and Families," in *Growth Groups*, chapter 9. Describes a variety of growth experiences for children, parents, and families.

Howard J. Clinebell and Charlotte H. Clinebell, "Developing Parent-Child Intimacy," in *The Intimate Marriage*, chapter 8. Explores ways of developing *creative* closeness between children and parents.

Evelyn Millis Duvall, *Marriage and Family Development*, 5th ed. (Philadelphia: J. B. Lippincott, 1977). An introduction to the family life cycle.

Thomas Gordon, *P.E.T. In Action* (New York: Bantam Books, 1978). Describes the basic methods of Parent Effectiveness Training, including learnings from parents who have used these techniques.

Bernard G. Guerney, Jr. et.al. *Relationship Enhancement: Skill Training Programs for Therapy, Problem Prevention, and Enrichment* (San Francisco: Jossey-Bass, 1977). Describes a skill-training program that can be used in marriage, family enrichment, and counseling.

Susan L. Jones, *Family Therapy: A Comparison of Approaches* (Bowie, Md.: Robert J. Brady Co., 1980). Describes the development of family therapies and compares seven approaches—integrative, psychoanalytic, Bowen, structural, interactional, social network, and behavioral.

David Kantor and William Lehr, *Inside the Family: Toward a Theory of Process* (New York: Harper Colophon Books, 1975). Reports on what trained observers discovered about how family systems actually function.

Shirley G. Luthman and Martin Krischenbaum, *The Dynamic Family* (Palo Alto, Calif.: Science and Behavior Books, 1974). A growth-centered approach to family therapy derived in part from Satir's theory and methods.

Del Martin, *Battered Wives* (New York: Pocket Books, 1976). A shocking report on the prevalence, causes, and treatment programs of domestic violence.

Salvador Minuchin, *Families and Family Therapy* (Cambridge, Mass.: Harvard University Press, 1974). An introduction to structural family therapy that seeks to change the organization of the troubled family.

_____ et al. *Families of the Slums: An Exploration of their Structure Treatment* (New York: Basic Books, 1967). The structure and treatment of disadvantaged families.

Clark E. Moustakas, *Psychotherapy with Children: The Living Relationship* (New York: Harper and Brothers, 1959). Chapter 8 describes how parents can do play therapy with their children.

Herbert A. Otto, ed., "Family-Centered Programs," in *Marriage and Family Enrichment: New Perspectives and Programs* (Nashville: Abingdon Press, 1976), chapters 3-6.

Letty Cottin Pogrebin, *Growing Up Free: Raising Your Child in the 80's* (New York: Bantam, 1981). A guide for parents on how to raise liberated children.

Virginia Satir, *Peoplemaking* (Palo Alto, Calif.: Science and Behavior Books, 1972). A book to help parents develop growth-nurturing families.

_____*Conjoint Family Therapy* (Palo Alto, Calif.: Science and Behavior Books, 1964). A classic on the theory and practice of family therapy.

Margaret M. Sawin, *Family Enrichment with Family Clusters* (Valley Forge: Judson Press, 1979). A guide to setting up family learning and enrichment clusters in congregations.

Arlene Skolnick, *The Intimate Environment: Exploring Marriage and the Family* (Boston: Little, Brown & Co., 1973). A textbook exploring the changes, problems, and future of the family.

Arlene S. Skolnick and Jerome H. Skolnick, eds., *Family In Transition* (Boston: Little, Brown and Co., 1971). A collection of readings on traditional and changing family patterns, sexuality, and child rearing.

J. C. Wynn, *Family Therapy in Pastoral Ministry* (San Francisco: Harper & Row, 1982). Provides both an overview of family therapies and practical applications for the parish minister.

CHAPTER 12

Referral Counseling

> Referral is not a pastoral failure. It is a subtle and important helping art. . . . I propose that we think about it as illustrative of the more generally useful skill of helping people to focus their needs and clarify their feelings.
>
> —THOMAS W. KLINK[1]

Skill in the art of referral is indispensable in a minister's caring and counseling. As Wayne Oates declares, "One of the reasons that pastors do not have time to do their pastoral ministry is that they insist on doing it all themselves. . . . They have failed to build a detailed knowledge of their community as to the agencies, professional and private practitioners, etc., who could help them in their task."[2] By default, the "lone ranger" pastor often deprives troubled people of needed specialized help that is readily available in the community. C. W. Brister hits the heart of the matter: "The minister calls upon community resources, not in order to pass the buck, but because he wishes the best for all persons concerned."[3]

Because many people trust a pastor's judgment and turn to him or her spontaneously when trouble strikes, a minister is in a strategic position to assist them in finding competent, specialized help. A review of the empirical research on counseling by clergy came to this significant conclusion: "Clergy bridge the gap between informal social support systems and more specialized formal helping professionals. Clergy have day to day contact with their parishioners and are highly visible in their communities when compared to agency or private therapists. . . ."[4]

A wise referral is one of the most significant services a pastor can render a suffering parishioner. A family who, in the midst of a traumatic problem, is guided by their minister to effective help, is usually eternally grateful to her or him. A minister can multiply his or her service to the troubled manyfold by using all the helping resources of her or his community to the hilt.

Unfortunately some ministers feel that to refer is to admit inadequacy or failure. A nationwide study of where people take their problems revealed that "the helping process seems to stop with the minister and physician in the majority of cases, and far more so with the minister than with the physician."[5] In fact, physicians referred eight times as many persons to mental health facilities and practitioners as did ministers.[6] Obviously some ministers have much to learn about the importance of "pastoral care by referral," as Klink has phrased it. At the other extreme, there are a few ministers for whom referral is as automatic and as mechanical as the salivation of Pavlov's dogs. Because of this too-rapid referral reflex, their unique helping potentialities as ministers are not used fully. They miss some of the deeper satisfactions of their profession by not attempting to establish healing relationships with those who may need precisely what they have to give. Troubled parishioners get the feeling that ministers are passing the buck (because they are)!

Properly conceived, referral is a means of using a team effort to help a troubled person. It is a *broadening* and *sharing,* not a total *transfer* of responsibility. It employs the division-of-labor principle that is the basis of interprofessional cooperation. Only by drawing on the specialized helping skills of others can ministers have time and energy to fulfill their unique *pastoral* function as *spiritual* growth enablers for an entire congregation.

Whom To Refer

With what persons should a minister utilize referral to broaden the base of help?

(1) Those who can be helped more effectively by someone else.

(2) Those with problems for which effective specialized agencies are available in the community.

(3) Those who do not begin to use pastoral help in four or five sessions.

(4) Those whose needs obviously surpass the minister's time and/or training.

(5) Those with severe chronic financial needs. Public welfare agencies with trained social workers are appropriate referrals.

(6) Those who need medical care and/or institutionalization.

(7) Those who need intensive psychotherapy.

(8) Those about the nature of whose problem one is in doubt.

(9) Those who are severely depressed and/or suicidal.

(10) Those toward whom the minister has a strong negative reaction or intense sexual attraction. The anxiety that often underlies strong antipathy will tend to vitiate one's counseling effectiveness with such a person. If the pastor can discover what is causing this reaction and work through the negative counter-transference feelings, she/he may do effective counseling and grow as a result of the experience. It is very difficult for any counselor to maintain the healthy objectivity needed in a counseling relationship if he or she is experiencing intense sexual attraction to a counselee.

It is important for pastors to build working relationships with one or more physicians in their community. A counselee who has not had a physical check-up recently should be strongly encouraged to do so if the pastor has any suspicion that the person may need medical attention. If there is the slightest suspicion that neurological, endocrine, or other medical problems may be lurking behind or complicating psychological or interpersonal conflicts, the pastor should *insist* that the person consult a doctor. A close collaborative relationship with a physician is also vital in counseling with those who have psychosomatic problems, severe depression, suicidal tendencies, alcoholism, other addictions (including food addiction), menopausal problems, physical handicaps, chronic or terminal illness, severe sexual problems, geriatric problems, pronounced mood swings, or severe anxiety. In my experience, many physicians will welcome collaborative relationships with competent counseling pastors. In such mutually helpful relationships, referral becomes a two-way street, as it should be. Counselees' permission to consult with their doctor (or therapist) should always be obtained before doing so.

Here are some of the signs of severe mental disturbances indicating a need for referral to a mental health facility or a psychotherapist:

(a) Persons believe (without any basis in reality) that others are attempting to harm them, assault them sexually, or influence them in strange ways. (b) They have delusions of grandeur about themselves. (c) They show abrupt changes in their typical patterns of behavior. (d) They hallucinate, hearing nonexistent sounds or voices, or seeing nonexistent persons or things. (e) They have rigid, bizarre ideas and fears, which cannot be influenced by logic. (f) They engage in . . . repetitive patterns of compulsive actions or obsessive thoughts. (g) They are disoriented (unaware of time, place, or personal identity). (h) They are depressed to the point of near-stupor or are strangely elated and/or aggressive. (i) They withdraw into their inner world, losing interest in normal activities.[7]

When these signs appear the minister should help such persons' families get them mental health treatment as soon as possible. The recovery rate from severe mental disturbance is higher if intensive treatment is instituted at an early stage. Family physicians are the minister's and family's logical allies in such situations. They can administer sedation or psychic energizers, or other emergency medical care and also can make arrangements for hospitalization. Often they are an effective link with a psychiatric facility or individual psychiatrist.

The question of *ego strength* has an important bearing on what type of referral to make.[8] As was pointed out in chapter 7, persons with weak egos generally respond best to help that is primarily supportive rather than uncovering. The goals of such therapy are to help persons gain strength by blocking regression, limiting their impulsive "acting-out," and helping them handle their adult responsibilities and use their personality strengths (rather than trying to erase their liabilities). Social casework agencies often are able to provide this form of ego-adaptive therapy. Persons with psychoneurotic problems and a reasonable degree of ego strength often are able to utilize the various forms of uncovering psychotherapy in growthful ways.

Consultation or Referral

Clergy can counsel safely and productively with many people they otherwise should refer, if they have regular access to competent consultants. There is growing awareness among pastoral counseling specialists and mental health professionals that providing consultation to the "care-giving professions," including ministers, is essential if the yawning gap between the supply of and the need for trained therapists is to be even partially bridged.[9] Regular or even occasional case conferences with a specialist in pastoral counseling or other competent psychotherapist, can extend the range of pastors' helping abilities, give them expert assistance in handling counseling crises, and alert them to subtle dangers in certain counseling relationships. Because they understand the ministry from the inside, pastoral counseling-therapy specialists usually make excellent consultants for those in general ministries. Because of their medical training, psychiatrists also are valuable as consultants provided they are also well-trained in psychodynamic theory and psychotherapy. Clinical social workers often bring extensive knowledge of community resources to consultations. Clinical psychologists offer expertise in psychological testing and evaluation.

Where to Refer

John L. Mixon, an experienced social worker, once declared: "The two most important aspects of a good referral are: (1) a knowledge of the resource, its program, functions, intake policy, etc., and (2) the use of sound counseling procedures in interpreting the resources and the possible help the individual might expect to receive."[10]

Pastors should begin to prepare themselves for an effective referral ministry soon after arriving in a new parish. This involves doing two things—(1) assembling a growing referral file of community resources and (2) building relationships with the social agencies and helping professionals. An organized referral file becomes increasingly useful as the minister accumulates information about social agencies; directories of pastoral counseling specialists, psychiatrists, clinical psychologists, marriage counselors, and AA groups etc.; phone numbers of pastoral counseling centers, emergency psychiatric facilities, mental health clinics, suicide prevention centers, etc.

A minister should check to see if the community has a welfare planning council or other community agency that provides a directory (and perhaps a phone information service) of community services. Copies of such directories should be in the pastor's study and in the church library.

What are the major problem areas where the minister needs to draw on community resources in counseling? One referral manual by Marcus Bryant and Charles Kemp, *The Church and Community Resources* (St. Louis: Bethany Press, 1977) includes helping resources in these areas: adoption and child placement, alcoholism, financial assistance, business problems, child guidance, child welfare, child abuse, crisis intervention, day care, correctional institutions, deafness, crime and delinquency, dental services, disaster relief, drugs, education, employment, family life, the handicapped, health, housing, industrial problems, legal assistance, mental health facilities, minority groups, older persons, planned parenthood, problem pregnancies, retirement, single parents, sex counseling, speech problems, transients, retardation, veterans, vocational guidance, youth services. This manual also includes a directory of national resources—church related, governmental, voluntary and a section where pastors may enter their own working list of local phone numbers and addresses. Parish pastors would do well to keep a manual such as this at their fingertips.

Accurate evaluations of the competence of the various counselors, psychotherapists, and agencies in one's community often are difficult to acquire. The reputation that therapists or agencies have among physicians, counselors, and ministers provides a reasonably reliable guide. Beyond this it is helpful for ministers to become personally acquainted with as many as possible of their community's therapists and social agency personnel. In my experience, the most trustworthy evaluations of therapists' personal authenticity and professional competency come from direct contact with them and from observing the outcome of referrals to them. By having coffee or lunch with such persons, visiting the local child guidance or mental health clinic, and attending the open meetings of AA and Al-Anon, pastors build relationship bridges that can prove immensely useful when they need to make a referral. As they work with these persons in helping troubled parishioners, the relationshp often grows stronger.

A cooperative team spirit among the helping professions of a community does not happen by accident. Someone must take the initiative. In order to do pastoral work optimally, ministers need such a team. What is more, pastors are in an ideal position to take the initiative in this, perhaps starting with a monthly breakfast meeting of a small group of helping professionals in one's congregation and community. Such meetings enhance communication of mutual concern and build working relationships. Participants may begin to ask the pastor for assistance in helping their clients or patients deal with value and meaning problems, as well as overtly religious issues. Thus collaboration between clergy and other professionals becomes a two-way street as it should be. To work effectively with physicians and mental health professionals, pastors may need to resolve self-esteem and authority problems that cause them to give their power away to these professionals.

How To Refer

The minister of a rural church recognized that a man who came to him "for help against a conspiracy" was suffering from paranoid delusions. A psychiatric referral, though obviously essential, was difficult since this particular illness, by its very nature, made the man unaware of his need for help. Only by counseling with his family and collaborating with their physician over a period of weeks was an appointment with a psychiatrist and subsequent involuntary hospitalization accomplished. In the interim, the pastor maintained a supportive role with the man. He listened and did not attempt to dissuade him from his delusions, although he did raise some gentle questions concerning whether the man felt that all the threatening aspects of his situation were objectively real or partly within his feelings. He did not challenge the man's paranoid defenses, but only tickled them. He stayed close to the burdened family while they were arranging, with the doctor's help, for hospitalization.

This is an example of *stopgap supportive counseling*, the valuable help a minister gives until more basic help becomes available. Because of frequent resistance to psychiatric help and the length of some agency's or therapist's waiting lists, the gap that must be "stopped" often extends over weeks or longer.

Here are some guidelines for effective referral counseling:

(1) *Create this expectation.* The function of assisting persons in finding specialized help should always be mentioned when the minister's availability for counseling is described in the church bulletin or newsletter.

(2) *Mention the possibility of referral early in counseling relationships where it is likely to occur, explaining why specialized*

help may be needed. Persons who have mustered their courage to come to their pastor expecting help, usually feel some degree of rejection if it becomes necessary to refer them. This is true even if they understand intellectually why the referral is necessary. The longer the pastor waits to plant the seed of the possibility of referral and the greater the dependence that has developed, the more likely referral will arouse feelings of rejection.

(3) *Start where persons are in their perceptions of their problems and the kind of help needed.* Until ministers understand these perceptions and expectations, they are in no position to make a referral. Counselees' inner pictures of their problems and their solution is often very different from the counselors' perceptions of the nature of the problems and the type of help needed.

(4) *Work to bring counselees' perceptions of their problem and their solutions close enough to the counselors' perceptions to permit referrals to take.* This may require several sessions of counseling. Referral efforts often fail because counselees' perception of their situation is fundamentally different from that of the referring pastor. Such persons naturally resist referral by not going to the helping resource or by not continuing long enough to receive benefits.

(5) *Help counselees resolve their emotional resistance to the particular helping person or agency recommended.* Tom Klink emphasizes the linking of two vital helping processes—*acceptance of feelings and support of reality testing*—in enabling persons to accept referral. The pastor should ask about persons' feelings about a particular referral while helping them move toward accepting the reality of the need for specialized help. Attempts to refer persons, without clarifying and accepting their feelings, and enabling them to become more realistic about their need for other help, usually fail.

Before suggesting that persons with drinking problems go to AA, it is important to find out how they see their problems (guideline 3). Do they feel that drinking is a cause or only an effect of (or even a solution of) their other problems? Do they have any desire for help in stopping their drinking? If so, AA is appropriate. In suggesting AA it is important to ask persons what they have heard and how they feel about that group. This query, about any agency to which one is making a referral, is a valuable means of discovering the fears, misinformation, and emotional resistance that otherwise may sabotage the referral. Dealing with these inner blocks often takes time, but it is an essential part of *motivating* a person to accept the help recommended.

(6) *Interpret the general nature of the help that persons may expect to receive, relating it to their own sense of need.* Do this without making the mistake of overselling the potential help—a mistake that makes the therapist's or agency's work more difficult—or committing the agency or therapist to a specific treatment approach.

(7) *Establish strong enough rapport with persons to develop a bridge over which they may walk into another helping relationship.* The use of this trust bridge is facilitated if counselees know that their minister is personally acquainted with the persons or agency to whom they are being referred. The minister is fortunate if she/he can say, "The therapist I want you to see is a person I know and trust." In any case, the pastor should say, "If you would like, I'll talk with the therapist about your situation so that she/he will know something about it before you go." This is a way of breaking the ice and smoothing the transition. Here is how the bridge principle was used in referring an alcoholic to AA. The pastor says: "Mac, if I understand what you're saying, you are beginning to suspect that you have a problem with drinking. I'd like for you to chat with a friend of mine who has been through the mill himself on this problem. He's found an answer that works for him. Let's see if he's free to drink a cup of coffee with us, OK?" At the three-corner coffee klatch that follows, the AA member (who is also in the minister's church) offered to take Mac to an AA meeting.

In making referrals to therapists and social agencies, it is generally wise to *let persons make their own appointment.* This keeps the initiative with them and, in addition, allows the relationship with the new helping person to begin on the phone. Talking with a therapist or an intake worker on the phone may help allay a person's anxiety about going for help. If possible the minister should check with a therapist or agency before suggesting that referral, to make sure that the person referred can be seen. It is also wise to ask persons to phone the pastor after making an appointment and after being seen for the first time. If a person does not call, the minister should phone to see how things went.

This procedure expresses continuing concern and allows the pastor to follow through with those who resist obtaining the specialized help recommended.

(8) *Encourage referred persons to really try a given therapist or agency, even if they are only mildly willing.* A skilled psychotherapist may be able to reduce resistances to help that have not yielded to previous efforts. With alcoholics, I first do all I can to reduce their resistance to AA. Next, I urge them to expose themselves to an AA group regularly for at least a month, whether or not they particularly like it. In some cases this exposure allows the warmth and the informal group therapy of AA to make an "end run around their defenses." Their resistances gradually dissolve as they experience the satisfaction of sobriety and the warm acceptance of the AA group. If one waits until alcoholics are completely ready for help, they may be in mental hospitals or cemeteries first. The same applies to many other problems. Of course, it is not wise to push persons beyond a certain point—the point at which the backlash phenomenon makes them more resistant to help.

(9) A final guideline is *to let persons know that one's pastoral care and concern will continue after the referral.* One of the unique strengths of referral by a pastor is that a pastoral *care* relationship can and should continue following a referral. This helps to lessen the sense of rejection. A "Pastor's Guide to Community Services" makes this wise recommendation:

> After you refer continue to show Christian concern and friendliness. Keep in touch with the agency . . . so that you can work together effectively to help the client. No community agency can take the place of a pastor or the fellowship of the church. In a healthy, collaborative working relationship, both the agency and the church should feel free to express any question or criticism of the other so that there can be better mutual understanding and appreciation.[11]

A collaborative interprofessional relationship may not be easy to maintain, but such a relationship often is in the best interests of the person being helped. In making referrals for psychotherapy, it often is necessary for the pastor to gradually diminish her/his supportive counseling in order to motivate the persons to move into another relationship. A person who is in psychotherapy should not to be allowed to drain off problems by continuing to counsel with the pastor. The relationship should be one of *pastoral care*, not pastoral counseling. Otherwise the person may attempt to use one parent figure against the other in a self-defeating manner. It usually is appropriate for the pastor to ask occasionally how things are going in therapy. If that relationship is unproductive, another therapist can be recommended.

When Referral Sources Are Lacking

Lack of essential community referral resources should do more than frustrate ministers. It should touch our prophetic nerve and motivate us to help create the needed resources. If enough people of goodwill are informed of the unmet needs, and if some individual or group takes the initiative, referral resources can be created. A minister or a dedicated layperson in a helping profession is in a strategic position to spark and lead such a community project.

Pastors in rural and small remote communities often find that making referrals and creating new resources is difficult if not impossible. Having knowledge of the *closest* helping facility or professional is crucial in such situations. Correspondence with state mental health departments or with the national voluntary organization focusing on a particular problem usually brings reliable information concerning the most accessible help. A minister working collaboratively with other pastors and community leaders, may help a state health agency recognize the need for a mobile clinic or therapeutic service in that area on a regular basis.

The lack of mental health referral resources on an ability-to-pay basis constitutes an acute need in many communities, both for middle and lower income groups. A study of five socio-economic classes in New Haven revealed that the bottom group—the poor—had a rate of psychiatric illness almost three times that of any other class.[12] Poor people are more likely to be diagnosed "psychotic" and sent to mental hospitals than are middle-class people with similar symptoms. The latter more often are given a less stigmatized diagnoses and offered private psychotherapy that the poor obviously cannot afford. But the high cost of private therapy makes it unavailable, on any extended basis, to many middle-income people. A needed expression of pastoral care through the prophetic ministry is challenging and working to change the medical and mental health delivery systems so that all persons will have the preventive and therapeutic help they need. Establishing a church-related counseling service where skilled pastoral counseling and therapy are available on an ability-to-pay basis is one way of helping meet this need.

Reality-Practice Session

PARISHIONER'S ROLE: You are Ed and Sally Wright, the parents of seventeen-year-old Jim, who has taken money from the cash register at the store where he worked after school. You have two teen-age daughters younger than Jim. You are deeply disturbed by what appears to be Jim's "delinquency" and willing to do whatever is necessary to obtain help for him.

PASTOR'S ROLE: Sally and Ed come to your office and tell you of Jim's problem. You sense that Jim's behavior may be a symptom of a hidden pain in the family and that the parents should be referred (and perhaps the whole family) with Jim to the local pastoral counseling center or family service agency. Attempt to make this referral after inviting Jim and his parents in for a talk, following the guidelines in this chapter.

OBSERVER-COACH'S ROLE: Help the pastor to be more effective in enabling the couple to clarify their feelings, and understand their need for specialized help by a particular counseling agency.

In another session, practice referring an alcoholic to AA and the spouse of an alcoholic to Al-Anon.

Recommended Reading

Marcus D. Bryant and Charles F. Kemp, *The Church and Community Resources (St. Louis: Bethany Press, 1977)*. Describes how to use community resources. Gives a handbook of available resources and an outline for compiling a local church's handbook of resources in its own community.

Ronald R. Lee, "Referral as an Act of Pastoral Care," *Journal of Pastoral Care*, 30 (Sept. 1976), pp. 186-97. Describes the initial, middle, and terminating phase of referral, pointing out that the skills involved are like those used in brief psychotherapy.

Robert L. Mason, Jr., Carol B. Currier, and John R. Curtis, *The Clergyman and the Psychiatrist—When to Refer* (Chicago: Nelson-Hall, Inc., Publishers, 1978). Uses case examples to explore the basic needs for help of persons with eight types of problems.

Thomas W. Klink, "The Referral: Helping People Focus their Needs," *Pastoral Psychology*, Dec. 1962, pp.10-15.

Wayne E. Oates and Kirk H. Neely, *Where to Go For Help* (Philadelphia: Westminster Press, 1972). Describes the major helping professions and gives list of helping resources on fifteen problems.

William B. Oglesby, Jr., *Referral in Pastoral Counseling*, rev. ed. (Nashville: Abingdon Press, 1978). Deals with when, how, and where to refer and what to do when referrals fail.

CHAPTER 13

Educative Counseling

Get Wisdom; get insight
Do not forsake her, and she will keep you;
love her, and she will guard you.

—PROVERBS 4:5-6

He taught them as one who had authority.

—MARK 1:22.

In our "race between education and catastrophe" we need the ministry of creative education. Every local church and every hard-pressed family becomes a center for creative learning in the midst of the realities and concrete dilemmas we face. On the scale of urgency to survive we must grow or perish. Learning is the first and last business of every growing-dying, time-bound finite person.

—PAUL E. JOHNSON[1]

A high school youth talks with his pastor about an emotionally charged vocational choice. A couple comes for their premarital conferences. A young man seeks help with a perplexing theological issue. His rigid, negative beliefs seem to reinforce his deep self-esteem problems and spiritual emptiness. A social action committee asks for the minister's help in planning its approach to a complex injustice issue in their community. All these situations have one thing in common—to meet the needs of the persons involved, the ministers must be able to function simultaneously as teachers and counselors. They must be *teacher-counselors*.

Many of the finest counseling opportunities that ministers have require a blending of the skills of creative education and dynamic counseling. This type of help is called *educative counseling*, a helping process that integrates the insights and methods of two pastoral functions with the single objective of fostering the wholeness of persons. This approach involves the personalized communication of certain knowledge, beliefs, values, and coping skills as an essential part of the counseling process. Educative counseling goes far beyond merely imparting information. By utilizing counseling skills and sensitivities, it helps persons understand, evaluate, and then apply the relevant information to coping with their particular life situations.

There are, of course, educative ingredients in almost all types of pastoral counseling. In certain types of counseling—referral, vocational, sexual, premarital, prebaptismal, divorce, mid-life, and retirement counseling—educative elements loom so large that it is appropriate to label these types "educative pastoral counseling."[2]

This is a natural form of counseling for pastors. As their professional role is defined, they are both counselors *and* educators with a certain message and *Weltanschauung* to be communicated. Educative counseling methods are among their most valuable tools for helping people. They are particularly useful in *preventive group counseling*—small group experiences designed to prevent future problems by preparing people to meet "developmental crises" constructively (e.g., marriage, childbirth, going to college, retirement, dying). The concept of "educative counseling" helps to resolve the unnecessary conflict in some ministers' minds—between their roles as counselors and as teachers and proclaimers of the gospel. This conflict is often the result of the image of the counselor as relatively passive and value free (as in client-centered counseling theory) and of the false dichotomy between knowledge and feelings in the Rogerian approach. The conflict is resolved when transmitting relevant knowledge and dealing with feelings are seen as complementary, interacting factors in the helping process. This view is emphasized in the newer cognitive therapies, which provide rich resources for both the theory and methodology of educative pastoral counseling.[3] The concept of educative counseling is the bridge that links pastoral counseling with the entire growth-nurturing educational program of a church. Education and counseling become natural allies with a common goal—to maximize whole-person growth. Counseling and therapy are simply methods of reeducation to help persons replace faulty learning with creative learning of attitudes, ideas, relationship skills, and values.

The Goals of Educative Counseling

Educative counseling shares the common elements of all pastoral counseling described in chapter 4. It becomes educative as it moves toward three goals: (1) *discovering what facts, concepts, values, beliefs, skills, guidance, or advice are needed by persons in coping with their problems;* (2) *communicating these directly or helping persons discover them* (e.g., through reading); (3) *helping persons utilize this information to understand their situation, make wise decisions, or handle problems constructively.*

To discover what may be relevant to a person's needs obviously requires listening and interacting with that person. It requires becoming aware of her/his inner and interpersonal reality. To give information and or advice in counseling prior to understanding the person's needs and feelings weakens the counselee's trust in the counselor. Ideally, the teaching aspects of counseling should be focused as sharply on the person's particular needs as is the medicine that a competent physician gives to a particular person for a specific malady. In discussing "guiding" as one of the historic dimensions of care, Clebsch and Jaekle state:

> Fundamentally, the guiding ministry assumes that useful wisdom, which edifies and illuminates the meaning and direction of a person's life, can be made available within the framework of the helping act. . . . The wisdom *must be fashioned or shaped to the immediate circumstances of the troubled person* in order that it may be appropriated and used in the context of the particular trouble at hand. Guiding as a pastoral function does not develop ethical principles . . . for general application to the process of living, but rather forges decision-guiding wisdom in the heat of specific troubles and strives to facilitate its use in particular situations.[4]

Ministers should share those aspects of their experience, insight, and knowledge that they sense, from their awareness of persons' problems, will be helpful to them as *tools or building materials* in their constructing a workable approach to their situation. Counselors should not try to sell counselees on certain approaches to their problems. Instead they should encourage persons to wrestle with the material communicated, to use what "speaks to their condition," and ignore the rest. The subject matter of educative counseling, as in all counseling, is *the person* and not the ideas *per se*, however valid. The cognitive input of educative counseling provides resources for the person's own thought processes by which she/he searches for constructive approaches to current problems or demanding future ex-priences— e.g., marriage, parenthood, moving, surgery, retirement. Guidance commonly employs two identifiable modes. *Eductive guidance* tends to draw out of the individual's own experiences and values the criteria and resources for such decisions, while *inductive guidance* tends to lead the individual to adopt an *a priori* set of values and criteria by which to make his or her decision.[5] Educative pastoral counseling blends *inductive* and *eductive* methods of guidance in varying proportions. The minister communicates information in this spirit: "Here is some information (concepts, values, or approaches) which, from my experience and understanding, are valid. I believe they may be useful to you in meeting your needs, so I share them for you to consider. If you wish I will help you evaluate their relevance and apply them to your situation." The method is inductive in that it draws on the minister's store of knowledge and insight from her/his religious tradition, study, and experience. It is eductive in that it seeks to draw out the person's inner problems *and wisdom*, effecting encounter between these and the ideas presented. Counseling methods are used to help the person diminish emotional blind spots and inner conflicts that otherwise would prevent her/him from understanding, evaluating, selecting, and then utilizing the ideas that are relevant. The minister-counselor should not be timid about sharing relevant knowledge acquired by disciplined study and sharing whatever wisdom about life she/he has derived from counseling others and from personal growth struggles. The difficult but crucial goal is to find, in Granger E. Westberg's words, "a healthy balance between real authority based on expert knowledge, and the person's right to work through human problems in a free and empathetic relationship."[6]

The educative counselor is a kind of coach whose function is to assist the person in acquiring skills in coping constructively with problems. Most coaches don't play the game, but they do share the expert knowledge they possess about it. Often the minister is like a "player-coach" (Elton Trueblood's phrase) who plays but also guides others.

A devout and conservative Protestant young woman consults

her pastor for help with a difficult decision—whether to terminate a romantic relationship obviously moving toward marriage with a Catholic man. To make an informed decision, such a person needs accurate knowledge about the basic views of the two traditions on the Bible, the church, religious authority, birth control, and freedom. She needs to face realistically tensions and conflicts that characterize most mixed marriages. From her training and experience, the minister had at least some of the knowledge the woman needed to make a constructive decision. Complete objectivity is impossible, particularly in such emotionally laden decisions, but possessing reliable facts can increase the degree of objectivity.

Sharing information (however accurate) is seldom, if ever, enough. Almost always powerful feelings, interpersonal dynamics, fears, and prejudices are present. These must be dealt with if a person is to make a wise decision. Information becomes useful only as it is related to *that* person's inner world of meanings. Skilled counseling in the case described above involved the integration of relevant knowledge with the person's feelings, attitudes, beliefs, values, and her relationship with this man. Only such *integrated* knowledge is really useful in decision making and problem solving.

The Dynamics of Educative Counseling

The fundamental question that must be answered to ascertain the possibilities and limitations of educative counseling is this: *What is the function of knowledge in causing and curing human problems?* As Rogers states, "Most maladjustments are not failures in *knowing*" but root in emotional blocks.[7] It does not follow from this that the communication of information is unimportant in much counseling and therapy.

Misconceptions, distorted beliefs, and unconstructive values often are significant, even crucial dimensions of troubled people's problems in coping. Seldom are they the *only* factor but they can be the crucial factor. Lack of accurate knowledge is sometimes a *cause* and frequently a *complicator* of interpersonal problems. Mrs. E's realistic fear of an unwanted pregnancy formed a vicious cycle with her conflicting sexual attitudes. This fear produced diminishing returns in the couple's sex life, which strained their interpersonal relationship. Their pastor referred Mrs. E. to a competent gynecologist who recommended a more effective contraceptive method for her. This diminished the fear of pregnancy and together with the pastor's couple-counseling on their sexual and communication problems, improved their relationship.

The *extent to which persons are actually able to use knowledge depends on their degree of wholeness*. No amount of information about reality will, in itself, transform a pyschotic's deep distortions in perceiving reality. And yet, as remotivation therapy has shown, even regressed schizophrenics have some conflict-free areas of their psyches. By starting in these areas and providing cognitive resources and reality-oriented coping skills, the healthy parts of the psyche grow stronger as these are exercised.

Six assumptions constitute the theoretical foundation of educative counseling:

(1) Intellectual knowledge is an important resource for handling reality constructively.

(2) Most counselees have sufficient conflict-free personality areas to allow them to make *some* use of information derived from educative counseling sessions and reading assignments between sessions.

(3) A minister possesses knowledge, values, and skills that can be useful to many counselees.

(4) Counseling skills can help a person *utilize* relevant information.

(5) Facts, insights, values, and skills can help many persons cope more effectively with the challenges they confront. Constructive coping strengthens their sense of identity confidence, and worth.

(6) Some of the most effective teaching a minister does (in counseling and elsewhere) is done by modeling constructive attitudes, beliefs, values, and behavior. For example, relating to women clients in nonsexist ways (as full human beings first and women second) tends to produce learning and growth, which can be reinforced by a didactic statement on this issue.

In her study of how normal children cope with stressful situations, Lois Barclay Murphy made this discovery:

Over and over again we saw how the impact of a new challenge intensified the child's awareness of himself; his capacity to meet such a challenge enhances his pleasure, his sense of adequacy, and his pride. . . . Through his coping experiences the child discovers and measures himself. . . . We can say that the child creates his identity through his efforts in coming to terms with the environment in his own personal way.[8]

The Dangers of Educative Counseling

In educative counseling the minister faces several serious pitfalls. The most ominous is subtly *manipulating the counselee*. It requires considerable emotional maturity to present ideas for which one feels conviction (in theology, for example) without subtle pressure on the counselee to conform. Such pressure communicates disrespect for the person's precious right to choose her/his own meaningful philosophy of life. A closely related danger is slipping from *rational authority*, the healthy authority of competence (Erich Fromm), into authoritarianism, the authority of using power coercively, in ways that diminish personality growth. Another pitfall is that of regarding information *per se* as adequate to help troubled persons. This leads to what could be called "salvation by words," an ineffective, advice-giving approach to counseling. It is important to listen for the hidden cries for help that often come disguised in innocuous appearing requests for information.

As noted in discussing supportive counseling, giving advice and sharing information are useful ways of nurturing persons under stress by gratifying dependency needs. The danger is that with markedly dependent people such approaches may *foster even greater dependency*. When a minister senses that this is happening, her/his task is to wean the person by being gradually less advising and guiding. This is often difficult because the dependent person's emptiness makes her/him long to be led and fed.

A final danger is that the pastor will *equate transmitting information with genuine learning* on the counselee's part. As Nathaniel Cantor makes clear: "Significant learning stems from the self-directed motivation of the learner who wants something positive and creative for an unexpressed or unfulfilled need."[9] Genuine learning will occur only when a person's sense of need and certain ideas come together. In educative counseling, *the person's own sense of need is always the place to begin*. Through the process of counseling, that person's understanding of what she or he needs often expands.

Authoritarian educative counseling can stifle the sacred spark of learning and growth. Cantor declares:

> Most of us learn how *not* to learn. That is, we learn very early how to avoid tangling with the authority of adults who are significant in our lives. . . . We learn to curb self-expression a good deal of the time. We learn how to submit, run away, cut corners, rationalize, defend ourselves, and to distort. . . . In brief, we are driven "to adjust" to threats, anxieties, and fears.
>
> *Behavior which lessens anxiety is adjustive not integrative*. The essence of integrative behavior is the capacity to exercise one's curiosity, to derive positive satisfaction from the *spontaneous* expression of one's skills and powers. Motivation which leads to the spontaneous expressions of one's self is different from the kind of learning which seeks to lessen anxiety and avoid threat.[10]

Educative counseling should aim at stimulating integrative learning—the kind that enables persons to discover and develop their God-given gifts and capacities.

The Methodology of Educative Counseling

Ministers have a strategic opportunity to help couples prepare for good marriages. Because premarital guidance is the parish minister's most frequent educative counseling opportunity, I will use it to illustrate the methodology of this type.[11]

There are two categories of educative counseling: (a) *those situations in which people come at the minister's request—e.g.*, premarital, prebaptismal, church membership preparation, and (b) *those where the counselee takes the initiative*, seeking guidance on vocational, theological, or other problems. The rule of thumb is that minister-initiated types of educative counseling often require a greater proportion of direct *instruction* than do counselee-initiated types.

Most premarital sessions are actually *individualized education or personalized training sessions*. They usually are not counseling in that the couples are not motivated by a desire for help with particular problems. But most couples are *open* to training and coaching (in relationship-building skills) that affirms their basic strengths and responds to their desire to develop the best possible marriage relationship. Personalized education can be helpful to many couples if counseling skills and sensitivities are integral to the process. The pastor who learns to do counseling-oriented education will find increasing opportunities to do actual counseling with some premarital couples. Here are some useful methods:

(1) As in other counseling, *relate warmly, empathetically, and openly so that a sturdy relationship with the couple will grow*. Establishing a trustful and (if possible) ongoing relationship with the couple is the overarching goal of prewedding sessions. Such a relationship bridge helps make the minister emotionally accessible to them if they need and want help with a problem, now or in the future.

(2) As in other counseling, *establish a clear contract for how the session will be used*.

> **Pastor:** I'm sure you both want to keep your love growing as fully as possible through your years together. Building a good marriage takes the loving skills of two people who are willing to work and play at it—to keep it growing. As your pastor, I'd like to help you in this exciting and demanding process (response by the couple). I hope that these sessions will prove helpful to you in discovering more of the hidden strengths that you want to develop in your relationship. What would each of you like to get out of these sessions?

After the couple has described their interests and needs, the pastor may mention (by way of seed planting) other topics or skills on which it may be helpful to focus— e.g., tension areas in their relationship; family backgrounds; their understanding of marriage and of men-women roles; spiritual issues and growth in their marriage; sexual pleasuring skills; birth control methods; relating to relatives; love-nurturing communication skills; negotiating (and revising) a mutually fair marriage covenant (contract); conflict resolution skills; handling money issues; balancing autonomy and togetherness; conflicting values in their marriage; children—to have children or not and dividing responsibility for their rearing; developing a support group; mutual need satisfaction; outreach to their community; first year adjustments; and the meaning of the wedding as a celebration of their committed and growing relationship. On the basis of what the couple *and* the minister want and hope for from the sessions, a flexible schedule of topics can be set up. This collaborative structuring helps to reduce the initial anxiety that many couples bring to the first session.

(3) *Allow rapport to develop by asking low-threat, open-ended questions, beginning with informational queries about positive aspects of their relationship.*

> **Pastor:** Since I'm going to have the privilege of sharing in this important experience in your lives, it seems right that we should get better acquainted. Tell me, how did you meet?

Continuing to gently ask low-threat leading questions helps the couple talk about how their relationship began and developed. In the process a tentative picture emerges of their current interaction and of their parental families that shaped it. This modification of Virginia M. Satir's method of taking a "family life chronology" can be very useful in premarital sessions.[12] Threatening questions should be avoided until considerable trust has grown in the relationship with the pastor.

> **Pastor:** One reason we're meeting is to help you launch your marriage in the most creative direction possible. As you've been thinking about the kind of marriage you want, what thoughts have come to your minds?

If a couple does not respond by opening up issues that they are interested in, the pastor can prime the pump by asking leading questions or by mentioning some common issues related to one of the topics on the tentative agenda:

> **Pastor:** As we meet for these three sessions I'll have some suggestions to share about the issue we agreed on, but I'll save as much time as you want for the questions that come to your minds. We'll go through the ceremony step-by-step, to discuss its meaning as well as the mechanics. At some point I'd like to share some thoughts from my experience about how couples can keep their love growing over the years. How does all this sound to you?

What about the use of psychological inventories in premarital sessions? Psychological tests or inventories of any type tend to raise the anxiety level in counseling relationships. Their potential usefulness must be weighed against this limitation. Inventories such as the Taylor-Johnson Temperament Analysis Inventory and

PREPARE (Premarital Personal & Relationship Evaluation) can be useful in increasing a couples' awareness and opening up discussion of factors in each partner's personality that may influence their relationship.[13] To use such inventories meaningfully, pastors should read carefully the manual that accompanies particular instruments and also do background reading to acquire general understanding of personality inventories. Background information forms can be used by pastors to prime the pump of discussion with couples of significant issues. Joan and Richard Hunt's *Growing Love in Christian Marriage* includes several useful checklists.[14] Such instruments are easily used, are less threatening than personality inventories, and provide an abundance of information quickly. A pastor's perceptive eyes may pick up clues that point to fruitful topics of discussion and areas where a couple need accurate information. The "Sex Knowledge Inventory" (SKI) can be a helpful resource particularly with couples who are inhibited in discussing this area openly. Their responses to the eighty multiple choice questions (on Form X of this inventory) identify gaps or inaccuracies in their knowledge about sexual relationships and suggest emotional hangups areas that need to be discussed in the prewedding sessions.[15] (For a discussion of the use of tests in premarital counseling, see Stewart's *The Minister as Marriage Counselor*, pp. 55-58).

(3) *Do everything possible to reduce any sense of threat so that a couple will feel free to reveal their real needs and worries*. In addition to building rapport and providing structure, threat reduction involves communicating to the couple that they are not on trial. At the outset the minister may say, "I consider it a privilege to share in the launching of your marriage." This initial reassurance cannot be given of course until the minister is certain that there are no insurmountable obstacles to the marriage or to her/his participation.[16]

Reducing the threat to open communication is often difficult on two frequently encountered issues—living together and pregnancy. In most areas of North America, it is safe to assume that the majority of couples in premarriage sessions have had intercourse and many are living together. A high percentage of teen-age couples are pregnant before marriage. It is important to create a *climate of acceptance* (transcending differences in sexual standards) that will free couples to talk openly rather than remaining defensive as they try to hide the fact that they are sexually active, living together, and/or pregnant. The fact that many young people talk so freely about sex today does not necessarily mean that they have accurate knowledge, constructive attitudes, or skills in full-body, mutual pleasuring. Premarital sessions with couples living together in committed relationships have many similarities with marriage counseling. They tend to be very different from sessions with couples who have not had such mini-marriages.

If a minister suspects that a couple is pregnant, it is important to check this out by a simple question (when the issue of children is discussed). "When do you expect to have your first?" If they are pregnant, the pastor should explore their feelings—e.g., guilt, anxiety, blame, joy—about this fact and check to see if they're being pressured to marry. Helping them evaluate their readiness for marriage is important so that they can consider alternatives, such as adoption or abortion if they are clearly not yet capable of establishing a constructive marriage. The most important thing is to surprise couples who expect a minister's judgment with loving acceptance and an opportunity to learn how to cope healthily with the enormous challenges they face.

(4) *Become aware of the couple's learning readiness and their awareness of problems related to their relationship*. This is done by responding to their feelings as these emerge and by gradually asking more feeling-centered and relationship-probing questions; for example, "How do you respond when she/he is very late for a date?"

Couples who answer in cliches, revealing only positive or surface-level feelings, either are unaware of deeper dimensions of their relationship or feel they *must* put their best foot forward with the minister. The latter type couple will bring their less socially acceptable feelings and real problems out of hiding only when they feel safer in that relationship.

A useful method of surfacing conflicted areas in a relationship (adapted from marriage counseling) is to scrutinize specific vignettes of interaction involving conflict.

Pastor: (After rapport is well-established) What happens when you disagree over something you both feel strongly about? Could you think of an example we could look at together?

(5) Learning readiness varies greatly in different areas. It is helpful, therefore, *to open up various key topics, watching for increased-energy responses that indicate awareness of need*. Obviously this should not be done in lectures but briefly and informally and in a personalized way.

> **Pastor:** Most of us have some trouble with open communication. Larry and Sue (our hypothetical couple) have been married about a year. Sue gets her feelings hurt when Larry is preoccupied with business. She has trouble letting him know what is really bugging her. Does this happen to ring any bells with you?

Brief discussion by the pastor of the areas of the couple's heightened interest is essentially a seed-planting operation.

(6) When the signs of interest appear in a couple's responses, *concentrate discussion on that area for a while, encouraging them to examine it, and seeking to communicate constructive attitudes and relevant information*. Begin with what *they* are interested in and build on that, sharing ideas, experiences, (including personal experiences in one's own marriage), and relationship-building and communication skills that seem relevant to the couple's needs. Dialogue is invited around the axis of their needs. After brief, informal sharing, feedback is encouraged by asking, "How does this relate to *your* experience?" or "How do *you* feel about this?" It is important to focus on a given topic long enough to give the couple ample opportunity to understand and discuss it. If a topic proves fruitless, move on to another. As one sows seeds in this way, some of the seeds will fall on the fertile soil of the couple's emerging interests and perceived needs. In the give-and-take of this dialogic method, the couple may gradually learn ways of growthing their relationship. As Nathaniel Cantor observes, "Learning probably takes place in small increments which accumulate into insights."[17]

Some topics are so vital, from the minister's viewpoint, that a general orientation should be given even if the couple shows little or no sense of need in those areas. Such presentations, done in moderation, will not diminish the quality of the relationship with the couple. Some of the seeds sown in this way may fall on receptive soil. One of my "must" topics is the importance of *their* working out (and writing down) a fair working agreement, a marriage covenant, providing equal opportunities for both persons to develop their potentialities and share in both the satisfactions and responsibilities of the marriage.[18] Other important topics include communication and conflict resolution skills, sexual attitudes and techniques, and changing women-men roles.

(7) *Discussion should focus on present feelings and current issues more than on anticipated future problems*. In Peace Corps training, "anticipatory guidance" was found to be most effective when it dealt with current experiences of trainees in handling the minor crises of the training program—e.g., their feelings of deprivation resulting from leaving their families and their resentments arising from constantly being tested and observed during training. These feelings were similar to those which they would have overseas. Concentrating on these allowed the small training groups to work with *live feelings*.[19] A similar approach to premarital guidance gives attention to how the couple copes with tensions, feelings, and problems arising during the prewedding period, including the anxieties of the premarital sessions themselves.

A couple's worries abut the future are, of course, *present* feelings and should be examined thoroughly. When a couple chooses to reveal their problems or worries, premarital sessions become counseling in the full sense of the word. It is usually unproductive to dwell on possible future conflict areas of which they have no awareness. To do so usually seems, from their view, to be irrelevant or an inaccurate prophecy of gloom. It is much better to concentrate on learning how to cope growthfully with current issues and problems, and on developing their assets, strengths, and hopes for their marriage.

(8) *Take time to teach couples useful communication skills, letting them practice these during as well as between the sessions*. It is important to coach a couple as they actually practice a communication tool during a session and then to talk briefly about how they can use such a tool on their own to enrich their relationship. The most important communication exercise to teach couples before marriage is the International Relationship Method (discussed in chapter 10). This communication paradigm is useful in several crucial areas of a marriage—mutual affirmation, need-satisfaction, conflict-resolution, and revising their marriage contract.

(9) *Carefully selected book chapters and articles should be assigned as homework to be read and discussed together between sessions.* This exposes the couple to awareness-stimulating material and increases their communication time with each other. During the next session after such an assignment, the pastor can ask: "How did the ideas in that chapter you read tie in with what you have experienced in your relationship?" A book such as *Equal Marriage* by Jean Stapleton and Richard Bright provides excellent homework assignments.[20]

(10) *A primary goal of the prewedding sessions is to relate the couple to the church's ongoing program of marriage enrichment.*

> **Pastor:** Following the wedding, I would like to invite you to meet with me after six months and one year, to chat about how things are going. . . . Most couples find these sessions worthwhile.[21]

A date should be made for the first such "healthy marriage checkup." Couples should also be encouraged to participate in a church-sponsored marriage enrichment class, workshop, or retreat at least once a year for a refresher course to help keep their marriage growing.

(11) A line-by-line discussion of the wedding ceremony helps lessen couples' anxieties about the mechanics of that service and provides a natural entrée to a discussion of its deeper meanings, including the crucial spiritual dimension of their relationship. The minister should strongly recommend the deletion of any sexist and patriarchal elements that are still present in some wedding liturgies—e.g., the practice of fathers giving their daughters away, vows that are not mutual, a ring given only to the woman, and other obsolete symbols of unequal status and power in marriages.

A minimum of three sessions should be spent with each couple. Discovering in the first session that a minister is a caring, nonjudgmental human being may enable couples to open up areas of real pain and conflict in subsequent sessions. The number of sessions a pastor needs to spend with each couple may be reduced dramatically if couples have been a part of a pre-marriage class, workshop, or retreat. Much of the premarital training and instruction can be done more effectively and efficiently in small groups than individual sessions with couples. Those who have been through a weekend pre-marriage/marriage enrichment retreat or a four to six session enrichment class co-led by the pastor often do not need more than one individual session before the wedding.

Throughout premarital counseling, the minister should bear these *goals of the process* in mind: (a) instructing them in the mechanics of the wedding; (b) giving them some practical guidelines for the early adjustment stages of marriage; (c) strengthening their sense of adventure and joy within some awareness of the complexities, conflict, and struggles of marriage; (d) strengthening their interpersonal competence based on effective communication skills; (e) giving them a juicy taste of a deeper level of communication than they have hitherto experienced; (f) setting an example for them of communication openness on topics that are still taboo issues for some couples—e.g., sex and anger; (g) introducing them to the "language of relationships" (Reuel Howe); (h) supplying them with sound information and guidance to help them develop a satisfying, growing relationship; (i) helping them experience the wonder of the real presence of the love of God in their love; (j) helping them understand the differences between holy matrimony and just getting married; (k) making oneself emotionally available so that, if they choose, they may use the relationship with the pastor for more extended counseling, before or after the ceremony and (l) seeking to involve them in the caring community of the congregation and in its ongoing program—including the marriage and family enrichment events. The minister should hold to these goals with a very light grip, remembering that if only the *master goal* is achieved—the establishment of a warm, caring, trustful relationship with the couple—the premarital sessions have been eminently worthwhile.

High Motivation Educative Counseling

Those forms of educative counseling where parishioners, impelled by the pain of their problems, seek counseling be described as "high motivation" counseling. Maintaining a significant level of dialogue in such counseling is much less difficult than in forms of educative counseling where parishioners come because the minister or the church require it. To illustrate the role of positive guidance and sound knowledge in high motivation educative counseling, one aspect of divorce counseling will now be briefly discussed. Persons in both pre- and post-divorce counseling are typically highly motivated by a sense of failure and interpersonal pain—particularly if children are involved.[22] With more than one million divorces per year in the United States involving over half a million children, pastors should be much more involved than most are in helping minimize the personality damage to children and maximize the potentialities for learning by parents in these crises. Since only one fourth of divorced persons remain single longer than five years, most divorce counseling is also preparation for remarriage.

Here is a closer look now at the *contents* of one facet of divorce counseling—that of minimizing emotional damage to children—with some of the recommendations that the pastor should help divorcing parents implement:

(1) Avoid senseless rancor that will expose children to added trauma.
(2) Obtain counseling to deal with their own resentments, guilt feelings, rage, hurt, and grief, so that they will not attempt to use children as therapists or a battleground for getting at the ex-spouse.
(3) Obtain psychotherapy, after the acute crisis has passed, to discover and resolve the emotional problems and change the behavior patterns that contributed to the disintegration of the marriage. This will help free persons to function more constructively as parents and also enable them to learn from their divorce, thus lessening the possibility that they will repeat dysfunctional relationship patterns in future relationships.
(4) Help children avoid blaming themselves for their parents' problems.
(5) Be honest with children about what is happening.
(6) Get therapy for the children (play and/or talk therapy, depending on their ages), to work through conflicted feelings.

These additional recommendations are offered by a psychiatrist on the staff of a children's hospital: Don't inform young children about an impending divorce until definite plans for their future have been agreed upon. Don't ask children under twelve to make the choice concerning which parent they will live with. Don't separate siblings. The child should be placed with whichever parent is able to provide a more secure, nurturing relationship and home. One household should be established as home for the child, with the other as a place to visit. Parents should not use the child as a confidant or a spy. "Every effort should be made to help them retain whatever feelings of love or respect they may have for both parents."[23]

Because of the intensity of their angry and hurt feelings, many divorcing couples are unable to implement sound recommendations such as these until they have extensive counseling. Educative counseling with such parents includes communicating the best of what is known about minimizing the damage to children in the process of divorce. Equally important is helping them work through the emotional blocks particularly the hurt and hostility that otherwise interfere with their taking constructive action in the situation.

Educative Counseling on Social Problems

Educative counseling skills are valuable assets in the prophetic ministry. They are useful tools in implementing the Gandhi-King-Day-Lee principle by dealing constructively with community problems and issues of institutional injustice. The methodology of effective social action must utilize but go beyond the educative counseling model to include political methods designed to influence the power structures of one's community. There are, of course, no easy ways to transform prejudicial attitudes, effect reconciliation between estranged groups, or stop the exploitive use of power by institutions. But precisely because of the psychological-sociological complexities involved, it is imperative that insights and methods from the fields of group dynamics, social psychology, group counseling, and organizational development be applied to these societal problems.

The CR (consciousness raising) group model can be applied productively in a congregation's educative and prophetic ministry. Such a group is an instrument of both personal and social liberation. The CR group approach began in the "radical therapies" during the sixties. Subsequently, it has been developed and used extensively in the feminist liberation movement. Here is a description of feminist CR groups:

> In their unmodified form CR groups have no professional "leader" or "therapist"; they are explicitly not "therapy" (with the connotations of privatized sickness, and passivity in receiving help from a one-up professional that that word connotes for many people). But, as the experience of countless women demonstrates, an effective CR group *can* be very therapeutic. CR groups illustrate the remarkable healing-growthing power of lay, self-help groups that are flourishing in many places.[24]

The authors of a manual on setting up CR groups state the philosophy of feminist consciousness raising:

> The key to all that happens in CR . . . is the phrase "from the personal to the political." In the CR meeting the members will begin by discussing their own experiences, being as personal as they can and wish; but with the guidance of the leader they will recognize the common denominators of their experiences and see the social implications of whatever is happening in their own lives. . . . "Political" . . . in this context refers not to political parties or voting, but to the concept of power in society: who has it, how it is used, how can one get it, how society is managed. Unless the political point is made for each topic discussed in CR, there is a danger that the women will not genuinely have their consciousness raised; they may—or may not—achieve some relief from tension or pain, but until they see the connection between what happens to them as individual women and what happens to all women in a sexist society, they are not experiencing real feminist CR . . . The other kinds of group activity labeled CR miss the essence of the feminist approach when they concentrate solely on ways the individual woman can improve her situation or beef up her personal "copability"; however valuable these may be, they are at best temporary expedients and at worst illusory, since they coax the woman to work on herself rather than society. There are no personal solutions to social problems—only adjustment, accommodations, temporary loopholes—and pain. Nothing a woman can do for herself alone will solve her basic problem of being female in a society rigged against her.

They conclude with this affirmation of the values of the process:

> Feminist consciousness raising will enrich a woman's personal life with sisterhood, support from other women, intellectual and emotional stimulation; but its most important contribution will be

that it shows her how to work to free herself and other women through feminist understanding and action. Real CR is inevitably tremendously exciting and genuinely liberating. It is worth all the effort it takes.[25]

In an in-depth analysis of CR groups as an alternative to traditional psychotherapy for women Barbara Kirsch cites a study describing four stages in the group process: (1) *Opening up*—Each member tells personal experiences as a woman in a nonjudgmental atmosphere of support and acceptance of feelings; group closeness and mutual trust develop rapidly. (2) *Sharing*—Through deeper expressing of feelings, needs, and experiences, the individuals discover that many of their problems are shared by other women; this leads to the awareness that their problems root in society's problems more than in their individual inadequacies. The sense of group cohesion grows stronger with this awarness. (3) *Analyzing*— The group reaches beyond personal experiences and focuses on the devalued position of women in society. This leads to new objective understandings, which are integrated with the member's personal experiences as women. (4) *Abstracting*—The group members evolve a new vision of their potentials as women, and the group begins to see itself as a means for changing social institutions so that the potentials of women can be realized more fully.

Some feminist therapists have discovered that the CR group's philosophy and methods can be integrated with professionally led group therapy in ways that deepen the growth-enabling effects of both.[26]

I have written elsewhere about using counseling insights and methods in the prophetic ministry. Let me summarize the six steps of effective social action showing how educative counseling methods are integral to this process.[27] I will use the feminist CR group to illustrate how this approach helps to bridge the gap between personal growth and social change.

Step 1: *Recruiting and Training a Growth-Action Task Force:* To change institutional structures (the essential goal of social action) usually requires a team effort. The most effective instrument for this is a well-prepared task force with a focused change target. There are several substeps within this first step: (A) *Awakening awareness of the need for change:* Growth-action task forces in churches offer an ideal setting within which conscienti-zation (consciousness raising) regarding community problems and injustices can occur. As task force members encounter firsthand the victims of racism, sexism, classism, agism, militarism, economic injustice, and other forms of growth oppression in their community, their awareness of the need for change increases.

The feminist CR group is a personal growth and empowerment group—not a task force for social action. But its ways of increasing the awareness of its members of the destructive impact on their lives of the pervasive sexism of our society offers methods of consciousness raising in growth-action groups generally. Such a group is a growth group within which an awareness develops of the societal context and causes of the damaged self-esteem suffered by most women. The "click experience" in such a group occurs when an individual becomes aware of a powerful and transforming fact—that many of her painful experiences and feelings are shared by the other women in the group and that these problems result to a considerable degree from their socialization as women in a society that treats them as second-class persons. The awareness that their personal problems are also social and political problems helps to increase a woman's sense of worth and her sense of inner power. In growth-action groups generally, the awareness of group members that *their* lives are somehow diminished (directly or indirectly) by particular social evils, seems to be the heart of the kind of consciousness raising that motivates continuing commitment to social action. For example, it is not until men sense that they *too* are oppressed, that their own becoming is diminished by their social programming as men in our male-dominated society—that they are motivated to work for self-liberation and for the full liberation of women. Conscientization of those in power (such as men) is much more difficult than is the case of those who are obvious victims of social oppression. When men have the click experience, they discover that they are the oppressed oppressors! This awakens their awareness of need for liberating their personal relationships with women and changing society's institutions in which they participate (including marriage) so that they will nurture the full becoming of both men and women.

(B) *Team building:* To work together effectively, a social action group must develop a sturdy sense of mutual trust and belonging. One ecumenical project designed to train lay persons as agents of social change in their communities discovered that unless a sense of belonging developed within a training group, many members did not finish the training, and there was little chance that those who did would move into social action. In an effective feminist CR group, a sense of group bonding and sisterhood deepens rapidly and with this comes empowerment and a sense of identifying with the struggles for liberation of women generally.

(C) *Learning change agent skills:* Social action groups frequently stumble over their own communication and relationship problems. It is crucial therefore that conflict-resolution and communication skills be taught in the training. In addition, training should include learning the skills of using one's assertiveness effectively in working with others to change power structures. Feminist CR groups have developed effective ways to reverse the learned helplessness and passivity of women. They do this by enabling them to get in touch with their justified, constructive anger (at their oppression) and by helping them mobilize their sense of inner competence and power.

Step 2: *Deepening Understanding of the Problem:* The first and the second steps both involve major cognitive as well as experiential elements. An understanding of the social issue on which a group has chosen to focus, can be enhanced by disciplined study, input by those with expertise on the problem, and firsthand encounter with the victims. In a feminist CR group, information about the social, historical, and political roots of women's problems helps awaken awareness of the need for action and increases understanding of the complex issues involved. The political (power) dynamics that sustain our oppressive male-dominated institutions must be understood. Feminist CR groups may include discussion of the historical and sociological roots of current sexist attitudes and practices. Increased understanding of the ways in which patriarchal institutions developed and continue to constrict the growth options of women is a force for self-liberation.

Step 3: *Deciding on Action Goals:* As understanding of a problem deepens, various action goals are considered. Most social problems have many facets crying out for action. Through group decision making, one or two of these facets should be selected and realistic change goals developed by the group. It is important to select "workable problems"—smaller parts of the larger social issue about which something concrete can be done, and which the task force members are motivated to tackle.[28]

In feminist CR groups, action goals frequently emerge spontaneously as consciousness raising increases and group support grows stronger. These goals have to do mainly with two areas: personal-relational issues (e.g., how to relate to a man without giving one's power away) and wider institutional-societal issues (e.g., how to get involved in the struggle to eliminate *de facto* discrimination against women in one's place of employment). At this point, CR groups occasionally decide to work together to accomplish one or more social change objective (which means they are no longer primarily CR groups). More often, certain members of a CR group get involved in existing feminist action projects. They do so with the motivation, understanding, and interpersonal skills acquired in their CR group experiences.

Step 4: *Developing an Action Plan:* When goals are agreed on, a growth-action group needs to devise a plan for achieving them. A workable plan: (1) identifies a measurable result, (2) names the action to be taken to accomplish it, (3) sets a date by which it will be completed, and (4) says who will do what.[29] All key decisions in growth-action groups—e.g., about goals, how to mobilize available resources, acquire allies, and divide responsibilities—should be made by group process. Each person needs to know that her or his views are heard and valued by the group and taken into consideration in developing the action plan. Group ownership of an action strategy depends on the use of this person-respecting, often time-consuming process.

Step 5: *Taking Action:* The group's *esprit de corps* and sense of mutual support become crucial when action begins to impact a community's customs, laws, or institutions in even a small way. When the "flak begins to fly" from defenders of the *status quo*, strong mutual support is essential. Social change of almost any kind is an uphill struggle. Open communication and mutual support within the group are therefore vital.

Experience in social action has demonstrated that the very act of working with others to change growth-constricting community problems tends to strengthen the participant's self-esteem and sense of competency. Personal healing and growth of the kind one would hope for in effective counseling often occur as a result of being involved in the struggles and successes, large or small, of a social change team![30]

Step 6: *Evaluating and restrategizing:* Midway through an action project, it is important for a team to do critical evaluation, particularly if things are not going well. On the basis of this evaluation, a mid-course correction of strategy can be made. At the conclusion of an action project or a major phase of a project, in-depth evaluation allows a group to learn from its mistakes and its achievements. This provides a basis for restrategizing and for choosing the next action goal and planning strategy. It may be necessary to go back to step 2 to acquire more facts about the part of the larger problem that has been chosen as the new change target. The growth-action group may need to be reconstituted from persons with a dynamic interest in working for change in relation to the new action goal.

The effectiveness of the prophetic ministry of a congregation can be enhanced significantly if the *personal growth-social change group* model is utilized. Pastoral leadership that combines the skills of the creative educator, the effective group facilitator, and the political activists can help a church become a more significant influence for social change. Educative counseling methods, combined with social change strategies, can help liberate the potential of a congregation to be a greater influence for transformation in its community and world, to the end that all persons will have an opportunity to develop more of their God-given potentialities!

The CR group is one of the most significant innovations in the whole field of group theory and practice, (the focus of the next chapter).

> Because this model integrates personal growth and social-political change, the CR group is a valuable innovation for the whole field of therapy and growth work. Effective CR groups blend processes that help to restore a sense of personal self-esteem, power and competency, together with conscientizing processes that help people become aware of the role of societal oppression in their problems and empower them to join with others in social change efforts. The CR group model can be used for therapeutic-growth-liberation work with any oppressed group. It may be the key to creating indigenous socio-therapies among those in pockets of poverty in affluent countries and among economically and poltically oppressed people in the developing countries.[31]

The CR group approach is one key to helping pastoral counseling transcend its middle-class origins and become an instrument of *empowerment* for social as well as personal change.

Reality-Practice Session

PARISHIONER'S ROLE: You are a young couple who have grown up in the same church, are well-known to the minister, and are previously unmarried. You have been living together for several months, are pregnant, and have decided to get married.

PASTOR'S ROLE: Give premarital guidance to this couple.

OBSERVER-COACH'S ROLE: Give feedback on how the pastor might be more effective in integrating needed information with counseling methods.

Recommended Reading

Creative Education

George J. Brown, ed., *The Live Classroom* (New York: Viking Press, 1975). Innovative teaching and learning approaches using confluent education and gestalt.

Nathaniel Cantor, *Dynamics of Learning* (East Aurora, N.Y.: Henry Stewart, 1946). A classic statement of the principles of creative teaching-learning.

George Leonard, *Education and Ecstasy* (New York: Dell, 1969). Ways of making learning an exciting process.

Carl R. Rogers, *Freedom to Learn* (Columbus, Ohio: Charles E. Merrill Publishing, 1969). Describes the relationship factors that facilitate self-directed learning.

Cognitive Therapies

Aaron T. Beck, *Cognitive Therapy and Emotional Disorders* (New York: International Universities Press, 1976). Integrates cognitive and behavioral approaches.

John P. Foreyt and Dianna P. Rathjen, eds., *Cognitive-Behavior Therapy: Research and Application* (New York: Plenum Publishing, 1978). A collection of papers on the use of cognitive behavior methods with a variety of types of problems.

Personal Growth-Social Change

James A. Ashbrook, *In Human Presence—Hope* (Valley Forge: Judson Press, 1971). Notes the pastor's work with individual and social change.

Howard Clinebell, *Contemporary Growth Therapies*, chapter 10, "Growth Resources in Feminist Therapies."

_____ *Growth Counseling*, pp. 30-36, "Growth in Relation to Organizations and Institutions."

_____ *Growth Groups*, chapter 10, "Training Change Agents to Harmonize Society (with special emphasis on ecology)."

_____ *The Mental Health Ministry of the Local Church*, chapter 5, "The Prophetic Ministry and Mental Health."

Speed Leas and Paul Kittlaus, *The Pastoral Counselor in Social Action* (Philadelphia: Fortress Press, 1981). Two social action specialists utilize insights and methods from pastoral psychology and counseling to increase the effectiveness of social change ministries.

Harvey Seifert and Howard Clinebell, *Personal Growth and Social Change* (Philadelphia: Westminster Press, 1969). Explores the creative interdependence of personal growth and social action.

Preparation for Marriage

Howard J. Clinebell, Jr., *Growth Counseling for Marriage Enrichment, Pre-Marriage and the Early Years* (Philadelphia: Fortress Press, 1975). Chapter 6 describes a growth-oriented marriage enrichment paradigm for preparing for marriage; chapter 7 suggests ways of continuing the enrichment process into the early years of a marriage.

David R. Mace, *Getting Ready for Marriage* (Nashville: Abingdon Press, 1972). A book for couples that can be used as "homework" between pre-wedding sessions. Includes an annotated bibliography of other books a couple may find helpful.

Robert F. Stahmann and William J. Hiebert, eds., *Klemer's Counseling in Marital and Sexual Problems*, 2nd ed. (Baltimore: Williams and Wilkins, 1977). By twenty-five professionals in marriage counseling, this volume includes six chapters on premarital counseling.

Charles W. Stewart, *The Minister As Marriage Counselor*, rev. ed. (Nashville: Abingdon Press, 1970). Chapters 5 and 6 deal with premarital counseling.

Charles A. Wood., Jr., "Premarital Counseling: A Working Model," *Journal of Pastoral Care*, 33, No. 1, March 1979.

CHAPTER 14

Group Care and Counseling

For where two or three are gathered in my name, there am I in the midst of them.

—MATTHEW 18:20

That their hearts may be encouraged as they are knit together in love, to have all the riches of assured understanding and the knowledge of God's mystery.

—COLOSSIANS 2:2

Group caring and counseling methods constitute the single most useful resource for broadening and deepening a church's ministry of healing and growth! Group approaches applied to a wide spectrum of crises and issues in living can allow a church to become an increasing force for preventing personality problems by stimulating growth toward wholeness. Exciting developments are occurring in the use of small groups in some congregations. But most churches have only scratched the surface of the rich possibilities for small group ministries.

The Key Role of Groups in Caring and Counseling

Small groups are a natural and time-tested methodology in the church. Church historians have noted that the use of small groups has been a dynamic factor in every major surge of new spiritual vitality in the church. Christianity grew through the spread of its "network of new and tough groups."[1] In his doctoral dissertation, "Group Therapy as A Method for Church Work," Robert Leslie identifies these significant points at which small groups played a vital role in church history:

Christ and his disciples, the Apostolic chuch, Montanism, monasticism, the Waldenses, the Franciscans, the Friends of God, the Brethren of the Common Life, German pietism, the Anabaptists, the Society of Friends, the Wesleyan revival, the Great Awakening, the Iona Community, the Emmanuel Movement, the Oxford Group Movement (from which AA came).[2]

The contemporary renaissance of small groups in churches follows a familiar path. In places where the church has been persecuted in recent history, Christians have rediscovered the power of small (forbidden) group meetings in homes.[3] This time-tested Christian strategy for personal empowerment and transformation has been discovered in recent years by secular-psychotherapists and by the human potentials movement.

> Groups, large and small, are the fabric from which a church's program is woven. Many church groups provide rich opportunities for developing interpersonal skills, leadership abilities, spiritual depth and intellectual discipline. The existence of a variety of sizes and types of groups in a local church is an invaluable asset in fulfilling its ministry of growth, healing, service, reconciliation, training for service, and proclamation of the good news! The spiritual vitality of a local church is directly correlated with the health of its groups—particularly its small groups where heart-hungers are most apt to be satisfied. Here a sense of Christian community can flourish.[4]

As pointed out earlier, a pastor is the leader of a social organism or system composed of a network of subsystems and small groups.[5]

For pastors, small groups are a natural form of caring ministry. Whatever pastors or seminarians can do to increase their knowledge of group dynamics (the forces that make groups "tick," well or poorly) and their skills in facilitating groups, will strengthen their ministry to persons at many points. Such knowledge and skills will be assets both in enchancing the growthfulness of existing groups and in helping to create new ones. Effective growth groups and regular growth events (such as marriage enrichment) can produce a creative leavening effect on the interpersonal climate of a whole congregation.[6] As a means by which *koinonia* or the shalom community becomes an experienced reality, small groups are essential to effective caring ministry.

> If a church is to be "a creative cell in our mass society," it must offer people abundant opportunities to experience Christian community. Large groups have a vital function in achieving the

instructional and inspirational objectives of a church. Think, for example, of the spiritual lift which comes from being a part of a congregation singing the mighty Easter hymns of resurrection. But a church's smaller groups are the settings in which lonely people can best experience the reality of religion as creative relationships—with self, others, God and creation. In "house churches", retreat centers, in denominational and local church camps, youth assemblies, parent education and Bible study groups, thousands of persons are discovering the excitement of life-to-life communication in small groups. Many are finding a fresh baptism of the biblical experience as a small, honest group becomes a channel of God's grace for them. There is no doubt that the small group is a powerful factor in the recovery of the power of personal growth and social transformation in the church. [7]

George Webber holds that any congregation that is really in mission "will make basic provision for its members to meet in small groups (as well as corporate worship), not as a sidelight or option for those who like it, but as a normative part of its life."[8] I agree.

A church of any size can meet many of its members' pastoral care needs by a variety of small sharing groups. Each member of a church should have such opportunities to experience a warm nurturing sense of belonging. In larger churches a network of small groups is essential to an effective teaching and caring ministry. Some larger churches develop a geographical network of neighborhood "Sharing and Caring Groups." Others offer a smorgasbord of interest, study, growth, and action groups designed to respond to the varied needs and interests of their members. In Korea—many Methodist churches are seeking to relate each member to a small "class meeting," a contemporary version of the small groups created by John and Charles Wesley as the Methodist church was being born in eighteenth-century England. These groups engage in Bible study, prayer, mutual caring, and service to the community.

Small groups are particularly important in our period of history. It is psychologically true as in John Donne's familiar line, that "No [one] is an island, entire of itself." But the fact is that millions of persons experience themselves as islands, cut off from the continent of humanity. Many are not aware of the depth of their loneliness. They live in what Tennessee Williams describes as "a lonely condition so terrifying to think about that we usually don't." Cut off from real communication with others, they feel like grains of sand, washed back and forth by the waves of impersonal forces, having friction with others but no organic relatedness. In this kind of society, small, lively groups in a church offer sorely needed opportunities for persons to drink deeply from the fresh springs of relationship, discovering the reality of the New Testament experience of being "members one of another."[9]

A key weakness of many churches today is identified by Robert Leslie: "It is rather ironical that the church is often the last place where people talk with freedom and openness about the concerns that touch them deepest."[10] Small sharing and growth groups are the most effective way of restoring transforming power to a church.

Five Types of Church Groups

Five types of groups can serve important functions in a church's ministry of healing and growth (a) task, service, and action groups; (b) study groups; (c) supportive-inspirational groups, (including corporate worship); (d) growth groups; (e) crisis counseling and therapy groups. Many ongoing church groups combine the functions of service, study, mutual support, and inspiration in varying proportions. For reasons that will become clear, therapy groups are (and should be) relatively rare in churches. The most exciting frontier in the church's group program is in the areas of crisis support and grief healing groups (discussed in chapter 8) and growth groups (educative counseling groups).

This chapter will focus on two issues: How can existing organizations and groups become more wholeness-enabling? And how can new groups with healing and growth as their central purpose be created to broaden and deepen the caring ministry of a congregation?

The Advantages of Group Caring and Counseling

Group caring and counseling have several significant advantages over individual methods. First, much of the counseling and even more of the caring now done individually can be done *more effectively* in small groups. Most of the methods described in this book can be used in groups, often with more effectiveness than when used individually. As psychiatrist Jerome D. Franks says: "Intimate sharing of feelings, ideas and experiences in an atmosphere of mutual respect and understanding enhances self-respect, deepens self-understanding, and helps a person live with others. Such an experience can be helpful to persons as any level of illness or health."[11]

A second advantage is that it is obviously better stewardship of a pastor's or lay leader's time to help five to ten people simultaneously than to spend the same time helping one individual. This is crucial in the light of the heavy demand on most pastors' time. The growth group approach is *one* key to broadening a church's general caring ministry. Pastors who learn how to organize and facilitate growth groups have an efficient method for providing mutual support, challenge, and help to scores of people hungering for the nourishing food of a small community of mutual caring!

A third advantage is that groups allow helpers to *help themselves by helping each other*. The unique element in group counseling and therapy is the presence of mutually "giving" relationships as distinguished from the largely "taking" role of clients in individual counseling and therapy. Counseling or growth group participants are often *helper* and *helped* in the same session. The group climate of interdependency facilitates the growth that comes when one becomes an agent of healing in the lives of others, even while one's own healing is being nurtured by them. Group caring and counseling are closer to the reciprocity of everyday life. As a way of releasing the potentialities that are dormant in most people, caring and sharing groups are contemporary ways of implementing the ancient injunction, "Bear one another's burdens" (Gal. 6:2). In effective counseling or growth groups the group as a whole becomes an instrument of healing and growth. This tends to distribute the dependency of needy individuals onto group members, rather than concentrate it on an individual pastor.

A fourth advantage is that a small group is the most productive milieu for *short-term educative counseling*. Three sessions of prebaptismal counseling with a group of four to six couples often stimulates learning that exceeds that of a couple-by-couple approach because the couples learn from each other and are nourished by the group's *esprit de corps*. By modeling openness, the less inhibited couples encourage the others to open up about their real problems.

The fifth advantage is that small groups can be used to help many who will not come for formal counseling. A man who descibes himself as "not the type who would go to a minister for counseling" reports that two years of participation in a "depth Bible study" group (which incorporates growth group methods) has helped him in profound ways.

Creating Growthful and Healing Groups

In the psychological sense, a group is not just a collection of individuals in geographical proximity.[12] Fifty people packed like sardines in a subway train do not constitute a true group. A group comes into existence when, through interaction, there is a partial overlapping of the "psychological field" or "life space" of the individuals. The significant world of each is to some extent involved in the other. There are definite, predictable stages through which an aggregation of people go in the process of becoming a true group. When this process is well advanced, there is a strong sense of group identity, of group boundaries and of cohesiveness, interdependency, and belonging.

Although the process of becoming a group is a natural one, certain factors in our society tend to block it—for example, competitiveness, fear of intimacy, and general reluctance to relax our defensive masks. Consequently, many so-called groups meet in churches for years without achieving more than superficial interaction. Unfortunately, glib talk about "Christian fellowship" will not produce it. Only as a group satisfies the conditions under which vital interpersonal relationship can grow will genuine fellowship be experienced.

A group tends to develop a distinctive "personality"—a persistent emotional climate and style of relating which distinguishes it from other groups. Many groups have "personality problems." Since groups can be robust or sickly, energetic or anemic, it behooves church leaders who work constantly with groups to be able to diagnose and treat the factors which limit group health.

For any group to come into existence there must be "physical, social, and interactional proximity."[13] Physical proximity must be combined with continuity of meeting. It takes time together to develop a sense of group identity. Social proximity refers to the common goals or interests which bring certain individuals together. The sense of group identity grows as mutual need-satisfaction develops and psychological fields overlap through interaction. Emotional involvement in the group flowers as its members communicate and share meaningful experiences. The more intense the experience in which they participate, the more powerful the bond—witness the rapport among men who have been through a battle together.

In the growth of a healthy group, openness and honesty of communication are essential. Speaking of small groups in the churches, John Casteel declares: "The vitality of the group's life together depends upon the freedom, honesty, and depth with which members come to share their questions, problems, insights and faith with one another."[14] The kind of participation which produces emotional involvement is based on the awareness that one's feelings and opinions are recognized, valued, and taken into account in group decisions.

A unique aspect of a church group which contributes to its health is its vertical as well as horizontal reference. The growth of individual group members is seen in relationship to God and the needs of the world. This helps to balance the necessary introspective aspects of a sharing group. In her description of the spiritual pioneering of the Church of Our Savior in Washington, D.C., Elizabeth O'Connor put the issue squarely: "The group does meet for the nurture of its own members, but it also meets in order that God may have an instrument through which His life may break in new ways for the world."[15]

Growth-Nurturing Leadership

Although few if any church groups should be "therapy groups", all church groups should have a therapeutic (healing) effect on the lives of their members. The most crucial factor in determining the healing and growth effects of a group is the nature and quality of its leadership. In an authority-centered group, open communication tends not to occur. Members hide their real feelings and withhold themselves from wholehearted participation. The more leaders assume responsibility for what happens in groups, the more the group lets them carry the ball. In a leader-centered group, members give only enough of themselves to "get by." Uncreative conformity and its Siamese twin, passive resistance or "foot-dragging," flourish. Coercive devices such as penalties and rewards become increasingly necessary to keep the wheels turning.

Various studies have shown that authority-centered patterns of leadership produce negative effects on personality health. The morale of workers and the emotional stability of children have been found to be enhanced by job situations and homes, respectively, in which they participated in some of the decisions affecting them.[16] The distribution of leadership in the "therapeutic community" approach in mental hospitals (including patient self-government) has produced impressive therapeutic results.

The leadership model which maximizes the growth-stimulating effects of groups is described by Thomas Gordon in *Group-Centered Leadership: A Way of Releasing the Creative Power of Groups*. Here are some of the functions of a growth-enabling leader:

> (1) Seeks the maximum distribution of leadership among the group members. (2) Sees that all members of the group have an opportunity to participate in group decisions. (3) Encourages freedom of communication. (4) Seeks to increase opportunities for participation. (5) Attempts to create a nonthreatening group climate in which feelings and ideas are accepted. (6) Conveys feelings of warmth and empathy, thus encouraging others to do likewise. (7) Sets the tone by paying attention to the contributions of others, perhaps of reflecting what they are saying with, "Let's see if I understand what you mean. . . ." (8) Helps build group-centered (as contrasted with self-centered) contributions by a linking function in which he or she points to the relationships among various individuals' contributions to the discussion.[17]

Such a leader is a catalyst and facilitator of the group process. As group-centeredness grows, dependence on the leader decreases and the functions of the leader are gradually taken over by the group. It is important to emphasize that the degree to which members give of their abilities to the group's thought and work is determined by their emotional ownership, elicited through the distribution of leadership and meaningful participation.

Group-centered leadership is not the same as *laissez faire* leadership or leader passivity. Group-centered leaders actively help the group to release its own potentialities. They know that the only way this can happen is by not doing the things for the group that they can learn to do for themselves. Their respect for persons and for the group process assures them that they can depend on the group's discovering its identity and power. As a midwife they help in a "natural childbirth" process by which a creative group is born. Their job is to help the group achieve an emotional climate and a level of communication, which will facilitate the growth of all group members.

The spirit rather than the mechanics of leadership is at the heart of this matter. An authority-centered person can misuse a knowledge of group dynamics (or even the methods of group-centered leadership) to manipulate a group in subtle ways. In contrast the leader who believes that the group-centered approach releases human potentialities, will carry this spirit into those situations requiring more directive approaches. Church groups require a variety of leadership styles, including the constructive use of authority. Like counseling, leadership calls for different facets of a leader's personality in different situations. On the same day, a minister may function with a family temporarily paralyzed by a tragic loss, a ministerial association meeting involving numerous routine administrative matters, and a planning retreat for her church leaders. The use of any one leadership style in all of these situations would miss the needs of the other two. The first calls for a firm warm supportive approach. The second needs efficiency in leadership in order to save the group's time for important matters. In the third situation—the planning retreat—group-centered methods are essential in order to reduce leader dependency and allow each person the freedom and incentive to contribute her or his creativity to the planning.

Leadership Training and Growth

A major challenge facing pastors and lay leaders is how to help existing church groups become more healing and growth-nurturing. The most effective way of accomplishing this is a leadership training program combining growth group methods and experiential learning of leadership skills—e.g., guiding a training group through a process of role playing effective decision making on a knotty problem. Such training can be done in a variety of ways—e.g., an intensive weekend "Leader Effectiveness Retreat"; a Friday evening, all day Saturday mini-retreat for group leaders or teachers (church school and/or public teachers); or a four to six session, weekly "Training and Enrichment Group" for group leaders and/or teachers. To make a church's overall group program more growthful, a pastor needs to involve leaders and teachers in regular leadership training events and other growth groups.[18]

Several churches with which I am familiar have added spiritual growth and relationship-strengthening exercises to their church board's annual program planning workshop and to their monthly meetings.[19] In one church, lay officers took turns at their meetings giving a brief description of their work and how they were seeking to express their faith through it. At the beginning of a planning retreat at another church, leaders were invited to share on the theme, "My most painful and most joyful experience last year," and "My most meaningful spiritual experience last year." Rich, relationship-building communication followed this sharing. Leaders of an inner city church facing difficult problems in a changing neighborhood, agreed to devote the opening session of a weekend planning retreat to communication exercises designed to deepen relationships among them. Those who wanted to "get on with our business" were reluctant to spend time in this way. But the group discovered that their struggles to solve the problems their congregation faced were unusually productive after this opening session.

Another strategy for enlivening the caring and growth ministry of existing groups is to focus on this concern at an evaluation and planning session of the groups' officers. In one West Coast church, each group within the congregation was asked to do a self-study of its effectiveness as a caring community. A group Vitality Check List was made available to leaders to assist them in the process. It contained items such as the group's growth in size; attention to newcomers, absentees, and members experiencing illness and other stresses; rotation and distribution of leadership and decision making; depth of sharing feelings and significant life experiences; and the degree of warmth and caring experienced within the group. One result of these group self-evaluation was a request from several group leaders for a leadership training course. This was held subsequently.

Groups with low levels of mutual support often can develop new warmth and caring through a renewal retreat spent in a remote spot. Such retreats aim at rethinking the group's purposes and guiding vision, including the caring and growth dimensions of this vision. During the fun times as well as the serious discussions, interpersonal barriers are lowered and relationship bridges are strengthened.

Creating New Groups

A church should develop new sharing and caring groups to meet the changing needs of persons in our contemporary society.

In evaluating its present group structure, a church's leaders need to ask themselves questions such as these:

> What are the gaps in group structure, when viewed against the need for healing and growth of our particular congregation and community? Is it possible for persons of every age, with a wide range of interests and needs, to find nurturing group experiences in our church? What new groups should we create to respond to unmet needs? Who will take responsibility for developing these new groups?

Among the growth experiences that should be available in every congregation are classes, workshops, retreats, or groups devoted to: a) leadership training and growth; b) teacher training and growth; c) marriage/pre-marriage enrichment; d) healing of bereavement (from losses of all kinds); e) spiritual growth. If such group opportunities do not exist, their development should be given high priority.

Group Counseling and Therapy

Paralleling its conventional, ongoing groups, every church ought to have several groups with explicit healing goals. These should include groups to give support and spiritual healing during personal crises; seek solutions to common problems in living (e.g., being a single, two-in-one parent, relating constructively with a rebelling teen-ager, etc.); and increase interpersonal effectiveness. Objectives such as these often are realized as byproducts in other groups, but these goals should be the primary *raison d'etre* in some church groups.

Group therapy describes a cluster of varied group approaches to psychotherapy. Being a client in an effective therapy group can be an invaluable training and growth experience for seminarians and pastors. But doing therapy with a group (like doing individual psychotherapy) requires a high level of therapeutic awareness and skills that comes from advanced training. In some ways, group psychotherapy is more complex than individual psychotherapy. Powerful positive and negative transference reactions may occur and there is sometimes an acting out of these transference feelings. It takes a skilled therapist to handle such incidents constructively. Pastors with limited counseling and group training should not attempt to lead group psychotherapy. If a church has a minister of counseling or a mental health professional with group therapy training, it may be appropriate to provide this form of intensive help to people with deeper psychological problems. If such leadership is not available, a church should concentrate on the vitally important ministry of growth groups and group crisis counseling. The latter consists of relatively short-term counseling in groups aimed at helping people handle losses or crises constructively.[20]

Varieties of Growth Groups

The mainstream of any church's group caring should be directed, not at those who need group therapy, but at the host of people who can profit from growth groups. In any church there are many persons in this broad category—those who have garden-variety problems and unhappiness, and those who wish to grow spiritually, improve their relationships, develop their creativity, and discover what "life in all its fullness" can mean in their life stage and situation.

A growth group is any group, whatever its name or other purposes, which has these characteristics:

(1) The dominant (though not exclusive) purpose is the personal growth of participants—emotionally, interpersonally, intellectually, spiritually, physically. (2) A group centered growth-facilitating style of leadership is used—first by the designated leader and gradually by the entire group so that the group itself becomes an instrument and environment of growth. (3) The growth-orientation is the guiding perspective; the emphasis is more on unused potentialities, here-and-now effectiveness in living, and future growth, than on past failures or present hang-ups and problems, though these are not excluded from consideration. Growth groups are primarily mutual care groups, not counseling or therapy groups. (4) The group is composed of relatively functional people so that its aim is "making well people better." (5) It is small enough to allow group trust and depth relationships to develop. (6) There is a back-and-forth movement from sharing of personal growth issues to considering content (ideas or relational skills) which is relevant to the growth needs of participants. It is *group educative counseling* which blends personalized education with group counseling methods. Constructive changes in both attitudes and feelings on the one hand, and in behavior and relationships on the other are encouraged in growth groups. Concern for *spiritual*

growth, understood as the heart of all human growth, should be a central thrust in all church-related groups. Empowerment to enable the growth of others, should be one expression of the growth individuals achieve in such a group.[21]

The versatility of the growth group approach can be suggested by listing some of the types of groups that have proved to be feasible and growth-producing in various churches:

Youth groups to work through unfinished personal identity.

Preparation for marriage groups.

"Keeping Our Marriage Growing" groups (recently married).

Marriage enrichment groups for parents of young children; for parents of adolescents (middle marrieds); and for empty-nest marriages.

"Making the Most of Maturity" groups (over-forty groups).

Creative singlehood groups.

Play-for-growth groups for children and parents.

Parent-child and parent-youth dialogue groups.

Preparation for childbirth (leaving home, retirement, and other developmental crises) groups.

Study-growth groups with a focus on intellectual growth (often centering on a book).

Liberation groups for women, for men, and for couples desiring fresh approaches to changing female/male roles.

Creativity groups using drama, poetry, painting, pottery, body movement (creative dance), yoga, etc. as a stimulus to growth.

Sharing groups for mutual help in coping constructively with common causes of stress, e.g., aging parents, physical handicaps, a handicapped child, "adolescing" children.

Action-growth groups with a dual focus on personal development and training for some significant task such as community service and social action.

Spiritual growth groups and Bible-study aimed primarily at growth in the areas of meanings, values, beliefs and one's relationship with God.

Ecology groups for tuning in on nature and saving the environment.

Multiple-family growth networks.

Bereavement recovery groups.

Youth groups searching for nondrug ways of turning on.

Career choice, planning and transition groups.

Follow-up groups for persons who have completed counseling or therapy.[22]

This list is only suggestive. The possible applications of the growth-group approach are limited only by one's imagination and leadership resources available.

A complementary relationship should exist in a church between pastoral counseling and growth groups. Each should strengthen the other. Growth groups often facilitate referral for counseling or therapy. Confronting personal and relationship issues openly in growth groups makes some people aware of their need for deeper help. By increasing awareness of these needs, growth groups may enable people to enter therapy considerably sooner than they otherwise would. Conversely, referral to a growth group is an ideal follow-on experience for persons who have completed counseling or therapy (individual or group). The healing and growth that occurred as a result of therapeutic experiences can best be consolidated and continued in the nurturing environment of a growth group. Participation in a growth group concurrently with individual or couple counseling often accelerates the growth that occurs in counseling. The long-range growth effects of pastoral counseling can be multiplied significantly if linked with growth groups.

Leadership for Growth Groups

Providing adequate leadership is one problem that prevents some churches from developing the sharing and growth groups their people need. Most pastors did not have formal training in group dynamics and group counseling in seminary. Some therefore feel inadequate to launch growth group programs in their congregations. Fortunately, ministers with good interpersonal awareness and individual counseling skills can equip themselves to lead growth groups by this process:

Step 1: *Experiencing several growth groups.* This aspect of training has a dual purpose—to maximize one's personal growth and to learn various growth-enabling styles and techniques by experiencing these as a group member.[23]

Step 2: *Learning the basic working concepts of interpersonal and group dynamics, group methods, and facilitator skills, by reading several key books in the field.* The books by Bob Leslie, Clyde Reid, and myself in the Recommended Reading section give basic information on such crucial issues as publicizing and recruiting a growth group; the group size, length, frequency, and format; developing a workable group contract; the stages in the life of a group; facilitator functions and methods; spiritual growth in groups; coping with common group problems; and methods of evaluation in groups. Learning the theory of small groups illuminates what one experiences in such groups. Thus one acquires the "cognitive maps" needed by a group facilitator.

Step 3: *Co-leading one or more groups with an experienced facilitator*. This enables one to learn both from observing the other facilitator and from getting supervisory feedback (after each session) on one's own facilitating.

In many communities a pastoral counseling specialist or a mental health professional with training in group methods can be recruited by a pastor to co-lead a growth group. If it is not possible to involve an experienced co-leader, solo-leading of a group should be begun under the supervision of a competent group counselor. Recording group sessions (with the group's permission, of course) and playing segments of these in supervisory sessions increases the value of the supervision.

The full range of growth groups that a congregation should have to meet the varied needs of its people cannot possibly be led by any pastor. Fortunately much of the leadership for sharing and growth groups can be provided by carefully selected and trained lay persons. One reason why it behooves pastors to learn group facilitator and supervisory skills is so that they will be equipped to train and give backup support to lay facilitators. Thus pastors become facilitators of facilitators, enabling the impact of their caring skills to be multiplied through the ministries of these growth group leaders. Persons selected to receive training for this important work should be warm, aware, congruent, and growing. One of the best ways to identify potential lay facilitators is to be aware of how people respond as members of existing growth groups. As the facilitating functions begin to be shared by group members, it will become apparent who has natural facilitator aptitudes and therefore will be most trainable.

The process of training lay group facilitators follows the three steps described above. But a fourth step should be added—ongoing supervision by a pastor or other professional with group expertise should be built into any growth group program using lay facilitators. (For criteria for selecting trainable persons, see chapter 15.)

Growth Groups Through the Life Stages

Ideally a church should develop a *ladder of growth groups* to help people at each major life stage cope constructively with the new problems and develop the new possibilities of their current stage. Small educative counseling groups can help people prepare for and handle constructively the stress periods in their life journey. Gerald Caplan calls the work of such groups "anticipatory guidance" or "emotional innoculation:"

> In small-group or individual discussions, the specialist then draws their attention to the details of the impending hazard and attempts to evoke ahead of time a vivid anticipation of the experience, with its associated feelings. . . . He then helps them begin to envisage possible ways of solving the problems, including mastery of their negative feelings. When the experience itself arrives, the hazards will be attenuated because they have been made familiar by being anticipated, and the individuals will already have been set on the path of healthy coping responses.[24]

To show the usefulness of this approach to a life-cycle caring ministry, here are some examples of educative-counseling groups designed to respond to the needs of persons during each of the eight stages outlined by Erik Erikson:

Stage 1—*Infancy* (birth to 15 months). A *"Preparation for Parenthood Groups"* can help pregnant couples and those planning on adopting a child increase their readiness for the demanding, rewarding role of parenting; "New Parents Sharing Group" can help couples learn to nurture the foundational feeling of basic trust in their child. Such groups can provide valuable peer support and learning from each other as well as input from professionals with knowledge about infants. A marriage enrichment component should be included in all preparation for parenthood and new parents groups to help couples cope creatively with the heavy pressures on their marriages of having an infant. Educative growth groups for staff of church school nurseries (and each of the subsequent levels of the church school) are also important.

Stage 2—*Early Childhood* (15 months to 2½ years). A "Parents Study Sharing and Support Group" can help parents learn how to respond to needs of children in this stage, particularly how to nurture their child's need for growing autonomy, the growth goal of this stage. In one church, a young couples' Sunday School class chose to follow a child study theme for several years, under the leadership of a child psychologist in that community. The sharing in this class became deep and helpful to many of these parents.

Stage 3—Play age (3 to 6). A growth group for parents of children at this stage can help parents learn how to nurture a child's sense of initiative, the central growth goal of this life stage.

> A Long Island church of which I was pastor used the growth group approach in its continuing program of child-study for mothers of preschoolers. After preliminary discussion of the need for such a group, the nursery superintendent and the minister invited all the mothers of preschool children to an exploratory meeting. Those who responded decided to start a "Child-study Nursery Group" which would meet one morning a week throughout the school year. They elected a steering committee with a rotating chairperson. This committee planned the child-study program in consultation with the minister and the superintendent after circulating an "Interest Finder" questionnaire among the entire group. Here is a sampling of their programs: systematic study of a mental health film, a talk by a pediatrician, a trip with their children to a zoo, a talk by the minister on "Handling a Child's Fear of Death," and a panel of members on "Sex Education of Young Children."
>
> While the mothers met in the church parlor, their children attended nursery school in the basement under the supervision of trained volunteers. Each mother contributed financially to cover costs of nursery school equipment as well as coffee and juice. Occasional evening meetings were scheduled so that fathers could share in choice programs. In the evaluation session at the close of the first year, comments such as these were voiced: "This group has given me self-confidence as a mother. I don't feel so pushed around by what others on my street think." "Our family is spending more time together and *liking* it! We went on our first picnic in the country last week."
>
> This group continued for a number of years. Some dropped out as their children reached school age. Other mothers joined, keeping the group at about twenty-five. This group was effective because it met real needs of mothers and children. It allowed the mothers an opportunity to deal with their feelings and attitudes as well as acquire useful information. It was self-directed so that it stayed close to the needs and interests of the participants. The group association helped to overcome the loneliness often felt by mothers whose activities are confined by small children.[25]

This group illustrates the potential values of a growth group for parents of children in all three preschool stages. It also shows a way that a church can provide growth group experiences for children. The social skills the children acquired through their play together, and all that they learned through the use of art, storytelling, and music, made this a significant growth experience for the children. This Child Study-Nursery Group was to me as a pastor-participant, the most exciting experience with a growth group during my parish ministry. In retrospect (and with a raised consciousness) I now realize that this program would have been strengthened significantly if we had devised a strategy for involving dads and whole families more regularly in growth experiences.

Psychotherapists and developmental psychologists have given us convincing evidence that the preschool years are the foundation-laying years. The future wholeness of children, adolescents, and adults is deeply influenced, for better or for worse, by the quality of a child's relationship during this crucial period. Churches have a unique entrée to many family systems with children in these formative stages. This gives congregations strategic opportunities to develop growth groups to strengthen, inform, and energize fathers and mothers of children in these stages. Whatever a church does to respond to this opportunity through its education program and growth groups will pay psychological and spiritual dividends far into the future.[26]

Stage 4—School Age (6 to 12). Growth groups for parents and for children of this stage should focus on enabling movement toward the children's primary growth goal—to acquire the basic tools and relational skills for living productively in their culture. While he was a pastor, Edgar N. Jackson frequently encountered a sense of need among parents of preadolescents. So he invited a cluster of six to eight couples to meet for eight sessions to discuss matters of mutual concern. He began each session with a brief statement on some aspect of the psychology of preadolescents or of parent-child relationships. This precipitated spirited discussion of the parents' feelings and problems. This simple approach can be applied to a variety of "Parent Enrichment Groups." During the preadolescent stage and beyond, growth experiences for children with their peers become increasingly valuable.[27]

Stage 5—Adolescence. There is no life stage when small sharing groups can be more growth-producing than adolescence. Growth groups can be used to help teens strengthen their sense of identity (their key growth goal); develop new relationship skills with persons of the other sex; enhance their feelings of self-worth; keep the Adult side of their personality in the driver's seat of their lives;

affirm and guide their blossoming sexuality; and develop their own viable faith and responsible ethical values. Elsewhere I have described a variety of growth group models used by churches with youth.[28] Educative counseling approaches can be used productively with membership training groups and confirmation classes for youth.

Stage 6—Young Adulthood. Growth groups that are relevant to this stage include "Creative Singlehood Groups," "Preparation for Marriage Workshops," "Preparation for Parenting" classes, "New Parents Growth Groups," and "Creative Marriage and Sexuality Enrichment groups."

"Growing Together," a marital enrichment group for young adults in the first few years of marriage, was offered by a West Coast church of which I was minister of counseling. Role playing of typical adjustment problems of new marriages was used to help the group focus on their real growth issues quickly. With one exception, the couples came to the group not because their marriages were in deep trouble, but because they desired to make good marriages better. This was an example of preventative pastoral care.

As suggested earlier, to be more responsive to the needs of persons who have never been married, divorced or widowed— churches should devise "singlehood enrichment" programs including growth groups. Such groups are effective ways of providing mutual care and growth for the young adults who in increasing numbers are choosing singleness as a life-style or choosing to delay getting married. Groups can strengthen the communication and relationship-building skills that can make singlehood truly creative.

Stage 7—Middle Adulthood. During Mid-Years I, the years with adolescents in the home, a sharing group for parents can help them handle the challenges of those relationships constructively.[29] Transgenerational Teen-Parents communication events are also useful. "Generativity Groups" can help mid-year adults develop the creative outreach dimension of their lives, which is the central task of those years.

Mid-Years II, empty-nest years, confronts couples with new issues, needs, and possibilities. Growth groups should have a different orientation during this stage. A mid-years minister in Southern California sensed that one group that was needed to meet the needs of his people was an Empty-Nest Marriage Enrichment Group.[30] He and his wife served as co-facilitators for a group of five couples, which met for six weekly 2½ hour sessions, plus an all-day Saturday retreat. The contract developed by the group included these purposes for the group:

> To enable couples "to understand the dynamics of the empty nest stage of marriage, both as a crisis period and as highly creative, productive years; to help couples increase their communication skills and their experiences of the many facets of intimacy; to increase the spiritual quality of their relationships including Christian values; to develop a network of support and trust among them and a sense of outreach to other couples.[31]

This group illustrates some of the rich possibilities of marriage enrichment groups during Mid-years II, when many of us need to revitalize our marriages to enhance growth and generativity during the latter mid-years and beyond. Spiritual growth around value and meaning of life issues is often centerstage in the needs of persons in both Mid-years I and II. "Preparation for Creative Retirement" groups also serve an important function in Mid-years II.

Stage 8—The Mature Years. The minister of a New York church drew a retirement group together informally by simply inviting ten men on the verge of retirement or recently retired, to meet with him for six times to share ideas on "Making the Most of Retirement." The interaction was vigorous and helpful. Retirement growth groups should be available to both men and women, and also to couples since the retiring of one or both partners usually impacts marriages with new stresses and possibilities.

Educative counseling methods have proved effective with many small groups of seniors.[32] There is no life stage when the growth perspective on one's life is more difficult or crucial. Groups for spouses and other relatives of the terminally ill can be very helpful. One minister in the Seattle area has formed several "Living with Dying" groups to help members of her congregation face the fact that all of us are living-dying creatures. Elisabeth Kübler-Ross's *On Death and Dying* is used as a resource, with group members agreeing to read certain chapters between each session. The pastor who facilitated these groups divided the two-hour sessions equally between discussion of particular topics and experiential exercises designed to help people get in touch with their feelings and attitudes about death. These exercises included writing one's own epitaph and imagining that one has only a few months to live.

Which life stage growth groups are most needed in a particular church can be determined by analyzing the age distribution of that congregation and community. In addition to life stage growth experiences, a church has a unique opportunity to offer a variety of growth group experiences that cut across age categories. I recall a marriage enrichment retreat where the oldest couple had been married nearly forty-five years, and the youngest only four months, with the other couples sprinkled unevenly between. At first the wide age and marriage experience gaps seemed to present an unbridgeable communication chasm. It was a beautiful moment of mutual discovery when the longest married couple talked openly about an issue they were working on currently and the newlyweds reported in astonishment that they were confronting a similar issue.

Classes and groups focusing on common interests and needs tend to attract participants from various life stages. As Bob Leslie astutely observes:

> The most natural way to introduce the note of sharing into small groups is through study. Church people are used to the idea that study is done best in a class and hence have little resistance to coming together in a group. Almost every successful attempt at meaningful group life has involved study. Indeed, as groups grow in intimacy and in appreciation of each other there tends to develop a felt need for material really to grapple with in order to keep growing in depth. [33]

Principles of Effective Growth Groups

(1) These factors seem to be involved in attracting members to growth groups: (a) The group goals are designed to respond to the *felt* needs of a particular group of persons in the congregation. (b) A nonthreatening name and growth-oriented publicity are used. (c) A personal invitation is extended by the minister or a trusted lay leader to selected individuals. (d) The group's purposes are stated clearly (psychologically and theologically) in all publicity and recruiting.

(2) An effective growth group must be small enough to permit frequent participation and face-to-face communication among all its members.

(3) At the outset, the leader should ask members to say what they each hope to get from the experience. This gives the facilitator a tentative impression of the group's needs and learning readiness. Initial input by the leader should be brief and immediately relevant to the felt needs of the group. It is important to develop a group contract and agenda of topics and issues, reflecting the needs and interests of the group. Long lectures are verboten because they kill dialogue. After six to ten minutes of seed-planting input, the leader should invite feedback and keep raising pertinent questions until the group members become involved. The leader may increase feeling-level involvement on the part of group members by personalizing an issue with a hypothetical but true-to-life case, or by sharing her or his own personal experience. The bulk of growth group sessions should be spent in the group's wrestling with the issues related to each person's situation and growth goals.

(4) Having a resource book, a topic, or a flexible outline of how the sessions will be used tends to reduce group (and leader) anxiety as well as provide a flowchart of the group's plan and topics. The less structure a group has, the higher the anxiety level tends to be. Too much structure curtails group spontaneity and reduces personal involvement. An excess of instruction tends to trap a group in leader-centered dependence, which defeats the purpose of a growth group. Group-centeredness is generated by throwing the group on its own resources, gently refusing to carry them, and involving the maximum number in decisions, goal-setting, program planning and participation, and evaluation and re-contracting.

(5) Leaders should function in the group-centered manner described earlier in this chapter. They should attempt to create a warm, accepting climate; listen closely and responsively to what each person says; encourage openness of communication; draw less assertive members into the interaction by asking, "How do you feel about this matter, Carl?"; build group-centeredness by linking what various people say, pointing to the connections or contrasts in their positions. Leaders may occasionally summarize what has been said, giving the group an overview of its process and content. Leaders should encourage feeling-level communication by sharing their own feelings and responding to feelings of others as they emerge. When someone opens a door to a deeper level of

interaction by mentioning a personal issue, the leader helps the group walk through that door by focusing on the issue.

(6) The leaders may suggest tools that the group can use to enhance interaction. For example, persons can be asked to "draw your childhood family," using different-sized circles to represent the relative influence of each and the distance between persons. Each group member then shares and comments on what he or she has drawn. The same can be done with current family constellations. Both stimulate rapid involvement. Another useful tool is role playing. To illustrate, a young man who consistently failed to get jobs for which he was interviewed brought up this problem during a young adult growth group. The minister-leader suggested that the man reenact the interview of the day before, a group member taking the company personnel director's part. It was immediately apparent to the group that the young man unwittingly was sabotaging his chances by his behavior during the interview. Another group member than played the young man's role allowing him to stand off and see himself making a negative impression. In this case the person did not need to discover the underlying causes of his self-defeating behavior in order to change his approach enough to obtain the next job for which he applied. Thus he interrupted his failure cycle.

(7) Leaders should attempt to be aware of the group as a whole, as well as of each individual. They may suggest that an observer-feed back person be selected to help the group become aware of its own process and interaction. This is rewarding, but threatening at first, and it should be suggested only after a group gains some sense of mutual trust. The contemporary rediscovery of the power of small groups is an exciting development in the churches. Clearly the imaginative use of such groups is one of the major frontiers in pastoral care and counseling.

Reality-Practice Session

PARISHIONER'S ROLE: (Three to five persons needed) Constitute yourselves as members of a sharing and caring group, whose goal is to communicate on a level that is mutually helpful and group-building.

PASTOR'S ROLE: Facilitate this group using the growth-enabling style of leadership described in this chapter.

OBSERVER-COACH'S ROLE: Give feedback concerning how the facilitator deepens the communication within the group.

Recommended Reading

Philip A. Anderson, *Church Meetings That Matter* (Philadelphia: United Church Press, 1965). Principles of understanding and improving ordinary church groups; the "Christian Group Life" inventory, pp. 50-52 is an excellent instrument for evaluation by a group.

Phillip & Phoebe Anderson, *The House Church* (Nashville: Abingdon Press, 1975). A useful introduction to the house church approach.

Dorwin Cartwright and Alvin Zander, *Group Dynamics: Research and Theory*, 3rd ed. (New York: Harper & Row, 1968). A classic on group dynamics.

Casteel, John L., *The Creative Role of Interpersonal Groups in the Church Today* (New York: Association Press, 1968). Fifteen papers on developing and leading a variety of types of small groups in the church.

Howard Clinebell, *Growth Groups* (Nashville: Abingdon Press, 1972). Describes the formation and leadership of growth groups, and shows their use in enrichment marriages, parent-child relationships, singles, youth, social action, women's and men's liberation.

Gerald Corey, *Theory and Practice of Group Counseling* (Monterey, Calif.: Brooks-Cole, 1981). Various approaches to group counseling.

Edgar W. Jackson, *Group Counseling: Dynamic Possibilities of Small Groups* (Philadelphia: Pilgrim Press, 1969). Describes the uses of group methods with persons in different stages of the life cycle.

David W. Johnson and Frank P. Johnson, *Joining Together: Group Therapy and Group Skills*, 2d ed. (Englewood, N.J.: Prentice-Hall, 1982). Reviews group dynamics, leadership, group goals, conflict, and coherence in groups.

Harold I. Kaplan and B. M. Sodock, eds., *New Models for Group Therapy* (New York: Jason Aronson, 1972). Describes a variety of types of therapy groups including TA, behavior therapy, and existential groups.

Robert C. Leslie, *Sharing Groups in the Church* (Nashville: Abingdon, 1971). A basic guide for using small groups in a church.

Thomas C. Oden, *The Intensive Group Experience: The New Pietism* (Philadelphia: Westminster, 1972). Provides a historical and theological evaluation of the small group movement.

Clyde Reid, *Groups Alive—Church Alive* (Harper & Row, 1971). Has helpful chapters on group dynamics, contracting, leadership, and church group problems.

Carl Rogers, *Carl Rogers on Encounter Groups* (New York: Harper & Row, 1971). Describes the process, facilitive skills, application, and research and encounter groups.

David L. Williamson, *Group Power: How to Develop, Lead, and Help Groups Achieve Goals* (Englewood Cliffs, N.J.: Prentice-Hall, 1982). A summary of small groups' dynamics and leadership skills in a developmental framework.

Pastoral Psychotherapy

The purpose in a [person's] mind is like deep water, but a [person] of understanding will draw it out.

—PROVERBS 20:5

Ful wys is he that can him-selven knowe.

—GEOFFREY CHAUCER[1]

The essence of therapy is . . . helping a person discover the depths of his own being and express this in symbols that carry vital meaning . . . Living religious language does have a place . . . language which picks up and expresses vital experiences with which the person is struggling.

—CARROLL A. WISE, *PASTORAL PSYCHOTHERAPY*[2]

Pastoral psychotherapy is a long-term helping process aimed at effecting fundamental changes in the counselee's personality by uncovering and dealing with hidden feelings, intrapsychic conflicts, and repressed, early life memories. It is the use by ministers of psychotherapeutic methods to enable people to change basic aspects of their personalities and behavior patterns to make these more constructive and creative. The uniqueness of *pastoral* psychotherapy is that it regards changes in one's spiritual life, one's values, meanings, and ultimate commitments, as central and essential to the depth transformations that are the goal of all psychotherapy. Pastoral psychotherapy is a healing process seeking to help people remove blocks (within themselves and their relationships) to their growth toward Spirit-centered wholeness. The terms "insight counseling," "pastoral psychotherapy," "depth pastoral counseling" are roughly synonymous. Depth methods seek to increase self-understanding and thus produce basic intrapsychic changes or growth.

It should be emphasized that the depth of the counseling

process is a matter of degree. Significant insight and change can occur on all levels of counseling interaction. New and helpful self-understanding may be achieved during short-term crisis counseling. But generally "the longer the period, the deeper the material that tends to emerge."[3]

Up to this point in the book, I have emphasized short-term caring and counseling approaches that are best adapted to parish counseling. These approaches provide treatments of choice for the majority of those seeking pastoral help. Effective short-term crisis methods often produce long-term beneficial results. Some people, however, *require* longer-term counseling if they are to be helped. Intense unconscious conflicts sabotage their efforts to cope with crises or improve their relationships. Psychotherapy is essential to help them resolve these inner conflicts and enhance self-awareness and self-esteem.

What should the minister do to be of help to such persons? Seward Hiltner states: "There is no inherent reason why extended counseling could not be a part of a pastor's work—if he [or she] were trained, had the time, and did not in the process step out of his [or her] role as pastor. That is, extended counseling is not inherently foreign to pastorship, but in a practical sense it is rarely wise or appropriate for most pastors to engage in it."[4]

As Carroll Wise points out, the word "psychotherapy" has deep roots in our biblical tradition. In the New Testament, the Greek word *psyche*, which is sometimes translated "soul," actually means "the living person as a total reality and unity," not a spiritual dimension distinguished from the physical and mental aspects of persons. "Therapy" is from the Greek *therapeuo*, which in the New Testament is used to mean "to serve and also to heal" (as in Jesus' commission to "heal the sick" in Matthew 10:8 and Luke 10:9).[5] Pastoral psychotherapy is one means of reclaiming our biblical heritage of healing and depth transformation using the insights and methods of contemporary psychotherapies.

But depth counseling is a complex, time-consuming process. As suggested earlier pastoral psychotherapy should be done mainly by those in specialized ministries of counseling and therapy. The pastor with limited training in counseling should refer persons needing such help to a competent pastoral or secular psychotherapist. Even if pastors are well-trained as depth counselors, they are wise to invest most of their available counseling time in the crisis opportunities that occur so frequently in pastoring. Over the years they can give significant help to many times the number of persons they could assist by majoring in long-term pastoral psychotherapy.

The levels at which ministers counsel should be determined to some extent by the points where their skills intersect the needs of those who seek help. In many nonmetropolitan settings, clergy with even limited counseling training have more training than almost anyone else in their communities. In such therapy-poor areas a minister who has skills in deeper pastoral counseling may be the only resource available to those who desperately need such help. In most situations, clinically-trained pastors have many opportunities to make some use of their depth-counseling skills, to whatever extent their time permits.

In addition to providing a valuable service to the troubled, doing a *limited* amount of deeper pastoral counseling tends to strengthen one's total ministry. To relate to even one or two persons at a time in the depth required to do pastoral psychotherapy helps to provide a deeper dimension to one's ministry, diminishing the occupational hazard of shallowness in relationships. Pastoral psychotherapy is demanding, both in time and emotional energy. It is also highly rewarding when done effectively. But overinvestment in depth counseling weakens one's total ministry by consuming a disproportionate amount of a pastor's time, which could be spent in helping many more persons by short-term counseling and other person enhancing ministries.

In this chapter I will give only a brief introduction to insight-oriented psychotherapy, the dominant form of pastoral psychotherapy up to the present. I will discuss the use of Transactional Analysis, since I have referred to this approach several times elsewhere in this book, applying it to marriage counseling. Many of the newer psychotherapies (see streams two, three, four, and five below) are rich sources of insights that can be utilized in pastoral care, education, and short-term pastoral counseling by parish pastors. They provide valuable resources for broadening and strengthening the conceptual foundations of pastoral psycotherapy. Those who wish to explore these therapies in more depth may consult *Contemporary Growth Therapies*.

Depth Understanding

A distinction should be made between depth *understanding* and the practice of depth therapy. All pastors need sufficient knowledge of the goals and methods of psychotherapy to make skillful referrals. Furthermore, whether or not they have the training and time to do pastoral therapy, their total work with persons will be strengthened and enriched as they increase their understanding of the deeper forces in persons influencing all thoughts, beliefs, and behavior profoundly. Some understanding of psychodynamics will enhance their effectiveness in all aspects of ministry.

The insights of depth psychology are indispensable for ministering to persons in our age of alienation and brokenness.[6] The psychoanalytic views of psychosexual (Sigmund Freud) and psychosocial (Erik Erikson) development are valuable pastoral resources for understanding behavior, beliefs, and relationships—of oneself and one's parishioners. The insights of Freud and his successors illuminate vast areas of human life, which otherwise are shadowed enigmas. The contributions of Jung, Adler, and Rank, the interpersonal schools of depth psychology (Sullivan, Fromm, and Horney in particular), and the existentialists in psychotherapy supplement and/or correct the view of Freud at crucial points. The feminist psychotherapists have critiqued and helped to correct the profound male biases in Freud and in most other psychotherapeutic approaches. These biases distort the therapist's understanding of and attempts to help women. By studying depth psychologies and the psychotherapies based on them, pastors can increase their understanding of the amazing depths and heights within themselves and the persons with whom they have the privilege of being in ministry.

The Five Streams of Contemporary Psychotherapies

The most creative and effective psycotherapists—pastoral or secular—are those who have developed an *integrated eclecticism* that utilizes insights and methods from a variety of therapeutic approaches. To be used effectively, these resources must be integrated around a consistent core of assumption about the nature, process, and goals of healing and wholeness. In the early years of my specialized ministry of counseling, I used (as do many pastoral psychotherapists) the psychoanalytic, ego psychology system as a unifying conceptual framework. At the present time, I find the principles of growth counseling (which include many ego psychology insights) to be a more change-producing system of integration.[7]

A rich variety of therapies is blossoming today like flowers in a spring meadow offering both the generalist pastor and the pastoral therapist unprecedented resources for facilitating wholeness. These psychotherapies can be understood as representing five categories or streams, which complement and overlap as well as conflict with each other at many points. Growth-oriented pastoral counselors and psychotherapists can draw on all five of these streams, to gain appropriate resources for the unique healing/growth needs of particular parishioners or clients:

Stream 1: *Traditional Insight-oriented Therapies*. This stream, beginning with the pioneering work of Sigmund Freud, encompasses most of the therapies developed prior to the last two decades. Included are Freud and the Ego Analysts, Alfred Adler, Otto Rank, Erich Fromm, Karen Horney, Harry Stack Sullivan, and Carl Rogers. Pastoral counselors and therapists will continue to derive invaluable resourcs from the therapies in this stream.

Stream 2: *Behavioral, Action, Crisis Therapies*. This cluster of diverse therapies is linked by the shared assumption that maladaptive learning is the root cause of problems in living and that behavioral and/or cognitive relearning therefore is the heart of therapeutic change. In contrast to insight therapies, behavior therapies view the painful symptoms that motivate people to seek help as the real problems to be treated rather than surface manifestations of deeper, hidden causes. The goal is to change overt, maladaptive behavior or, in the case of the cognitive therapies, the covert behavior (thoughts, feelings, beliefs, fantasies). Included in this stream are the various behavioral approaches to individual therapy (e.g., Joseph Wolpe, Skinnerian therapies); the behavioral marital therapies (e.g., David Knox); the cognitive therapies (e.g., Albert Ellis's "Rational Emotive Therapy" and Aaron Beck's "cognitive therapy"); Reality Therapy (William Glasser); crisis counseling; and the sex therapies, pioneered by William Masters and Virginia Johnson. Using models and methods from the therapies in this stream is one of the challenging opportunities facing counseling pastors and pastoral psychotherapists in the next decade (see Howard Stone's book in Recommended Reading).

Stream 3: *Human Potential Therapies.* This stream includes a variety of nonanalytic therapies whose explicit goal is to help people actualize their full potentialities—e.g., transactional analysis, gestalt therapy, and the body therapies. The therapies from this stream have enriched the field of pastoral care and counseling immensely in the past fifteen years and undoubtedly will continue to do so in the future.

Stream 4: *Relational, Systems, and Radical Therapies.* This stream includes all those therapies aimed at freeing small or larger social systems so that all their members can be free to live more constructively. Among these approaches are the various group therapies (including group counseling, growth groups, and self-help groups); conjoint marriage, family and multiple-family therapies; the radical therapies (including the feminist therapies) that aim simultaneously at enabling people to experience healing of their individual and relational psychic wounds, empowering them to work with others to change the social roots of their problems—sexism, economic injustice, racism, and class oppression; and the systemic approaches (including organizational development and social action) that aim at changing the oppressive structures and the interpersonal climate of larger face-to-face systems such as schools, churches, and industries—making them more nurturing of wholeness. Since ministers are natural relational and systems counselors, this stream offers abundant resources for pastoral counselors and psychotherapists. The "radical therapies" seeking to *liberate* and *empower* people to change growth-oppressive social structures can provide counseling pastors with concepts and methods that help bridge the pastoral and prophetic ministries.

Stream 5: *Spiritual Growth Therapies.* This stream includes the various therapies that view spiritual healing and growth toward spiritual wholeness as central to all healing and growth. The approaches of Carl Jung, the existentialist therapies, psychosynthesis, pastoral psychotherapy, and the eastern approaches to enhancing consciousness are all a part of this stream. These therapies offer many resources directly relevant to the spiritual work of pastoral care and counseling.

The Goals of Pastoral Insight Psychotherapy

The ways that therapeutic goals are conceptualized varies from one approach to another, as was evident in the above overview. The insight therapies seek intrapsychic changes to enable persons to become more "fully functioning" (Rogers). Here are some directions of change sought by these therapies.

Persons are helped to move toward:

—Self awareness—listening to their own feelings and experiences.

—Insight—depth understanding of their feelings and relationships, freeing them from the dominance of past experiences in the present.

—Permitting the therapist to care about them as persons of worth and thereby coming to perceive themselves in this way.

—Letting go of the proctective facades that had prevented them from developing their authentic humanity and genuine, mutually-fulfilling relationships.

—Autonomy, self-directedness, choosing their own goals, trusting their own organism with its awareness, needs, and values.

—Increasing self-acceptance that enables them to accept others more fully.

—Being the self one truly is (Kierkegaard).

—Constructive changes in behavior stemming from a more aware, congruent, authentic, and alive self.[8]

To these changes within persons, the interpersonal therapies add these changes in their relationships:

—Enhancing and strengthening need-satisfying and conflict-resolving communication between persons.

—Enabling persons to establish creative intimacy and interdependency (without loss of identity and autonomy) in caring relationships where growth is mutually nurtured and inner freedom is enhanced.

After extensive pastoral psychotherapy, one woman could report: "I feel something is complete. For the first time in my life,

I have access to the full range of my feelings. Having access, it is up to me what I do with them. Before I had no choice." She had experienced liberation from the stranglehold of obsolete experiences, feelings, and relationships on her present life. Her growth had opened up alternatives in her inner life and her relationships. Spontaneity had become a prominent characteristic of her feelings and her behavior. She had a stronger sense of her unique identity, and a greater sense of aliveness. Abraham Maslow declares: "Self-actualizing people have a wonderful capacity to appreciate again and again, freshly and naïvely, the basic goods of life, with awe, pleasure, wonder and even ecstasy, however stale these experiences have become to others."[9] Persons are alive psychologically and spiritually, to the degree that they are aware of and in relationship with the many facets of their own inner lives, and with other people, nature, and God. Self-awareness is the path to greater aliveness. By this path one moves beyond *knowing* to *being* and *accepting* one's authentic self.

The distinctive and ultimate goal of all pastoral psychotherapy that is truly pastoral is a more open, growing, and loving relationship with God. Augustine's prayer notes this well: "O God . . . may I know myself, may I know thee."[10] Christian pastoral therapy has as its goal the healing of the deep alienation within and between persons, and the nurturing of their growth in all six dimensions of their wholenesses. It seeks to help them grow toward the full blossoming of wholeness represented so clearly in Jesus. His aliveness, self-affirmation, inner freedom, and profound love of God and persons were wonderfully contagious, enabling those with whom he related to become more whole.

The Methods of Insight Psychotherapy

In general, insight-oriented approaches to pastoral psychotherapy employ methods that enable persons gradually to become aware of and change those out-of-awareness (repressed) feelings, images, impulses, desires, memories, and conflicts, which limit their effectiveness in living. Insight emerges within the context of a trustful, empathetic relationship where the troubled person feels safe enough to become aware of and explore these painful residuals from the past. By "working through" deeper and deeper levels of these life-constricting inner forces, persons gradually diminish inner blocks to aliveness and self-acceptance. They deal with obsolete, inappropriate feelings and resolve growth-blocking inner conflicts from the past. Long-sealed doors to hidden rooms in the recesses of their early lives may gradually open. The "ghosts" of feelings and experiences from their childhood have haunted them, causing them to be alienated from the strengths of their adult, reality-oriented personalities. These ghosts from the past are gradually shorn of their "demonic" power by being exposed to the light of present adult reality. A passage from Lewis Carroll's *Alice's Adventures in Wonderland* illustrates the way we are tyrannized by our past: "Alice knew it was the Rabbit coming to look for her, and she trembled till she shook the house, quite forgetting that she was now about a thousand times as large as the Rabbit and had no reason to be afraid of it."[11]

The psychotherapeutic relationship and process allow persons to stop frightening themselves by their hidden rabbits. Healing comes by reexperiencing the painful feelings and self-perception from early-life relationships and, in a trustful therapeutic relationship, working through to a more self-valuing and constructive here-and-now identity. Pastor Oskar Pfister wrote to Freud: "You yourself have always taught that what matters is not remembering but *reliving* . . . You have always insisted that memory is not sufficient, but that it must be charged with affect."[12] The therapeutic relationship permits the repair (to some degree) of personality crippling caused by inadequacies in parent-child relationships. It allows persons another chance to experience and learn more self-affirming attitudes toward themselves and others. The therapist goes down with people into their "little private hells," allowing them to face their inner "devils" and find liberation from them.[13]

Near the conclusion of long-term pastoral therapy with a female psychotherapist, a young adult woman reported that she was no longer engulfed by negative feelings toward her mother: "For the first time in my life I can feel real compassion for her because I am free enough from her not to feel crippled by her crippledness. Poor thing! All her life she suffered from feelings of powerlessness. She was trapped in traditional women's roles that didn't let her use her brains and creativity fully. No wonder she felt a need to put others down and control them." The woman commented on the meaningfulness of her relationship with the therapist adding: "Before I felt so cheated by not feeling close to my parents I kept trying to gulp in from others what I didn't get from my folks and couldn't feel myself—which pushed other people away of course." Experiencing the therapist's acceptance had enabled her to find and accept herself as a person, separate from her parents. Self-acceptance allowed her to accept her parents, with all their limitations and take responsibility for her own life rather than continuing to stay dependent by blaming them. This illustrates the way that psychotherapy can provide emotional and relational reeducation, producing personal liberation and growth at a deep level.

Effective therapy reduces inner conflicts and liberates for better use the life energy they have squandered. It makes one more sensitive to the dynamics of both one's inner life and one's relationships. Pastoral psychotherapy can help people become more aware of their longing for deeper, more meaningful relationships with their own depths, with other people, and with God. Equally important, it can help them develop the skills to relate in more mutually-growthful ways. Therapy can liberate persons by helping them learn how to live more fully, relate more constructively, and handle the inevitable problems and losses of living more creatively. It can help empower them to initiate needed changes in their own lives and in their communities.

Transactional Analysis

TA's conceptual tools are useful in teaching and in growth groups, in short-term counseling as well as longer-term therapy with both individuals and couples. When the TA approach is used in marriage counseling, the basic concepts should not be presented until strong rapport is established and the presenting problems explored in a preliminary way. Here is an example of how this approach may be presented:

Pastor: We're beginning to get a clearer picture of some of the patterns in your ways of relating that are causing you both a lot of pain. It might be helpful, at this point, for me to share some ideas, which I have found useful to several couples like yourselves.

Couple (Jean and Joe): (Indicate interest.)

Pastor: These ideas may help you understand and change your relationship. First, let me draw a diagram. (Takes a sheet of paper and draws the circles as in figure 1.) This represents the three sides of anyone's personality. The P in the top circle stands for our inner Parent. We all have a Parent part of our personalities, which is the way we experienced our parents when we were small chilren. Our inner Parent has two sides—the *nurturing* side that lets us take care of our children (or others) and the *prohibitive* side that says no and sets limits much as our parents did. This prohibitive or prejudicial side is the part of us that may get punishing and dominating occasionally. Know what I mean?

Figure 1

 Parent
Adult
Child

Jean: Yes, I catch myself using the same harsh tone with my children when they get in my hair, that my mother used when she got annoyed with me when I was small.

Pastor: That's your prohibitive Parent voice, Jean. We all have a whole set of attitudes, feelings, and behavior patterns that resemble our parents as we perceived them early in our lives.

Joe: Yeah, and do I get the critical treatment when I get slightly loaded and fool around a bit at a party!

Pastor: I'm glad you mentioned that. It has to do with the bottom-circle—with the C. Each of us has a playful, creative, pleasure-seeking side of our personalities. Eric Berne, the psychiatrist who devised this approach, called this the "Child ego state." The everyday way of saying it is that "we all have a little boy or girl inside us." When this side of us is activated, our feelings and ways of responding to others are similar to what they were at a certain stage of childhood. Did you ever notice how you feel and behave when you're called on the carpet by the boss or a police officer gives you a ticket? That's your Child side in action.

Joe: Yeh, I stutter and stammer like a five-year-old—feel about two-inches high. But (annoyed) what's that got to do with the critical way Jean comes on when I enjoy myself at a party?

Jean: Is it that the Parent side of me gets upset when Joe's Child side runs wild?

Joe: (with anger) Aw, come on now! There you go exaggerating again!

Pastor: You feel that Jean is making too much of the party incidents.

Joe: Damn right! She makes a federal case out of my having a good time!

Pastor: I wonder if you could tell me how you felt just now when Jean used the words "runs wild." (The pastor is seeking to activate the husband's Adult.)

Joe: Made me burn! Felt like, "There she goes again criticizing me unfairly!"

Pastor: In TA terms, what came through to you as Jean's critical Parent side got a strong response from your inner Child, Joe. I might point out that the opposite happened in our last session when your inner Child, Jean, responded to Joe's "making like big daddy," as you put it; remember that?

The pastor encourages them to express their reactions and to think of other examples of Parent-Child transactions in the vignettes of interaction they had discussed previously. To stimulate their thought the pastor gives an example of P-C interaction from her own marriage: "My husband and I find that my inner Parent gets turned on when . . . and this tends to turn on his inner Child. Like the other night. . . ." Although autobiographical examples should be used sparingly, they do serve to show the counselees that the pastor is not talking *down* to them from what they may imagine to be a peaceful pedestal of perfect marital bliss.

Pastor: The Child ego state is a very influential side of us, a carry-over from our childhood. It is most apt to be activated by the presence of someone else's active Parent Ego State. Most marital conflicts are Parent-Child and Child-Parent interaction. We could diagram what occurred a minute ago when you got mad at Jean's use of the words "runs wild," Joe. (Draws another set of circles as in figure 2.) The arrow (2) between your Child, Joe, and Jean's Parent show what

Figure 2

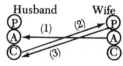

happened when you responded. What would have happened if I hadn't intervened by asking you to look at what was occurring?

Jean: My parental side would have snapped back at him that I *wasn't* exaggerating and that he *was* misbehaving in an irresponsible way. (Pastor draws arrow (3) from wife's Parent to husband's Child.)

Joe: And that would have turned on my Child side some more, and we would have been off to the races for two days of fighting.

Pastor: Uh huh. The side of your personalities that lets you stand off just now and become aware of what was going on is represented by the middle circles—your Adult ego states. This is the part of your personality that can deal more objectively and realistically with the way things are—making decisions on the basis of probable consequences. Adult to Adult relationships tend to focus on how real issues can be handled constructively. Incidentally, your observation about your response to Joe's activities at parties, Jean, may have been intended as an Adult to Adult communication, (as indicated by line 1) but Joe's inner Child got turned on by your tone or choice of words.

Jean: (Laughs) Maybe it *was* my Parent that chose those words!

Joe: (Also laughs) Could be! (Both persons' Adult and playful Child sides are activated.)

Pastor: I appreciate your awareness of that, Jean. And the fact that you can both laugh at what happened. It was each of your Adult sides, which allowed you to interrupt the Parent-Child fight.

Wife: Should we try to get rid of our Parent and Child sides so that our marriage will be all Adult?

Pastor: No, I can understand how you might have received that impression from what I've said. Actually, all three ego states are permanent and valuable parts of our personalities. Each has an important role in a good marriage. The Child in us is very important—it brings enjoyment and spontaneity to a relationship. Our nurturing Parent enables us to *be* adequate parents to our children and to nurture each other when we need help. They also provide guidelines in thousands of routine matters by giving us the "this is the way it's done" information. The goal of counseling is to strengthen the Adult side so that it can guide the activities of the Parent and Child. When one's Adult is weak or inactivated, the inner Parent and/or Child usually runs things—into the ground, I might add. Having a robust inner Adult in charge most of the time lets one keep a healthy balance among the ego states. How does all this strike you?

The above case (in condensed form) shows how the basic concepts of the structural analysis part of TA can be presented in marriage counseling, using the live interaction of the session. As in this case, some couples begin to use these conceptual tools almost immediately. Others simply do not respond to this approach. The counselor should be guided by the clues in counselee responses. If a couple grasps the tools immediately, counseling progress often is accelerated. The effect of introducing this couple to the TA approach was to gain the cooperation of their Adult sides early in the counseling process. Their inner Adults became the active allies of the pastor's Adult.

In TA terms, interactions between persons consist of "transactions," including *pastimes, games,* and *scripts.* A pastime is a transaction without ulterior motive. Common pastimes include "General Motors" (comparing cars), "Do You Know?" (so-and-so), and "Who Won?" (sports). Berne defines a game as "an ongoing series of complementary *ulterior* transactions progressing to a well-defined, predictable outcome."[14] Games are profoundly serious matters, their functions being to provide psychological "stroking," preserve psychic equilibrium, and avoid psychological intimacy. Games are essentially manipulative and operate unconsciously. Children learn their dominant games in early relationships. Family life and married life, as well as life in organizations such as churches, may be based on variations of the same game year after year.[15]

Almost any game can provide the structure for marriage interaction, but certain games tend to be more prevalent. The all-time favorite marriage game, "If It Weren't for You," is present in most marital wrangles. Another marital game, "Look How Hard I've Tried," is often played with an unsuspecting counselor. "Uproar" is a popular game for escaping sexual intimacy by pre-bedtime fights. By provoking mutual rejection, both parties avoid the feared intimacy without loss of self-esteem. "Courtroom," a three-handed marital game involving a plaintiff, a defendant, and a judge (e.g., wife, husband, counselor), begins with the plaintiff saying, "Let me tell you what he or she did."[16]

Games are segments of more complex patterns of transactions called *scripts,* which are unconscious master plans determining the overall direction of a person's life. Awareness of the existence of such unconscious determinants can alert the counselor to the magnitude of the problem involved in changing the behavior resulting from scripts.

Here are some of the values of TA for the pastoral counselor:

(1) It provides fresh ways of understanding the dynamics *and* interrelationships of individual behavior and of relationships—husband-wife, parent-child, pastor-parishioner, counselor-counselee, etc.

(2) It uses nontechnical terms (on its simpler levels) that can be readily understood by the counselee and are less threatening than technical jargon. It has a sane, whimsical quality, which appeals to many people.

(3) It provides a rapid means of interrupting runaway (Parent-Child) cycles of interaction. Its working concepts are easily taught.

(4) It provides tools with which the counselee's Adult can cooperate with the counselor's Adult, during and between sessions.

(5) It encourges the conscious effort to become aware of one's ego states, and games; this effort tends to strengthen the Adult through exercise.

(6) It provides a way of discovering how early life experiences continue to influence one's current relationships—i.e., through one's inner Child and Parent.

(7) It integrates well with some other therapies such as gestalt.

An Overview of Other Useful Therapies

Gestalt therapy, which grew from the work of psychiatrist Fredrick Perls, is one of the most innovative contemporary therapies. It provides an abundance of resources for counselors, psychotherapists, teachers, and group facilitators. Its basic philosophy is nonanalytic, holistic, existentialist, and growth-centered. Many of its insights are relevant to the work of minister counselors, both generalists and specialists. It is particularly useful in helping functional people increase their awareness, deepen their relationships with themselves and others, affirm their own identity, and claim their power as persons. Growth as understood in gestalt therapy has two interdependent poles—increasing awareness of and contact with one's whole mind-body organism, and increasing awareness of and contact with other people and the world. Increasing awareness is both the means and the goal of growth. Many of gestalt therapy's insights can be used to help people move from growth-blocking to growth-supporting religious experience.[17]

Psychosynthesis, a therapeutic approach developed by Italian psychiatrist Roberto Assagioli, is a valuable source of insights and methods for pastoral counseling and psychotherapy. Psychosynthesis is both growth-oriented and spiritually-centered. When queried about the differences between his approach and psychoanalysis, Assagioli responded with this striking metaphor:

> In one of his letters Freud said, "I am interested only in the basement of the human building." We try to build an elevator which will allow a person access to every level of his personality. After all a building with only a basement is very limited. We want to open up the terrace where you can sun-bathe or look at the stars. Our concern is the synthesis of all areas of the personality. This means psychosynthesis is holistic, global and inclusive . . . it insists that the needs for meaning, for higher values, for a spiritual life, are as real as biological or social needs.[18]

The self of everyday experience is not our ultimate identity. It is a reflection of our transpersonal Self. Psychosynthesis regards this higher Self as our creative center and essence. Making this true Self the integrating center of our being is the primary goal of therapy. The fundamental resources for growth come from the higher Self, which has potent superconscious spiritual energies, with a transforming, regenerating influence on the whole personality. The Self is the source of inner wisdom and the therapist's main ally. The will and the imagination are essential resources for wholeness in psychosynthesis.

There are three levels of growth in psychosynthesis. The first is *personal synthesis,* which aims at the synthesis of the various conflicting "subpersonalities" around the conscious self or ego. The second level called *spiritual synthesis* aims at integration of the whole person around the higher Self, enabling one to tap the superconscious capacities of human personality—the potential for meaning, values, love, altruism, and for scientific, aesthetic, and spiritual creativity. The third level is *transpersonal synthesis,* which aims at helping persons get into harmonious relationships with other persons, with the whole human family, with the cosmos, and with the spiritual reality called God.

The influence of psychosynthesis on pastoral counseling theory and practice in the past has been relatively small, even though it is potentially invaluable for our field. One of the exciting challenges facing pastoral counseling in the next decade is the fuller incorporation of insights and methods from this remarkable therapy.

The so-called "body therapies" are a constellation of therapies and growth approaches—all of which emphasize working directly with the body to increase its vitality and aliveness. Included among these therapies are Alexander Lowen's bioenergetics; autogenic training and other deep relaxation methods; dance and movement therapies; and such Eastern body disciplines as T'ai chi and hatha yoga. Gestalt therapy and some feminist therapies also have a strong emphasis on body awareness and empowering.

The body therapy perspective holds that the basic alienation that impoverishes us mentally and spiritually as well as physically is estrangement from our bodies. Our technological, left-brain society tends to overvalue rationality, cognitive knowledge, control, analysis, and work, and to undervalue body awareness, intuition, synthesis, play, and other right-brain functions. Alienation from experiencing and affirming our bodies diminishes our capacity for feeling deeply and for sensuousness, playfulness, and creativity. The body therapies seek to help people awaken their dulled senses, recover awareness in their whole bodies, and rediscover the spontaneity, playfulness, and wonder that have been buried under a load of lopsided rationality and overcontrol. Any approach to pastoral care and counseling, which is really holistic, must help people affirm and enliven their bodies. The body therapies, like the holistic health movement, can help us recover the ancient Hebrew view of body-mind-spirit-community wholeness. They can help us feel and shout a resounding Yes! to all dimensions of our humanity including our bodies.

While drawing on the rich resources of various secular psychotherapies, pastoral psychotherapy in the years ahead also could develop its own theo-therapeutic methods, using biblical metaphors, stories, and images, and other religious resources to facilitate wholeness centered in Spirit. As Carl Jung observes, many of the images of the Bible are archetypal in that they are related to universal human experiences and to the resources of the unconscious. To illustrate how this may be used—in some counseling, a direct route to the person's central problem via a simple question, "What is your favorite or least liked Bible story?" Jane, a bright adolescent who was failing in school, responded, "The Adam and Eve story is the one I most dislike."

Counselor: Tell me about it.

Jane: Adam and Eve were in the garden and ate the fruit of the tree of knowledge. That was the beginning of their trouble. They got kicked out and had to take care of themselves after that!

Counselor: Are you saying, Jane, that when we gain knowledge, pain often follows?

Jane: Uh huh.

In subsequent sessions, Jane began to see that succeeding in school was equated in her feelings with growing up and leaving the dependency relationships of childhood, her personal Garden of Eden. As she faced and worked through her fears of adulthood, her schoolwork improved.

Church-Related Counseling, Therapy, and Growth Programs

The emergence of pastoral psychotherapists as specialists within the ministry and the mushrooming of church-related counseling and growth services are significant and complementary developments in the contemporary religious scene. There is now within the life of the churches a growing network of ministers who, through advanced clinical and academic training and personal therapy, have developed high levels of psychological awareness and therapeutic skills; they make this healing-growthing work their primary ministry. This network is a creative leavening influence within the churches and ministry generally. They practice their specialized ministries in a variety of settings including counseling centers and programs sponsored by individual churches, denominations, and ecumenical counseling programs; mental health, crisis, and career guidance centers; theological seminaries, college chaplaincies, and medical schools.

Pastoral counseling-therapy specialists represent a significant resource for accomplishing four things in the life of the church: (a) They provide pastoral counseling and psychotherapy services at the high level of competence that specialized training makes possible. As such they are a vital service arm of the churches. (b) They are doing creative research, experimentation, theory-building, and writing, which help develop and illuminate the unique contributions of pastoral counseling pastors and to the other healing disciplines. (c) They are developing a network of training programs in many places where seminarians and parish ministers can increase their counseling skills by participating in pastoral case conferences, supervision, consultation groups, and continuing education events. (d) An increasing number of seminaries and pastoral counseling centers also providing graduate training and supervised internships for those preparing for specialized ministries of counseling.

Reflecting on the uniqueness of pastoral counseling specialists among psychotherapists, John Patton declares:

> Part of the pastoral counselor's calling is to remind the counselee and the community of the religious dimension of life—that there is more to health than symptom relief. The goal of pastoral counseling is never simply unimpaired function, but function *for* something, for one's commitments and meanings. The pastoral counselor is not the only health practitioner who has this understanding of healing. He or she is, however, the only one whose role and identity, as well as function, represent this understanding. The pastoral counselor offers an identifiable witness to Christian meanings and commitments and their relevance for health care.[19]

One major Protestant denomination has included specialized pastoral counseling in what it calls "extension ministries"—an outreach of the Christian community in response to the special needs of persons. "Thousands of persons who go to pastoral counseling centers would not go near a parish church. For thousands of others the pastoral counseling center is an intermediate church structure that can be used as an entryway to a more traditional form of Christian community."[20]

In 1913, when the negative responses to Freud's discoveries were at their peak, Henri Bergson wrote: "To explore the more sacred depths of the unconscious . . . that will be the principal task of psychology in the century which is opening. I do not doubt that wonderful discoveries await it there, as important perhaps as have been in the preceding centuries the discoveries of the physical and natural sciences."[21] It is fortunate for the church, for suffering people, and for the advancement of the psychotherapeutic art that some ministers are obtaining training allowing them to participate in these discoveries. In 1936, Anton Boisen, the foreparent of the clinical pastoral education movement expressed this hope:

"Instead of allowing the psychiatrist to remain the exclusive keeper of the lower regions, I am hoping and laboring for the day when the specialists in religion will be able with his help to go down to the depths of the grim abyss after those who are capable of responding, those in whom some better self is seeking to come to birth."[22] Pastoral psychotherapists are now helping Boisen's hope to become a reality.

Around the turn of the century, a warmhearted Swiss pastor named Oskar Pfister wrote a paper protesting "the sin of omission toward psychology of present-day theology." In 1909 he encountered the writings of Freud and, shortly afterwards, the man himself. Thus began a lifelong, mutually enriching friendship. Pfister was a frequent and welcome visitor in the Freud household in Vienna. In writing to thank him for a gift, Freud commented that it would remind him of "a remarkable man who came to see me one day, a true servant of God, a man in the very idea of whom I should have had difficulty in believing, in that he feels the need to do spiritual good to everyone he meets. You did good in this way even to me."[23]

Pfister was a pastoral psychotherapist who, in contrast to most of his present-day counterparts, remained a parish pastor. He served the Zurich circuit until his retirement in 1939, much loved by his congregation. He used psychodynamic insights and methods in his pastoral counseling and also made significant contributions to the development of psychoanalytic theory and practice in its applications to children, adolescents, and education. His lifelong appreciation of Freud's genius did not cause him to adopt Freud's metaphysical views. Following the publication of *The Future of an Illusion*, he wrote Freud candidly:

> Thus there remains between us the great difference that I practice analysis within a plan of life which you indulgently regard as servitude to my calling, while I regard this philosophy of life, not only as a powerful aid to treatment (in the case of most people) but also the logical consequence of a philosophy that goes beyond naturalism and positivism, is well based on moral and social hygiene, and is in accordance with the nature of mankind and the world.[24]

Pastoral psychotherapists can do in our day what Pfister did so well in his under more difficult circumstances—bring together three mighty streams of healing—the time-tested resources of our religious heritage, the illuminating insights of the depth psychologies, and the methods of the psychotherapeutic disciplines. Pastoral therapists are in a position to help develop a creative synthesis of these streams out of which can be born new therapeutic approaches to facilitating Spirit-centered wholeness. Because of the depth and riches of their spiritual heritage, pastoral therapists have many unique assets as depth healers and growth enablers. The full development of these precious gifts by specialists in pastoral counseling and therapy is one of the exciting challenges of the next two decades!

Recommended Reading

John C. Carr, John Hinkle, David M. Moss III, eds., *The Organization and Administration of Pastoral Counseling Centers* (Nashville: Abingdon Press, 1981). Discusses the organization, standards, clinical, training, supervision, and research aspects of centers.

Howard Clinebell, *Contemporary Growth Therapies: Resource for Actualizing Human Wholeness* (Nashville: Abingdon Press, 1981). Highlights insights and methods, which are useful for facilitating growth from a variety of therapies including—Freud, the ego analysts, Adler, Rank, Fromm, Horney, Sullivan, Jung, the Existentialists, Rogers, the behavioral therapies, TA, Gestalt, biofeedback and the body therapies, family system therapies, feminist therapies and psychosynthesis. An annotated bibliography for further exploration of these approaches is at the end of each chapter.

Pilgrimage: The Journal of Pastoral Psychotherapy, David O. Bristow, ed., 427 Lakeshore Drive, N.E., Atlanta, Ga. 30307. A journal devoted to articles on developments in pastoral psychotherapy.

Howard W. Stone, *Using Behavioral Methods in Pastoral Counseling* (Philadelphia: Fortress Press, 1980). Describes how pastors can use behavioral methods in a variety of types of counseling.

Carroll A. Wise, *Pastoral Psychotherapy* (New York: Jason Aronson, 1980). An introduction to the theory and practice of insight-oriented pastoral psychotherapy. (The author, unfortunately, calls all pastoral counseling "psychotherapy," which confuses the distinction between counseling and psychotherapy.

Training Lay Persons for Their Caring Ministries

Bear one another's burdens, and so fulfil the law of Christ.
—GALATIANS 6:2

Any emphasis on the ministry of the laity means not only training but a special kind of pastoral care. Laymen and women should be encouraged to use the pastoral gifts that many of them possess. Mutual care of members by each other as well as by the clergy is needed in the Church. Christians have many natural opportunities for the pastoral care of neighbors, workmates and others.
—REPORT OF THE SECOND ASSEMBLY OF THE
WORLD COUNCIL OF CHURCHES[1]

In recent decades there has been a dramatic rediscovery of a striking fact—*all Christians have a ministry because they are Christians*, whether or not they are ordained! This awareness gives laypersons a new self-image. They are no longer second-class Christians who leave spiritual work to the pastor. They have a vital, unique ministry to the world beyond their church—to their neighbors, their business associates, their union, their friends, their enemies, and especially to the disadvantaged, rejected, and exploited in their community. The vitality of the ministry of the laity may be reaching a level that has not existed since the early decades of the Christian movement.[2] The potentialities of this development are almost unlimited. It is like a fresh wind blowing across the church, awakening a growing group of lay men, women, and youth to their exciting ministry to persons.

This lay renaissance is based on the rediscovery of the New Testament understanding of the church—the *people of God*, the *body of Christ*, and the *community of the Holy Spirit* in which each member has her or his ministry. The New Testament word *laos*, from which "laity" is derived, refers to all Christians! The "ministry of reconciliation" (described in II Corinthians 5:17) was entrusted to the whole church, not to a set-apart professional ministry.

What, then, is the function of the clergy? We are, by our training and ordination, equipped and designated to function as leaders, trainers, and specialists in that which is the work of every Christian. Instead of being one-person bands who play each Sunday for passive congregations, pastors should be conductors of orchestras, who help each person make his/her unique contribution to the symphony of the good news. The key role of clergypersons is described in Ephesians—"to equip God's people for work in his service" (4:11-12, NEB). Our job is to train, inspire, guide, coach, and work alongside the lay ministers as "teachers of teachers," "pastors of pastors," and "counselors of counselors."[3]

Implications for Pastoral Care and Counseling

The implications of the lay renaissance for pastoral care and counseling are profound and challenging! Pastoral care, rightly understood, is a function of the entire congregation. A local church should strive to become a healing, growth-stimulating redemptive organism. The aim of the church's pastoral care program should be to develop a dynamic climate of mutual, loving, enlightened concern, which gradually leavens the whole congregation. Church administration and the small group program should be oriented toward this objective. To the extent that *koinonia* exists in a congregation, mutual ministry occurs spontaneously as individual members seek to give themselves, in Luther's words, *"as a Christ to my neighbor."*[4] Every member has pastoral care opportunities that are uniquely hers or his. Only as increasing numbers of us accept this challenge can our churches fulfill their mission as training and empowering centers for healing and liberation, wholeness and justice!

The caring ministry of the laity is essentially *a ministry to persons in need*—in the congregation and in the community. The challenge of Jesus' parable of the man who was robbed and beaten beside the Jericho Road was directed to all his followers. The criteria in his description of the last judgment were all matters of loving service: "For I was hungry and you gave me food, I was thirsty and you gave me drink, I was a stranger and you welcomed me, I was naked and you clothed me, I was sick and you visited me, I was in prison and you came to me" (Matt. 25:35-36).

As the *"pastorhood of all believers"* (Hiltner) becomes a reality in a congregation, laypersons escape from their "spectatoritis" and begin to fulfill their personal ministries. Their own spiritual growth is stimulated as they put their faith to work in direct service. The unmet human needs in every church and community are so numerous and varied that a pastor working alone cannot possibly meet more than a small fraction of them. A church's caring ministry to the community's lonely, sick, aging, bereaved, home-bound, stranger, insitutionalized, exploited, socially and economically oppressed, can be quadrupled by involving trained laypersons fully in caring work. When dedicated laypersons become informal pastors to their neighbors, associates, and fellow church members, *they become the church*—the body of Christ serving those in need.

Two persons, who have developed a lay training program, declare:

> Enabling lay people in the caring ministry of the church involves far more than "getting a few people to help the minister with calling." We believe lay pastoral care manifests the very nature and foundation of the church as a caring community with its common priesthood of all believers. It provides a place in the life and ministry of the church for those who hear and believe, and want to put their faith into practice in a visible, tangible way.[5]

Lay training for caring is one of the keys to the revitalizing and growth of a congregation. Research on church growth and decline shows that a robust and comprehensive ministry of caring is a crucial variable in the health and growth of a congregation. Such a ministry is not possible unless trained laypersons are deeply involved in caring within a congregation and its community.

The resistances in the feelings of many pastors to involving lay persons in this way must be resolved or at least reduced before an effective program of lay caring can be fully implemented. Some ministers feel guilty when they ask others to do pastoral care tasks. The "indispensibility complex" makes sharing this ministry with the laity threatening. Some pastors allow themselves to be so overloaded by the demands and needs of their people that the time to train lay carers seems like an impossible additional burden. Furthermore, most ministers in seminary were not shown the crucial importance of training lay carers, nor did they learn the supervisory skills required. Consequently many ministers feel and some *are* inadequate in this area of ministry. Ministers' self-images must be rethought and their supervisory skills increased so that enabling lay ministry can be both a central and satisfying part of their task.

Resistances in pastors are reinforced by certain attitudes prevalent in most congregations. The initial response of some church members, when the idea of training lay carers is presented is, "We hired our pastor to give us pastoral care, not to teach someone else to do it."[6] Some parishioners feel that they are getting second-class help from amateurs, when a lay person calls on them. Both pastors and congregations need to learn that training lay carers is not a pastor's way of passing the buck but a powerful way of deepening, broadening, and sharing the ministry of caring with the whole congregation. It does not replace pastoral care by a pastor, but rather complements and greatly augments it.

An appropriate concern of pastors is with the *quality* of lay caring and helping programs. Is it really possible for lay persons to give effective help to burdened, hurting people? Fortunately studies have confirmed the effectiveness of lay and paraprofessional helping persons. Robert R. Carkhuff, a pioneer in the field of training lay helpers, makes this striking (and disturbing to some professionals) statement about the research literature comparing the effectiveness of lay and professional training and treatment: "Briefly, the available evidence indicates that lay training programs have been more effective in demonstrating change on indexes that measure constructive helpee change."[7] Experience with lay caring programs in churches has shown that inadequately trained and unsupervised lay persons *can* do harm, particularly if they try to work with individuals or families who need counseling or therapy. (The same could be said of inadequately trained and unsupervised ministers and other professionals, of course.) But the clear evidence is that in doing pastoral *care*, well-trained lay persons can make a constructive and unique contribution to the total caring ministry of a church, hospital, or other institution!

Types of Lay Caring Ministries

Ministries of lay caring are blossoming in many places. In one midwestern city, a council of churches conducted a workshop to train laypersons to visit the elderly. This led several congregations to "adopt" a nursing home. Residents were visited regularly and given caring services by the laypersons. A church in the San Francisco area sponsors a halfway house for young adults in outpatient mental health treatment and those recently released from mental hospitals. Twenty-three laypersons completed a sixteen week training course to prepare for their roles in this project. In Southern California, an ecumenical group of laywomen call regularly on the families of prisoners.[8]

Churches in may countries have set up Lifeline Centers where trained volunteers give crisis help to those who phone. This worldwide lay caring program was started in Sydney, Australia, by a minister, Alan Walker and his staff.[9] The training in this program is extensive and rigorous; it involves careful supervision and consultation with mental health professionals and ministers who are trained in counseling.

Kenneth Haugk, a pastor and clinical psychologist in St. Louis, was troubled by the lack of ownership by parishioners of his church's overall ministry. He began to wonder what would happen if phrases like "priesthood of all believers," "body of Christ," and "equipping God's people for work in his service" became not theological cliches but the basis around which to build a congregation's ministry. "What would the church look like if people really did minister to each other? If a congregation was really marked by 'rejoicing with those who rejoice, weeping with those who weep?' What if it didn't depend so heavily on one overworked pastor? What if we could develop a whole churchful of pastors?"[10]

Seeking an answer, Haugk began to train a small group of his parishioners for doing lay caregiving with others in that congregation. This was so effective that two of those trained, believing that "this is too good to keep to ourselves," urged their pastor to share it with other congregations. Eventually the "Stephen Series" was developed (named after Stephen in the New Testament) to train interested pastors and laity to do lay training in their own churches. Numerous congregations in a variety of denominations have participated in this "Pastoral Care Team

Ministry" training program. As in other effective lay training, this approach includes regular meetings of the carers (after the initial training) for group support, supervision (usually by the pastor), and ongoing training. Haugk observes that many lay caring programs fall flat after a year or less because continuing support and training isn't provided. He also has found that lay carers receive a good response from 90 percent or more of those to whom they reach out, if the pastor prepares them (the helpee) for the call.

Howard Stone has developed an uncomplicated model for training lay carers (descibed in *The Caring Church: A Guide for Lay Pastoral Care*). The eight sessions focus on these topics and skills: What is lay pastoral care? (The ABC method of crisis is presented); establishing a care relationship by effective listening; responding in facilitative ways; making hospital and shut-in visits (calls in a nursing home are assigned during this session); caring in grief situations; discussing the visits trainees have made; solving problems and referring; wrapping up including structuring the lay caring program in the church. Stone emphasizes that most pastors who develop lay caring programs do not reduce their own pastoral care load thereby. But they have the satisfaction of knowing that their people's pastoral care needs are being served far more fully than they could possibly do alone.

Diane Detwiler-Zapp and William Dixon have developed a multifaceted approach to lay training (described in *Lay Caregiving*). They emphasize ways of utilizing the pastoral care opportunities in already existing parish activities—evangelism and incorporating new members, hospital visitation, bereavement care, visiting the elderly and homebound, canvasing for annual stewardship pledges, Sunday School classes, and women's groups. They offer suggestions for the structuring, content, and supervision of training. From their broad experience in training carers, Detwiler-Zapp and Dixon declare:

"One of the most caring things you can do for a church and for yourself is to enable others in caregiving. Putting theology into practice in this way can visibly change the whole life of a congregation. We believe that you will be awed and inspired by the gifts, talents, and commitments that lay people will bring to this mutual ministry."[11] In commenting on the positive reception of lay carers, Dick Watts whose congregation uses the Stephen Series program says, "I'm reminded of the comment by the actress

Melina Mercouri: 'In Greece we are too poor to have psychiatrists. And so we have friends instead.' "[12]

How to Implement a Lay Caring Ministry

Here are some suggestions for developing a lay caring ministry in your congregation. It is important to recognize that there are different kinds and levels of lay training in caring, all of which are needed in the life of a church. "Throughout their lives, most people encounter problems, unexpected crises, or troublesome transitions. The majority of individuals depend on their social network of family, friends, and neighbors as a major source of help."[13] Every member of a congregation is a part of some type of informal social support network. Therefore, everyone should be offered an opportunity to enhance their caring skills by learning, for example, how to listen in more depth. Pastors and mental health professionals in congregations can help raise the general level of caring within their congregation *and* within the supportive networks of individual members by an ongoing education-for-caring emphasis. This can utilize sermons, as well as lectures and training sessions with church school classes, youth groups, women's and men's groups, family events, etc.

A second and deeper level of training for caring should be focused on all the laypersons who call on others as a part of the church's program. Some churches in the Stephen program provide training in caring for those who do home evangelism, calling on newcomers and the unchurched to invite them to join the church. On one occasion in my church, I gave instruction in caring methods to the "stewardship team," those persons visiting church members to ask them to pledge financial support. They were given this training *before* they made their calls for three reasons—to help them heal the wounds of members who were angry and alienated from the church; to recognize and respond helpfully to the needs of persons going through crises; and to be alert and aware of situations where counseling by the pastor was needed. Training provided persons doing home visitation   a double benefit from their calls. The tasks of recruiting new members or underwriting the budget are accomplished more effectively, *and* a vital pastoral care ministry occurs.

In-depth training of a Pastoral Care Team is a third essential level of a caring congregation's program. Although pastoral care *is* the function of the whole congregation, some group or groups need to be selected and trained to spearhead this ministry. Every church member should be challenged to become a part of the caring network of supportive, growth-nurturing relationships that is the church at its best! But within a church there should be one or more task forces (depending on the size of a church) of those committed to pastoral care as their primary lay ministry. Ministers do not need to wait until they can launch a formal training program in their churches. Many parishioners are already engaged in informal, spontaneous caring with persons who are in crises. When a pastor learns about this, she or he can give such persons encouragement, make suggestions aimed at improving their helping, and suggest a relevant book or article to help them make their caring be more effective.[14]

Whenever the pastor encounters an individual or family in crisis, it can be very helpful to link them with someone in the congregation who has weathered a similar situation and grown as a result of this struggle.[15] From personal experience I have learned that a person whose diabetes has just been diagnosed can be helped tremendously by talking with someone who has learned to live effectively with this frustrating metabolic problem. The two persons usually establish instant rapport. The more experienced one knows many of the other's feelings from the inside and therefore can give both empathetic support and practical suggestions for coping with the many new demands imposed by the problem (particularly if the person is insulin-dependent). The linking of persons with similar losses, crises, and life situations in informal diads or clusters of mutual support is one of the simplest and most helpful strategies a pastor can use to enable lay caring. A lay person who is sensitive, caring, and informed about the issues other parishioners are facing can be used to coordinate such a mutual ministry, in partnership with the pastor.

Individuals and couples who have graduated from pastoral counseling or therapy and have grown as a result of coping with the crisis that brought them to help, can be used as informal resource and support persons (befrienders) to others going through similar problems. In such cases the pastor should do the *linking*—clearing first to see if both persons would be open to such a relationship. The names of the other person should not be mentioned until the pastor has that person's permission, since to do so would violate the professional confidentiality essential in all caring and counseling. Using persons who have had counseling and therapy in this way often facilitates their continuing growth, as well as giving peer support to other persons wrestling with similar dilemmas.

Many churches have an existing group that does pastoral care with hospitalized, homebound, or elderly members. Some denominational structures give special responsibility for care of the ill and others in special need to a particular committee or to a group such as stewards. It is the minister's role to help these groups maximize their effectiveness in fulfilling their responsibilities by means of an ongoing program of training and supervision such as the one described below. In situations where there is no such group, or a group exists but concentrates in only a limited area of caring (e.g., hospital calling), the maximizing of caring action by the laity can best be enabled by recruiting and training a *pastoral care team*. Such a team can enrich and spearhead the general caring ministry of a congregation. They should work under the direction and with the coaching of their pastor (or another professional member of the church staff) as lay co-pastors.

Let me describe a process by which a pastoral care team can be developed. This approach is derived primarily from experience I have had in two lay training programs—one in a United Church of Christ and the other in a United Methodist congregation.

Step 1: Selection and recruitment: In a church Robert A. Raines was serving, lay pastoring developed as a result of the spiritual deepening of a network of spiritual growth groups engaged in depth Bible study. A depressed, convalescing woman was helped so much by a visit from a friend in her group that, quite informally, she took up a lay ministry to the sick and hospitalized. Raines reports:

> One morning in a sermon I mentioned what this woman was doing and asked any persons who were interested in this kind of ministry to speak to me. The response was amazing. I discovered that a veritable well of compassion existed which had only been waiting to be tapped. Approximately twenty-five persons said they wanted to take up this ministry. I am now working with them, informing them when people are hospitalized, sending them to visit the sick, shut-ins, those in hospitals, new mothers, and in some instances bereaved families.[16]

In most situations it is necessary to recruit team members actively. To do so has the clear advantage of allowing one to invite persons with natural caring aptitudes. Those with natural healing-growthing personalities—in Paul's words, who have "gifts of healing"—(I Cor. 12:28, NEB) should be identified and urged to participate. In every congregation there are persons with a high degree of those personal qualities that nurture creative change in close relationships—self-respect and caring for others, and the capacity for empathetic understanding and authenticity or congruence.[17] Such individuals are growing persons who possess personal warmth, a love of people, sturdy self-esteem, contagious aliveness, a dynamic faith and trust in the universe, and a demonstrated capacity to grow from their own losses and painful experiences.

Other people feel more whole in their presence. They are natural care-givers. The pastor or a committee recruiting potential caring team members can identify these persons simply by recognizing those to whom others turn spontaneously for help. Those who should *not* be recruited for a caring team (and who should be gently but firmly channeled into other services, if they volunteer) are so-called "do-gooders." Such persons are strongly motivated by a self-aggrandizing need to be of service, but they usually lack the openness required to be teachable. Equally important to avoid are persons who do not keep confidences. It is *crucial* that all team members be able to keep privileged communication absolutely confidential!

Among those recruited for a caring team, it is important to include persons of both sexes, and of varied ages and life experiences.[18] In addition it is helpful to have AA members of each sex with stable sobriety, an experienced member of Al-Anon, a physician, an experienced business person, a member of one or more of the counseling-therapy professions—including a social worker or staff member of a community agency who knows the referral resources of the community. It also is important to recruit persons who have grown from the losses and tragedies in their own lives, e.g., persons who have lost a child by cancer, experienced divorce or the death of a spouse, survived a major accident or surgery, etc. Such people often have a hidden asset of which they are unaware. They can relate as "wounded healers" (Henri Nouwen) to others going through crises.

At the time trainees are recruited, it is important to ask them to commit themselves to completing the basic training. But it should be made clear that the decisions concerning their ongoing participation will be made by them (in consultation with the trainers) at the end of the initial training. Fortunately, experiencial training itself is an excellent natural screening process. Some people discover during the training that they are not particularly effective in caring work. They should be encouraged to serve in areas of the life of their congregation that do not require a high degree of interpersonal skills. Persons who choose not to continue after training should be able to leave the training group without a sense of guilt or failure. Whatever caring skills they learned will be used productively in their own relationships.

The effectiveness of lay caring programs is directly correlated with the selection of teachable trainees and the rigor of the training program. Even persons with strong natural caring aptitudes need to develop these by continuing in-service training. Since any effective lay caring team must work closely with the pastor, it is advantageous that she or he be involved in the selection and training. If the responsibility for selecting and training is given to a lay task group, they should function in close consultation with the pastor. If the pastor has a strong background in pastoral psychology and counseling, he or she can well be the primary trainer of the team. In any case, the pastor should provide theological-biblical input and help define the role of the team in that congregation's total pastoral care program. There are few, if any ways that ministers can invest their professional expertise that pay richer dividends than helping to equip lay carers. In my experience, the awareness that one is multiplying one's ministry by geometric progression, by helping to train, inspire, and coach a team of co-ministers, is deeply satisfying. The sense of colleagueship and mutual ministry that develops within a caring team can nurture and energize the pastor as well as team members.

Step 2: Basic training—Most of the varied formats used in training programs begin with a period of intensive team-building and training in fundamental helping skills. The basic training of the UCC group mentioned above consisted of two weekend training retreats at a church camp in the mountains, one month apart. To give a picture of the flow and content of one approach to lay training, I will describe the process used with this group. After supper on Friday evening of the first weekend, we did a get-acquainted exercise, and then we co-trainers dialogued briefly on our hopes and expectations for the training emphasizing the following points:

> The purpose of these training events is to increase our abilities to relate in ways that help and strengthen others. In order to do this, we need to become as aware as possible of *our* relationships, including blocks, feelings others stir in us (and vice versa), of better ways of communicating. Therefore, we'll be concentrating on self-other awareness. Another purpose is to understand the ways in which helping relationships are established and to be aware of the theology of such relationships. The training also will aim at the acquisition of certain helping skills which are useful in relationships. These skills will be the main thrust of our second weekend, after we have worked together in building a foundation of awareness and relationships. However, since the essence of any helpful relationship is a rich, full mutual experience of relating, we'll keep working on that throughout our training.[19]

Trainees were then invited to say what they hoped to get from the training. A tentative group contract, spelling out the aims of the weekend and how the time would be used, was developed, reflecting the hopes and goals of both the trainees and the trainers. Two hours were spent on Friday evening in communication exercises designed to increase self-other awareness and to build trust within the group.[20]

On Saturday morning, after a period of tuning in spiritually through prayer, meditation, and guided imaging, there was a dialogue "lecturette" by the co-leaders on "the process of growth in sharing groups." Three hours were then spent in two subgroups where the trainees worked on their own feelings and relationships. These persons had been chosen for their aptitudes as helpers, but (not expectedly) the opportunity to share honestly brought their human pain and loneliness to the surface quickly. The debriefing of the morning showed that the depth of the communication had been powerful and trust building for many.

The grief experience, as a universal crisis, provides an ideal context for the teaching of helping skills. After lunch and volleyball, the co-trainers talked candidly about some of their own recent experiences of loss. Then, in growth groups of six, centering on the biblical words, "Blessed are those who mourn for they shall be comforted," each person was given an opportunity to share something that caused him or her grief or pain. It was suggested that comforting by group members should be done nonverbally to allow the use of a wider range of ways of communicating strong feelings. These powerful sharing groups elected to meet again on Saturday evening; one continued until 2 a.m.

On Sunday, the training focus shifted to explicit skill-practice. After a few comments on the centrality of listening skills in all caring, the co-trainers demonstrated *responsive listening* by taking turns responding with empathy to each other's live feelings.[21] Then the trainees divided into triads for reality practice, taking turns expressing their feelings, being listener-responder and observer-coach. The trainers circulated among these small groups to provide coaching. This was followed by a session on "the theology of helping relationships" where group members shared the biblical insights that had come alive for them during the weekend. A lively discussion then ensued on "what our church and community need from a Samaritan group."[22] Tentative action goals were drawn up by the group as it discussed the possible uses of their training in caring work. Then came a group evaluation of the weekend and discussion of homework to be done before the next training retreat—i.e., to practice responsive listening daily, to reflect further on the caring needs of their church and community, and to read one of the books suggested.[23] After lunch the group closed the event by an outdoor worship celebration planned by a small group of trainees to pick up the main learning from the weekend. Never in my experience have I seen a group more turned-on and sensitized-to-caring relationships, after so brief a time together!

The meaningfulness of the first weekend was indicated by the fact that only one person missed the second weekend a month later. In the opening "reconnecting" session on Friday night, there was sharing of significant happenings in trainees' lives resulting from the first training event—e.g., two women reported that they had been able to listen in new ways to their teen-agers. The remainder of Friday evening was spent in a meeting of the two growth groups followed by creative-movement-to-music session. Most of Saturday morning was spent introducing the group to the

ABCD method of crises help (described in chapter 8). Here is how this approach was presented:

First, the co-leaders presented the ABCD model as the "basic caring and helping tool that can be adapted to help people cope constructively with many types of crises." Then the trainees did an overview of the four steps, concluding with "You have already learned the first step. Responsive listening *is* the main way a relationship of trust is established and strengthened."

Second, as a live demonstration of how to use the ABCD method, my co-trainer counseled with me to help me deal with a mini-crisis I was facing at that time (the painful rejection of a manuscript by a publisher).

Third, most of the remaining time on Saturday morning was spent in the two groups doing reality-practice. Trainees had an opportunity to use the ABCD method as they worked with each other's actual struggles and pain. The co-trainers coached the reality practice groups. After an early afternoon hike, the trainers helped the whole group apply the ABCD model to three common types of human crises—being a newcomer in a community, hospitalization, and bereavement.

On Saturday evening, the whole group brainstormed the question, "What action should our group take to respond to the unmet needs for caring in our church and community?" Ideas were pooled and a committee chosen to set priorities and recommend next steps. This was followed by a time of singing and very lighthearted socializing. When the committee reported on Sunday morning, discusson was intense. An action plan was agreed on by the group and the basic training was then concluded with a worship-celebration of the growth we had experienced and the commitment the group had developed to the ministry of wholeness and caring.[24]

The approach to basic training used in the United Methodist church employed many of the methods and exercises described above. But the training format consisted of two, seven-hour mini-retreats (Sunday afternoon and evening) held at the church two weeks apart.[25] There was a stronger emphasis than in the U.C.C. training on the explicit task of developing a caring program for the congregation. Some intensive time was used for group-building and near the begining of that training project. This is essential as a foundation for any lay training.

Step 3: Supervised training calls—After completing the basic training, trainees should exercise their option of deciding whether or not to continue in the ongoing caring program. Those who elect to do so should be asked to begin making calls on persons in need of caring and to participate in a regular monthly or bimonthly supervisory group focused on learning from their calls.[26] To maximize learning, team members should be encouraged to write brief verbatim accounts of significant interchanges between themselves and the persons being visited. These are used in supervisory sessions.

It is wise to assign newly trained persons to situations that are likely to be low threat—e.g., the newcomer, the homebound, or the aged—rather than persons known to be in major crises. As lay carers grow in confidence and competence, they can be assigned calls requiring more sophisticated crisis-helping skills—e.g, the bereaved, the sick, families of terminally ill persons, those going through separation and divorce, or parents with a severely handicapped child. Special instruction on caring in particular problems should be provided by the pastor or other trainer(s) before and after calls are made on those suffering from those problems. Persons with special expertise should be invited to be resource persons during supervisory sessions dealing with particular issues—e.g., an AA and an Al-Anon member can brief the team on working effectively with alcoholics and their familes.

The initial anxiety of lay carers is usually painfully high even if the types of calls they are asked to make seem unthreatening from inside the pastor's role. To help them keep their anxiety from interfering with their effectiveness, it is well to suggest that they make their calls in pairs to give each other support. This also tends to increase significant learnings by allowing the two persons to debrief the call immediately, giving each other feedback concerning the strengths and weaknesses of what each said and did. Writing verbatim accounts of important segments of calls, to use in coaching sessions, is initially threatening but very valuable to most trainees.

In using a verbatim in training, robust affirmation of its strengths and only gentle criticism of its weaknesses should be given.[27] After examining crucial interchanges of a verbatim report (written or oral) the person who presented the verbatim should be invited to role play the helpee while others try various approaches to caring.

It is essential that the pastor stand beside lay persons who get involved in lay caring especially during the early stages of their calling. In many cases they find it much more difficult than they had imagined. The minister should let lay carers know that he or she is glad to be contacted whenever the carer feels uncertain about what to do or whenever a helpee seems to be in need of assistance by the minister or some other trained professional. The lines of communication should always be open with the pastor and other backup professionals for consultation and referral!

The ongoing training design that the U.M. team found most helpful was built around meeting for three hours once a month (on a Sunday afternoon). Information from the pastor about persons needing calls was shared at the outset. Team members then chose two names; calls were made in twos during the next hour and fifteen minutes. Then the whole team reassembled at the church to receive supervision of their calls and share their personal feelings and issues. Although this format precluded the opportunity to write verbatims, the two team members who had made a call sometimes role played perplexing or effective segments of the call they had just completed. At the end of each supervisory session, the members chose a particular problem that had emerged during one of the calls on which to focus the next time. The trainers suggested between-session reading on that problem.

Step 4: Annual refresher event and recontracting—At least once a year a caring team should hold a Friday night-Saturday or whole weekend retreat to evaluate their service to others, strengthen their resources for caring, renew their commitment to the program (if they elect to continue for another year) or do their leave-taking if they decide not to continue, and integrate additional persons into the caring team.[28] Both the UCC and the UM groups became small caring communities for their members including their trainers. A strong bond grew among us, strengthened both by sharing the ministry to others and by the mutual caring that developed among us. During the first year of the UM group, two of the members experienced the loss of parents and one discovered that her long bout with malignancy had taken a turn for the worse. We discovered that only as we responded caringly to each other's needs were we able to reach out effectively to persons outside the group.[29] Outreach-to-others and personal support and growth within the group need to be kept in balance.

If lay caring team members are to function well, their satisfactions must outweigh the anxiety and frustrations of the experience. The satisfactions that people can derive include:

The enjoyment of the openness, honesty, and pro-life atmosphere that comes to characterize the group, involvement in a team learning and doing significant things; the satisfaction of growth in interpersonal competence—discovering that one *can* relate more helpfully; the opportunity to be a part of the emerging church—a creative network of mutual caring, support, and growth—and to infiltrate the present church with this new spirit; being part of a support group which helps trainee and leaders cope constructively with their personal pain and loneliness.

Here are some significant learnings from these two training experiences: It is important to have the "contract" between the leaders and the group members clear and mutually acceptable from the beginning. This requires an explicit statement by the leader-trainer regarding the goals of the group—e.g., that it is primarily for training for helping others and for the personal growth needed to make helping effective . . . It is important to blend and balance, from the beginning, the three basic ingredients in effective lay training—input of functional concepts; personal growth and relationship-building experiences; skill practice and supervision . . . Inductive teaching of helping skills is the most effective approach. This means beginning with a learning experience of some kind (e.g., a role play, live demonstration or a verbatim of a call) and then, through group reflection, deriving the principles of caring which are operative in that experience . . . It is well to use only simple operational models—e.g., the ABCD method of crisis help—in the input and skill practices sessions . . . Teaching understanding of human dynamic can best be accomplished by focusing on a few common problems that the trainees have experienced—e.g., bereavement, sickness, aging, moving . . . Try to use the ability and ideas of all trainees from the beginning by involving them in planning their own learning goals and experiences. Frequent evaluative group discussion during the training is important. The trainer must be open to renegotiating the original group contract to keep it related to emerging needs—the group's, her or his own, and those of the congregation and community. Theological resourcing should occur throughout the training. It is important for the leaders to be open about what is theologically meaningful to trainees with respect to the *why* of their caring, the need to incarnate theological truths in caring relationships, and the need to live in pro-life partnership with the creative Spirit of the universe in caring work. Theological reflection by the group can help them capture the learnings which are potentially available in those precious moments when the theological truths implicit in all close relationships, become most transparent—moments when time stands still and one knows that one stands on holy ground! Those involved in personal caring ministries encounter such moments frequently—e.g., when they are with persons who are standing in the valley of the shadow of death or persons on some mountain top, celebrating a milestone in their lives.[30]

Self-Help Groups

The flowering of self-help groups is an exciting development in the contemporary caring and counseling scene. It shows that the lay renaissance is a lively reality, not just in the churches, but in the whole field of healing and health.[31] The power of mutual healing available in nonprofessional persons and groups, is increasingly evident in the self-help groups of many types that are flourishing in most communities. Think for a moment of the tremendous implications of what has happened in Alcoholics Anonymous, the grandparent and model for many other self-help groups. In 1980 the more than one million recovered alcoholics in AA, in some one hundred ten countries were living miracles, demonstrating the healing power of spiritually centered self-help groups. The effectiveness of self-help groups is a dramatic confirmation of the wisdom of making *mutual* ministry of, by and for the laity, a dominant thrust in the caring program of a church. There is a largely undiscovered gold mine of caring and helping that can be developed by increasing the lay, self-help groups in any church. The self-help group model can be applied in a variety of forms to strengthen a congregation's caring program.

Earlier in this chapter, it was suggested that persons who have grown as a result of having weathered painful life problems should be linked with others who are encountering similar problems to give them support and an insider's understanding and practical guidance in constructive coping. A natural extension of the practice of linking individuals for mutual care, is to create informal clusters of three or more persons struggling with similar problems, handicaps, losses, and crises. When such clusters become mutually helpful, they draw others with similar needs to them. The potential lay leadership for such *caring clusters* is already available in most congregations. With minimal coaching and ongoing back-up and support from the pastor, many people who have used their problems as growth opportunities can learn the skills of leading a mutual help group. Whenever a pastor discovers two or more individuals or families with a common problem, he or she can invite them to meet informally to share what they have learned. [32] Such persons usually discover that they can help each other in different ways and, in some cases, *more* than professionals who have not experienced their problems.

The variety of human situations where the self-help group model can be applied productively is almost limitless. Every church should have caring clusters for persons going through the stress of divorce, unemployment, raising a handicapped child, retirement, moving, living with an alcoholic or emotionally disturbed person, (and most of the other problems listed on the Holmes-Rahe Stress Scale). Caring clusters should also be developed for persons whose growth-potentials are constricted by oppressive economic, institutional, or social prejudices and practices—e.g., women, minority group members, the aging—to combine support with consciousness raising.

In small and medium-sized congregations, a single sharing group for persons experiencing any type of crisis or loss can be formed. Larger congregations may find it feasible and helpful to have separate caring clusters for those going through such common losses as divorce. A church should be bold and imaginative in experimenting with a variety of self-help groups in its caring program, as well as in opening the use of its facilities to self-help groups in the community.

What should the role of pastors and other helping professionals be in relation to self-help groups in the church? They should recognize that they cannot be the ongoing leader of such a group unless they have experienced the type of problem that has drawn the group members together. A pastor (or other professional) can serve these functions: (1) inviting persons with a common personal issue together to form the nucleus from which a self-help group can grow; (2) giving continuing moral support to the group and its leaders; (3) referring other persons to the group; (4) being available as a consultant when invited by the group—e.g., on spiritual growth issues; (5) asking for the guidance of group members when counseling with persons facing the problem on which a particular group focuses.

Among the self-help groups that churches should experiment

with is a group where the twelve-step recovery and growth program of AA is applied to other problems of living with which some church members are struggling. The AA steps represent a systematizing of some of the basic thrusts of our religious tradition—awareness of need, repentance (surrender of narcissism), openness and dependence on God, self-examination, honest confession, restitution, and renewal, deepening one's contract with God, and sharing the new life one has found with others in need. It may well be that these steps provide a path by which a distinctively religiously oriented approach to group counseling eventually will be evolved.[33]

As groups like Al-Anon, Gamblers Anonymous, Overeaters Anonymous, and Neurotics Anonymous have discovered, the AA steps are readily adaptable to nonalcoholic problems. The difficulty in developing such groups for normal people (with better-hidden problems) is that many of them are unaware of how much their lives are diminished by their problems. To be effective, a group should be composed of persons who are *hurting* in some area of their lives and *aware* of their pain. The leadership of such a group should rotate. Leaders should have a lay perspective. That is, they should make their own needs clear and be full participants in the group's search for healing and help. They cannot stand apart as a leader or therapist, without damaging the basic therapeutic dynamic of a self-help group. Professional persons who have experienced and found workable solutions to problems similar to those shared by most of the group make ideal leaders, provided they have genuine humility and are aware of their own need for continuing growth. Without these qualities they will alienate others by an unrealistic I've-got-it-made attitude. Leaders should serve as a model of openness in discussing their own continuing struggles, as well as in sharing what has worked for them. Such openness is contagious. Perparation for leading an AA-patterned self-help group should include study of the AA principles and attendance at a number of open meetings of that fellowship.

The words of the Second Assembly of the World Council oi' Chuches are still full of power and relevant in our day: "The Church is sent into the world as a ministering community, not only in the sense that the parts serve each other, but that all serve the world."[34] The entire lay caring program of a church should be an outreach ministry to persons in need, in the wider community and the world as well as within the congregation. As the pastorhood of all believers is taken seriously and implemented in the churches, a new healing force is released into the life of a community!

Reality-Practice Session

PARISHIONER'S ROLE: You are a lay person receiving training in methods of lay caring (a small group of two to five people is ideal).

PASTOR'S ROLE: Instruct the lay person(s) in the training session how to use the ABCD method of crisis intervention.

OBSERVER-COACH'S ROLE: Give feedback on the training methods that the pastor uses, particularly the blending of cognitive instruction and experiential practice of methods.

Recommended Reading

Robert R. Carkhuff, *Helping and Human Relation: A Primer For Lay and Professional Helpers* (N.Y.: Holt, Rinehart & Winston, 1969). A classic in the field of lay training. Vol. I deals with selection and training; vol. II with practice and research.

Howard Clinebell, "Experiments in Training Laity for Ministry," *Pastoral Psychology*, 22, No. 215, June 1971, pp. 35-43. Describes three models used to train persons for pastoral care and—in the case of one model—social change.

*Gary Collins, *How to Be A People Helper* (Santa Ana, Calif.: Vision House Publishers, 1976). Describes the basics of friend-to-friend helping and gives guidance on referral, help in crisis, telephone help, and helping yourself.

*Diane Detwiler-Zapp and William Caveness Dixon, *Lay Caregiving* (Philadelphia: Fortress Press, 1982). A practical guide to lay training based on their broad experience in the Fort Wayne, Indiana, area.

John W. Drakeford, *People To People Therapy* (San Francisco: Harper & Row, 1978). The roots, principles, and processes of self-help groups.

Bernard G. Guerney, Jr., *Psychotherapeutic Agents: New Roles for Nonprofessionals, Parents and Teachers.* (New York: Holt, Rinehart & Winston, 1969). A collection of papers on the use of peers, parents, teachers in therapeutic roles in mental health.

*Harvey Jackins, *The Human Side of Human Beings* (Seattle: Rational Island Publishers, 1965). The principles of "re-evaluation counseling," a mutual help approach.

Hendrik Kraemer, *A Theology of The Laity* (Philadelphia: Westminster Press, 1959). A theological foundation for lay ministry.

Francine Sobey, *The Nonprofessional Revolution in Mental Health* (New York: Columbia University Press, 1970). Describes the recruitment, training, supervision, and evaluation of nonprofessionals in the mental health field.

*Howard W. Stone, *The Caring Church: A Guide for Lay Pastoral Care* (San Francisco: Harper & Row, 1983). The theology and methodology of lay training.

Samuel Southard, *Comprehensive Pastoral Care: Enabling The Laity to Share in Pastoral Ministry* (Valley Forge, Pa.: Judson Press, 1975). Describes a variety of training programs for lay caring.

*Bruce Turley, *Being There for Others—A Pastoral Resource for Lay People* (Melbourne, Australia: Joint Board of Christian Education of Australia and New Zealand, 1976). The principles of lay caring ministries and help in such care in specific problems—e.g., sickness, dying, bereavement, alcohol abuse, suicide.

Chad Varah, ed., *The Samaritans* (New York: The Macmillan Co., 1965). Describes the church related programs of suicide prevention and crisis help.

Charles A. Van Wagner, II., "Supervision in Lay Pastoral Care," *Journal of Pastoral Care*, 31, No. 3, Sept. 1977, pp. 158-63. Describes methods of lay supervision.

How to Keep Your Caring and Counseling Skills Growing

Teachers of pastoral counseling are occasionally queried by pastors and theological students who ask, "Where should I go from here? I'm aware of my need for greater competence in caring and counseling. How do I keep growing in this pastoral art? What other skills and sensitivities do I need and what training experiences are most helpful in acquiring these?" This chapter is my attempt to answer these important questions.

The Key—The Pastor's Personality

Empirical studies have identified three crucial counselor characteristics—often called the "therapeutic triad."[1] When they are present in a helper and are perceived by the helpee, the relationship tends to be used by that person for healing and growth. They are—*congruence, nonpossessive warmth* (caring and respect), and *empathic understanding.*[2]

Congruence, in this context, means inner genuineness, integration, and openness. Rogers observes: "The most basic learning for anyone who hopes to establish any kind of helping relationship is that it is safe to be transparently real."[3] The opposite of congruence is "being a phony" or "putting on an act." In such persons there is an incongruence between their words and their real feelings.

Persons who have had to hide their real feelings from others for extended periods in order to feel accepted, eventually become unaware of many of their own feelings. These repressed feelings produce emotional blind spots, frequently in the areas of hostility, aggressiveness, sexuality, and tenderness. A counselor's emotional blind spots prevent him/her from being inwardly congruent in those areas—from being the self she/he truly is. This keeps the person from relating therapeutically to others in these blocked-off areas. "Each person is an island unto himself. . . . He can only build bridges to other islands if he is first of all willing to be himself."[4]

To experience unconditional positive regard (Rogers term for nonpossessive warmth) is to experience the human equivalent of grace in a relationship. Grace is the love one does not have to earn because it is already *there* in a relationship. Rogers declares:

> Actually it is only the experience of a relationship in which he is loved (something very close, I believe, to the theologians' *agape*) that the individual can begin to feel a dawning respect for, acceptance of, and finally, even a fondness for himself. It is as he can thus begin to sense himself as lovable and worthwhile, in spite of his mistakes, that he can begin to feel love and tenderness for others.[5]

Unconditional positive regard is a blend of warmth, liking, caring, acceptance, interest, and respect for the person. A significant study by Julius Seeman "found that success in psychotherapy is closely associated with a strong and growing mutual liking and respect between client and therapist."[6] The counselor becomes a companion-guide in a warm, human relationship that helps clients find courage to face their situation, bear their load, or go on the often frightening journey into the unexplored areas of their personhood. Unconditional positive regard, in Buber's terms, is the counselor's ability to establish I-Thou relationships.

Empathic understanding means entering into the person's inner world of meanings and deep feelings through listening with caring awareness. The counseling pastor's continuing prayer might well be the hymn line, "Take the dimness of my soul away." Fortunately for most of us, even a "bumbling and faulty attempt to catch the confused complexities of the client's meanings" often is helpful to her or him.[7]

One of the barriers to empathic understanding is our defensive narcissism. To the extent that we are overly invested in ourselves we find it impossible to enter into another's inner world. Self-absorption and depth self-awareness are opposite psychological conditions. Self-centered persons are aware mainly of their own painful insecurity, inferiority feelings, and demanding need for affirmation and attention. Their consuming question, "Will I get *my* needs for approval satisfied?" blocks awareness of their own deeper feelings and limits their capacity for empathy.

In addition to the three counselor qualities just described, I would add *a sturdy inner sense of one's identity* as a person. A theological student, reflecting on a reality-practice session where she was the "parishioner," said of the counselor: "I felt his compassion but not the hope that his strength and know-how would help me pull myself together and set me up for a working-together relationship. I felt I had pulled him down in the hole with me." To avoid this, pastors need that firm sense of their identity and personal worth that are at the nucleus of ego strength. Counselors are able to be sensitive and responsive to the needs of others to the degree that they possess this centered awareness of their own value and personhood. Persons who are not centered are out of touch with the only secure locus for stable self-esteem and identity. They "give their power away" (as gestalt therapists put it) by allowing others to define their worth by external evaluations.

A fifth essential counselor quality (mentioned earlier) is the therapeutic attitude described by Henri Nouwen as that of the *"wounded healer."* This results from a vivid awareness of one's affinity with the sickness and sin, loneliness, alienation, and despair of the disturbed person. This attitude begins to dawn as we ministers sense, in the presence of the person with alcoholism, psychosis, or suicidal impulses, that "there but for the grace of God (and some good fortune perhaps) go I!" It emerges more fully when we move beyond this to the deflating awareness—*"There go I!"* This feeling somehow lowers the walls that block the flow of healing forces in relationships. Retaining this acceptance of our only partially-healed brokenness is often difficult when one is "the helper." To identify with the essential humanness of a despairing person threatens our fragile defenses against our own despair. To recognize that the regressed catatonic in a mental hospital is more like than different from oneself shakes the very foundations of our defensive self-image.[8] To accept this truth at a deep level requires an inward surrender of subtle feelings of self-idolatry and spiritual superiority. One of my students referred to this as "getting off the omnipotence kick." A potential advantage of growing older is that the accumulating blows of life may shatter to some degree our defensive facade of pseudo-omnipotence—which was easier to maintain during our young adult years. Even a partial surrender of one's defensive superiority feelings helps to open the door to mutually healing relationships. Somehow it melts a hole in the icy barrier of pride that keeps people—especially disturbed people—at a distance from us.

A sixth essential quality in counselors is *personal aliveness*. If pastoral counselors are enliveners—enablers of life in all its fullness in others—our most important (and often most difficult) task is to learn how to stay as fully alive as possible! Aliveness is contagious! So is deadness! Think for a moment of how weighted-down you feel after spending even a short time with certain people. Compare this with the zestful aliveness that fills you after the same amount of time with others.

Depth Training for Creative Counseling

What kinds of learnings enable ministers to use the many facets of their complex personality more creatively? Which experiences will enhance their inner congruence, warm caring, and empathic understanding; their sense of identity and worth; their capacity to use their brokenness as a healing resource; their sense of aliveness? Carroll A. Wise puts his finger on the key: "The pastor needs to *know himself* [or herself] as well as to understand the dynamic processes of personality as they find expression in the counselee."[9] Being able to form a helping relationship with another is dependent on forming a "helping relationship to myself."[10] Our self-awareness catalyzes the process of increasing self-awareness in others. Our inner freedom helps awaken the freedom of the spirit in others. Rogers summarizes: "The degree to which I can create relationships which facilitate the growth of others as separate persons is a measure of the growth I have achieved in myself."[11] Grace-communicators must have experienced grace. Growth-facilitators must be growing persons. Renewal agents must know firsthand the struggles, discipline, and joy of ongoing personal renewal. To stay alive requires continuing to grow through all of our lives, in our awareness of here-and-now experience, particularly of our own inner depths. As Dag Hammerskjöld observes, "The longest journey is the journey inwards."[12] We can establish deep, transforming relationships with others only to the degree that we are in touch with our own depths and are open to continuing transformation within ourselves.

What experiences available to pastors stimulate personal growth most effectively? Academic courses, seminars, and books (including this one) *per se*, usually have limited effects on this level, although they be valuable on cognitive and skill-building levels. There are six types of experiences providing, in varying degrees, the deeper *self-encounter* that accelerates the counselor's personal growth: psychotherapy, clinical pastoral education, supervision of one's counseling, growth groups, reality-practice, and spiritual disciplines. The learning accruing from these experiences, to quote a choice Shakespearean line, "adds a precious seeing to the eye."[13] It increases the capacity for "thou-ness" in relationships.

Optimally, *personal psychotherapy* should be an integral part of the training of every pastor. Anyone's ministry can be deepened and enriched by it. Psychotherapy tends to sharpen one's interpersonal awareness and makes previously unused facets of one's personality available for more person-enhancing relationships. A minister's personality is her or his only instrument for communicating the Good News (through relationships). Psychotherapy is a means of removing the inner blocks that diminish the ability of one's personality to be the fine, effective instrument it can be. Psychotherapy cannot and need not eradicate all inner blocks and conflicts. It can make one aware enough of those which remain to reduce drastically their interference with growthful relationships. Without personal therapy some ministers distort their counseling by projecting their inner conflicts and repressed impulses onto relationships without realizing it.

For many pastors, group therapy is more effective than individual psychotherapy because it offers wider opportunities to become aware of interpersonal distortions and transference problems, to be confronted with one's unconstructive attitudes and behavior, and to experiment with more creative relating in the group. Individual therapy is indicated where distortions in relating stem mainly from need deprivation in the preschool years. Group therapy is ideal for rectifying distortions derived primarily from later inadequacies in peer relationships. Ideally, a seminarian's or minister's training therapy should include both.

It is imperative that psychotherapy, individual or group, be done by a highly trained professional person—a specialist in pastoral counseling, a psychiatrist, social worker, or clinical psychologist. Because of the extensive training required, and the relative scarcity of qualified therapists, the cost is usually high. Ordinarily, group therapy is less expensive than individual. But, whatever the cost, personal psychotherapy is a valuable investment in one's future and in one's ability to relate more growthfully in all dimensions of ministry. Pastors often have to make financial sacrifices to obtain therapy. But those who do so usually discover that it is the most valuable learning experience of their entire education, paying rich dividends in subsequent years—both personally and professionally.

To help ministers experience healing and growth, therapists should be thoroughly trained in depth psychotherapy. This should include their own personal therapy. They should be skilled in dealing with unconscious material—dreams, fantasies, free associations, transference feelings. Based on my experiences through the years with several therapists who had a variety of orientations, I would recommend an eclectic therapist who understands psychodynamics theory from the depth psychologists (particularly Freud and Jung) but who uses the more active methods of the contemporary therapies, especially gestalt, psychosynthesis, and the body therapies. These methods tend to facilitate more rapid healing and growth than do unmodified psychoanalytic methods. To the minister contemplating therapy, I would pass along the words that Fritz Kunkel inscribed on the fly leaf of my copy of one of his books: "Good luck on the journey down and up!" (I didn't understand his words until years later.)

Clinical pastoral education (CPE) also provides a depth encounter with oneself. In some four hundred accredited centers in North America, mainly in general and psychiatric hospitals and in correctional institutions (but also in a few parishes), theological students and ministers spend eleven weeks or longer working under supervision (by a chaplain supervisor) with people in crisis.

Clinical training has many values. It forces the student to ask searching and sometimes disturbing questions concerning the dynamic meaning of religion in troubled people's lives. It raises the confronting question of relevancy: "How is my understanding of religion relevant to the real needs of this mental patient (or delinquent, drug addict, cancer patient)?" CPE helps reveal the strengths and weaknesses of one's pattern of relating in all aspects of one's ministry. It provides opportunities to learn to work with the other helping professions, and to define one's unique professional function and pastoral identity in relation to them and in the light of one's tradition. CPE also involves participation in a personal growth group that usually is very valuable.

Parish ministers who take a three-month sabbatical from their churches for CPE (as I did after nearly a decade in the parish ministry), usually find it to be one of the richest learning experiences of their lives. Some accredited centers offer extended quarters on a two days per week basis, for those who cannot arrange to take full-time CPE. Clinical training, both full- and part-time, offers unique opportunities to strengthen one's total ministry to persons, not just one's counseling. [14]

One of the finest resources for enhancing interpersonal skills is at the fingertips of most pastors: The opportunity to obtain *supervision of one's pastoral relationships—including one's counseling*.[15] Competent supervision is the most direct and efficient way of upgrading interpersonal skills. To help seminarians and pastors shape and strengthen their professional identity, it is important that at least a part of one's supervision be done by trained and experienced clergy supervisors who understand and appreciate the church context, the faith perspective, and the pastoral role in the faith community. Any minister who lives within reasonable driving distance of a well-trained pastoral psychotherapist or chaplain supervisor may obtain this valuable training by a modest investment of time and money. The procedure is simply to arrange with that person to have weekly or biweekly supervision sessions of one's caring, counseling, growth group leadership and other pastoral relationships.

Most pastoral counseling specialists and mental health professionals welcome the opportunity to do supervision and consultation with pastors. Small groups of ministers (two to eight) can make arrangements for group supervision dividing the cost among them. As described in chapter 15, significant new resources for enabling parish ministers to increase their counseling skills have emerged in recent years in the training programs developed by a growing number of church-related counseling centers. Ideally, church-related counseling programs should devote at least one-fourth of their staff time to providing continuing education and training for pastors!

A West Coast pastoral counseling center sponsors pastoral case conferences following this pattern: The group, limited to ten parish ministers, meets once a week for two hours. The leader is the center's director, a pastor with advanced training in counseling. At each session one minister makes detailed presentation of one of his or her counseling cases. Emergency counseling problems are discussed as they are raised by group members. Occasionally the leader highlights some new development in pastoral counseling. Audio and videotapes of actual counseling sessions are used in the supervision, as are reality-practice techniques. Each minister pays a modest sum per session to the center for this service.

Supervision is more widely and readily available potentially than any other form of counselor training. In many situations all that is required is for the minister to take the initiative in arranging with a therapist for such an experience. In ongoing supervisory groups, the interaction often approaches the group therapy level. Depth understanding of any counseling relationship throws as much light on the counselor as on the counselee. Like CPE, supervision can sharpen a minister's self-awareness as it strengthens her/his ability to help the troubled. Supervision groups often also become peer support groups, thus helping to meet one of the most pressing needs of many pastors.

Growth groups offer another valuable learning experience for pastors, though they are not a substitute for personal therapy, clinical training, and in-depth supervision. Such groups are widely used in workshops and human relations labs to enhance the participants' skills in relating. For over a decade the seminary where I teach required a group experience called "Personal Growth Through Group Interaction" for all first year theological students. The aim of these sharing groups was to enhance students' abilities to communicate and relate in healing, growthful ways. A research project that studied these groups and comparable groups at two other seminaries demonstrated the value of even two-semesters in growth groups as part of preparation for person-centered ministry.

The ministry can be a lonely and depleting profession, because of the multiplicty of contacts with needy people. One way to refuel one's own energies is to establish a peer support-nurture group. To be effective, pastoral support groups must learn how to interrupt the "games which ministers play" and relate to the real hopes and hurts, the real needs of persons in our demanding profession. Pastors and their spouses should do whatever is necessary to find or co-create (with other individuals and couples) a support group in which they are not the leaders. One's spouse can give valuable support but having a support group where both of you receive as well as give nurturing care, is also important. A support system is especially helpful in one's early ministry and when one is going through a crisis in one's personal life or ministry.

Practicing the spiritual disciplines of prayer and meditation is vital to the continuing enlivening of the minister. It is by keeping open to our true spiritual center—the high Self within us—that we are in touch with the artesian spring of God's Spirit, the Source of aliveness. Learning a simple method of meditation can enrich experiences of prayer and help one open the sluice gate on the inner channel through which flows the renewing energy of God's love—within us and through our relationship to others.[16]

Here are some suggestions for self-nurture, for the pastoral care of pastors. (They are ways to enjoy avoiding ministerial burnout.) (1) Make some time in your daily schedule for yourself, to do something you find satisfying and renewing. Let your inner Child (in TA terms) play regularly. Give yourself several mini-vacations each day—a few minutes to do something really fun (that will feel frivolous to your inner Parent). No one can be a nurturing Parent and/or Adult all the time. (2) Give yourself a gift each day—something you find nurturing. (3) Take a full day off each week, the equivalent of a long weekend off each month with no professional duties, and a study leave in addition to a vacation each year. You may have to get away from your home-base and the telephone to have these renewal breaks. (4) Try to be realistic in the goals for your ministry and your life. Stop trying to be the "bionic minister"![17] (5) Jog and/or do some yoga each day (or some other form of enjoyable exercise) to reduce tension and tune-up your body, particularly your cardiovascular system. (6) Develop various techniques of stress reduction—and inner quieting, which work for you and practice at least one of them every day. (Here are some I enjoy—meditation; "floating" in music; resonating to nature as I work in the garden; sitting in a warm bath with a book I enjoy.) (7) Find a person or small group with whom you can let down your hair, relax your professional "persona," ventilate the frustrations that have built up, discuss personal as well as professional issues, and get affirmation and objective feedback. (8) Let yourself laugh regularly—with others and at yourself. Someone has called laughing "internal jogging." It's therapeutic, stress-reducing effects are well-documented. (9) Risk letting your vulnerability show more. Sitting on a ministerial pedestal is not only lonely, it keeps one from receiving the mutual nuture of close relationships. (10) Treat yourself to regular experiences of enlivement, such as a stimulating workshop and continuing education courses, time to immerse yourself in an exciting book, or a long refreshing conversation with a close friend. (11) When your inner flow of creative energy gets blocked, treat yourself to a "therapeutic retread," some reenergizing sessions with a competent therapist.

Understanding of Basic Concepts

I have discussed clinical learning and personal growth first to emphasize their foundational importance in any sound approach to counselor training and renewal. The deepening of one's ability to relate is essential if conceptual tools are to be useful. Otherwise the mastery of concept can make one a clever technician but not a growth-enabler. But as pastors grow as whole persons, their conceptual grasp of psychodynamics and counseling theories become increasingly valuable in ministering to the troubled. Through disciplined reading and study, including continuing education courses, a minister or theological student should acquire a workable understanding of the following:

(1) *Normal personality growth and development* (including child, adolescent, and adult psychology). Erik Erickson's stages and more recent studies of the special aspects of the adult life stages[18] and the unique development of women,[19] are useful for understanding the life cycle.

(2) *Marriage and family dynamics, enrichment and counseling,* including changing women's-men's identities, relationships, and roles.

(3) *Group dynamics.*

(4) *Psychopathology* (abnormal psychology).

(5) *Methods of individual counseling.*

(6) *Growth groups and group counseling methods.*

(7) *Community referral resources.*

(8) *Personality and cultures* (socio-economic-political forces as they influence personality health and growth in one's own culture and others).

(9) *History and theory of pastoral care.*

(10) *Theology and counseling,* (including the theology of counseling, and the dynamic role of religion in human wholeness and brokenness).

This list may arouse the response expressed by Chaucer's line: "The lyf so short the craft so long to lerne."[20] But these are fundamental subject areas that should be mastered at some point during a minister's education—in college, seminary or continuing education—if she/he is to be equipped for growthful work with people in *all* dimensions of ministry.

As a major study of theological education stated:

> When one considers the revitalization of much in the theological curriculum today through new emphases in psychology and pastoral counseling, it must be concluded that a significant new turn in the education of the ministry has been taken. Powerful new resources are available throughout the curriculum because of work in this field.[21]

Much has happened in seminaries and in continuing education during the last few decades to make these powerful resources more available to seminarians and pastors. However, much more needs to be done, particularly in supervised education, before seminary graduates in general will enter parishes with the basic psychological understanding and competence in counseling, which they sorely need. Theological students should be urged to take at least one quarter of CPE during their seminary career, preferably after the first year. Pastors who are aware of needing more counseling skills should explore, with nearby seminaries, CPE supervisors or pastoral counseling centers with training programs, the possibility of setting up the continuing education opportunities they need. Most D. Min. (Doctor of Ministry) programs offer pastors the option of focusing in pastoral psychology and counseling. Seminary Ph.D./Th.D. programs in pastoral counseling are designed to equip specialists to staff pastoral counseling centers (and other specialized ministries).

Denominational leaders have a key role in helping enhance the quality of the interpersonal ministry (including pastoral care and counseling) by their clergy. Increasingly ministers are sensing that intentional career planning and lifelong continuing education must include personal and professional growth experiences that enable them to learn the new concepts and methods that are emerging continually in the counseling field. Denominations should provide experiential learning events focusing on new approaches to this pastoral art. In addition, denominational decision makers should make personal therapy and marriage counseling readily available to clergy and their families when this kind of help is needed.[22] Nine United Methodist Annual Conferences now have directors of pastoral care and counseling to serve their ministers both by providing counseling for them and their families, and by offering frequent continuing education and supervision experiences.[23] Such pastoral counseling specialists know the frustrations, problems, and rewards of the ministry from the inside. They have this distinct advantage over secular therapists in helping clergy and their spouses deal with the common issue of role identity and conflict.

Counseling, of course, is only one aspect of the work of pastors. But if ministers sense the crucial importance of these skills in the lives of burdened people, their motivation to grow in this area is strong. Many ministers are realizing that to be too busy to participate in such experiences as personal therapy, supervision, refresher courses, and workshops on counseling, is to be something like carpenters who are too busy to sharpen their tools. Fortunately these professional growth experiences help to enhance one's communication and relationship skills generally, which tends to strengthen and deepen all dimensions of one's ministry.

To keep abreast of new thinking and research in the field of pastoral psychology and counseling, pastors should read one or both of the two leading journals in the field—*The Journal of Pastoral Care*, published by several professional associations in the pastoral care field, including the Association for Clinical Pastoral Education, and the American Association of Pastoral Counselors, and *Pastoral Psychology*, sponsored by Princeton Theological Seminary and published by the Human Sciences Press, 75 Fifth Avenue, New York, NY 10011.

Pastors who emphasize counseling in their ministry should join the American Association of Pastoral Counselors as pastoral affiliates or as members, depending on the category for which their training in the field qualifies them.[24] A primary goal of AAPC is to help raise the general level of training and practice of pastoral counseling in all settings where it occurs. Participation in the national convention and regional meetings, and reading the newsletter of this professional association can help a counseling pastor keep in touch with innovative developments in this field. A growing network of AAPC accredited training programs and centers offers opportunities to keep one's caring and counseling tools sharp through individual and/or group supervision, workshops, and other training experiences.

Some Final Perspectives

In the practice of the counseling art, it is helpful to remember these perspective-giving facts:

(1) The pastor's focus on the acute needs of individuals who seek counseling should always be balanced by developing a broad ministry of pastoral care, by lay carers as well as the minister.

(2) One can help many troubled people without becoming a specialist in pastoral counseling and therapy. At every level of growth in caring skills—professional and lay—there are countless opportunities to be of genuine help.

(3) Every pastoral counselor, however skilled, fails to help some people. It is well to remember the human limitations of all of us counselors and all helping relationships. Jesus' lack of success with Judas, in spite of his close association, is a case in point. As in Jesus' parable of the sower, the seeds in counseling do not always fall on receptive soil. The counselor's job is to keep sowing, trusting the God-given growth forces in people and relationships, and remembering that, at best, he/she is an imperfect instrument for communicating healing resources beyond her/himself.

(4) Increasing one's caring and counseling skills is a continuing, lifelong challenge. One never "arrives." The heart of the counseling art can be learned only by experience. However, this learning is accelerated immensely if one's experience is exposed to systematic reflection and evaluation. This is why supervision, consultation, and reality-practice can be so fruitful.

(5) Having examined a variety of theories and methods of counseling, it is important to reemphasize the heart of the matter. This was put well in Jung's advice to psychotherapists: "Learn your theories as well as you can, but put them aside when you touch the miracle of the living soul. Not theories but your own creative individuality alone must decide."[25] Engraved in every pastor's mind should be these words: *Caring Relationships—the Instruments of Help!*

Without a warm, accepting relationship, the methods of counseling described in these pages become mere techniques— sterile, manipulative, and ineffective. But when skillfully employed *within an accepting, energized, caring relationship,* they become means by which that relationship's healing power is released.

(6) Finally, it is liberating to remember that all healing and all growth are gifts of the creative Spirit of life whom we call God. When healing and growth occur in counseling relationships, it is because persons have become more open in their minds and bodies and relationships to the re-creating energies of Spirit. As I am often aware in my counseling, healing and growth may occur in spite of, not because of, what a counselor says or does. This awareness is no excuse for doing poor counseling. It is a reminder that at best a counselor is a finite and often fractured channel for the healing power of the universe! Paul Tillich once declared:

> The power which makes acceptance possible is the resource in all pastoral care. It must be effective in him who helps, and it must become effective in him who is helped . . . This means that both the pastor and the counselee . . . are under the power of something which transcends both of them. One can call this power *the new creature or the New Being.* The pastoral counselor can be of help only if he himself is grasped by this power.[26]

The pastor who thus has been grasped becomes a channel through which this power becomes an *experienced reality* in the life of a congregation—and through the shared ministry of this congregation brings release of the prisoners, recovery of sight to the blind, and freedom for the broken victims!

With all the encouraging developments in the field, the helping potential of the ministry of caring and counseling has only begun to be released. As more and more of us strengthen our competence as counselors, this potential wellspring of healing and growth will become more available to the millions who desperately need what it can give. The challenge that confronts each of us is to help release this potential by becoming *incarnational counselors*—persons whose imperfect relationships somehow enable the liberating Word to become flesh and dwell in and among us with healing power—healing *us* as well as those with whom we minister.

Our heritage from the past is rich indeed! Developments in the present show that the field is alive and growing. The future is pregnant with exciting possibilities for new ministries to people. The continuing rebirth of this art of ministry depends on the willingness of people like you and me to dream and to do, to use our imaginations and invest our energies in developing innovative ministries of caring and counseling. The living Spirit calls us to participate joyfully in co-creating a future in which the church's tremendous undeveloped potentialities for healing and wholeness can be actualized.

Planning Your Growth Journey

I recommend that you now—

(1) Develop a list of the personal and professional growth goals toward which you need to move in order to maximize your effectiveness in caring and counseling. Write down these goals.

(2) Prioritize your goals in terms of their importance.

(3) Decide on the immediate steps you will take to enable you to grow toward your high priority goals.

(4) Commit yourself to a concrete plan, with a realistic time schedule for doing those things that will keep your caring-counseling skills growing.

I wish you joy and shalom on your continuing journey as a growing enabler of wholeness!

Recommended Reading

Charles L. Rassieur, *Stress Management for Ministers: Practical Help for Clergy Who Deny Themselves the Care They Give to Others.* (Philadelphia: Westminster Press, 1982). Describes the nature of clergy burnout and how to prevent or treat it.

John A. Sanford, *Ministry Burnout* (New York: Paulist Press, 1982). Includes suggestions for "feeding the soul" and recovering the energy and joy of creative service.

NOTES

Chapter 1

1. This parable originally appeared in an article by Theodore O. Wedel, "Evangelism—the Mission of the Church to Those Outside Her Life," *The Ecumenical Review*, October 1953, p. 24. The above paraphrases the original by Richard Wheatcroft, which appeared in *Letter to Laymen*, May-June 1962, p. 1.
2. The concept from transactional analysis will be discussed in chapter 15.
3. William R. Clebsch and Charles R. Jaekle, *Pastoral Care in Historical Perspective* (Englewood Cliffs, N.J.: Prentice-Hall, 1964), p. 79.
4. Ibid.
5. For a more comprehensive discussion of various therapies, see Howard Clinebell, *Contemporary Growth Therapies* (Nashville: Abingdon Press, 1981).

Chapter 2

1. Paradigm, from the Greek *paradeigma* meaning "to show side by side," is a pattern or archetypal model.
2. Howard Clinebell, *Growth Counseling* (Nashville: Abingdon Press, 1979), pp. 17-18.
3. Herbert A. Otto estimates that most human beings function at 10 percent or less of their potential. See Otto, ed., *Human Potentialities: The Challenge and the Promise* (St. Louis: Warren H. Green, 1968), p. 3.
4. For an in-depth exploration of these six dimensions of growth, see Clinebell, *Growth Counseling*, chapter 1.
5. Dorothy Day was a courageous leader of the Catholic workers' movement; Tai-Young Lee is Korea's first woman lawyer, a dedicated and courageous defender of human rights, and of women's rights in particular.
6. The concept of the higher Self is from psychosynthesis.

7. Clinebell, Growth Counseling. For a fuller discussion of "Growth Counseling through the Stages of the Life Cycle," see pp. 156-81.

8. See James Ashbrook, "Postcritical Ministry: Beyond Critical Coolness and Uncritical Warmth," *Foundations*, Jan.-Mar. 1977, p. 61.

9. Clinebell, *Growth Counseling*, p. 20.

10. See Howard Clinebell, *The Mental Health Ministry of the Local Church* (Nashville: Abingdon Press, 1972) for a fuller discussion of the growth and healing potentialities of all dimensions of ministry.

11. See John T. McNeill's *A History of the Cure of Souls* (New York: Harper & Brothers, 1951) for a history of pastoral care. Don S. Browning's *The Moral Context of Pastoral Care* (Philadelphia: Westminster Press, 1976) includes in chapters 2, 3, and 4 a history of pastoral care emphasizing the central place of moral guidance. E. Brooks Holifield, *From Salvation to Self-Realization: Protestant Pastoral Counseling in America* (Nashville: Abingdon Press, 1983) is a comprehensive and critical history of the pastoral counseling movement up until about 1970.

12. Russell Dicks was my first teacher of pastoral care and counseling.

13. Clebsch and Jaekle, *Pastoral Care in Historical Perspective*, p. 33. The authors acknowledge their indebtedness to Seward Hiltner for his delineation of the first three functions; Ibid., pp. 8-9.

14. See Daniel Yankelovich, *New Rules: Searching for Self-Fulfillment in a World Turned Upside Down* (New York: Random House, 1981).

15. Ibid., p. 3.

Chapter 3

1. Paul Johnson, one of the pioneers in the modern period of pastoral care, wrote these words in a paper entitled "Where We Are Now in Pastoral Care" (*Christian Advocate*, 23 Sept. 1965, p. 7). I am saddened and impressed with how precisely these words still describe the massive alienation of our contemporary world!

2. These are the words of a psychiatrist who is also a devoted churchman. He calls for "a more intensive *in*reaching mission" to these persons. C. W. Morris, "The Terror of Good Works," *Pastoral Psychology*, Sept. 1957, p. 25.

3. Wayne E. Oates, *An Introduction to Pastoral Counseling* (Nashville: Broadman Press, 1959), p. vi.

4. The results of this study were reported in *Americans View Their Mental Health* by Gerald Gurin, Joseph Veroff, and Sheila Feld (New York: Basic Books, 1960).

5. Joseph Veroff, Richard A. Kulka, Elizabeth Dorran, *Mental Health in America*, (New York: Basic Books, 1981).

6. Ibid., p. 79.

7. Ibid., p. 134.

8. Ibid., p. 138.

9. Ibid., p. 151; p. 147.

10. David Roberts, *Psychotherapy and a Christian View of Man* (New York: Charles Scribner's Sons, 1950), p. 142.

11. See Gerhard van Rad, *Genesis: A Commentary*, trans. John H. Marks (Philadelphia: Westminster Press, 1961), p. 56.

12. Rollo May, *The Courage to Create*, (New York: Bantam Books, 1975), p. 134.

13. See Douglas J. Harris, *The Biblical Concept of Peace: Shalom* (Grand Rapids: Baker Publishing House, 1970).

14. James Cone, *A Black Theology of Liberation* (Philadelphia: Lippincott, 1970), p. 170.

15. For a discussion of the glasses of growth, see Clinebell, *Growth Counseling*, pp. 52-55.

16. Paul Tillich, *Systematic Theology*, II (Chicago: University of Chicago Press, 1957), p. 60.

17. See Clinebell, *Growth Counseling*, pp. 140-41.

18. Daniel Day Williams, *The Minister and the Care of Souls* (New York: Harper & Row, 1977), p. 15.

19. H. Wheeler Robinson, *Redemption and Revelation* (New York: Harper & Brothers, 1942), pp. 232-33.

20. Williams, *The Minister and the Care of Souls*, p. 13.

21. See Pierre Teilhard de Chardin, *The Future of Man* (New York: Harper & Row, 1964).

22. See Clinebell, *Growth Counseling*, pp. 143-51.

23. Rosemary R. Ruether, *New Woman-New Earth: Sexist Ideologies and Human Liberation* (New York: Seabury Press, 1975), p. 65.

24. See Leonard Swidler, "Jesus Was a Feminist," *Catholic World*, Jan. 1971.

25. See Richard H. Niebuhr, in collaboration with Daniel Day Williams and James M. Gustafson, *The Purpose of the Church and Its Ministry* (New York: Harper & Brothers, 1956), p. 31.

26. Norman Pittenger, *Making Sexuality Human* (Philadelphia: Pilgrim Press, 1970), chapters 2, 3, and 4.

27. Williams, *The Minister and the Care of Souls*, p. 17.

28. Erich Fromm, *Psychoanalysis and Religion* (New Haven: Yale University Press, 1951), p. 87.

29. Ulrich Sonnemann, *Existence and Therapy* (New York: Grune and Stratton, 1954), p. 343.

30. Dietrich Bonhoeffer, *Letters and Papers from Prison* (New York: The Macmillan Co., 1972), p. 124.

31. Wayne E. Oates, *Pastoral Counseling* (Philadelphia: Westminster Press, 1974), pp. 11-12.

32. Address at the National Conference of Clinical Pastoral Education, Atlantic City, New Jersey, Nov. 1956).

33. Anton T. Boisen, *The Exploration of the Inner World* (New York: Harper & Brothers, 1936), p. 285.

34. See Clebsch and Jaekle, *Pastoral Care in Historical Perspective*, pp. 4-5.

35. Transference is the projection of strong archaic feelings of love and hate from one's relationships with parents or other persons from one's early life onto persons perceived as authority figures. These

projections occur, to some degree, in most if not all relations with ministers. But transference is apt to occur with great intensity in longer-term counseling or therapy. Either positive or negative transference attachments can be emotionally demanding and difficult to resolve. Persons who "fall into love" with their pastor usually are in love with the image of her or his parent of the other sex, with whom the persons had an unsatisfying relationship. The same is true of those persons who develop irrational feelings of hatred for a pastor. Reducing the danger of transference relationships is one reason why ministers should not attempt long-term pastoral psychotherapy unless they are well trained in this work.

36. The development of walk-in crises clinics to which distressed persons can go without appointments for immediate help in crises, indicates that the mental health professions have become aware of the value of what has been the minister's approach through the centuries.

37. See Donald C. Houts, "Pastoral Initiative: Why Wait for George/Georgia to Do It?," *Journal of Pastoral Care*, 37, No. 1, Mar. 1983, pp. 33-41.

Chapter 4

1. Dietrich Bonhoeffer, *Life Together* (New York: Harper & Brothers, 1959), pp. 97-98.
2. See Seward Hiltner, *Pastoral Counseling* (New York/Nashville: Abingdon-Cokesbury Press, 1949).
3. From the Greek word *maieutikos,* "midwife."
4. Sonnemann, *Existence and Therapy,* p. 343.
5. Carl R. Rogers, *Client-Centered Therapy* (New York: Houghton Mifflin, 1951), p. 45. For a discussion of this view by a student of Buber, see Maurice Friedman, *Martin Buber: The Life of Dialogue* (New York: Harper & Brothers, 1960), p. 192.
6. William Shakespeare, *Henry IV*, Part II, Act I, Sc. I, 1. 139.
7. I am indebted to Robert L. Brizee for this way of describing an important aspect of counseling. Undisciplined listening consists of allowing counselees to ramble through their inner world, without helping them begin to find the pattern in what they are saying or to focus on what seems to be significant issues. For an insightful discussion of listening in depth, see Thomas W. Klink, *Depth Perspectives in Pastoral Work,* pp. 22ff.
8. Flanders Dunbar, *Mind and Body: Psychosomatic Medicine* (New York: Random House, 1955), p. 249.
9. Paraphrased from Heinz Kohut, "Pilgrimage," *Journal of Pastoral Psychotherapy*, 5, No. 1 (1977).
10. "Psychotherapists' Expressions as an Index to the Quality of Early Therapeutic Relationships," unpublished Ph.D. diss., University of Chicago, 1950. Cited by Carl R. Rogers in *On Becoming a Person* (Boston: Houghton Mifflin, 1961), p. 44.
11. Lynn Bush, School of Theology at Claremont, June 1965.

12. Paul W. Pruyser, *The Minister as Diagnostician* (Philadelphia: Westminster Press, 1976).
13. Carl R. Rogers, *Counseling and Psychotherapy* (Boston: Houghton Mifflin, 1942), p. 131.
14. Warmth does not mean effusiveness, of course. People who need emotional distance and are afraid of being overwhelmed by others will retreat from the effusive pastor's verbal aggressiveness.
15. Letter from Warren A. Nyberg, 5 July 1965.
16. See Robert R. Carkhuff and William A. Anthony, *The Skills of Helping* (Amherst, Mass.: Human Resources Development Press, 1979); Gerald Egan, *The Skilled Helper* (Belmont, Calif.: Wadsworth Publishing Company, 1975); Gerald Egan, *Exercises in Helping Skills* (Monterey, Calif.: Brooks-Cole, 1975); and Allen E. Ivey and Jr. Authier, second ed., *Microcounseling* (Springfield, Ill.: Charles C. Thomas, 1978). For a report on the greater effectiveness of this training method as contrasted with my reality practice method alone, see H. Terry Kiesel, "Training in Basic Counseling Skills: A Comparison of a Microtraining Approach with a Skill Practice Approach," *Journal of Pastoral Counseling*, 31, No. 2, June 1977, pp. 125-33.
17. Adapted from Elias H. Porter, *An Introduction to Therapeutic Counseling* (Boston: Houghton Mifflin, 1950), p. 201.
18. Adapted from Porter, p. 12. Here is the key to the above exercise: (1) Interpretive, (2) Supportive, (3) Evaluative, (4) Understanding, (5) Advice Giving, (6) Probing.
19. Dale White, "Mental Health and the Poor," *Concern*, 15 Oct. 1964, p. 6.
20. Ibid., pp. 6-7. The study was done by Frank Riessman of Columbia University.
21. Ibid., p. 7.
22. See Charles Kemp, *Pastor Care of the Poor* (Nashville: Abingdon Press, 1972).
23. Edward P. Wimberly, *Pastoral Care in the Black Church* (Nashville: Abingdon Press, 1979), pp. 20-21; Ibid., p. 84.
24. Inge K. Broverman et al., "Sex Role Stereotype and Clinical Judgments of Mental Health," *Journal of Consulting and Clinical Psychology*, 34, No. 1, pp. 1-7.
25. Phyllis Chesler, *Women and Madness* (New York: Avon Books, 1973).
26. Clinebell, *Contemporary Growth Therapies*, p. 250.
27. Charlotte Holt Clinebell, *Counseling for Liberation* (Philadelphia: Fortress Press, 1976), pp. 22-23.
28. For further insights concerning cross-cultural counseling, see Derald W. Sue et al., *Counseling the Culturally Different: Theory and Practice* (New York: John Wiley and Sons, 1981); Elaine S. Levine and Amado M. Padilla, *Crossing Cultures in Therapy* (Monterey, Calif.: Brooks-Cole, 1980); and Paul B. Pedersen, ed. et al.,

Counseling Across Cultures, rev. ed. (Honolulu: University of Hawaii Press, 1981).

Chapter 5

1. "Charmides," The Dialogues of Plato, trans., Benjamin Jowett (New York: Random House, 1937), I, p. 6.
2. This study was done in 1972 by Morris Taggart. See "AAPC Membership Information Projects," Journal of Pastoral Care, 26, Dec. 1972, pp. 219-44. Since many AAPC members do their counseling in situations detached from congregations, it may be that the percentage of persons with explicit spiritual problems seen by pastors is higher.
3. Wayne E. Oates, Religious Factors in Mental Illness (New York: Association Press, 1955), pp. 6-7.
4. Hiltner, Pastoral Counseling, p. 17; Geoffrey Brunn, Saturday Review of Literature, 5 Jan. 1957, p. 20; Herman Melville, Moby Dick (New York: The Modern Library, 1950), p. 1.
5. Gerald Sykes, The Hidden Remnant (New York: Harper & Row, 1962), p. 72.
6. Carl Jung, Modern Man in Search of a Soul (New York: Harcourt, Brace & Co., 1933), p. 269; Erich Fromm, ed. et al., Zen Buddhism and Psychoanalysis (New York: Harper & Brothers, 1960), p. 91.
7. Newman S. Cryer and John M. Vayhinger, Casebook in Pastoral Counseling (Nashville: Abingdon Press, 1962), pp. 240-45.
8. Margaretta K. Bowers et al., Counseling the Dying (New York: Thomas Nelson and Sons, 1964), p. 2.
9. Howard Clinebell, "Philosophical-Religious Factors in the Etiology and Treatment of Alcoholism," Quarterly Journal of Studies on Alcohol, Sept. 1963, p. 477. (Adapted to remove sexist language.)
10. Bowers, Counseling the Dying, p. 21. The source is Martin Heidegger, Being and Time (New York: Harper & Row, 1962).
11. See Paul Tillich, The Courage to Be (New Haven: Yale University Press, 1952), chapter 2; Tillich, Systematic Theology, I (Chicago: University of Chicago Press, 1951), p. 193.
12. Paul Tillich, "The Theology of Pastoral Care," Clinical Education for the Pastoral Ministry, Proceedings of the Fifth National Conference on Clinical Pastoral Education, Nov. 9-11, 1956, Ernest E. Bruder and Marian L. Barb, eds. (Advisory Committee on Clinical Pastoral Education, 1958), p. 3.
13. See J.F.T. Bugental, The Search for Authenticity (New York: Holt, Rinehart & Winston, 1956), p. 15.
14. Tillich, The Courage to Be, p. 67; Ibid., p. 151.
15. Bugental, The Search for Authenticity, p. 25.
16. Jung, Modern Man in Search of a Soul, p. 264.
17. Søren Kierkegaard, The Concept of Dread (Princeton: Princeton University Press, 1944), p. 104; Ibid., p. 142; see Fred Berthold, Jr., "Anxious Longing," in Constructive Aspects of Anxiety, Seward

Hiltner and Karl Menninger, eds. (Nashville: Abingdon Press, 1963), p. 71.

18. From Nikos Kazantzakis, *Zorba the Greek,* quoted by Frederick J. Streng in *Understanding Religious Man* (Belmont, Calif.: Dickenson Publishing Co., 1969), opposite p. 1.
19. See Clinebell, *Growth Counseling,* pp. 109-26.
20. Augustine's *Confessions,* Book I.
21. For a discussion of spiritual and value crises in mid-years persons, see Howard Clinebell, *Growth Counseling for Mid-Years Couples* (Philadelphia: Fortress Press, 1977), chapters 4 and 5.
22. For a historical overview of spiritual direction, see Kenneth Leech, *Soul Friend: The Practice of Christian Spirituality* (London: Sheldon Press, 1977), chapter 2; Ibid., p. 86.
23. Ibid., p. 34.
24. Ibid., p. 37-38.
25. See Ruth Tiffany Barnhouse, "Spiritual Direction and Pastoral Counseling," *Journal of Pastoral Care*, 33, No. 3, Sept. 1979, pp. 149-63; Ibid. p. 154.
26. William A. Barry, "Spiritual Direction and Pastoral Counseling," *Pastoral Psychology*, 26, No. 1, Fall 1977, pp. 4, 5-6.
27. See James W. Fowler, *Stages of Faith* (New York: Harper & Row, 1981), part 4.
28. Adapted from Clinebell, *Growth Counseling,* pp. 107-9.
29. For a discussion of RET, see Clinebell, *Contemporary Growth Therapies,* pp. 142-44. For a discussion of ways to change self-damaging beliefs, see Howard Stone, *Using Behavioral Methods in Pastoral Counseling* (Philadelphia: Fortress Press, 1980), chapter 3.
30. William E. Hulme, *Pastoral Care and Counseling* (Minneapolis: Augsburg Press, 1981), pp. 11-12.
31. John B. Cobb, Jr., *Theology and Pastoral Care,* Howard J. Clinebell and Howard W. Stone, eds. (Philadelphia: Fortress Press, 1977), p. 61; see William B. Oglesby, Jr., *Biblical Themes for Pastoral Care* (Nashville: Abingdon Press, 1980).
32. See Wayne Oates, *The Bible in Pastoral Care* (Philadelphia: Westminster Press, 1953); see also Carroll Wise, *Psychiatry and The Bible* (New York: Harper & Brothers, 1956).
33. Donald Capps, *Biblical Approaches to Pastoral Counseling,* (Philadelphia: Westminster Press, 1980), p. 44.
34. David K. Switzer, *Pastor, Preacher, Person* (Nashville: Abingdon Press, 1979), p. 104.
35. See Hulme, *Pastoral Care and Counseling,* pp. 122-24.
36. Switzer, *Pastor, Preacher, Person,* p. 133.
37. See Jay Adams, *Competent to Counsel* (Grand Rapids: Baker Book House, 1970).
38. Hulme, *Pastoral Care and Counseling,* p. 113.
39. See William A. Barry, "Spiritual Direction and Pastoral Counseling," pp. 6-7.

40. See Herbert Benson and Miriam Z. Klipper, *The Relaxation Response* (New York: William Morrow & Co., 1975); see Morton Kelsey, *The Other Side of Silence: A Guide to Christian Meditation* (Ramsey, N.J.: Paulist Press, 1976).

41. "The Use of Religious Imagery as a Cognitive Restructuring Technique," a paper presented at the American Psychological Association convention, Sept. 3, 1977 in New York City.

42. The first part of this exercise is my adaptation from the method described in *The Relaxation Response*.

43. Thomas R. Blakeslee, *The Right Brain* (New York: Anchor Press/Doubleday, 1980) gives the findings of split brain research, applying these to education, creativity, and the unconscious.

44. See Carol P. Christ and Judith Plaskow, eds., *Womanspirit Rising: A Feminist Reader in Religion* (New York: Harper & Row, 1979), pp. 273-87.

45. Niebuhr et al., *The Purpose of the Church and Its Ministry*, p. 11.

46. Bugental, *The Search for Authenticity*, p. 20.

Chapter 6

1. Don Browning, *The Moral Context of Pastoral Care* (Philadelphia: Westminster Press, 1976), p. 109.

2. Ibid., p. 98.

3. Clebsch and Jaekle, *Pastoral Care in Historical Perspective*, p. 63.

4. Ibid., p. 66.

5. Ibid., p. 81.

6. Ibid., p. 82.

7. Edmund Bergler, *The Battle of the Conscience* (Westport, Conn.: Associated Booksellers, 1948), p. VII.

8. I am indebted to Geoffrey Peterson's delineation and discussion of several of these types of conscience problems in *Conscience and Caring* (Philadelphia: Fortress Press, 1982).

9. For Freud the superego was primarily the *unconscious* internalized prohibitions of one's parents. He used the term "ego ideal" to describe the internalized positive values of parents.

10. Victor W. Eisenstein, ed., *Neurotic Interaction in Marriage* (New York: Basic Books, 1956), p. 15.

11. From Erich Fromm, *Man for Himself* (New York: Holt, Rinehart and Winston, 1947), p. 100.

12. This is John C. Ford's term for the process of overprotecting alcoholics.

13. Browning, *The Moral Context of Pastoral Care*, p. 77.

14. For a discussion of the twelve steps, see *Alcoholics Anonymous*, 3rd ed. (New York: AA Publishing Co., 1976), pp. 58ff, and *Twelve Steps and Twelve Traditions* by a co-founder of AA (New York: Harper & Brothers, 1952).

15. William Glasser, *Reality Therapy* (New York: Harper & Row, 1965), p. 60.

16. Philip Anderson, "A Ministry to Troubled People," *The Chicago Theological Seminary Register*, Feb. 1965, p. 5.
17. Ibid.
18. Peterson, *Conscience and Caring*, p. 41; see pp. 41-54 for an illuminating discussion of the confused conscience.
19. Paul Tillich summarizes the impact of our times: "The anxiety which, in its different forms, is potentially present in every individual becomes general if the accustomed structures of meaning, power, belief, and order disintegrate. These structures . . . keep anxiety bound . . . In periods of great changes these methods no longer work" (*The Courage to Be*, p. 62).
20. Rollo May, ed. et al., *Existence: A New Dimension in Psychiatry and Psychology* (New York: Simon & Schuster, 1967), p. 17.
21. Peterson, *Conscience and Caring*, p. 44.
22. Freud regarded the gaining of freedom from dependence on parental authority as "one of the most significant but are also one of the most painful psychical achievements." *Three Essays on Sexuality: Collected Works* (New York: Macmillan Publishing Co., 1953), 7, p. 227.
23. Peterson's discussion of the dynamics of the self-righteous conscience is illuminating.
24. Ibid., pp. 62-63.
25. Ibid., p. 10.
26. Sigmund Freud and Oskar Pfister, *Psychoanalysis and Faith: The Letters of Sigmund Freud to Oskar Pfister*, Eric Mosbacher, trans. (New York: Basic Books, 1963), p. 123; see Erik Erikson, *Insight and Responsibility* (New York: W. W. Norton, 1964).
27. Howard Clinebell, *Mental Health Through Christian Community* (Nashville: Abingdon Press, 1965), pp. 232-33. This represents a form of supportive counseling in that the counselee draws on the inner controls of the pastor to support her inadequate controls. Thomas Klink says: "The Modern Pastor must represent transcendent values to persons who live in settings untouched by traditional controls" (*Depth Perspectives in Pastoral Work*, p. 65).
28. Stanley W. Standal and Raymond J. Corsini, *Critical Incidents in Psychotherapy* (Englewood Cliffs, N.J.: Prentice-Hall, 1959), p. 84.
29. From a communication from Billy Sharp, cf. Robert A. Blees in *Counseling with Teen-Agers*, (Englewood Cliffs, N.J.: Prentice-Hall, 1965) describes his method of limit setting in counseling with those in the middle teens, pp. 65-80.
30. Glasser, *Reality Therapy*, p. 21.
31. Standal and Corsini, *Critical Incidents in Psychotherapy*, p. 249.
32. Glasser, *Reality Therapy*, p. 11.
33. Ibid., p. 31.
34. See Peterson, *Conscience and Caring*, p. 39.
35. Robert C. Leslie, *Jesus and Logotherapy* (Nashville: Abingdon Press, 1965), p. 75.
36. Ibid., p. 14.

37. Peterson, *Conscience and Caring,* p. 40.
38. Adapted from Clinebell, *Growth Counseling for Mid-years Couples,* pp. 36-38.
39. James A. Knight, "Confrontation in Counseling with Special Emphasis on the Student Setting," *Pastoral Psychology,* Dec. 1965, p. 48.
40. Ibid., p. 49.
41. Ibid., p. 49.
42. See Hobart O. Mowrer, *The Crisis in Psychiatry and Religion* (Princeton, N.J.: D. Van Nostrand, 1961) and *The New Group Therapy* (Princeton, N.J.: D. Van Nostrand, 1964).
43. Browning, *The Moral Context of Pastoral Care,* pp. 108-9.
44. See Capps, *Biblical Approaches to Pastoral Counseling,* pp. 131-38.
45. Ibid., p. 131.
46. See Carol Gilligan, *In a Different Voice: Psychological Theory and Women's Development* (Cambridge, Mass.: Harvard University Press, 1982); Peterson, *Conscience and Caring,* pp. 67-75.
47. See Jean Baker Miller, *Toward a New Psychology of Woman* (Boston: Beacon Press, 1976).
48. *Growth Counseling for Mid-Years Couples,* p. 39.
49. See Jonathan Schell, *The Fate of the Earth* (New York: Knopf, 1982).
50. I am indebted to Edith Cole for helping to raise my awareness of these crucial matters.

Chapter 7

1. Clebsch and Jaekle, *Pastoral Care in Historical Perspective,* p. 80.
2. Franz Alexander, *Psychoanalysis and Psychotherapy* (New York: Norton, 1956), pp. 55-56.
3. Franz Alexander used the psychiatric term "abreaction" rather than "catharsis"; "manipulating the life situation" was his way of stating point 5.
4. Lay members of a pastoral care team (chapter 16) can be used to give such practical services as part of their ministry.
5. Prescribing an activity is not helpful, of course, in cases where the person responds to a trauma by hyperactivity, another way of attempting to avoid facing one's pain.
6. Sigmund Freud used the term "ego defenses" to describe the unconscious mechanisms that a child's ego adopts early in life to protect itself and deal with conflict. These defenses operate automatically outside conscious control. They include repression, regression, projection, rationalization, fixation, denial of reality, introjection, dissociation, and reaction formation. See Anna Freud, *The Ego and the Mechanisms of Defense* (New York: International Universities Press, 1946).
7. There are three categories of personality disorders described in traditional psychiatric nomenclature—psychoneurotic, psychotic, and character problems. The neurotic internalizes conflicts, whereas the character problem type externalizes—acting out conflicts in

relationships. The psychotic's fragile defenses have collapsed, to some extent, allowing portions of the ego to be overwhelmed by impulses from the unconscious.

8. Many over-sixty-five persons have strong egos, but egos that have become less flexible with age. This is why supportive rather than uncovering methods are often indicated with older persons.

9. Many persons gain inner strength for coping by identifying with their minister as he or she functions as priest (worship leader), preacher, teacher, and leader of their congregation. Some people in a church feel much closer to the pastor than she or he feels to them. There is something very sustaining in this identification with a minister.

10. After a period of stable sobriety and of resocialization in the group, some AA's seek psychotherapy because they are uncomfortable or dissatisfied with their growth and want deeper help. Some alcoholics who do not achieve sobriety through AA alone are persons with underlying psychopathology requiring psychotherapeutic help in addition to AA.

11. Psychiatrist Lewis R. Wolberg writes: "An individual handicapped by a disturbing symptom often loses self-respect. He withdraws from people. . . . The symptom becomes his chief preoccupation. . . . Here, the removal of a symptom may alter his whole pattern of adjustment." *The Technique of Psychotherapy* (New York: Grune and Stratton, 1954), p. 22.

12. This is analogous to the case of a person who relies on an orthopedic brace permanently rather than doing the exercises that would render the brace unnecessary.

13. A minister's ability to support people in growth-stimulating rather than growth-stultifying ways depends on the resolution of their own dependence/indepedence struggle; the inability to resist manipulative people is usually an indication of low self-esteem of which the fear of not being liked is a painful expression.

Chapter 8

1. Wayne E. Oates, *The Christian Pastor* (Philadelphia: Westminster Press, 1964), p. 1. This book illuminates the pastor's birth-to-death crisis ministry.

2. See Veroff, Kulka, Dorran, *Mental Health in America,* pp. 228-32.

3. Viktor Frankl, *Man's Search for Meaning* (New York: Washington Square Press, 1963), p. 121.

4. See Erich Lindemann, "Symptomology and Management of Acute Grief," *American Journal of Psychiatry,* Sept. 1944.

5. Gerald Caplan, *Principles of Preventive Psychiatry* (New York: Basic Books, 1964), pp.. 26-55.

6. Ibid., pp. 40-41.

7. For a discussion of Erikson's eight life stages, see *Childhood and Society* (New York: W. W. Norton, 1950), pp. 219-33.

8. Caplan, *Principles of Preventive Psychiatry,* p. 43. Italics added.

9. Thomas H. Holmes and R. H. Rahe, "The Social Adjustment Ratings Scale," *Journal of Psychosomatic Research,* 2 (1967), pp. 213-18.

10. It should be emphasized that there are no sharp lines dividing general pastoral care, precounseling (Hiltner's phrase), and informal counseling. These pastoral activities tend to overlap. Precounseling, the relationship-building with a pastor, which helps prepare persons to accept or ask for help, often occurs during general pastoral care. Relationships may move gradually from precounseling/pastoral care to informal counseling as persons become more aware of their need for help.

11. For a discussion of precounseling, including the issue of when the minister should take the initiative and go to people offering help, see Hiltner's *Pastoral Counseling,* pp. 125-48.

12. Those who sense or recognize only in retrospect that they are frequently missing such clues should arrange to have personal psychotherapy or clinical pastoral education to defog their perceptive sensitivities.

13. Adapted from Cryer and Vayhinger, *Casebook in Pastoral Counseling,* pp. 276-83.

14. See Ibid., pp. 157-61, for a verbatim account.

15. Wayne Oates, *An Introduction to Pastoral Counseling* (Nashville: Broadman Press, 1959), p. 111.

16. Franz Alexander and Thomas Morton French et al., *Psychoanalytic Therapy* (New York: Ronald Press, 1946), p. 164.

17. Hiltner, *Pastoral Counseling,* p. 83.

18. See Clebsch and Jaekle, *Pastoral Care in Historical Perspective,* pp. 49-56.

19. Adapted from Howard Clinebell's "Ego Psychology and Pastoral Counseling," *Pastoral Psychology,* Feb. 1963, pp. 33-34.

20. One way of ascertaining the prognosis of a person in crisis is to discover the relative adequacy of his pre-crisis functioning. Persons who have a history of some success in coping can usually be helped to recover their previous equilibrium (or better, in some cases) in a relatively short time using supportive, ego-adaptive counseling methods. But even those with limited pre-crisis adequacy may have latent coping resources that can be mobilized.

21. W. E. Morley, "Treatment of the Patient in Crisis," Benjamin Rush Crisis Center, 5 May 1964 (unpublished manuscript).

22. Eric Berne, *Transactional Analysis in Psychotherapy* (New York: Grove Press, 1961), p. 146.

23. Warren A. Jones, "The A-B-C Method of Crisis Management," *Mental Hygiene,* Jan. 1968, p. 87. These steps are comparable to Robert Carkhuff's four phases of helpee activity—involvement, exploration, understanding, and action. See *The Skills of Helping* (Amherst, Mass.: Human Resources Press, 1979).

24. Clinebell, *Growth Counseling,* p. 156.

25. See Clinebell, *Growth Counseling,* chapter 6 and *Growth Counseling for Mid-Years Couples,* chapters 1 and 2.

26. The 1980 census found that the median age was almost exactly 30.
27. See Morton Kelsey, *Healing and Christianity* (New York: Harper & Row, 1973).
28. See Clinebell, *Contemporary Growth Therapies*, chapter 8. I am indebted to Donald B. Ardell, *High Level Wellness* (Emmaus, Pa.: Rodale Press, 1977) for his elaboration of the principles of holistic health.
29. Adapted from O. Carl Simonton, Stephanie Matthews-Simonton, and James Creighton, *Getting Well Again* (Los Angeles: J. P. Tarcher, 1978) pp. 131-2; 135-6.

Chapter 9

1. Albert Camus, *Actuelles*, 3 vols. (French and European Publishers, 1950-58).
2. Wayne Oates, *Pastoral Care in Grief and Separation* (Philadelphia: Fortress Press, 1976), p. 4.
3. Erich Lindemann, "Grief and Grief Management: Some Reflections," *Journal of Pastoral Care*, Sept. 1976, 30, No. 3, p. 198.
4. Lindemann, "Symptomology and Management of Acute Grief," *American Journal of Psychiatry*, Sept. 1944.
5. There is a variety of ways of delineating the progressive stages of grief. I find it useful to focus on the essential tasks that must be accomplished by a person in order to complete the healing.
6. Questions suggested William M. Clements.
7. Caplan, *Principles of Preventive Psychiatry*, pp. 45-46.
8. William E. Hulme, *Pastoral Care and Counseling*, p. 160. The pastor was John Oman.
9. See Clinebell, "How to Set Up and Lead a Grief Group," *The Christian Ministry*, Nov. 1975.
10. *Colleague*, a paper Kemper publishes occasionally. (March 1978, p. 5.)
11. Ibid.
12. Lois agreed to have me record our conversation. The essence of her insights are included in "Helping and Being Helped by the Dying," cassette course IIA in *Growth Counseling, Part II: Coping Constructively with Crises.*
13. See Elisabeth Kübler-Ross, *On Death and Dying* (New York: Macmillan Publishing Co., 1969), chapters 3, 4.
14. Lisl M. Goodman, *Death and the Creative Life* (New York: Springer Publishing Co., 1981), p. 164.
15. Cicely Sander's foreword to Jack M. Zimmerman, *Hospice: Complete Care of the Terminally Ill* (Baltimore-Munich: Urban and Schwarzenberg, 1981), p. ix.
16. See Paul Bohannan and Rosemary Erickson, "Stepping In," *Psychology Today*, 11, No. 8, Jan. 1978, p. 53; see Gay C. Kitson et. al., "Divorcees and Widows, Similarities and Differences," *American Journal of Orthopsychiatry*, April 1980, pp. 291-301; of divorced

people, 80 percent remarry and of these marriages, 60 percent involve a parent with custody of one or more children. In 1977, 13 percent of all children under eighteen (an estimated fifteen million) live with a remarried parent and a stepparent. See Emily B. Visher and John S. Visher, *Stepfamilies* (Syracuse, N.J.: Lyle Stuart, 1980), p. xviii.

17. Oscar Dowdler, "Help for the Divorced," *The Interpreter*, Sept. 1976, p. 60.

18. See Mal Krantzler, *Creative Divorce: A New Opportunity for Personal Growth* (New York: M Evans & Co., 1974); and Henri Nouwen, *Reaching Out: The Three Movements of Spiritual Life* (New York: Doubleday, 1975).

19. See J. A. Snyder, "The Use of Gatekeepers in Crisis Management," *Bulletin of Suicidology*, No. 7, (1971) pp. 39-44; and Cooper B. Holmes and Michael E. Howard, "Recognition of Suicidal Lethality Factors by Physicians, Mental Health Professionals, Ministers, and College Students," *Journal of Consulting and Clinical Psychology*, 48, No. 3, (1980) pp. 383-87. Ministers in this study were no better in recognizing suicidal persons than the lower division college students used as a control group!

20. This discussion of the signs of potential suicide is condensed from Clinebell, "The Suicide Emergency," in *First Aid in Counseling*, C. L. Mitton, ed. (Edinburgh: T. and T. Clark, 1968), pp. 149-51.

21. Karl A. Menninger, *The Human Mind* (New York: Alfred A. Knopf, 1947), p. 122.

22. *Suicide Prevention Center: Manual for Handling Telephone Calls* (Los Angeles, 1963), p. 4.

Chapter 10

1. Gurin, Veroff, Feld, *Americans View their Mental Health*, pp. 91-92.

2. Jean Stapleton and Richard Bright, *Equal Marriage* (Nashville: Abingdon Press, 1976), p. 19.

3. A 1976 study reported in Veroff, Kulka, Dorran, *Mental Health in America* found that 57 percent of those who sought pastoral counseling did so for marriage or family problems. This included 45 percent who had gone for help with marriage problems, 8 percent for problems with children or youth, and 4 percent for other troubled family relationships (see p. 135).

4. This is Virginia Satir's apt phrase.

5. See Charles W. Stewart, *The Minister as Family Counselor* (Nashville: Abingdon Press, 1970), chapter 1; Jessie Bernard, *The Future of Marriage* (New York: Bantam Books, 1972). Chapters 2 and 3 document the negative effects of marriage on women.

6. Charlotte Holt Clinebell, *Counseling for Liberation*, p. 34.

7. Arlo D. Compaan, "A Study of Contemporary Young Adult Marital Styles," Diss. School of Theology at Claremont, 1973. Available from University Microfilms International, P.O. Box 1764, Ann Arbor, Mich., 48106.

8. Henry Stack Sullivan, *The Psychiatric Interview* (New York: W. W. Norton, 1954), p. 171.

9. One study revealed that individuals in egalitarian marriages reported greater marital satisfaction than those in traditional marriages. See L. Bailyn, "Career and Family Orientations of Husbands and Wives in Relation to Marital Happiness," *Human Relations*, 23 (1970), pp. 97-113.

10. Adapted from Howard Clinebell, *Growth Counseling for Marriage Enrichment, Pre-Marriage and the Early Years* (Philadelphia: Fortress Press, 1975), p. 24.

11. Ibid., p. 23.

12. Ibid., p. 25.

13. The names and addresses of qualified marriage therapists in your area can be obtained by AAPC or AAMFT (addresses given on page 259).

14. A detailed description of how to use this communication tool with couples will be found in Clinebell, *Growth Counseling for Marriage Enrichment*, chapter 2, and with families in *Contemporary Growth Therapies*, pp. 233-34.

15. Nathan W. Ackerman, *The Psychodynamics of Family Life*, (New York: Basic Books, 1958), p. 22.

16. This is discussed in *Between Man and Man* (New York: The Macmillan Co., 1947), pp. 203-5. Buber wrote: "A soul is never sick alone, but always through a betweenness, a situation between it and another existing being." Freedman, Buber, *The Life of Dialogue*, p. 191.

17. Sullivan, *The Psychiatric Interview*, p. 13.

18. Eisenstein, ed., *Neurotic Interaction in Marriage*, p. 18.

19. Ethel M. Nash et. al., eds., *Marriage Counseling in Medical Practice: A Symposium* (Chapel Hill: University of North Carolina Press, 1964), p. 278.

20. The concept of healthy "release," which I learned from Al-Anon, is useful in all marrige counseling. Releasing one's spouse involves doing four things: (1) Letting go of attempts to manipulate, control, or change the spouse's behavior; (2) Neither punishing nor overprotecting the spouse from the painful consequences of irresponsible behavior; (3) Abandoning the subconscious assumption that improvement in one's own life depends entirely on changes in the spouse; (4) Owning and caring for oneself—this includes developing a more fulfilling life for oneself and children, whatever the other spouse decides to do or not do.

21. Hilda M. Goodwin and Emily H. Mudd, *Marriage Counseling in Medical Practice*, Ethel M. Nash et al., eds. (Chapel Hill, N.C.: University of North Carolina Press, 1964), p. 279.

22. William H. Masters and Virginia A. Johnson, *The Pleasure Bond: A New Look at Sexuality and Commitment* (Boston: Little, Brown and Co., 1974), pp. 107-8.

23. For an elaboration of these guidelines, see *Growth Counseling for Mid-Years Couples*, chapter 6.

24. See John R. Landgraf, *Creative Singlehood and Pastoral Care,* (Philadelphia: Fortress Press, 1982), pp. 22; 58.
25. Adapted from Clinebell, *Growth Groups,* p. 111.
26. Landgraf, *Creative Singlehood and Pastoral Care,* p. 22.

Chapter 11

1. Stewart, *The Minister as Family Counselor,* p. 11.
2. Ackerman, *The Psychodynamics of Family Life,* p. 17.
3. Nathan W. Ackerman, "Emergence of Family Psychotherapy on the Present Scene," in *Contemporary Psychotherapies,* Morris I. Stein, ed. (Glencoe, Ill.: Free Press, 1961), p. 231.
4. Clinebell, *Contemporary Growth Therapies,* p. 219.
5. Ackerman, *The Psychodynamics of Family Life,* pp. 21-22.
6. Ibid., p. 218.
7. Satir, *Conjoint Family Therapy* (Palo Alto, Calif.: Science and Behavior Books, 1964), chapter 5.
8. Martin Grotjahn, *Psychoanalysis and Family Neurosis* (New York: W. W. Norton, 1960).
9. Stewart, *The Minister as Family Counselor,* pp. 173-75.
10. Anderson, "The Family Growth Group: Guidelines for an Emerging Means of Strengthening Families," *The Family Coordinator,* Jan. 1974, p. 7.
11. Ibid., pp. 7-8.
12. Sawin, *Family Enrichment with Family Clusters,* pp. 30-31.
13. Stewart, *The Minister as Family Counselor,* p. 176.
14. See Ibid., pp. 176-78 for a fuller description of this retreat.
15. Charlotte Holt Clinebell, *Meet Me In the Middle: On Becoming Human Together* (New York: Harper & Row, 1973), p. 80.
16. Ibid., p. 88.
17. See Susan L. Jones, *Family Therapy: A Comparison of Approaches* (Bowie, Md.: Robert J. Brady Co., 1980).
18. Jay Haley, "Whither Family Therapy?," *Family Process,* March 1962, p. 70.
19. See Satir, *Peoplemaking,* (Palo Alto, Calif.: Science and Behavior books, 1972), pp. 26-27.
20. Clinebell, *Contemporary Growth Therapies,* pp. 222-23.
21. Couple counseling involves three interactional axes (pastor-husband, pastor-wife, husband-wife) of which the counselor must have awareness. Family counseling with a couple plus one child doubles the interactional axes (to six). A couple plus two of their children in a session increases the axes to ten, and a couple plus three children raises it to fifteen interactional axes.
22. I have described Healthy Family Enrichment Sessions and illustrated them with segments from an interview with a family in audio-cassette course IIIB in *Growth Counseling: New Tools for Clergy and Laity,* Part I.

23. Adapted from Clinebell, *Contemporary Growth Therapies,* p. 226.
24. Stewart, *The Minister as Family Counselor,* p. 103.
25. The IFM is described more fully as an experiential exercise in Clinebell, *Contemporary Growth Therapies,* pp. 233-34.
26. Adapted from Charlotte H. and Howard J. Clinebell, *Crisis and Growth: Helping Your Troubled Child,* chapter 2.
27. For a full description of how to do parental play therapy, see Clark E. Moustakas, *Psychotherapy with Children: The Living Relationship* (New York: Harper & Brothers, 1959), chapter 8.
28. Adapted from Clinebell, *Growth Groups,* p. 98.
29. Anderson, *New Approaches to Family Pastoral Care,* pp. 5-6.
30. See Del Martin, *Battered Wives,* (New York: Pocket Books, 1976); Susan Brownmiller, *Against Our Will* (New York: Simon & Schuster, 1975); and Diana E. H. Russell, *Rape in Marriage* (New York: The Macmillan Co., 1982).
31. This understanding of the sociological causes of violence against women and children is documented in Martin's *Battered Wives.*

Chapter 12

1. Thomas W. Klink, "The Referral: Helping People Focus Their Needs," *Pastoral Psychology,* Dec. 1962, p. 11.
2. Wayne E. Oates, *Protestant Pastoral Counseling* (Philadelphia: Westminster Press, 1974), pp. 112-13.
3. C. W. Brister, *Pastoral Care in the Church* (New York: Harper & Row, 1977), p. 162.
4. J. David Arnold and Connie Schick, "Counseling by Clergy: A Review of Empirical Research," *Journal of Pastoral Counseling,* 14, No. 2 (Fall-Winter 1979), p. 96.
5. Gerald N. Grob, ed., *Action for Mental Health* (New York: Basic Books, 1961), p. 104.
6. Quoted by Klink in "The Referral: Helping People Focus Their Needs," p. 10.
7. Adapted from Clinebell, *Mental Health Ministry of the Local Church,* p. 244. (See pp. 242-60 for a discussion of "Helping the Mentally Ill and Their Families.")
8. For an insightful article on this issue by a pscyhiatric social worker, Minnie L. Waterman, see "Pastoral Decision: To Counsel or Refer," *Journal of Pastoral Care* (Spring 1960), pp. 34-38.
9. See Caplan, *Principles of Preventive Psychiatry,* pp. 212-65 for an excellent discussion of types and methods of mental health consultation.
10. Personal communication; John L. Mixon suggests these principles for making good referrals to social agencies: "(a) Secure basic information regarding the agency. This should include an understanding of the purpose, functions, and intake policy. To guess at possible services to be rendered by an agency resulting in indiscriminative referrals is a

waste of everybody's time and frustrating to the person to be served. (b) Do not commit an agency to a specific service or solution. The agency must be free to assist within the limits of its resources and in relation to the real needs of the applicant. (c) Provide such information as you may have to the agency called upon, either by letter or by phone. (d) Follow up all referrals. This will enable you to evaluate the services for the future. Your understanding of what took place will assist you in further consultation if the person returns to you" (personal communication).

11. Produced by Protestant Community Services of the Los Angeles Council of Churches, 1965. The paragraph quoted is from the introduction.

12. A. B. Hollingshead and F. C. Redlich, *Social Class and Mental Illness: A Community Study* (New York: John Wiley & Sons, 1958).

Chapter 13

1. Paul E. Johnson, "Where We Are Now in Pastoral Care," *Christian Advocate*, 23 Sept. 1965, p. 8. Dynamic education should "bring us alive to the new possibilities of humanness." (Joseph Matthews, address, School of Theology at Claremont, November 15, 1965).

2. Educative counseling could also be called "counseling-oriented education." Counseling-oriented education and education-oriented counseling actually form a continuum. Awareness of this allows the minister to move freely toward a greater emphasis on the educative or the counseling dimensions as the needs of a particular person, couple, or family require. A synonym for educative counseling is "pastoral guidance."

3. For a description of the cognitive or learning-theory therapies, see Clinebell, *Contemporary Growth Therapies*, chapter 5 and the books by Foreyt and Rathjen in Recommended Reading.

4. Clebsch and Jaekle, *Pastoral Care in Historical Perspective*, p. 50. Italics mine.

5. From *educare*, "to lead forth", "to rear" (Latin); Clebsch and Jaekle, *Pastoral Care in Historical Perspective*, p. 9. Client-centered therapy is a relatively pure eductive approach. The inductive approach in the church has traditionally used codes of ethics, moral theology, and advice giving.

6. Granger E. Westberg, *Minister and Doctor Meet* (New York: Harper & Brothers 1961), p. 18.

7. Carl R. Rogers, *Counseling and Psychotherapy* (Boston: Houghton Mifflin, 1942), p. 29. Rogers was reacting to an older approach to counseling consisting of exhorting, advising, and persuading. He retained the either/or, feeling/knowing dichotomy of that approach, but opted for feeling instead of knowing. Educative counseling seeks to move beyond the either/or to a both/and position.

8. Lois Barclay Murphy, *The Widening World of Childhood: Paths Toward Mastery* (New York: Basic Books, 1962), p. 374.

9. Nathaniel Cantor, *Dynamics of Learning* (East Aurora, N.Y.: Henry Stewart, 1946), pp. xiv-xv.

10. Ibid., pp. xiii-xiv.

11. For a more in-depth discussion of a growth-oriented approach to preparation for marriage, see Clinebell, *Growth Counseling for Marriage Enrichment: Pre-Marriage and the Early Years*, chapter 6.

12. See Satir, *Conjoint Family Therapy*, pp. 112-35.

13. The Taylor-Johnson is available from Psychological Publications, 5300 Hollywood Blvd., Los Angeles, CA 90027. PREPARE is available from PREPARE, Inc., P.O. Box 190, Minneapolis, MN 55440.

14. A *Pastor's Manual* by Antoinette and Leon Smith, designed to be used with Joan and Richard Hunt's *Growing Love in Christian Marriage* (Nashville: Abingdon Press, 1981) provides excellent suggestions on group preparation for marriage, the theology of marriage, and the content of the five sessions they recommend.

15. The SKI (revised, 1979) is available with a manual for its use by Gelolo McHugh, from Thomas McHugh, Family Life Publications, P.O. Box 427, Saluda, N.C. 28773.

16. I am thinking of severe emotional disturbance on the part of one or both, and of the ecclesiastical strictures in some denominations against remarriage of divorced persons.

17. Cantor, *Dynamics of Learning*, p. 281.

18. See Clinebell, *Growth Counseling for Mid-Years Couples*, pp. 26-29, for a description of the process or creating or revising a marriage contract or covenant.

19. Caplan, *Principles of Preventive Psychiatry*, pp. 84-85.

20. See Jean Stapleton and Richard Bright, *Equal Marriage* (New York: Harper & Row, 1977).

21. Clinebell, *Growth Counseling for Marriage Enrichment*, p. 50.

22. Frequently individuals drop out of pastoral counseling when one or both parties decides to end the marriage. Divorcing persons often avoid pastors because of their guilt and then fear of being judged. It is important to urge such persons to continue in counseling in spite of their pain. A special pastoral effort is necessary even to maintain contact with such individuals. The minister should take the initiative in offering them the opportunity for counseling aimed at helping them divorce nondestructively.

23. Graham B. Blain, Jr., "The Children of Divorce," *Atlantic Monthly*, March 1963, pp. 98-101.

24. Clinebell, *Contemporary Growth Therapies*, p. 253.

25. Harriet Perl and Gay Abarbanell, *Guidelines to Feminist Consciousness Raising* (Washington, D.C.: National Organization for Women, 1975), p. 2.

26. Clinebell, *Contemporary Growth Therapies*, p. 255.

27. These steps are explored in more depth in Clinebell, *Growth Groups*, pp. 150-58.

28. See Speed Leas and Paul Kittlaus, *The Pastoral Counselor in Social Action* (Philadelphia: Fortress Press, 1981), pp. 40-58, for a helpful discussion of the process of defining problems and setting goals.

29. Ibid., p. 57.

30. See Peggy Way, "Community Organization and Pastoral Care: Drum Beat for Dialogue," *Pastoral Psychology*, March 1968, pp. 25-36, 66.

31. Clinebell, *Contemporary Growth Therapies*, p. 253.

Chapter 14

1. George Homans, *The Human Group* (New York: Harcourt, Brace & Co., 1956), p. 658.

2. Robert C. Leslie, unpublished Ph.D. diss. Boston University, 1948.

3. Robert C. Leslie, *Sharing Groups in the Church* (Nashville: Abingdon Press, 1971), p. 19.

4. Adapted from Clinebell, *The Mental Health Ministry of the Local Church*, p. 149.

5. See Mansell Pattison, *Pastor and Parish—A Systems Approach* (Philadelphia: Fortress Press, 1977.)

6. In a paper, "Theological Dimensions of Renewal through Small Groups," *Pastoral Psychology* (June 1964), pp. 23-32, James B. Ashbrook holds that the vitality of church life depends on the presence of a number of "cellular units," which are discovering new life in the Spirit. He describes the way in which his church developed ten small groups paralleling the regular organizational structure but not formally a part of it. Their purpose was to seek the authentic life of the Spirit. Each group had its own life history. When a group had outlived its usefulness, it was allowed to die so that new life might come into being. The idea of creating vital parallel groups, at the same time one works to energize existing "institutionalized" groups, has much to commend it.

7. Adapted from Clinebell, *The Mental Health Ministry of the Local Church*, p. 152; "A Creative cell in our mass society" is quoted from Alan Walker, address at Garrett Theological Seminary, August 1957.

8. George Webber, *The Congregation In Mission* (Nashville: Abingdon Press, 1964), pp. 116-17.

9. Clinebell, *The Mental Health Ministry of the Local Church*, pp. 153-54; Tennessee Williams, *Cat on a Hot Tin Roof* (New York: New Dimensions, 1955), p. vi.

10. Leslie, *Sharing Groups in the Church*, p. 14.

11. Jerome D. Franks, "Group Methods in Therapy," Public Affairs Pamphlet 284, pp. 3-4.

12. This section and the next are adapted from Clinebell, *The Mental Health Ministry of the Local Church*, pp. 154-57.

13. Quoted from Eugene Jennings of Michigan State University in *You Can't Be Humans Alone*, p. 6.

14. John Casteel, ed., *Spiritual Renewal Through Personal Groups* (New York: Association Press, 1957), p. 201.

15. Elizabeth O'Connor, *Call to Commitment* (New York: Harper & Row, 1965), p. 37.
16. Thomas Gordon, *Group-Centered Leadership: A Way of Releasing the Creative Power of Groups* (Boston: Houghton Mifflin, 1955), pp. 8-9.
17. Paraphrased from Thomas Gordon, "Group-Centered Leadership and Administration," in Carl R. Rogers, *Client-Centered Therapy* (Boston: Houghton Mifflin, 1959), chapter 8.
18. The pastor of a church where Charlotte and I co-led a couple enrichment retreat, focused his recruitment efforts on his key lay leaders and church school teachers. This was a strategy to strengthen support for an ongoing marriage enrichment and growth group program in his congregation and also a way of enriching the leaders and teachers of his church.
19. See Clinebell, *Growth Groups*, pp. 48-52 for a description of such exercises.
20. See chapter 9 for a description of grief groups and chapter 16 for a description of mutual help groups for those coping with similar crises.
21. Adapted from Clinebell, *Growth Groups*, pp. 3-4.
22. Clinebell, *Growth Groups*, pp. 11-12.
23. (Persons like myself, who are not natural growth enablers, usually require extensive growth experiences, starting with some individual depth therapy to overcome inner blocks to growth.)
24. Caplan, *Principles of Preventive Psychiatry*, p. 84.
25. Adapted from Clinebell, *The Mental Health Ministry of the Local Church*, pp. 167-68.
26. Parents of "exceptional children" (physically handicapped, mentally disturbed, retarded, and unusually intelligent) need a support and sharing group to help each other with the special problems and stresses they face.
27. See Clinebell, "Growth Groups for Children and Families," chapter 7 in *Growth Groups*, pp. 96-107.
28. Ibid. Chapter 6, "Youth Growth groups—Identity Formation," pp. 89-90.
29. The Mid-years, are really two life stages—Mid-Years I, when adolescents are in the home, and Mid-Years II, the empty nest years before retirement.
30. Edwin C. Linberg, Temple City Christian Church (Disciples of Christ), Temple City, Calif.
31. Clinebell, *Growth Counseling for Mid-Years Couples*, p. 68.
32. See Wilma H. Klein et al., *Promoting Mental Health of Older People Through Group Methods* (New York: Mental Health Material Center, 1965).
33. Leslie, *Sharing Groups in The Church*, p. 32.

Chapter 15

1. Geoffrey Chaucer, *Canterbury Tales*, "The Monk's Tale," 1. 3329.
2. Carroll Wise, *Pastoral Psychotherapy* (New York: Jason Aronson, 1980), p. xii.

3. Hiltner, *Pastoral Counseling*, p. 88.
4. Ibid., pp. 89-90.
5. Wise, *Pastoral Psychotherapy*, pp. 3-4; Ibid., p. 6.
6. "Depth Psychology" refers to the approaches to understanding the human mind that illuminate its subconscious and unconscious dimensions.
7. For a summary of the principles of growth counseling, see Clinebell, *Contemporary Growth Therapies*, pp. 16-18.
8. This list is paraphrased from Carl R. Rogers, *On Becoming a Person* (Boston: Houghton Mifflin, 1961), pp. 163-96.
9. Abraham Maslow, *Motivation and Personality* (New York: Harper & Brothers, 1954), pp. 214-15.
10. Augustine, *Soliloquia*, book II, chapter 1.
11. Lewis Carroll, *Alice's Adventures In Wonderland* (New York: Viking Press, 1975), p. 40.
12. Freud and Pfister, *Psychoanalysis and Faith*, p. 92.
13. This is Lewis J. Sherrill's apt description of the therapist's role.
14. Eric Berne, *Games People Play* (New York: Grove Press, 1964), p. 48. Italics mine. A game leads to a predictable outcome and payoff for each party.
15. Ibid., p. 17.
16. Unless this game is recognized by the counselor and interrupted, the counseling will be ineffective.
17. See Clinebell, *Contemporary Growth Therapies*, pp. 178-87.
18. Sam Keen, "The Golden Mean of Roberto Assagioli," *Psychology Today*, Dec. 1974, p. 98.
19. John Patton, "Pastoral Counseling Come of Age," *The Christian Century*, 4 March 1981, p. 230.
20. Ibid., p. 231.
21. From Henri Bergson *The Independent, 30 Oct. 1913. Quoted by Lancelot L. Whyte in The Unconscious Before Freud* (New York: Basic Books, 1960), p. 181.
22. Anton Boisen, *The Exploration of the Inner World* (New York: Willett, Clark and Co., 1936), pp. 266-67.
23. Freud and Pfister, *Psychoanalysis and Faith*, p. 24.
24. Ibid., p. 116.

Chapter 16

1. *The Evanston Report* (New York: Harper & Brothers, 1955), p. 170.
2. See Howard Grimes, *The Rebirth of the Laity* (Nashville: Abingdon Press, 1962). This movement has been called the "lay renaissance" by Hendrik Kraemer.
3. See Niebuhr et al, *The Purpose of the Church and Its Ministry*, pp. 83 ff.
4. John Dillenberger, ed., *Martin Luther, Selections from His Writings* (New York: Doubleday, 1961), p. 75.

5. Diane Detwiler-Zapp and William Caveness Dixon, *Lay Caregiving* (Philadelphia: Fortress Press, 1982), p. 5.

6. See Detwiler-Zapp and Dixon, *Lay Caregiving*, for a fuller exploration of this and other resistances to lay training and how to overcome them.

7. Robert R. Carkhuff, *Helping and Human Relations: A Primer for Lay and Professional Helpers* (New York: Holt, Rinehart, & Winston, 1969), vol. 1, p. 1.

8. For a fuller description see Clinebell, *The Mental Health Ministry of the Local Church*, pp. 252-53; Ibid. pp. 278-79.

9. See Alan Walker, *Help Is as Near as Your Telephone* (Nashville: Abingdon Press, 1967) for a description of this program.

10. This quotation and the description of this program is taken from *The Pastor's Letter*, Vol., Apr. 1980, No. 6 by Dick Watts of Lakewood, Ohio, a pastoral trained in the program. The address of The Stephen Series, Pastoral Care Team Ministries is 7120 Lindell Blvd., St. Louis, MO 63103.

11. Detwiler-Zapp and Dixon, *Lay Caregiving*, p. 80.

12. Dick Watts, *The Pastor's Letter*.

13. E. Litwak and I. Szelenyi, "Primary Group Structures and Their Functions: Kin, Neighbors and Friends," *American Sociological Review*, 34 (1969), pp. 465-81.

14. I am indebted to Diane Detwiler-Zapp and Will Dixon for this suggestion; they discuss several of these ideas in more detail in their book (see Recommended Reading).

15. Ibid.

16. Robert A. Raines, *New Life in the Church*, rev. ed (New York: Harper & Row, 1980), pp. 126-27.

17. See chapter 17 for a full discussion of these characteristics.

18. The UCC Samaritan task force (of which I was a co-trainer with my colleague Frank Kimper) was formed by the pastor in charge of "Christian outreach" selecting a list of some eighty persons who seemed to have the personal characteristic to make them easily teachable. Of these twenty-three accepted the invitation to participate in the training. In the case of the United Methodist group, a small task force worked with the Dirctor of Christian education to select and recruit sixteen men and women considered by them to be natural therapeutic persons. Both programs were developed with the approval of the pastor of the church, but both would have been strengthened if the pastor had participated actively in the training.

19. Clinebell, Howard, "Experiments in Training for Laity for Ministry," p. 36 (see Recommended Reading).

20. These included taking a trip in fantasy together, the familiar trust-fall exercise (with each person standing in the center of a small circle with closed eyes and falling backwards to be passed around the circle); mutual "gift giving" where each person was invited to go around a small group and give every other person a gift—e.g., an affirming

touch, an honest compliment, an embrace. After each exercise participants had an opportunity to define their feelings thoroughly.

21. When I work alone as a trainer, the live demonstrations of caring skills are done with volunteers from the group.

22. This name was drawn from the Samaritan movement, a crisis program that began in England under the leadership of Chad Varah (see Recommended Reading).

23. See book titles marked with asterisks in "Recommended Reading" at the end of this chapter.

24. Rather than setting up a separate caring team, the group decided to continue meeting for growth and training with the goal of infiltrating the many other groups in the church where they were already active, with caring concern and action. Over the next two years, they became a leavening influence in the life of their congregation, a mutual support group dedicated to doing everything they could to foster person-centeredness and growth in their entire church program. Eventually several other relationship training groups were formed for others who had heard about the training and wanted to participate. Two youth growth groups were organized and led by members of the original training group.

25. Charlotte Ellen and I were the co-trainers of the United Methodist Church group; in contrast to the UCC group, the UM trainees had been recruited with an explicit understanding that a lay caring team would be the outcome of the training.

26. It is important not to ask trainees to make calls before they have enough understanding and practice of caring skills so that their first experiences probably will not be failures (from their point of view). In the U.M. training group we made a serious timing mistake by asking trainees to make a call after the first seven-hour session. This was one reason why almost one-third of the group did not finish the training. By this premature assignment we overloaded their anxiety circuits and did not give them adequate emotional support.

27. The growth formula is useful in supervising lay trainees. In the early stages of training, the emphasis should be on caring, not on confrontation. As trainees become more confident, stronger confrontation with the areas in which they need to grow may be helpful.

28. The Life Line workers at the original center in Sydney have three all-day training conferences, and one live-in conference each year. They also attend "College for Christians" weekly classes to enhance their theological resources for caring.

29. A pastoral care group can become a kind of modern equivalent of the Methodist class meeting, where pastoral care was a function of lay persons.

30. This statement is adapted from Clinebell's "Experiments in Training Laity for Ministry," pp. 40-41.

31. See Francine Sobey, *The Nonprofessional Revolution in Mental Health* (New York: Columbia University Press, 1970).

32. See John Drakeford, chapter 9, "Establishing a Group," in *People to People Therapy* (New York: Harper & Row, 1978).
33. See *Alcoholics Anonymous* (New York: AA Publishing Co., 1955) and *Twelve Steps and Twelve Traditions*, by a co-founder of AA (New York: Harper & Row, 1952).
34. *The Evanston Report*, p. 70.

Chapter 17

1. Rogers, *On Becoming a Person*, pp. 47-49. Rogers relates these characteristics to personal maturity when he writes: "The optimal helping relationship is the kind of relationship created by a person who is psychologically mature" (Ibid., p. 56).
2. Charles B. Truax and Robert R. Carkhuff, after surveying research on the effectiveness of contemporary psychotherapies, conclude, "Research seems consistently to find empathy, warmth, and genuineness characteristics of human encounters that change people—for the better." *Toward Effective Counseling and Psychotherapy: Training and Practice* (Chicago: Aldine Publishing, 1976), p. 141.
3. Rogers, *On Becoming a Person*, p. 51. Counselors may choose not to verbalize certain of their own feelings, but they should be *aware of them*. Otherwise these feelings will interfere with the relationship in hidden ways.
4. Ibid., p. 21.
5. Review of Reinhold Niebuhr's *The Self and the Dramas of History* in *The Chicago Theological Seminary Review*, Jan. 1956, p. 14. It is not possible, of course, for acceptance and positive regard to be totally *unconditioned* in any of us. As human beings we embody agape or grace in only very partial ways.
6. Rogers, *On Becoming a Person*, p. 44.
7. Rogers, *On Becoming a Person*, p. 53.
8. One of my mentors, the late Frieda Fromm-Reichmann, once declared that effectiveness in dealing with psychotics is contingent on the therapist's awareness of this fact (lecture at the William A. White Institute of Psychiatry, 1948).
9. Carroll A. Wise, *Pastoral Counseling: Its Theory and Practice*, p. 11. Italics mine.
10. Rogers, *On Becoming a Person*, p. 51.
11. Ibid., p. 56.
12. Dag Hammarskjöld, *Markings*, Leif Sjöberg and W. H. Auden, trans. (New York: Alfred A. Knopf, 1964), p. 24.
13. William Shakespeare, *Love's Labour's Lost*, Act IV, Scene III, 1. 333.
14. Information concerning CPE centers can be obtained by writing the Association of Clinical Pastoral Education, 475 Riverside Drive, New York, NY 10027 or telephoning (212) 870-2558.

15. The September 1977 issue of the *Journal of Pastoral Care* included several insightful papers on supervision of pastoral counseling.
16. For a description of a method of meditation and other approaches to spiritual enlivening, see Clinebell, *Growth Counseling,* chapter 4.
17. William Rabior, "Ministerial Burnout," *Ministry,* March 1979, p. 25. Several of my suggestions are from this article.
18. See Roger L. Gould, *Transformations: Growth and Change in Adult Life* (New York: Simon & Schuster, 1978).
19. See Carol Gilligan, *In a Different Voice: Psychological Theory and Women's Development* (Cambridge, Mass.: Harvard University Press, 1982).
20. Geoffrey Chaucer, *The Parliament of Fowls,* l. 1.
21. H. Richard Niebuhr, Daniel Day Williams, and James M. Gustafson, *The Advancement of Theological Education* (New York: Harper & Brothers, 1957), p. 128.
22. This should be done with the assurance that therapists will not be asked to report to the judicatory officials on confidential aspects of the therapy.
23. Persons in such positions should be ordained with graduate-level clinical and academic training that qualifies them for membership in AAPC at a fellow or diplomate level.
24. The current requirements for membership in different categories can be obtained by writing the AAPC National Office, 9508A Lee Highway, Fairfax, VA 22031 (703-385-6967).
25. Carl Jung, *Psychological Reflections* (New York: Pantheon Books, 1953), p. 73.
26. Tillich, "The Theology of Pastoral Care," p. 4.

INDEX